JOHN FOWLES

JOHN FOWLES

A Reference Companion

JAMES R. AUBREY

Greenwood Press

New York • Westport, Connecticut • London

Library of Congress Cataloging-in-Publication Data

Aubrey, James R.
John Fowles: a reference companion / James R. Aubrey.
p.   cm.
Includes bibliographical references and index.
ISBN 0-313-26399-X (alk. paper)
1. Fowles, John, 1926–   —Handbooks, manuals, etc.   2. Novelists,
English—20th century—Biography—Handbooks, manuals, etc.
I. Title.
PR6056.O85Z52   1991
823′.914—dc20   91-9553

British Library Cataloguing in Publication Data is available.

Library of Congress Catalog Card Number: 91-9553
ISBN: 0-313-26399-X

First published in 1991

Greenwood Press, 88 Post Road West, Westport, CT 06881
An imprint of Greenwood Publishing Group, Inc.

Printed in the United States of America

The paper used in this book complies with the
Permanent Paper Standard issued by the National
Information Standards Organization (Z39.48-1984).

10 9 8 7 6 5 4 3 2 1

Copyright Acknowledgment

The author and publisher are grateful to Ashridge Management
College for granting permission to reproduce a photograph of
the college that originally appeared on the cover of their copyrighted brochure.

CONTENTS

ILLUSTRATIONS

PREFACE

I had not read any novels by John Fowles when I saw the film adaptation of *The Magus,* in 1969. I left the theater feeling bewildered but intrigued, so I returned the next night to see the film again, supposing that I had failed to understand it because I had missed something. The second viewing convinced me that the problem was with the movie more than with me, but I did borrow a copy of *The Magus* from the library, so that I could explore Fowles's world, which promised to be interesting, whatever else it might turn out to be. With the book, I was not disappointed.

I have gone on to read Fowles's other writings, and they are numerous. His seven books of fiction have attracted large numbers of readers and a great deal of attention from academic critics—an unusual combination. In 1977, novelist John Gardner went so far as to predict that "Fowles is the only novelist now writing in English whose works are likely to stand as literary classics." Fowles's nonfiction writing is less widely known but also noteworthy, ranging from a book of philosophical observations to a series of book reviews, from a geological note to a social diatribe. Indeed, Fowles's writings are so many and so diverse that compiling a comprehensive bibliography has been a challenge, but all the more necessary to do because so much is being written by and about him.

I have undertaken to describe the life of John Fowles in the first section, based largely on statements he has published or made in interviews, but also based on my own interviews and correspondence with acquaintances of his. The second section describes Fowles's works of nonfiction, which tend to illuminate the biographical material. In the third section, I have described and interpreted the fiction, and have included observations about the composition and the reception of each work. The fourth section examines the criticism about the fiction, especially essays written in the 1980s. I have arranged this material according to the critical approach used: biographical, psychological, deconstructive, historicist, feminist, reader-response, or formalist.

The fifth section is a long set of notes to the fiction. Fowles's novels are full of allusions to the arts, including other literature, and are written in British English, which sometimes can be obscure to an American reader—even one willing to use a dictionary. In the notes I explain British usages, I translate foreign-language phrases (which Fowles commonly uses but usually does not translate), and I explain references to cultural matters about which an American undergraduate reader might not know. The notes are arranged sequentially, by work, so that this book can be used as a "companion" volume by a reader who needs or welcomes the information. The appendix that follows is a census of characters from all Fowles's fiction, including their aliases and nicknames, for quick reference, as necessary. In all sections, references to the fiction include American hardcover and paperback page numbers, separated by a slash.

I have enjoyed the work of acquiring photographs and information for this book, as well as rereading the novels. I am particularly indebted to Larry Johnson of Metropolitan State College and Erlind Royer of the Air Force Academy, academic deans who provided support for this project at crucial stages. I also received help from librarians at different institutions: Constance Whitson of the Auraria Library in Denver, Sharon Johnson and Florence Klemm at the Air Force Academy Library, Roderick Dew at the Colorado Springs Fine Arts Center Library, Linda Perry at the University of Nevada at Reno, Betty Muirden at the Yale Center for British Art, and Elisabeth Bell at the Tate Gallery in London. Albert Brown and Dilys Vale of the Lyme Regis Museum were helpful, as were Arthur Nightall, Lionel Stephens, and R. G. Miller of Bedford School. John Wilcox and Joan Allen were especially generous with their recollections and their time. John Thomson gave me the idea of writing notes to the novels. Paul Farkas, Larry Langton, Annette McIlhiney, and Larry DiPaulo helped me to locate various items of hard-to-find information. Peter Brummage helped me to interpret various cricket statistics. In addition, I received help with foreign-language quotations from several people at various times: Elizabeth Holtze, Alain Ranwez, Owen Cramer, Joan Robertson, Tom Hasebe, Chiu Everett, Michael Everson, Dina Zainy, and Richard Lemp.

Finally, I must thank my family for tolerating my devotion to this project—at what must sometimes have seemed a lack of devotion to them.

JOHN FOWLES

LIFE OF JOHN FOWLES

In one of his first published book reviews, John Fowles compares readers to astronauts because, as they read one of Dickens' novels, they feel that they have landed on a new planet.[1] For Fowles, this astronaut metaphor is not just a structural device for one review, but an idea he will return to as he returns to certain themes in his novels. The idea enables him to think of reading as exploration on a global—indeed interplanetary—scale, and Fowles likes to think in such comprehensive terms not only when he creates a vast, imaginative world of a novel, but also when he discusses his relationship with the physical and social world outside himself. Drawing on the same metaphor of an astronaut from another planet, Fowles once remarked in an interview, "I like earthmen, but I'm not quite sure what they're at"; and on another occasion he adopted a similar perspective when he observed, "There is nothing nicer to me than sitting in a window over a street and just watching how these weird bipeds pass each other and speak to each other."[2]

Perhaps all good novelists need to be keen observers of their surroundings, but Fowles tries to critique human behavior from the outside, to view it as an anthropologist might—or a member of a different species. Perhaps he has taught himself this perspective, for his hobby is studying nature as an amateur field biologist; he has described himself as "a life-long ornithologist," and he likes to immobilize spiders for observation under a microscope by getting them drunk on tequila.[3] Watching birds and spiders resembles what a writer of fiction does with characters, watching how they behave as a novel develops.[4] Fowles has even suggested that the analogy holds in reverse, that "literary criticism ought to devote more time to its subjects' ethology: how living writers (off the campus) actually feel and behave," as if novelists were a sub-species of human for critics to observe "in the field."[5]

Fowles's remarks are an indirect invitation for others to observe him, as is the biographical criticism in *The French Lieutenant's Woman*, in which Fowles discusses the life of Thomas Hardy, his predecessor as Dorset novelist. In a review of an early deconstructionist book about Hardy, Fowles objects that the critic "virtually dismisses autobiographical data as irrelevant to the understanding of a writer"; he goes on to say, "Here, I am afraid, is where the practising novelist in his review begins to take exception."[6] The biographical "data" are particularly relevant for a writer such as John Fowles, whose narratives always have a significant, personal dimension.

LEIGH-ON-SEA (1926–1939)

John Robert Fowles (pronounced like the word *towels*) was born on March 31, 1926, in Leigh-on-Sea, a suburb of London at the mouth of the Thames River.[7] Although he has a sister, Hazel, she is more than fifteen years younger than he is, so John grew up as an only child.[8] This situation can only have made it easier for John to develop his stated preference for solitude over society, an attitude that, for a writer, can be a useful trait.[9]

Fowles describes his ancestors as "very ordinary," by which he seems to mean that none is noteworthy in any historical way.[10] He has described himself as one-fourth Cornish, perhaps with a shipwrecked Spaniard in his genetic history, but he considers his ancestry to be essentially "English," which he takes care to point out is not the same as "British" (Welsh, Scotch, Irish), with whom he believes he has little in common.[11]

Fowles once characterized his parents, Robert and Gladys, as "Victorian," but the disapproval he intended to convey seems to be based more on a judgment of their conventionality than on any lack of affection.[12] Fowles describes his father as "in the middle of the middle class" but wishing for more—for something like a large, Edwardian household.[13] Robert had returned from World War I to take over the Wills Tobacco Company, a family business that specialized in Havana cigars and its own line of cigarettes, from several London shops.[14] Unfortunately for Robert's ambitions, the business went into decline in the 1930s and never recovered, so John's parents kept the small, semidetached house John had grown up in at 63 Fillebrook Avenue.[15] John remembers that his father took the train to London and back every day, a typical commuter in his bowler hat, and this image of Robert's conventionality epitomizes what he now remembers with disapproval about his father.[16]

63 Fillebrook Avenue, Leigh-on-Sea, in Essex. Fowles lived in the second house from the left for his first thirteen years.

Robert also had an unconventional side, which John appreciated enough to characterize him in an interview as a "bit of an eccentric."[17] Robert especially liked German lyric poetry and was fascinated with philosophy, especially American pragmatism.[18] John reflects on his relation with his father in *The Tree*, in which Robert's cultivation of prize apples, espaliered in a tiny, enclosed garden, becomes an emblem for the way he hoped to direct the growth of his son. Robert seems never really to have understood how John, who likes wild gardens and dislikes cities, could have turned out so different from himself. Robert had spent three years as an artillery officer in Flanders during World War I, and there, John speculates, he developed a dislike of open country and disorder. Fowles notes that as trees must grow into spaces that are not already occupied, he necessarily became different from his father.[19]

About his mother, born Gladys Richards, Fowles has never said much, probably because, as he wrote to Robert Huffaker, their relationship was "perfectly normal, I hope."[20] Joan Allen, a woman who as a teenager helped to take care of the infant Hazel during the war, recalls that Gladys and Robert were "a smart couple." She was "tall and beautiful, even gorgeous, with black wavy hair." Allen recalls that Gladys was certainly "a good mother to John" during his teenage years, preferring to dote on her son but quite able to become cross if John didn't appear for a meal.[21] Fowles does mention his mother in *The Tree*, in a passage in which he remembers criticizing Leigh-on-Sea later in life, and observes that Gladys was "on my side" (against his father) in "loathing of [the town's] social and physical environment."[22]

Additional evidence of parental affection lies in the decision by Robert and Gladys to enroll John in a local school rather than to send him off to board at a "public" (private) school, as was (and to a lesser degree still is) common practice among prosperous, ambitious families in England. In September 1934 John was enrolled at Alleyn Court Preparatory School, a small, private academy for boys less than a mile from his house. Although Alleyn Court was primarily a boarding school in the 1930s, John would arrive every day on his bicycle, recalls the current headmaster, John Wilcox, son of the headmaster at the time.[23] Fowles is remembered as a hardworking student, who tried hard to fulfill his parents' expectations. He evidently was successful, for five years later, in 1939, Fowles was to be one of only three students in his class of thirteen-year-olds to win examination-based scholarships to prestigious boys' schools.

One teacher at Alleyn Court, Stanley Richards, took particular interest in John, no doubt in part because Stanley was his uncle (Gladys's brother). Fowles describes him in *The Tree* as "a keen entomologist . . . who took me on occasional expeditions into the country—netting, sug-

Alleyn Court Preparatory School, Imperial Avenue, Westcliff-on-Sea, Essex. Fowles was a day student here from age eight to age thirteen.

aring, caterpillar-hunting and all the rest of it—and taught me the delicate art of 'setting' what we had caught."[24] The school retains several display cases of butterflies collected by Stanley Richards, who evidently inspired John to take up the hobby and to produce what must be his earliest piece of published writing, in 1938 for *Alleyn Court Magazine.* Titled "Entomology for the Schoolboy," the short piece by Fowles and another boy begins with a description of the growth of butterflies and moths, tells how to catch moths, mentions alternative ways to kill an insect, and concludes with a few words of advice: "When you are setting a specimen, be patient, for it may not be possible to obtain another one."[25] Both the advice and the coolness of tone in the last two paragraphs anticipate the conclusion of Fowles's first novel, *The Collector,* whose narrator has captured a beautiful girl and inadvertently killed her, and is now looking for another victim.

Fowles says that he has "never since" collected butterflies, so the experience seems to have become one of the negative memories of Leigh-on-Sea that crystallized later. He told one interviewer that his attitude toward nature

has changed very considerably during my life, but it has always been important, I would now say vital, to me. I began by hunting and collecting it as a boy and adolescent, and rejected all that; but then fell into another trap—becoming a stock natural historian, obsessed with identifying and the quasi-scientific side. I would now call my relationship one of love, certainly one of need. What most people look for in human friends and contacts, I look for in nonhuman nature.[26]

The proper attitude is captured nicely by his phrase "seeing nature whole."[27] Comprehending nature is what Fowles believes that he did not learn to do during his "Suburban Childhood," as he calls one of his poems, which ends with the symbolic laying of a sewer through the nest of a skylark.[28] Such a destructive relationship with nature is part of the usual city dweller's inability to see nature at all, partly because there is less wildness to see in a suburban environment, but also because most suburban dwellers are blind to what Fowles calls the "hidden poetry" available, even on the monotonous Thames estuary.[29] No doubt Fowles enjoyed growing up in the town of Leigh-on-Sea more than he now admits, but the town subsequently became, in his mind, an emblem for all-too-common failure by people to get beyond conventional, blinkered ways of seeing life.

BEDFORD (1939–1941)

Having won what is known as a "House Exhibition" to Bedford School, Fowles left home in the fall of 1939.[30] Located about fifty miles north

Bedford School, Burnaby Road, Bedford, Bedfordshire. Fowles attended here as a boarding student, on a scholarship, from age thirteen to age eighteen. During his last year he was appointed Head of School, or "Head Boy."

of London, Bedford is a large boarding school, one of the classic English public schools, preparing boys for university—particularly Oxford or Cambridge—but in a larger sense for public service. In an interview, Fowles described Bedford School as "a proper English institution, which specialized in supplying the Foreign Service—a school traditional, academically demanding, and brutal."[31]

Although he had progressed well academically for two years, he had what he terms "a sort of nervous breakdown at the age of 15. From . . . not being able to cope." In a 1974 interview with the London *Times*, Fowles explained: "I was in the cram class, and I think we were worked savagely hard. And there was the general shock of boarding-school, you know, the brutality. Not that it was worse than anywhere else. One was caned or beaten with a slipper regularly every month. I really hated it like poison."[32] Academic studies alone can be cause enough for a psychological collapse, as the experience of philosopher David Hume at university attests. For Fowles to be a junior member of Bromham House in "the old flog-and-fag public school system," in addition, must have been stressful in something like the way an underclass cadet at one of the American military service academies comes to feel mentally beseiged.[33] In reaction to whatever pressures he was feeling, Fowles took a term off from school during the fall of 1941 and joined his family, by then living in Devon.[34]

IPPLEPEN (1941–1942)

John Fowles's parents moved to Devon, in southwest England, during June 1940, as part of an evacuation of civilians from the London area after the fall of France. Leigh-on-Sea was on the coast, where the Germans might land if they were to invade; furthermore, the nearby Thames served as a navigation route for German bombers on moonlit nights, and they could be expected to jettison their bombs in the vicinity if intercepted en route to London.[35] Residents were encouraged, not forced, to move, but a mild panic did set in that led some families to leave food on the table in their rush to evacuate.[36] Previous to that time, on vacations, Robert and Gladys Fowles had stayed with the Majors family at Croker's Farm in Ipplepen, Devon; so they arranged to live there, initially, as boarders.[37] A few months later they rented a small, detached cottage nearby, named Ashleigh. With their own boarders, a new daughter, a "mother's helper" from next door, and—between terms—John, the house must have been a busy place. For the next several years Robert made twice-weekly trips to London to look after the declining tobacco business and served as second in command of the local home guard.[38] The family remained at Ashleigh until the war in Europe ended, at which time Robert, Gladys, and Hazel moved back to Leigh-on-Sea.

Ipplepen is a farming community and, formerly, an apple-growing village—the place Fowles says that he fictionalized in his somewhat autobiographical novel *Daniel Martin,* and where he "learnt nature for the first time in a true countryside among true countrymen."[39] The learning process involved farm work and pursuit of game as well as solitary exploration for its own sake.

The Devon countryside was to become what Fowles later would describe as his "best friend."[40] He told an interviewer that "slinking into trees was always slinking into heaven," and coming to Devon for an extended vacation from Bedford was a particularly sublime pleasure for him. Fowles describes his stay in Devon as a "Huck Finn existence," a phrase similar to one he has used elsewhere to describe the main character's life in *Bevis,* by Richard Jefferies, the first book Fowles remembers reading and one that, he says, has haunted him all his life.[41] The novel recounts an English boyhood, as Bevis plays on a river with his raft and plays at war in the woods.[42] At age eight, when Fowles believes that he read *Bevis,* its rural world must have seemed wonderfully exotic, like a life on the Mississippi, wholly different from the environment Fowles was living in at Leigh-on-Sea. Years later, in the Devon countryside, Fowles was able to realize that childhood literary fantasy in the physical world, and he would come to recognize that pleasures similar to those of reading *Bevis* could be experienced in the natural world.

Joan Allen, a neighbor who worked as "mother's helper" to Gladys Fowles, remembers that John was "a deep-thinking boy—you never knew him. He had no particular friends but always wanted to be with the farmers in the field."[43] He evidently wanted to try everything, for he has written that he was once shown how to operate a thresher and, another time, overturned a wagon piled high with hay when he drove into a hidden tree stump.[44] He also developed a liking for the highly alcoholic Devon cider, a customary refreshment for field-workers at midday; Mrs. Allen recalls that "John would be gone at the first mention of cider—and a bit unsteady when he returned home."[45] When Fowles describes a wheat harvest in the first chapter of *Daniel Martin,* he evidently is drawing on firsthand experiences, probably acquired during his fall term away from school in 1941.[46]

When not working on Croker's Farm, Fowles spent a good deal of time pursuing wildlife. A local gentleman named Brealey, Fowles recalls, "took me under his wing and taught me to fish and shoot."[47] By his own account, Fowles became "a fanatical killer of birds, beasts, and also a keen fisherman."[48] He confesses to having poached when Brealey was not along, and has written that he regrets having shot several

Ashleigh, Croft Road, Ipplepen, Devon. Fowles spent various breaks from school living in this house, which his family rented from 1940 to 1944.

ravens.[49] Eventually Fowles lost interest in this way of being in nature, a change he dates from an accident in the Essex marshes when he nearly shot himself in the foot, around 1947.[50] He has since come to recognize that aggressive outdoor experiences can be valuable: "I am glad bird nesting and bug-collecting are no longer decent hobbies in small boys; yet can anything give a deeper adult love of nature than the experience of having once hunted and destroyed it?"[51]

Of this time in Devon, Fowles has written, "I thought I was learning to shoot and fish . . . , to botanize and birdwatch; but I was really addicting myself, and beyond curability, to the pleasures of discovery, and in particular of isolated discovery and experience."[52] Just the opportunity to be alone in nature provided the most valuable, formative experience for Fowles in these years, for he discovered in his solitary excursions the pleasures that, later in life, he would pursue by exploring imaginary worlds of his own creation, as a writer.

BEDFORD (1942–1944)

Fowles returned to Bedford in 1942, evidently restored. Not only did he play on the first team in cricket that spring and the next two seasons, but he was singled out for appointment as Head of School, or "Head Boy," during his last year in the sixth form, 1943–1944—in charge of the very disciplinary system he had formerly been shocked by. The irony does not escape him. He admits, "I had this awful taste of head-boy power, which you used to get in the old system. Police force of 60 under you, prefects and sub-prefects. You held court every morning and flogged the guilty." Although he now regards this system as "terrible" and seems to have learned from the experience what he does not want out of life, he had few doubts about his role at the time.[53]

Nor did anyone seem to have doubts about Fowles. Indeed, his later denunciations of the school system in a *Times* interview mystify those who knew him at Bedford. Lionel Stephens, one of Fowles's teammates, recalls that Fowles seemed "perfectly normal" during his last year at Bedford and was "surprised" to learn that Fowles later claimed to have hated school there.[54] In a profile of Fowles for the Bedford School magazine, *The Ousel*, in 1944, his successor as Head of School pays Fowles glowing tribute as a graduating student "endowed with an unusually attractive personality and a natural dignity" that enabled him "to deal in a cool and certain manner with the most difficult situations"; Fowles is described as "one of those born leaders who inevitably retain the respect even of those with whom they have to deal most hardly."[55] His intense dislike for the system he thrived in seems to have developed when he began to reflect more philosophically, in the later 1940s. Even though he once told *Current Biography* that, as a student, "even then only half of me believed in this beastly system," he admitted in a

1989 interview, "I wish I could say that a more sensitive side of myself had revolted against it at once. It did not. The power went to my head, and it was only afterward—when I had left the school—that I rejected it completely."[56]

Another reason Fowles was considered happy and successful at Bedford was his remarkable athletic ability. The 1944 profile notes that he "won his colours" on the rugby-football third team and the fives first team, and in cricket was captain of the eleven-man first team. As Fowles himself puts it, "You can't really hate school if you are in the top XI," which he was for three years.[57] The cricket statistics for 1944 show that Fowles did the lion's share of the bowling—the equivalent of pitching in baseball—and knocked down a respectable twenty-six wickets in thirteen matches. In one instance, a charity match described in detail, Fowles bowled a bit too well, and eliminated a world-famous professional cricket player whom everyone had come to see play, on his second time at bat.[58] As a participant in several sports, a sergeant in the Joint Training Corps, and a student of French and German under a teacher he highly respected, Fowles must have had small leisure at Bedford to worry about the nature of the school system.[59] Furthermore, the continuation of the war across the Channel and Fowles's intention to participate in it must have encouraged the outlook that everyone must get on with the work of defeating Hitler—an attitude unlikely to encourage reflection at that time about such a long-established social institution as the English public school.

EDINBURGH (1944–1945)

The November 1944 issue of *The Ousel* announced that Fowles was "now at a Naval Short University Course in Edinburgh," Scotland.[60] Having demonstrated leadership abilities at Bedford, where he had achieved the responsible rank of sergeant in the final course of the Joint Training Corps, Fowles was preparing to take a commission in the Royal Marines. He recalls, "I finished my recruit training on precisely the day, V.E. day," that the war in Europe ended, on May 8, 1945. Asked by an interviewer if he did not feel some guilt for having missed the war, Fowles replied that he—and others—were just "jolly grateful" that it was over.[61]

DARTMOOR (1945–1947)

Fowles must have been pleased to learn that he was being assigned to a training unit at Okehampton Camp, less than twenty-five miles from Ipplepen, in the Devon countryside he had grown to love. Okehampton is on the northern edge of Dartmoor, an isolated, wild area of rocky, barren hills, in which Fowles would be training younger marines in commando tactics. The commando unit was nicknamed the "Wisht Hounds," after the legendary haunters of the moor, and in his foreword to *The Hound of the Baskervilles,* Fowles tells of several experiences on Dartmoor, including one in which he is mistaken for a convict escaped from the prison at Princetown. Another anecdote, from the winter of 1946, tells of his search for some recruits who became lost during a training exercise, and of the moor's "isolation and the still potent sense of menace it can evoke when visibility turns bad."[62] For someone who loves the countryside, this kind of duty could not have been hard; indeed, Fowles has remarked about his time in the marines, "you spent most of your life wandering over Dartmoor, which was fine."[63]

Fowles has told several interviewers that he began to examine his life at this time, as he found much about military life distasteful—exercising authority, following orders, obeying rules.[64] To seriously question the need for such codes of organized behavior must have been almost unthinkable for someone who had been educated in a public school during years when virtually everyone was going into military service. A decisive event took place in 1947, when Fowles was assigned to escort the lord mayor of Plymouth while he visited the camp. At lunch in the officers' mess, Fowles told the mayor that he was undecided whether to stay in the marines or to attend university. Fowles has told one interviewer that the mayor "thought it was preposterous that anyone of any intelligence should want to stay in the armed forces." Fowles added: "This came as a shock to me. That a great dignitary and a famous man, at least locally, was anti the military."[65] That Fowles could be shocked suggests how thoroughly he had absorbed the public school codes of successful English behavior. Having been helped to see an alternative for himself, Fowles decided that year not only to leave the military, but also to leave off shooting wildfowl, which he saw were "bound up together," and he didn't want to kill any more.[66] In a larger sense, as Fowles explained to a different interviewer, up to the age of twenty, he had been "a very successful conformer"; around age twenty-one, he decided "consciously to revolt against his middle class background."[67] The idea of nonconformity has informed his thinking—and writing—ever since.

OXFORD (1947–1950)

The first novel Fowles wrote was *The Magus,* and its first-person narrator announces in the first paragraph, "I went to Oxford; and there I began to discover I was not the person I wanted to be."[68] Fiction is not necessarily autobiography, but Fowles has used much the same lan-

guage to describe himself after he left the marines: "I . . . began to
hate what I was becoming in life—a British Establishment young hopeful. I decided instead to become a sort of anarchist."[69]

Fowles did not foment revolution at Oxford, but he did begin to
discover a new side of himself. Donald Hall writes that, for Fowles,
"Oxford was an introduction to freedom and irresponsibility, and intellectual gaiety . . . with all-night incoherent philosophical discussions
combining seriousness and frivolity."[70] The philosophy that contributed to his self-exploration—and that helped him to articulate his
emerging, individualist views—was existentialism. He has made light of
the way they "all read Sartre and Camus and completely misunder-
stood them," and of the fact that existentialism "was a smart style to
adopt. To talk existentialist jargon was very much the norm" when he
was at Oxford.[71] Despite his downplaying of their seriousness, existentialist ideas and terms such as *authenticity* enabled Fowles to articulate
to himself as well as to others what he had found disturbing about in
his life before Oxford.

The Aristos, Fowles's 1964 book of philosophical observations, which
earned him the label "existentialist," dates from this period; although
the original, 1964 afterword states that it was begun "some ten years
ago," Fowles has twice revised the introduction; in the latest version,
he admits that "the jotting down of such 'thoughts' " was the first writing he attempted, while still an undergraduate at Oxford.[72] It was surely
the exuberance of self-exploration and self-discovery at this time, more
than Oxford's academic program, that prompted him to describe this
time at the university as "three years of heaven in an intellectual sense."

Sartre and Camus also influenced his decision to become a writer, at
least in the sense that Fowles began to think about writing because he
"felt the world was wrong."[73] In his last year at Oxford, he became
fond of starting to compose stories, but invariably dropped them; he
has since observed about writers of fiction, generally, "you haven't, in
your early twenties, seen enough of the world to be able to imagine
other worlds. And you haven't the command of language."[74] As he
once said about his own attempts at fiction while at university, "I had
the good sense to know how bad it was."[75]

Fowles was enrolled at New College. Rather than be content with a
basic degree, he enrolled in the Honours School of Languages and Literature for a degree roughly equivalent to an American master of arts.
He began to "read," or specialize in, both French and German, but
unhappy with the German faculty, he dropped that language to con-
centrate on French.[76] The regulations under which Fowles was graduated required him to take numerous examinations, as well as to write
weekly tutorial papers. All candidates "offering" a single language had
to show a competent knowledge of the contemporary language (spoken

The New Buildings, New College, Oxford, Oxfordshire. Fowles earned an honors degree in French here, from 1947 to 1950.

and written), the history of the language, the history of its literature, and designated works in the language. From various lists and options, Fowles took examinations on the periods 1530–1636 and 1690–1815; on early texts (*La Chanson de Roland, Le Roman de Tristan,* four *lais* by Marie de France, *Le Mystère d'Adam,* and poetry by Villon); on Montaigne and Pascal or Racine; on Hugo and Flaubert; on the evolution of the French language in the sixteenth and seventeenth centuries; and on French poetry from 1880 to 1914.[77] Fowles sat for these examinations for two weeks, six hours a day. He finished with a high "second" overall, out of four broad passing categories, and he once remarked that he "might have scraped a first" if he had really worked.[78] His performance must have been fairly impressive.

While at Oxford, Fowles continued to be interested in natural history as well as literature and philosophy. He has mentioned hunting for orchids, and no doubt enjoyed exploring nearby Ot Moor.[79] He played some cricket but chose not to try out for the varsity, so that he might spend his summers exploring the newly pacified continent, starting with France and Spain.[80] His greatest discovery at Oxford seems to have been a sense of personal identity.

POITIERS (1950–1951)

Fowles has never explained how he found himself lecturing in English literature at the University of Poitiers, except to say that "a position fell open."[81] Although he enjoyed his year in France, he found it inconvenient to know much more about French literature than about English literature. Fowles imagines that he must have been a terrible teacher, "mugging up desperately on Eliot and Pound in the evening and delivering a lecture the next day" to a group of 100 French students.[82] He was not so desperate, however, that he could not find time to teach himself Latin, or to do outside reading and even some writing, in imitation of Gide.[83] Whatever his merits as a teacher at Poitiers, he received two offers of teaching positions for the next academic year: "One was in the French department at Winchester and the other was from a ratty school in Greece. Of course, I went against all the dictates of commonsense and took the Greek job."[84]

SPETSAI (1951–1953)

Fowles was never happy with the program at the Anargyrios and Korgialenios School of Spetses, as it is still known, on the island of Spetsai, about sixty miles southwest of Athens. The school describes itself as "A Normal Panhellenic Educational, Civilizing and Athletic Center," but from 1928 to 1983, it functioned "as an educational insti-

Hotel Fume (academic hall), University of Poitiers, Poitiers, France. Fowles was a lecturer in the School of Languages and Literature here, from 1950 to 1951. Photograph by Kevin Whitman.

tution similar to Eton and Harrow Colleges in England."[85] As one of
the English masters there, Fowles evidently was expected to re-create
for Greek boys the kind of learning environment he had become disen-
chanted with at Bedford School. He has described the arrangement as
"very weird," and remarks in his introduction to *The Magus: A Revised
Version,* which takes place on a similar Greek island, "if I had attempted
a true portrait of [the school], I should have been committed to a comic
novel."[86] Events took a less than comic turn in early 1953 when he and
the other masters were all fired for "trying to institute certain moral
reforms" in the "appallingly corrupt school."[87]

The environment outside the school seems to have been much more
to Fowles's liking. After the war but before the tourists arrived, Fowles
has remarked, Greece was "magical," with shepherds on the hills and
silent pine forests, whose atmosphere influenced his writing of *The Magus.*[88] The villa Bourani, which Fowles discusses visiting in his foreword
to the novel, was actually called the Villa Yasemina (Jasmine), but it
has since become known locally as the "House of the Magus," according
to a travel guide.[89]

Fowles says that he wrote "hundreds of poems" when he was at Oxford, but the earliest ones he chose to publish were written on Spetsai
and collected as "Greek Poems" in his 1973 book of poetry.[90] In his
introduction to the poems, Fowles observes that it is more difficult to
keep one's private self out of a poem than a novel, and one of the most
autobiographical-sounding poems describes a group of non-Greeks
"sitting under pepper trees / swilling cheap wine."[91] This image evidently captures a central activity of his community of fellow exiles from
England, among whom there was an "extravagant amount of conversation and drink that flowed."[92] In these cafés, like one of the literary
expatriates of an earlier generation, Fowles was becoming a psychological exile from many traditional aspects of English society, even though
he was about to return to England.[93]

ASHRIDGE, HERTFORDSHIRE (1953–1954)

Fowles has remarked that he "taught at a variety of schools in England, ending up in London."[94] The only one he has mentioned specifically is Ashridge, near Berkhamsted and Little Gaddeston in Hertfordshire, about thirty miles northwest of the center of London, where
he says he taught for "a year or so."[95] The building is purportedly the
longest country house in England, and from 1929 to 1958, it served as
the Ashridge College of Citizenship. A brochure describes the program
in those years as "residential courses for adults, both party workers and
members of the general public, in political science, economics, current
affairs and civics," with an increasing effort after the war to serve the

Anargyrios and Korgialenios School of Spetses, Spetsai, Greece. Fowles taught English from 1951 to 1953 at this school, on which the Lord Byron school in *The Magus* is loosely based.

Ashridge Management College, Berkhamsted, Hertfordshire. Fowles taught here from 1953 to 1954. Photograph courtesy of Ashridge Management College.

educational needs of industry.[96] Fowles has never described just what
he taught at Ashridge, but in a letter to Robert Huffaker, he observed
that "most of the work there was to do with the management/trade
union courses; endless rhubarb about time-and-motion ergonomics. I
took strongly to the trade union and socialist side; and I haven't seen
reason to change my mind since."[97] In an interview, Fowles tells of
getting in a row over religion with the admiral in charge of the school.[98]
It is obvious that Fowles was working there only until he could find
something else.

LONDON (1954–1966)

On April 2, 1954, John Fowles and Elizabeth Whitton were married.[99] They had met on Spetsai, where she was married to another
teacher at the time. She has told an interviewer, "My marriage was
breaking up. There was a potential of doom, and John was the catalyst."[100] Whatever stage the chemical reaction had attained by the time
John had to leave the Anargyrios School, he must have found himself
unexpectedly apart from Elizabeth, even if she and her husband also
had returned to England. The separation may have helped Fowles to
become a novelist, for it was then that Fowles began to draft a novel
for the first time in his life. He has told an interviewer that he was
beginning to write *The Magus* when he left Greece and was writing it
when he was "back in London and missing Greece terribly."[101] If what
he was missing most was Elizabeth and his memories of her while there,
some of his other comments about writing *The Magus* sound less mysterious. One is Fowles's admission in a letter to David H. Walker that
"the novel carries traces of a personal sense of guilt Fowles was experiencing at the time he conceived it."[102] Another is Fowles's statement
in his foreword to the revised version of *The Magus* that an "unresolved
sense of a lack, a missed opportunity, led me to graft certain dilemmas
of a private situation in England on the memory of the island and its
solitudes."[103] At about the same time that Fowles was revising *The Magus,* he wrote an essay on Thomas Hardy in which he described the
importance of an absent woman as an object of desire in the mind of a
male novelist: "The difficult reality is that, if in every human and daily
way ('In one I can atone for all') the actual woman in a novelist's life is
of indispensable importance to him, imaginatively it is the lost ones
who count . . . because they are a prime source of fantasy and guid-
ance, like Ariadne with her thread, in the labyrinth of his other
worlds."[104] His first novel seems to have grown out of a wish to re-
create and to reexplore, in his creative imagination, the Eden from
which they had been expelled, with the absent Elizabeth as his muse—
or Eve—or Ariadne.

In September 1954, newly married and stepfather to Anna, Eliza-beth's daughter from the previous marriage, Fowles took a position at St. Godric's College, in Hampstead, London. Again he was to teach English as a foreign language, and he would serve for a time as de-partment head.[105] The students were female, many of them from other countries.[106] His poem "A Summer Class," composed in 1955, repre-sents a teacher who writes on the blackboard and explains gerunds while a student's "pale pink mouth constructs a yawn"; but Fowles has said elsewhere that he did enjoy "opening the minds" of his students to "the Anglo-Saxon liberties of the spirit."[107] Fowles left St. Godric's in April of 1963, when sales of his first published novel, *The Collector,* were doing well enough that he could afford to devote himself, full time, to writ-ing.[108]

Fowles had been training himself to become a writer since he re-turned from Greece. He was not sure what kind of writing he wanted to do, but he knew that he could not *not* write.[109] He started with *The Magus,* and continued working on it through "most of the fifties."[110] During the same period, Fowles has told an interviewer, he kept an enormous diary: "It trains you to analyze people's motives, to describe events. . . . Perhaps above all it can teach you to be honest about your-self."[111] The only writing he tried to publish during the 1950s was a travel book about Greece; his agent rejected it but praised part that was semi-fictional and advised Fowles to "try fiction."[112]

In late 1960, even though he had other novels drafted by then, Fowles began writing *The Collector,* confident that his ideas for the book would work well. In less than a month he had finished the first draft, but he revised for more than a year after that before he showed it to his agent.[113] Michael S. Howard, then publisher at Jonathan Cape, recalls an eve-ning in June 1962, when editor Tom Maschler visited him at his apart-ment with a pseudonymous manuscript in his hand. "Here," he said, "is an extraordinary first novel."[114] Howard agreed, as did everyone else, it seems; by the time *The Collector* appeared in the spring of 1963, the paperback rights had already been sold "for probably the highest price that had hitherto been paid for a first novel."[115]

Success as a writer brought other changes to Fowles's life besides freedom from teaching. One was both the opportunity and the obliga-tion to travel. John and Elizabeth spent two months in the summer of 1963 in Greece, after which they flew to the United States, "dragged here" by his publishers, Little, Brown, "to do the full publicity bit," he told the first American journalist to interview him.[116] Fowles returned several times in the 1960s, twice to live in Hollywood and collaborate on the filming of *The Collector,* released in 1965, and *The Magus,* re-leased in 1968.[117]

In 1964, the Fowles family moved a short distance to a new apart-

St. Godric's College, 2 Arkwright Road, Hampstead, London. Fowles taught at
this private school for girls from 1954 to 1963.

ment in London, in Highgate, on the other side of Hampstead Heath. Also that year, against the advice of his publisher, Fowles insisted that his second book published be *The Aristos*.[118] Meanwhile he began publishing essays and undertook to collate and rewrite previous drafts of *The Magus* for publication as his second novel, which appeared in 1965.[119]

In 1966, perhaps having waited until their daughter, Anna, was old enough to stay behind in London, John and Elizabeth moved to a farm in the West Country of England. They had considered moving abroad, to a tax haven, but did not want to leave England so much as to leave London. Fowles knew that he liked solitude, disliked middle-class society, and had no wish to join the London literary world. In addition, Fowles has said, there was his love for the wild places and creatures of the English landscape—what he refers to as this "nature business"— which he would have lost if they had moved to, say, Malta.[120] Moreover, as a self-described socialist who believes in "soaking the rich," he would have felt hypocritical if he had left to avoid paying taxes.[121] Finally, he has noted, the English climate is ideal for a writer because the weather forces one to stay indoors.[122] They decided to keep an apartment in Hampstead for convenience but to move their primary residence to a farm overlooking the English Channel, just inside Devon and a short walk from the town of Lyme Regis, Dorset.[123]

UNDERHILL FARM, DORSET (1966–1968)

Fowles described this property when he bought it as "a derelict farm" consisting of "thirty acres of scrub and rough pasture"[124] Built in 1847, the farmhouse is one-half mile southwest of Lyme Regis, where an extension of Ware Lane turns into a footpath to the west through the Axmouth–Lyme Regis National Nature Reserve—about four miles of totally wild coastline known as the "Undercliff."[125] The farmhouse was Fowles's model for "The Dairy" in *The French Lieutenant's Woman*, written during the second year the Fowleses lived there, and the woodland scenes of the film adaptation were shot—with difficulty—in the nearby Undercliff.[126]

The naturalist in Fowles was, as he had felt at Ipplepen, in a kind of heaven. Foxes nested in his garden, he has told an interviewer, and "at night, the roe deer made love outside with an appalling din."[127] He came to regard the nearby Undercliff as "not primarily a fascinating area geographically, or a wonderful nature reserve, but quite simply one of those places one always thinks of as one does of a poem or piece of music; not quite of this world; or, of this world as it should be, but alas so largely isn't."[128] But the total isolation of Underhill Farm proved too extreme. As he told another interviewer, "total solitude gets a bit monotonous. In winter from one week to the next not a soul would

Underhill Farm, near Lyme Regis. Fowles lived at this twelve-acre site along the Under-cliff (above), from 1966 to 1968. The farmhouse (below) figures as "The Dairy" in *The French Lieutenant's Woman*.

pass. That's an eerie feeling on the south coast."[129] He decided that he would welcome a certain amount of noise and people's voices around, so in 1968 they moved into the nearby town of Lyme Regis.[130]

LYME REGIS, DORSET (1968–   )

If one stands at the end of the wall known as the Cobb, which protects the harbor of Lyme Regis, one can see the conical tin roof on the tower of Belmont House, about one-third of a mile inland, clearly visible against the dark green lime tree behind it.[131] From the other direction, John Fowles must have an unobstructed view of the Cobb, which his "French Lieutenant's woman" has made famous. Located at the intersection of Cobb Road and Pound Street, the tower is attached to a large rectangular building finished in a pale yellow with white wooden trim. Belmont House was built in 1780 by Samuel Coade, a descendant of Lyme's former "Baptist 'aristocracy,'" who gave it to his niece Eleanor about 1784. Eleanor Coade was a woman industrialist who founded and managed a stone manufactory in London and who used Belmont as a summer villa.[132] The unpainted quoins and swags, the urns along the top of the facade, the stone gods and goddesses over the arched door and windows—all are of her manufacture, added at about the same time that the date 1785 was laid out at the front of the pebble driveway. Later it belonged to a seagoing doctor, who stocked the garden with "improbable" plants such as spiky palm trees.[133] It is not true, Fowles notes, that its stables were built on the site of a former Roman bath.[134] It is characteristic of John Fowles to have preserved such information—as well as the plants.

Fowles is pleased to have done almost nothing to maintain his two acres of "garden." From the street, his property appears to be an undeveloped, wooded hillside enclosed by a wall along the steep Cobb Lane. Even the small lawn directly behind the house, Fowles points out, is thickly woven with clover and is full of birds in the summer: "There is always something they can get off it."[135] The larger, wild section is various, like a small wood. Fowles points out that "it harbors five or six breeding mammals, a dozen or so species of nesting birds with many more as visitors, a good variety of butterflies and moths and a generally luxuriant insect life."[136] It also is a kind of demonstration garden, containing, for example, a large Scotch pine, beeches, apple trees, bamboo thickets, a Brazilian strawberry guava tree—even some sculpture.[137] One interviewer has called the place "bizarre."[138] Fowles no doubt smiled as he once remarked that his "system" is to "keep the main paths clear and let everything else go to wrack and ruin."[139] He considers the plants, animals, birds, spiders, and insects to be his "co-tenants," and he likes to watch them with microscopes or binoculars, which "open up new

Belmont House, Pound Street, Lyme Regis, Dorset. Fowles has lived in this late-Georgian house with two acres of garden, directly above the Cobb, since 1968.

worlds" (as fiction writing also does).[140] Fowles once compared his life
at home with that of a pastoral vicar, who needn't work too hard to
take care of his parish.[141] A more presumptuous comparison might
have been with a famous deity and his small garden east of Eden.

Inside, Belmont House has light and airy rooms, decorated with books
and small treasures. According to poet Donald Hall, who interviewed
Fowles at home in 1982, his "workroom" is on the second floor, with
large windows and a balcony facing south. He writes at a long mahog-
any table that was once a Victorian shop counter.[142] When he looks
out, Fowles must see the wild garden descending below him and, beyond it, the Cobb and the sea.

About his writing habits, Fowles has said, "I am not tidy."[143] Rather
than write every day, he waits for the proper mood—which "cannot be
induced."[144] He may wait as long as six months for it, doing cross-
words, reading detective stories, watching television, working in his
garden.[145] Once under way with a novel—probably with only a vague
idea of where he is going—Fowles virtually barricades himself in his
workroom and tunes out everything else.[146] "When I'm really on the
job, I work very hard, 12 to 16 hours a day," he has said, writing in
bursts for long hours and then drifting and dreaming.[147] He works on
problems as he is going to sleep and gets ideas as he is waking up.[148]
He has found that after 20,000 words or so, "you know whether you've
got a book or not because you feel its grip."[149] This period of sustained
concentration can last for months, during which time Fowles believes
that his whole life has been surrendered to the world he is trying to
create.[150] (Elizabeth, surrendering in her own way, felt that she had to
tiptoe around the house.[151]) During the process of composition, he observes, the good ideas seem to come from nowhere as he is writing.[152]
After a first draft is finished—or nearly so—he likes to set it aside for
at least six to nine months before he returns to it, more cold-bloodedly,
to revise—usually to cut—and to polish.[153] He likes to return more than
once, and some manuscripts sit on the shelf for years.[154] Indeed, Fowles
talks of many novels he has written but will never publish.[155]

While living in Lyme Regis, Fowles has come out with four new works
of fiction: a collection of short stories, *The Ebony Tower* (1974); a long,
realistic, somewhat autobiographical novel, *Daniel Martin* (1977); a short,
satirical fantasy, *Mantissa* (1981); and an eighteenth-century–style,
pseudo-documentary novel, *A Maggot* (1985). Fowles has continued to
write a great deal of nonfiction as well, much of which reflects his interest in local history and his involvement with the local museum. In
1978 he was appointed joint honorary curator, with Ann Jellicoe, of
the Lyme Regis (Philpot) Museum, and from 1979 to 1988, Fowles served
as sole honorary curator.[156] The term honorary does not mean that his
responsibilities were largely titular; on the contrary, the fact that a small

Lyme Regis (Philpot) Museum, Bridge Street, Lyme Regis, Dorset. Fowles served as curator from 1978 to 1988.

museum cannot afford a professionally trained curator means that an
unpaid paraprofessional like Fowles must do the work of a curator if
the museum is to thrive, and it was indeed thriving when he stepped
down in 1988, according to his successor, Liz-Anne Bawden.[157]

During his decade as curator, Fowles became something of an expert
in matters of local geological and social history. He joined the Geological Curators Group, and delivered a talk in 1982 to the Geological
Section of the British Association for the Advancement of Science.[158]
In *The Geological Curator,* one can trace Fowles's efforts to track down
the missing correspondence and fossil collection of James Harrison, an
important amateur paleontologist of the mid-nineteenth century whose
daughter had bequeathed the materials to the museum.[159] Other work
with historical documents has led to the publication by the museum of
several pamphlets composed by Fowles: *Three Town Walks* in 1982, *Medieval Lyme Regis* in 1984, and *A Brief History of Lyme* in 1985.[160] *A Short
History of Lyme Regis,* published as a book by Little, Brown in 1982, is
remarkable for the way it presents the town "rather more as a changing
and often precarious community than as a stage for a cavalcade of well-
known names and events."[161] Fowles's yearly *Curator's Reports* also are
full of interesting pieces of local history about Lyme Regis—for example, the inference from an old drawing that Bay Cottage (of Jane
Austen's *Persuasion*) was probably destroyed in the "great storm" of
1824.[162] Fowles has donated some of his own fossils to the museum,
and since 1974, he has been signing copies of his books for the local
bookstore, with proceeds from the surcharges going to the museum.[163]
Tom Gilbert, chairman of the Friends of the Museum from 1980 to
1986, expresses what must be a widely felt sense of "debt to John Fowles
(fortunately not literally) for putting his scholarship, his pen and so
often his pocket, and his time at our disposal."[164]

Fowles stepped down as honorary curator in March of 1988, after
having suffered a mild stroke. "My health really has given up," he told
the London *Times,* and he wrote in the *Curator's Report* for 1987–1988
that "things and facts hurtle past in an appalling jumble, and most
bearings are lost. I have to learn to simplify things, and that has not
been easy."[165] Later that year the acting chairman of the Friends of the
Museum wrote, "Although he has made a good recovery he is no longer
allowed to do so much work."[166] Fowles did agree to continue serving
as honorary archivist, and the report on his 1989 attempt to locate
"Jones's chair" (used for spying on Baptists in the Undercliff) indicates
that the stroke did not leave Fowles physically incapacitated.[167] The
effect on his writing has been serious, however, as he told *The Paris
Review:* "I can still enjoy reading, I feel I can still judge books. What
escapes me is composing fiction."[168]

As the most renowned citizen of Lyme Regis, whose resident population is less than 3,500, Fowles has had to reach what he calls "a sort of understanding with the town. They know I don't like being treated as famous."[169] For his part, Fowles has been willing to get involved in local politics, especially when preservation issues are at stake. Fowles's letter to the *Times* in 1973 about a dispute over the site of a sewage plant describes the customary political alignments in Lyme—around the town council on one side, oriented to low-cost solutions favored by the business community, and the Lyme Regis Society on the other side, oriented to preservation and aesthetics at any price.[170] With regard to the sewage plant, Fowles advocated compromise. On another issue, whether to restrict fossil-hunting along the coast, Fowles sided with the commercial collectors, against the idealists who would have regulated collecting, and his view prevailed.[171] On questions of whether to increase the commercial use of land, however, Fowles is a preservationist; his efforts are mentioned twice in the *Curator's Report* for 1988–89, once for helping to preserve Slopes Farm from development and, again, for having been "instrumental in persuading Mr. Attwood, owner of the Ware Cliff fields, to sell them to the National Trust."[172] In his more than two decades in Lyme Regis, Fowles has not behaved like a typical celebrity seeking privacy; he has been an active citizen and leading voice of the town.

CITIZEN OF THE WORLD

Fowles is considered reclusive, but his involvement with nature and history in Lyme Regis demonstrates that he is not antisocial. He may not be gregarious by temperament, but he cares deeply about society, not just on the local level, but nationally and globally. Fowles's description of John Aubrey as "essentially conservationist and public spirited" could be applied to Fowles himself.[173]

Conservationist does not mean conservative, politically. Indeed, Fowles must have been amused (or annoyed) when an early reviewer speculated that he must be a Tory, the party Fowles is not at all sympathetic toward.[174] He believes that it is an obligation of a novelist not to join political parties—or groups, or schools of thought—the better to critique them, to arrive at truths beyond their authority and categorizations.[175] He has referred to himself as "a socialist in my fashion," "an emotional Marxist," and an atheist, but he is not comfortable with labels—not even "novelist."[176] Fowles is conscious that everyone is embedded in the processes of ongoing social change, and he hopes to influence that process, even if only slightly.[177] His earliest essay as a professional writer opened with the declaration, "My first ambition has always been to alter the society I live in," and he has called the improvement of society "the duty of all art."[178] The society closest to his hand is English, but he sees himself "implicitly in exile" from much of England, in particular from the (international) culture of the middle class, which he told one interviewer is "outrageously selfish, aggressive, and stupid" in the preservation of itself.[179] The Marxist tenor of his critique echoes his statement in an interview that his "sympathies in most public matters are with the left."[180] Probably his liking for dissenters and eccentrics relates to the way they teach by example what Fowles has said novelists should teach with their fictions: resistance to fixed ideas.[181] Fowles's fiction occasionally is said to be "didactic" because readers can sometimes sense his urge to teach them to resist, to alter their views a little as he diverts them.

When Fowles intervenes more directly in political processes, he is guided by his larger social vision. He has tried to help improve conditions in the publishing industry by signing open letters in *The Bookseller,* one of them urging increases of pay for low-level workers in publishing houses and another protesting the hiring practices at Foyle's, London's largest bookstore, where new employees were being terminated just before they had worked there for six months and would have become eligible for benefits.[182] In the fall of 1970, Fowles even agreed to run for Parliament as a one-issue candidate, hoping to call attention to the campaign for a public-lending right intended to earn writers who were below a certain income level a payment each time one of their books was borrowed from a library.[183] When first approached about running, Fowles said no, but he changed his mind an hour and a half later, telling the organizer that he felt it was his duty to stand.[184] Seven other well-known writers had declined the quixotic honor, men probably less publicity-shy than Fowles, but without his highly developed social conscience.

Fowles's social vision is even more encompassing than the word *social* usually suggests. His experience as a field naturalist leads him to see human society in its relations with other societies, of other creatures. When he looks at the green English countryside, for example, he does not lyricize over the picturesque landscape, but worries over the way farmers have created "green deserts"—deserted, that is, by most wildlife.[185] In 1974, Fowles took over the chairmanship of the Allsop Memorial Trust, which in 1976 acquired Steep Holm—a fifty-acre island in the Bristol Channel—as a nature reserve in memory of Kenneth Allsop, a popular conservationist who had died that year.[186] Fowles took a personal interest in preserving the last of the wild peonies there, at the time thought to be the last ones in England. Out of worry about the near extinction of the species, Fowles subsequently raised several plants back in Lyme Regis, from seeds taken from the island, in an effort to help repropagate the species on Steep Holm.[187] The same attitude toward conserving a diverse natural environment led Fowles to persuade the Dorset Naturalists' Trust to erect a fence to keep cattle away from some rare spring snowflakes.[188] Fowles is not an uncompromising fanatic, however. He recognizes, for example, that writing his celebration of the Chesil Bank—eighteen miles of pebble deposits that form a long coastal lagoon east of Lyme Regis—could serve to blind readers to the threats it faces, one of which is visitors, but he writes anyhow and hopes that visitors will be "loving," that is, will have a caring attitude.[189] Nor is Fowles an advocate of return to some preindustrial relation with nature, an attitude he dismisses as "rural primitivism."[190] But he does not want to see more human awareness of the human situation in, not outside, the processes of nature.

In the old, positive sense of the word *amateur,* as Charles Smithson is an amateur paleontologist in *The French Lieutenant's Woman,* Fowles is an amateur ecologist. If he sometimes sounds as if he dislikes people, that tone can be the result of his refusing to share the usual human assumption of species superiority. He wrote a poem about the subject in 1972, in which he notes the irony and guilt he feels over having told his nephew that crabs get caught because their greed and stupidity lead them to take bait, at the same time not having pointed out that the oil slick surrounding their boat is evidence of the same traits in humans.[191] A few years later, Fowles angered at least one of his readers when he wrote, "I finished *Supership* in a state of sullen rage against the stupidity of my species"; his reply to the reader's letter included the statement, "I don't share his uniquely anthropocentric view of this planet."[192] What his view is, Fowles offers in his introduction to *Land:* "A huge majority of other members of our species are murdering nature and natural landscape, the world over, and some reflection of this must be seen" in serious art.[193] In what may be an extension of the Marxist view that people are situated in history, not outside it, Fowles considers people to be situated in a wider natural ecosystem.

If the human condition should be regarded as imbedded in the conditions of nature, one of his pronouncements takes on new meaning: "The key to my fiction, for what it is worth, lies in my relationship with nature."[194] He is not saying merely that his fiction is realistic because he wants to represent the world around him, but that it is realistic because he wants to express his deepest values and concerns, which involve the natural world of the planet. His favored metaphor of reader-as-astronaut appeals to Fowles because he is a writer-as-astronaut, exploring alternative worlds in fiction and hoping to improve the natural world in life. Fowles says that he once "hectored the Americans" on the need to provide wilderness in cities for the wildlife they attract, the way Hampstead Heath does in London.[195] Fowles's wild garden at Lyme Regis is a private wildlife "ghetto" of the sort he thinks public parks should be like, and a microcosm of the world as he would like it to be.

His "didactic" writing is analogous to his efforts to preserve what is left of the wild countryside of Dorset, to clean up the English Channel, or to save the wild peony. Historical explorations in many of his fictions are analogous to historical research at the Lyme Regis Museum. In seeing his writing activity as one of many related, integrated activities in his life, Fowles engages himself in the processes of natural and social evolution on his part of the planet.

NOTES

1. "Guide to a Man-Made Planet," review of *The World of Charles Dickens*, by Angus Wilson, *Life* (4 September 1970), p. 8.

2. Donald Hall, "John Fowles's Gardens," *Esquire* (October 1982), p. 101; Peter Conradi, unpublished interview in 1976 at the University of East Anglia quoted in *John Fowles*, Contemporary Writers (New York: Methuen), p. 24.

3. Robert Robinson, "Giving the Reader a Choice—A Conversation with John Fowles," *Listener* (31 October 1974), p. 584; Lorna Sage, "John Fowles," Profile 7, *New Review* (October 1974), p. 35.

4. Fowles describes himself as narrator, watching his characters with fascination and even surprise, in *The French Lieutenant's Woman*, p. 81, and earlier has described his male protagonist to be feeling like someone who has landed on a strange planet, p. 71.

5. "My Recollections of Kafka," *New Views of Franz Kafka*, ed. R. G. Collins and Kenneth McRobbie, in *Mosaic: A Journal for the Comparative Study of Literature and Ideas* 3.4 (Winnipeg: University of Manitoba Press, 1970), p. 32. Fowles describes the novelist as a subspecies in "Hardy and the Hag," in *Thomas Hardy After Fifty Years*, ed. Lance St. John Butler (Totowa, N.J.: Rowman and Littlefield, 1977), p. 29.

6. Little, Brown, 1969, pp. 271–72/215–16, "The Most Secretive of Victorian Writers, a Kind of Great Mouse," review of *Thomas Hardy: Distance and Desire*, by J. Hillis Miller, *New York Times Book Review* (21 June 1970), p. 4.

7. James Gindon, "Fowles, John (Robert)," *Contemporary Novelists*. 3rd ed., ed. James Vinson (New York: St. Martin's, 1982), p. 222. The pronunciation is noted in Mel Gussow, "Talk with John Fowles," *New York Times Book Review* (13 November 1977), p. 3, and observed by Michael Barber, *An Interview with John Fowles*, Audio-Text Cassette No. 38873 (North Hollywood, Calif.: Center for Cassette Studies, 1979).

8. Joan Allen, interview with author, Ipplepen, 20 June 1988.

9. In an interview, Fowles once remarked, "Most of my best friends are nonhuman"; Fred Hauptfuhrer, "His Stories Are Riddles Wrapped Inside an Enigma Named Fowles," *People Weekly* (7 April 1975), p. 57.

10. *The Tree* (New York: Ecco Press, 1983), p. 9. Fowles begins his poem "The Rain Took the Road This Winter" with the line "My ancestors are anonyms," in *Poems* (New York: Ecco Press, 1973), p. 86.

11. *The Aristos*, 2nd ed. (New York: NAL Penguin, 1975), p. 37; *Shipwreck* (Boston: Little, Brown, 1975), unpaginated [v]; Gussow, p. 3.

12. Ramon K. Singh, "An Encounter with John Fowles," *Journal of Modern Literature* 8 (1980–81): 191.

13. Mark Amory, "Tales Out of School," *Sunday Times Magazine* (22 September 1974), p. 33; *The Tree*, p. 10.

14. For the name of the company, I am grateful to Joan Allen, interview with author, Ipplepen, 20 June 1988.

15. They are listed at this address in 1965 in *Kelly's Directory of Southend-on-Sea, Leigh-on-Sea, Westcliff-on-Sea and Neighbourhood* (Kingston-Upon-Thames: Kelly's Directories, 1965), under "Fowles, R. J."

16. Some details as well as the recollections in this paragraph are from *The Tree*, p. 9.

17. Gussow, p. 84.

18. *The Tree*, p. 10.

19. Ibid., pp. 18, 21.

20. *John Fowles*, Twayne English Authors Series 292 (Boston: G. K. Hall, 1980), p. 36.

21. Allen interview, 20 June 1988.

22. *The Tree*, p. 19.

23. Interview with author, 24 June 1988.

24. *The Tree*, pp. 5–6.

25. J. R. Fowles and D. L. Erwood, *Alleyn Court Magazine* 9.2 (1938), p. 11.

26. Carol M. Barnum, "An Interview with John Fowles," *Modern Fiction Studies* 31 (1985): p. 188.

27. The phrase is Fowles's title for an essay in *Harper's Magazine* (November 1979), pp. 49–68, excerpted from *The Tree* (in which the idea is discussed on p. 72).

28. *Poems*, p. 50.

29. Introduction, *Land*, by Fay Godwin (Boston: Little, Brown, 1985), p. xix.

30. C. W. Edwards, profile, in "School Notes," *The Ousel* (10 November 1944), p. 95.

31. Hall, p. 94.

32. Amory, p. 33.

33. Fowles's house is identified by its initial under "Valete," in "School Notes," p. 97; the quoted phrase is from Fowles's essay "On Being English But Not British," *Texas Quarterly* 7 (1964): 156, and refers to the arrangement under which younger students are assigned to "fag" for older students (a role something like serving as personal valet) and to undergo physical punishment for their (inevitable) mistakes.

34. Fowles uses the word *term*, not *year*, to describe his absence, in Amory, p. 33. He was on the "first eleven" in cricket for three seasons, ending in 1944, according to the profile by Edwards, p. 95; so Fowles must have returned to Bedford in the spring of 1942.

35. John Wilcox, interview with author, 28 June 1988. By coincidence, the boarding students at Alleyn Court School also were evacuated to Devon.

36. Winifred Selby, interview with author, 24 June 1988. Mrs. Selby remembers counting more than 100 moving vans on the road to London in one hour.

37. Allen interview, 20 June 1988. The farmhouse was torn down in late 1987 to clear space for new housing.

38. Allen Dodd and Maria Dodd, interview with author, 20 June 1988.

39. *The Tree*, p. 14. Ipplepen has another literary association, with Arthur Conan Doyle, who wrote *The Hound of the Baskervilles* in nearby Park Hill House, according to village historian Reginald Honeywell, interview with author, 19 June 1988.

40. "Missing Beats," review of *Autobiography*, by Margiad Evans, *New Statesman* (13 September 1974), p. 352.

41. Sage, p. 32.

42. Tom Davies, "Moods in a Wood," *Observer* (14 October 1979), p. 52; Richard Jefferies, *Bevis: The Story of a Boy*, ed. Brian Jackson (1882; reprinted Harmondsworth, U.K.: Penguin, Puffin Books, 1974); Charles Monaghan, "Portrait of a Man Reading," *Washington Post Book World* (4 January 1970), p. 2.

43. Allen, 20 June 1988.

44. "Late Harvest," review of *The Worm Forgives the Plough*, by John Stewart Collis, *New Statesman* (26 October 1973), p. 612.

45. On drinking practices in the field, see n. 9, *Lyme Regis Museum Curator's Report: 1987–1988*, by John Fowles and Liz-Anne Bawden (Lyme Regis: Lyme Regis [Philpot] Museum, 1989), p. 11.

46. *Daniel Martin*, Signet Classics (New York: New American Library, 1977), pp. 1–18; Fowles has discussed the difference between his own feeling of enjoyment during the killing of the rabbits and the revulsion of young Daniel in the novel, in James R. Baker, "An Interview with John Fowles," *Michigan Quarterly Review* 25 (1986): 675.

47. He is named in Fowles's essay "Weeds, Bugs, Americans," *Sports Illustrated* (21 December 1970), p. 95; the quotation is from *The Tree*, p. 15.

48. Roy Plomley, *Desert Island Discs*, No. 1575, 10 January 1981, Radio 4 (London: British Broadcasting Corporation), p. 19.

49. "Weeds, Bugs, Americans," p. 95.

50. Fowles describes the incident in "The Blinded Eye," *Animals* 13.9 (1971): 388; my approximation of the year is based on his statement to an interviewer that he gave up wildfowling "right after the military service," in Norton Mockridge, "Smell of Success Makes Him Nervous," *New York World Telegram* (19 September 1963), p. 21.

51. "Country Matters," review of *Finches*, by Ian Newton, and *The Pollination of Flowers*, by Michael Proctor and Peter Yeo, *New Statesman* (27 April 1973), p. 620.

52. *The Tree*, p. 56. For another autobiographical account of childhood in wartime Devon, see the prologue to John Keegan's *Six Armies in Normandy* (New York: Penguin, 1982), pp. 1–19.

53. Amory, p. 33. Another student, Angus McCallum, evidently was head of school during the first part of that academic year, according to "Speech Day," *Ousel* (10 November 1944), p. 95.

54. Lionel C. Stephens, letter to author, 11 April 1989.

55. Edwards, pp. 95–96. The profile contains a photograph of Fowles at age eighteen.

56. *Current Biography Yearbook* (New York: Wilson, 1978), p. 160; James R. Baker, "The Art of Fiction CIX: John Fowles," *Paris Review* 111 (Summer, 1989): 44.

57. Amory, p. 33; John Fowles, "Cricket," *Ousel* (10 November 1944), p. 106.

58. "Cricket," pp. 106–07. Fowles describes another aspect of the charity match in "Making a Pitch for Cricket," *Sports Illustrated* (21 May 1973), pp. 108, 111.

59. Edwards, p. 95, mentions the paramilitary rank; Nightall writes that Fowles talked about Bedford in a radio broadcast, perhaps in 1987, and "mentioned in particular the influence upon him of A.G.A. Hodges, who specialized in French and German language and literature," letter to author, 17 August 1988.

60. Edwards, p. 96.

61. Barber, *An Interview with John Fowles.*

62. Foreword, *The Hound of the Baskervilles,* by Arthur Conan Doyle (London: John Murray and Jonathan Cape, 1974), p. 10. Fowles defines *wisht* to mean "melancholy and uncanny, wraithlike," in "Wistman's Wood," *Antaeus* 45/46 (1982): 90.

63. Plomley, p. 3. Fowles has never specified the location, but Camp Okehampton and nearby ranges of the Ministry of Defence are still to be found on detailed maps of the area.

64. Mockridge, p. 21; Amory, p. 33; Plomley, p. 3.

65. Amory, p. 33; elsewhere, Fowles represents the tone of the advice differently: "Anyone who's so stupid as to think he has a choice [between Oxford and the Marines] deserves to stay in the Marines," in Plomley, p. 4.

66. *Current Biography Yearbook: 1977,* ed. Charles Moritz (New York: H. W. Wilson, 1977), p. 163.

67. Richard Boston, "John Fowles, Alone But Not Lonely," *New York Times Book Review* (9 November 1969), p. 2. His attitude resembles that of his unnamed protagonist in *A Maggot,* of whom it is said, "he would break the world which bore him, and to which he owed all" (New York: New American Library, 1986), p. 452.

68. *The Magus* (1965; rev. ed. Boston: Little, Brown, 1977), p. 15/17.

69. "Imminent Victorians," interview and review of *The French Lieutenant's Woman, Time* (7 November 1969), p. 108.

70. Hall, p. 98.

71. Monaghan, p. 2; James R. Baker, p. 676.

72. *The Aristos: A Self-Portrait in Ideas* (Boston: Little, Brown, 1964), p. 229; revised preface, *The Aristos,* rev. ed. (London: Jonathan Cape, 1979), p. 11.

73. Mockridge, p. 21.

74. Singh, p. 184.

75. James Campbell, "An Interview with John Fowles," *Contemporary Literature* 17 (1976): 457.

76. Hall, p. 96.

77. Philip Moss, registrar, annotated copy of the Statute and Regulations, effective Trinity Term 1950, with a letter from John Pusey to the author, 10 June 1988.

78. Amory, p. 34.

79. Plomley, p. 5; Amory, p. 33.

80. Hall, p. 96; Plomley, p. 2.

81. Plomley, p. 5.

82. John Higgins, "A Fresh Mind on Molière's 'Odd Man Out,'" *Times* (6 April 1981), p. 6; Plomley, p. 5; Amory, p. 34.

83. In Monaghan, Fowles states that he went through a "Gide phase"; in Stolley, he says that he "imitated" Gide early in his career, p. 56, as he also did Lawrence, Flaubert, and Hemingway. His early experiments with fiction writing evidently were imitations of writers he admired.

84. Higgins, p. 6.

85. The Executive Committee, undated brochure, enclosed with letter to the author from Nikolaos Nikolidakis, 4 June 1990.

86. John Baker, "John Fowles," *Publishers Weekly* (25 November 1974), p. 6; foreword, *The Hound of the Baskervilles*, p. 7.

87. John Baker, p. 6; Madeleine Kingsley, "John Fowles: Collector's Piece," *Harper's and Queen* (6 October 1977), p. 151. Fowles has described the duration of his time there as "nearly two years," in Plomley, p. 5, and the total time in France and Greece as "almost three years," in Daniel Halpern, "A Sort of Exile in Lyme Regis," *London Magazine* (March 1971), p. 34.

88. John Baker, p. 6; foreword to *The Magus*, p. 8.

89. Arthur Eperon, *Eperon's Guide to the Greek Islands* (London: Pan Books, 1988), p. 66.

90. Hall, p. 96; *Poems*, pp. 1–19.

91. "Aboulia," in *Poems*, p. 8.

92. Sage, p. 31. For a description of what the expatriates called "the Aegean blues," see Halpern, p. 35.

93. Foreword, *The Magus*, p. 8/9.

94. Halpern, p. 34.

95. Amory, p. 34; Roy Newquist, "John Fowles," *Counterpoint* (New York: Rand McNally, 1964), p. 219.

96. Douglas Coult, *Ashridge: A Short Guide to the History and Principal Features of Ashridge in the County of Hertfordshire* (1971; reprinted Luton, U.K.: White Crescent Press, 1985), p. 7. In 1958, the school was renamed Ashridge Management College.

97. Huffaker, p. 30.

98. Amory, p. 34.

99. For the wedding date, which is given differently elsewhere, I have relied on Simon Loveday's chronology, which Fowles corrected in manuscript, *The Romances of John Fowles* (New York: St. Martin's, 1985).

100. Hauptfuhrer, p. 57.

101. Halpern, p. 35.

102. "Remorse, Responsibility, and Moral Dilemmas in Fowles's Fiction," *Critical Essays on John Fowles*, ed. Ellen Pifer (Boston: G. K. Hall, 1986), p. 57.

103. Foreword, *The Magus*, p. 9/9.

104. "Hardy and the Hag," p. 40.

105. John Loveridge, letter to author, 15 June 1988.

106. Plomley, p. 6.

107. Mockridge, p. 21; *Poems*, pp. 52–53.

108. Loveridge; Newquist, p. 219.

109. Plomley, p. 6.

110. Sage, p. 36; Plomley, p. 6; Campbell, p. 457.

111. Hall, p. 98 (ellipses in original).

112. Sage, p. 36; Plomley, p. 6. The agent was Paul Scott, subsequently a successful novelist himself.

113. John Fowles, "Collector's Item," *New Edinburgh Review* (August 1981), p. 7.

114. Michael S. Howard, *Jonathan Cape, Publisher* (London: Jonathan Cape, 1971), p. 299. Fowles's American publisher is Little, Brown; his Canadian publisher is Collins; his manuscripts are handled by W. Thomas Taylor of Austin, Texas; his literary agent is Anthony Sheil and Associates.

115. Howard, p. 300. Pifer mentions "several thousand pounds" from the sale of paperback, translation, and film rights (p. 314).

116. Mockridge, p. 21.

117. Kingsley states that Fowles rented a house in Santa Monica (p. 235), and James Baker specifies Mulholland Drive, in Hollywood (p. 7); these may be the locations of different rented houses during the two film shootings. Fowles told Richard B. Stolley that he had visited the United States three times before ("The French Lieutenant's Woman's Man: Novelist John Fowles" *Life* [29 May 1970], p. 57); but he was here at least one other time before 1970, when he was interviewed by Lewis Nichols in New York about *The Magus* (*New York Times Book Review* [30 January 1966], p. 8). Besides other travel in Europe, Fowles has mentioned visiting Morocco and Egypt: he once smoked *kif* in Tangier, according to Campbell (p. 459); and he describes a visit to Cairo in his introduction to *Miramar*, by Naguib Mahfouz, translated by Fatma Moussa-Mahmoud, edited by Maged el Kommos and John Rodenbeck, notes by Omar el Qudsy (1967; London: Heinemann, in association with the American University in Cairo Press, 1978), p. 9.

118. Campbell, p. 468.

119. Foreword, *The Magus*, p. 5/6.

120. Boston, p. 2.

121. Geoffrey Wansell, "The Writer As a Recluse: A Portrait of the Novelist John Fowles," *Times* (12 May 1971), p. 14.

122. John Baker, p. 6.

123. Michael McNay provides the general location of the flat in "Into the City's Iron Heart," *Guardian* (5 December 1970), p. 8. Stolley reports that, as of 1970, his occasional visits to London are usually to shop or to see the latest films (p. 56). John Baker reports that as of 1974 Fowles spends about one month a year in the flat (p. 7). Part of the "convenience" may have been easy access to nearby Hampstead Heath, London's nearest equivalent to a wilderness garden. Asked why he was moving to Lyme Regis, Fowles admitted to Wansell that he had been there only once, for a weekend some ten years before, and offered the less than compelling reason that he has "long family links with the West Country"—no doubt the Cornish grandmother and the great-grandfather who was a blacksmith from Yeovil, mentioned by Michael Thorpe

in "John Fowles," *British Writers*, Supplement, vol. 1, edited by Ian Scott-Kilvert (New York: Charles Scribner's Sons, 1987), p. 291.

124. *The Tree*, p. 22.

125. The date is in Fowles's foreword to *The Undercliff: A Sketchbook of the Axmouth-Lyme Regis Nature Reserve*, by Elaine Franks (London: J. M. Dent, 1989), p. 8. The distances are from the map on pp. 156–57.

126. Fowles, introduction, *The Undercliff*, p. 9. The film crew's T-shirts saying "I hate the Undercliff," Fowles observes, "summed up a lot of what is wrong with our world."

127. Halpern, p. 34; Kingsley, p. 151.

128. Introduction, *The Undercliff*, p. 9.

129. Amory, p. 36.

130. Halpern, p. 34; Hall, p. 101.

131. Fowles includes the name of his residence in "Fossil Collecting," a letter to the *Times* (30 September 1982), p. 11.

132. Fowles, in *Lyme Regis Curator's Report: 1987–1988*, n. 7, p. 9; John Fowles, *Lyme Regis: Three Town Walks* (Lyme Regis, U.K.: Friends of the Lyme Regis Museum, 1983), p. 12; "1780" is from Hall, p. 92.

133. Sage, p. 31.

134. John Fowles, in *Lyme Regis Curator's Report: 1989*, by Liz-Anne Bawden (Lyme Regis, U.K.: Friends of the Lyme Regis [Philpot] Museum, 1990), n. 6, p. 25.

135. J. Richard Munro, "Letter from the Publisher," *Sports Illustrated*, 21 December 1970, p. 5.

136. "Weeds, Bugs, Americans," pp. 90–91.

137. Hall, p. 102; Munro, p. 5; Leslie Garis, "Translating Fowles into Film," *New York Times Magazine* (30 August 1981), p. 52.

138. David Remnick, "Fowles, Following Form" *Washington Post* (12 September 1985), C1.

139. Hall, p. 102.

140. Sage, p. 34, to whom Fowles also describes studying spiders (p. 35); he also has told Davies that he likes to spend a half an hour a day in his garden, which he finds "replenishing"; Fowles once declared himself to be "a life-long ornithologist" to Robinson, p. 584; and he describes an experience hunting for dwarf geese with Sir Peter Scott (died 1972) near the Russian border with Norway in his interview with Jan Kjaerstad, "Romanens store frihet: Intervju med John Fowles," *Vinduet* 38.4 (1984): 5 (in Norwegian).

141. David North, "Interview with Author John Fowles, *Maclean's* (14 November 1977), p. 4.

142. Hall, pp. 92, 101; "Victorian" is from Hauptfuhrer, p. 58.

143. North, p. 6.

144. Stolley, p. 57.

145. Sage, p. 33; Gussow, p. 85.

146. Stolley, p. 59.

147. John Baker, p. 6; Stolley, p. 57.

148. Boston, p. 2.

149. Campbell, p. 456.

150. John Fowles, "Ordeal by Income," *Public Lending Right: A Matter of Jus-*

tice, ed. Richard Findlater (London and Harmondsworth: André Deutsch in association with Penguin Books, 1971), p. 105.

151. Stolley, p. 57.

152. Campbell, p. 457; Singh, p. 188.

153. Boston, p. 2.

154. Plomley, p. 11; Sage, p. 37.

155. Stolley, p. 57; Howard mentions that when Fowles submitted *The Collector* for publication, he had as many as twelve other novels drafted, one of which is evidently a Raymond Chandler–like thriller (p. 299).

156. Michael A. Taylor, "The Lyme Regis (Philpot) Museum: The History, Problems and Prospects of a Small Museum and Its Geological Collection," *GCG:The Geological Curator* 4.6 (1985): 310; John Fowles, preface, *Islands* (Boston: Little, Brown, 1978), p. 2. The curatorship is unpaid, according to John Fowles and Liz-Anne Bawden, *Lyme Regis Museum Curator's Report: 1987–1988,* p. 16.

157. Bawden, *Lyme Regis Museum Curator's Report: 1989,* p. 2. Mr. and Mrs. L. Pitts, members of the volunteer staff, agree that Fowles "did a fine job" as curator, interview with author, 20 June 1988.

158. "Fossil Collecting and Conservation in West Dorset: A Personal View," *GCG:The Geological Curator* 4.6 (1985): 325–29.

159. John Fowles, query number 66, *GCG: Newsletter of the Geological Curator Group* 2.5 (April 1979): 263; 2.6 (December 1979): 353; and *GCG: The Geological Curator* 4.3 (1984): 174.

160. Fowles also wrote an introduction to the facsimile of the 1817 *Picture of Lyme Regis and Environs,* reprinted in 1985. All four pamphlets are published by The Friends of the Lyme Regis (Philpot) Museum.

161. Foreword, *A Short History of Lyme Regis* (Boston: Little, Brown, 1982), p. 5. One of the book's illustrations (p. 29) reproduces a detail from the only known copy of a Cruikshank engraving and etching, representing a man on a rock watching the bathers through a telescope, which Fowles has admitted elsewhere to having "shamelessly adapted for my novel *The French Lieutenant's Woman,*" whose Dr. Grogan keeps a telescope on his table in the bow window, "for astronomical purposes only, of course"; Fowles's admission is in his "Introduction: Remembering Cruikshank," *Princeton University Library Chronicle* 35.1-2 (1973–74): xiii; the description of Grogan's study is in *The French Lieutenant's Woman* (1969; reprinted New York: New American Library, 1970), p. 123.

162. Note 20, *Lyme Regis Museum Curator's Report: With Notes on Recent Research and New Acquisitions: 1983* (Lyme Regis, U.K.: Friends of the Lyme Regis [Philpot] Museum, 1984) p. 16.

163. Taylor, p. 314; Marguerite Chapman, interview with author, 19 June 1988. In a similar move, Fowles signed 30,000 copies of a book club edition of *The French Lieutenant's Woman* for $1.25 each and donated the proceeds to charity. The original typescript for the same novel was donated to charity as well— either to the "War on Want," according to the *Times* (23 September 1977), p. 12, or to Amnesty International, according to David Leon Higdon, "Endgames in John Fowles's *The French Lieutenant's Woman,*" *English Studies* 65 (1984): 352 and note. The copyright for *The Tree* was given to the Association for All Speech-Impaired Children.

164. "Friends of the Museum," in *Lyme Regis Museum Curator's Report: With Notes on Recent Research and New Acquisitions: 1981,* by John Fowles (Lyme Regis, U.K.: Friends of the Lyme Regis [Philpot] Museum, 1982), p. 5. Gilbert's tenure is in the 1986 *Report,* p. 2.

165. "John Fowles Told to Rest," *Times* (11 March 1988), p. 16; Fowles and Bawden, p. 16.

166. Gwyneth Chaney, letter to the Friends of the Lyme Regis Museum, November 1988.

167. Fowles, *Lyme Regis Curator's Report: 1989,* n. 10, pp. 27–28; "John Fowles Told to Rest," p. 16.

168. James R. Baker, "The Art of Fiction CIX: John Fowles," *Paris Review* 111 (1989): 62.

169. Katherine Tarbox, *The Art of John Fowles* (Athens: University of Georgia Press, 1988), p. 172.

170. John Fowles, "Lyme Regis Sewage Plant," *Times* (23 August 1973), p. 15.

171. John Fowles, "Geology at Lyme Regis—A Museum Curator's View," *Circular of the Geologists Association of London* 829 (1981): 23; "Fowles Defends Fossil Collectors," *Times* (10 September 1982), p. 6; "Fossil Inquiry," letter, *Times* (30 September 1982), p. 11; "Fossil Collecting and Conservation," pp. 325–29 (based on a 1982 presentation).

172. Fowles and Bawden, n. 12, p. 13.

173. Foreword, *Monumenta Britannica: Or, A Miscellany of British Antiquities,* by John Aubrey, ed. John Fowles (Boston: Little, Brown, 1980), p. x.

174. Brian Moore, "Too Much Hocus in the Pocus," *New York Herald Tribune Book Week* (9 January 1966), p. 4, refers to the "sprinkling of Tory asides" in the novel; Fowles has written that he feels obligated "not to belong to any political party" in "I Write, Therefore I Am," *Evergreen Review* 8.33 (1964): 17; and he has stated, "I have no sympathy with the political Right at all" to Campbell, p. 468.

175. "I Write, Therefore I Am," p. 17.

176. "Lettre-Postface de John Fowles" [in English], in *Études sur "The French Lieutenant's Woman"* de John Fowles (Caen, France: Centre Régional de Documentation Pédagogique, 1977), p. 54; Richard Yallop, "The Reluctant Guru," *Guardian* (9 June 1977), p. 8; "I Write, Therefore I Am," pp. 16–17.

177. Barnum, p. 188.

178. "I Write, Therefore I Am," p. 17; "My Recollections of Kafka," p. 36.

179. Tarbox, pp. 193–94; Barnum, p. 188.

180. Barnum, p. 187.

181. Tarbox, p. 212.

182. *Bookseller* (9 April 1983), p. 1322, and (3 April 1982), p. 1323.

183. Wansell, p. 14; Fowles, "Ordeal by Income," pp. 106–7.

184. "No PLR Candidate for St. Marylebone," *Bookseller* (17 October 1970), p. 2099. The decision to field a candidate was reversed before the election was held.

185. Godwin, p. xiv.

186. Fowles provides the date—and a description of the island as habitat—in "The Man and the Island," in *Steep Holm—A Case History in the Study of Evo-*

lution, ed. Kenneth Allsop Trust and John Fowles (Sherborne, U.K.: Dorset Publishing Company, 1978), p. 22; although the 1976 date of acquisition is incorrectly reported as 1974, an otherwise interesting discussion of Steep Holm is provided by Matthew Engel, "Sisters Under the Squabbles," *Guardian* (18 June 1988), p. 19. Fowles describes his position in the letter "Preserving Peonies," *Times* (20 April 1977), p. 17.

187. "Preserving Peonies"; Rodney Legg, "A Herbal Flora," *Steep Holm—A Case Study in Evolution,* p. 54.

188. Fowles, *Lyme Regis Museum Curator's Report: 1987–1988,* n. 11, p. 12.

189. "The Chesil Bank," *Britain: A World by Itself* (Boston: Little, Brown, 1984), p. 27.

190. "A Lost World," review of *Lark Rise to Candleford,* by Flora Thompson, *New Statesman* (3 August 1973), p. 155.

191. "Crabbing," *Poems,* p. 116. The boy's age is one year too advanced for the oil to be the result of the Torrey Canyon disaster of 1967, though Fowles may have it in mind.

192. "Death on the Ocean Wave," review of *Supership,* by Noel Mostert, and of *Death Raft,* by Alexander McKee, *New Statesman* (4 July 1975), p. 22–23. The angry response appeared in *New Statesman* (11 July 1975), p. 54, and Fowles replied in *New Statesman* (18 July 1975), p. 82.

193. Godwin, *Land,* p. xv; Fowles is pictured in a news feature about *Coastline,* a book he had contributed to, published in association with Greenpeace, *Times* (18 September 1987), p. 20.

194. *The Tree,* p. 80.

195. "Unnatural Habitats," review of *The Unofficial Countryside,* by Richard Mabey; of *Insects of Britain and Northern Europe,* by Michael Chinery; and of *The Book of Flowers,* by Alice M. Coats, *New Statesman* (14 December 1973), p. 912.

NONFICTION OF
JOHN FOWLES

John Fowles is best known as a novelist, but that is not how he likes to think of himself. In his preface to *The Aristos*—his first book of nonfiction—Fowles writes, "I am a writer; I want no more specific prison than that I express myself in printed words. So a prime personal reason for this book was to announce that I did not intend to walk into the cage labelled 'novelist.' "[1] This opening move is typical of Fowles in several ways. For one, it assumes a personal stance rather then one that implies that he speaks with would-be scientific objectivity. He often begins an essay with this kind of provocative statement, or with some anecdote that reveals his eccentric side, partly to engage his reader, but also to confound his reader's expectations and, thereby, promote a theme important to him: intellectual dissent. His unwillingness to be labeled "a novelist" also reflects the influence of philosophy, both that of Existentialists, who see such categories as essentializing obstacles to finding one's authentic self, and that of Zen philosophers, who see words themselves as impediments to clear-seeing and self-discovery. The word *cage*, furthermore, for Fowles is not a dead metaphor, but an expression of his appreciation of wild nature and his ability to identify with other species—two capacities which make him hostile to zoos.[2] Finally, the idea of making such a pronouncement is consistent with the mask Fowles often assumes (in writing fiction as well as nonfiction)—that of teacher, who wants readers to grow, or evolve, like students in a private tutorial.

Fowles's nonfiction output is considerable. Indeed, he has written the verbal text for more books of nonfiction than of fiction, and his shorter nonfiction publications number well over 100.[3] Articles by Fowles have appeared in magazines and journals as diverse as *Cosmopolitan, Atlantic,*

The Edinburgh Review, and *The Geological Curator.* He has written introductions to work by others ranging from biography to photography,
from little-known fiction such as *Mehalah* to the extremely well-known
The Hound of the Baskervilles. Fowles has written reviews for several publications, regularly for *The New Statesman* between 1973 and 1977, and
for *The Irish Press* during 1978. He has undertaken various translations
from French, including a medieval *lai,* an illustrated *Cinderella,* a finely
bound edition of *Ourika,* and three plays. Fowles has even edited a massive facsimile edition of drawings and notes by seventeenth-century an-
tiquary John Aubrey, the long-awaited (three centuries) first publication of *Monumenta Britannica.*

   Diverse as Fowles's nonfiction writings are, they have some common
characteristics. In addition to the anecdotal openings, Fowles's essays
tend to be unabashedly personal; he recognizes that any writer has a
point of view, as does any reader, so he does not try to create an illusion of objectivity. His assumption that his readers are intelligent and
educated is implied not only in what he says, but also in how he says it:
with unusual words, foreign phrases, and references to paintings or
historical figures—usually without explanation. He would rather make
his readers use dictionaries than write down to them. His essays are not
difficult to understand, nor are they jargon-ridden, but they do demand a high level of cultural awareness from the reader.

   As with his fictions—or his wild garden—Fowles's nonfiction writings
constitute worlds that readers are invited to explore, even though they
will not feel perfectly comfortable in them. The metaphor of writer as
mental astronaut, exploring a fictive world as if it were an alien planet,
is embedded in "Notes on Writing a Novel," in which Fowles remarks
that writing about Charles and Sarah's love-making in *The French Lieutenant's Woman* is like writing science fiction because so little is known
about what Victorians said or did in such intimate moments.[4] Readers
also explore new worlds when they are reading—a point Fowles makes
directly in "Of Memoirs and Magpies," when he describes old books as
space machines for landing on another, inhabited planet, a kind of "science fiction in reverse."[5] Fowles uses the same idea to help a reader
appreciate difference, too, for example, when he suggests that tourists
looking for the England of Thomas Hardy might as well be "visitors
from outer space," so much has changed.[6] And the idea can help a
reader acquire distance from the familiar, as when Fowles points out
that a visitor from outer space would be puzzled by the discrepancy
between the egalitarian ideas expressed in words and the images of
privilege in the advertisements of England's liberal newspaper, *The
Guardian.* Fowles reverses the situation to make an ironic point about
anthropocentrism in his poem "Report from Starship 26," whose crew
of earthmen discounts the alien culture it has discovered because its

peaceable creatures are so different from themselves.[7] Finally, the metaphor of space explorer helps to enable one to think like an outsider, to gain the insights of an anthropologist as one observes human behavior as if from the outside. Such an explorer might be said to have assumed a cosmic, or Olympian perspective—terms that suggest another metaphor liked by Fowles, that of "the godgame," in which one plays god by objectifying and manipulating other people or characters in a fiction. This cluster of related metaphors implies that language—writing or reading—is a way of knowing, a means to explore ideas the way a field naturalist explores a habitat, not the way a logging company or a colonial enterprise would explore territory. By inviting readers to explore his worlds, created with language, Fowles hopes that they will gain a liberating self-knowledge, a humanized awareness that will make them more like astronauts or gods and less like manipulated puppets.

Various as Fowles's nonfiction writings are, like the plants in his wild garden, they can be grouped into some ten "species": philosophical essays, autobiography, biography, translations, reviews, literary criticism, art criticism, social criticism, cultural criticism, and essays about nature. Even though these categories inevitably overlap, they provide a useful way of organizing an exploration of Fowles's textual landscape.

PHILOSOPHICAL ESSAYS

Fowles's first essay, published after he retired from teaching in 1963, was something of a manifesto. The title is not modest: "I Write, Therefore I Am" echoes the seminal pronouncement of modern philosophy, Descartes' *Cogito ergo sum*—I think; therefore, I am.[8] Fowles assumes that readers will recognize the proposition, and his title suggests that his philosophical views will lay claim to major importance. In fact, the essay is more thoughtful observation and opinion rather than abstract, analytical philosophy, the reflections of an amateur philosopher who believes that "Ideas are the only motherland."[9]

"I Write, Therefore I Am" contains ideas that recur in later writings. The first three paragraphs anticipate his later preface to *The Aristos* as he explains why he thinks of himself as a "writer" rather than a "novelist," that is, because novel-writing often is considered to be less than "a central human activity." Fowles declares his first ambition to be to alter society, but recognizes that he is not a "doer."[10] So for Fowles, at age thirty-seven, writing seemed to be the means by which he was best equipped to undertake his aim.

In going on to describe the kind of writing he wants to do, Fowles mentions that writers tend to be entertainers or preachers. Like Horace, who thought that the best writing both delights and instructs, Fowles sees value in both but worries about a tendency to extremes. American novels, in general, he claims, are technically accomplished but lacking in content; the study of French literature has trained him to value content over style.[11] Fowles does not seem concerned that, philosophically considered, the two cannot be separated. He would grant that his own novels provide entertaining narratives and moral instruction, but his main purpose in this first essay is to establish that he wants to instruct more than he wants to entertain; the moral dimensions of both his fiction and nonfiction reflect that bias.

Fowles's first book of nonfiction, *The Aristos,* appeared later the same year, in the fall of 1964, with the subtitle "A Self-Portrait in Ideas." Based on notebook entries begun at Oxford and developed subsequently, the book contains enumerated, philosophical observations in the manner of Pascal's *pensées,* or enumerated "thoughts." In 1968 Fowles revised *The Aristos* to make it "shorter," "clearer," and less "irritating," as he remarked in the preface. He also made some changes in content that clarify the kind of social changes he would like to see.

The title of the book is one of many elaborations by Fowles of the pre-Socratic philosopher Heraclitus, whose own observations have survived as fragmentary "thoughts," some of which Fowles reproduces in an appendix. The *aristos,* Fowles explains in his preface to the revised edition, means roughly "the best for a given situation."[12] Having been accused of "crypto-fascism" for his earlier edition, Fowles takes pains to emphasize that he understands Heraclitus to mean by the "few" and the "many"—the usual translation of *aristoi* and *polloi*—a distinction based on biology and morality, not on hereditary rank. In the last chapter, whose revised title is "The Aristos in the Individual," Fowles further points out that the *aristos* is a characteristic exhibited at times by anyone, that people are sometimes of the many and sometimes of the few. Whereas most people are conditioned, "like an audience under the spell of a conjuror," the "best" are creatively authentic, like the magician.[13] Fowles admits that the idea of the few and the many is subject to abuse by those who would impose thought control, but anyone who suspects Fowles himself of totalizing impulses should remember that the book begins with an invitation for readers to disagree with him.[14]

The second edition of *The Aristos* was reissued with revised prefaces, in the United States in 1970 and in England in 1980, but the main text of the book has not changed since 1968.

The introduction to this second edition was cut from the original forty-eight paragraphs, or "notes," to just five. Many of the items dropped offered justifications that Fowles must have recognized were unnecessary or even off-putting, for example, "I write in English; but this is for no one country."[15] There and throughout the book he eliminated gnomic observations that made him sound too much like a would-be Zen master, such as "Pick up a stone and envy it," or "A fish water, a man hazard."[16] And he got rid of the numerous coinages that were more hindrance than help to the reader of the first edition, for example "parahades," "agora society," and "ISR" (for illicit sexual relationship).

The first chapter, "The Universal Situation," omits much abstract discourse to focus on an extended metaphor that represents the human condition: earth is like a raft, adrift, whose inhabitants feel a sense of loss but no sense of direction. The absence of meaning, or fundamental mystery of existence, he no longer describes as "The It," but as " 'God' "— in quotation marks because the only kind of deity compatible with personal freedom would be incompatible with established religion. Fowles's "God" would leave humans to "drift" rather than intervene. In a new section called "Atheism," Fowles explains that he does not consider himself to be an atheist, but behaves in all public matters as if he were.

In "Human Dissatisfactions," Fowles discusses the idea of life after death as a compensation fantasy for the perception that this life is not just. He adds a discussion of Pascal's wager, the argument for betting on an afterlife, to help make his case for the opposite, that one should accept responsibility for the shortcomings of this world. A one-word change, from "refugees" to "racialism," seems to indicate an evolution in Fowles's thinking about the relative importance of particular injustices between 1964 and 1968.[17]

"The Nemo" is elevated from a section to a chapter of its own in the second edition. Fowles defines this term as the opposite of Freud's *ego*, a feeling of lack of self-esteem, or a "pawn complex," that drives people to seek recognition in various ways—by adulating experts, assassinating public figures, or writing poetry. In the 1964 edition, Fowles wrote that there was "no way" to reduce the effects of this sense of powerlessness; in 1968, he suggests one practical means: frequent general votes on great national issues (with an improved system of educating and informing the electorate).[18]

In "The Relativity of Recompense," Fowles discusses the uniquely human awareness of inequality that robs them of an otherwise happy oblivion. Additions to this chapter in 1968 increase its political charge, as "happiness" and "envy" are discussed as conditions that allow communist and capitalist societies to manipulate people.

Fowles's chapter on "Doing the Good" begins with a discussion of free will and moves to an examination of good and evil actions. One new paragraph compares individuals with courteous judges, who are compelled to judge between right and wrong, even if those judgments are meaningless. The last section asks, "Why So Little Good?" and answers that most people seem to believe that doing nothing is better than doing good. With a surprising metaphor—and an even more surprising reversal of the terms as he used them in 1964—Fowles argues that "we should *evacuate* good—not *ejaculate* it," that acts of charity, kindness, and justice should be acts of hygiene rather than acts of pleasure.[19]

The chapter on "The Tensional Nature of Human Reality" is about oppositions that constitute the mental world everyone inhabits. Fowles, willing to consider even the thorniest of issues, examines beauty and ugliness as his model for the mechanism of tension. The 1968 version is completely revised and condensed, with new references to popular culture and with a debt to Zen Buddhism (for the concept of "virgin" beauty) made explicit. Another section of this chapter is devoted to the tensions of marriage, with material added in 1968 on aging and the "*de facto* polygamous institution" of the Western male remarriage practice.[20] Fowles describes as "the ultimate tension" the mysterious gap "between what we know and what we know we will never know," which "mystery," he points out, is not the sentimental idea people sometimes attach themselves to in order to avoid action.[21]

"Other Philosophies" considers Christianity, Lamaism, humanism, socialism, fascism, and existentialism. The revised discussion of Christianity adds an observation about the relation of religion to particular environments (and their consequent inadequacies in a different environment). On Lamaism, Fowles adds a long paragraph about why "the perennial philosophy" is untenable in a world "like ours, in a permanent state of evolutionary war."[22] In the revised discussion of humanism, Fowles makes the unorthodox case that Hebrew monotheism was a more artificial construct than Greek polytheism. Socialism is newly defined, at its best, as wishing "to achieve a maximum of freedom with a minimum of social suffering."[23] And existentialism, formerly in the middle of the chapter, is moved to the more emphatic last position, where Fowles concludes by observing that it is unsuited to political action or subversion because it can generate only individual resistance, "one personal expression of view; such as this book."[24]

In the chapter on "The Obsession with Money," Fowles discusses wealth and poverty, the monetization of pleasure, the effects of automation on workers, the duties of leisure, and the problem of overpopulation. It is a Marxian analysis, but gloomy.

"A New Education" offers something like a remedy. Fowles first argues that preparing students for economic success has preempted other valid aims of education. He proceeds to discuss tangentially related issues such as the need for a universal second language and his interpretation of the Adam and Eve myth. When he returns to education, as such, Fowles asserts that "present educational systems are all paramilitary" because they aim to produce "soldiers" who will be obedient and successful within the state as currently constituted.[25] What Fowles wants to see, first, is a program for developing "inward knowledge," including a personal, psychoanalysis of each student. He concludes the chapter with five new paragraphs about "synoptic education" which, in a world of inequalities, should aim to promote "a sense of discontent that is also a sense of moral purpose."[26]

"The Importance of Art" includes a new second paragraph that insists that science and art are complementary, not hostile, though which one he values more highly is evident from his observation that science is "constricting" and art "liberating." In another paragraph added to the 1968 edition, Fowles offers the view that even the most ritualistic of art is "therapeutic in intention," an assumption that seems to guide Fowles when he writes essays about other authors.

The first chapter, originally "The Aristos," is retitled "The Aristos in the Individual." The added phrase is Fowles's emphasis on the situational nature of equality and its accessibility to any individual, along with that individual's limited freedom. In a landscape of ideas, *The Aristos* locates Fowles in existential-humanist terrain; his revisions indicate that he is facing in a Marxist-socialist direction; his idiosyncratic approach places him in a particularly secluded preserve of his own.

His nonfiction writing during the 1980s shows no evidence that Fowles has changed his thinking much since he wrote *The Aristos*. His introduction to a collection of pieces from *The Guardian,* the left-liberal newspaper Fowles reads, praises it for "constantly questioning the prevailing system" and for its "open-forum quality, inside the general context of a liberal humanism."[27] Equally unsurprising is the content of Fowles's essay for *The Times* to launch a creative writing competition in 1985, in which he describes writing as a means for self-expression and self-discovery, not a means to best-sellerdom and prestige. He suggests that the necessary commitment to writing is a form of insanity, but that writing is wonderful therapy.[28] Fowles discovers who he is from what he writes—journals, essays, books; he asks that others decide who they are from reading and who he is from his writing. Fowles writes; therefore, he is.

AUTOBIOGRAPHY

For an instinctive storyteller like Fowles, it must feel quite natural to include autobiographical narratives in his nonfiction writing. Sometimes, as in *The Tree,* the autobiographical sections are extensive. In virtually every instance, Fowles recounts personal experiences to make some point beyond the purely autobiographical accounting for himself, in implicit hope of altering society.

Fowles makes a theoretical observation about the autobiographical dimension of literature in the introduction to his *Poems:* "Of course some poets wear masks . . . and of course there is an autobiographical element in all novels. Nonetheless, I think there is a vital distinction. It is rather difficult to put one's private self into a novel; it is rather difficult to keep it out of a poem."[29] He invites readers to consider his poems to be self-expressive, and his willingness to date them also implies that they are tied to a particular moment in his personal history. The poem "In Chalkwell Park," for example, represents the thoughts of a son who is walking with his aging, infirm father on a Sunday afternoon in October. The poem seems likely to be autobiographical, for there is a Chalkwell Park in Leigh-on-Sea and Robert Fowles died in a nursing home, where John recounts a visit to him in *The Tree*.[30] Some other poems are more fictive—"Report from Starship 26" is the obvious example—but all his poems seem to be attempts at personal expression rather than games with masks.

Fowles's thoughts about autobiography are revealed in a metaphor from an essay that originally was untitled, but later was republished as "Of Memoirs and Magpies."[31] In the essay, Fowles describes the way he accumulates books, especially accounts of old trials, travel narratives, and memoirs that "give me the sharp feel of the age [they were] written in." He explains that he does not collect in some systematic way, but more like a magpie, with the result that his bookshelves are "nonsense," full of "broken-backed detritus from the last four centuries, most of which the rest of the world has quite rightly consigned to oblivion." Elsewhere in the essay, Fowles connects his "magpie" book-buying practices with the way he reads, writes, and remembers: "I live the direct and present experience very intensely; but when it is over, it sinks very rapidly out of sight."[32] What he implies about autobiography is that the personal anecdotes in his essays also are representations of memories that have somehow retained the "sharp feel" of the original experience. These moments are something like a magpie detritus of a personal history, each piece without meaning except as re-created through the processes of an individual mind, what Fowles describes in *The Tree* as "another memory trace, already becoming an artefact, a thing to use"—or to let sink into the oblivion of the unconscious.[33]

In other essays, Fowles has discussed the origins of his novels, sometimes with reference to theories of depth psychology (implied by his use of the word *sink,* above). In "Collector's Item," Fowles describes conscious influences on his composition of *The Collector*—attending a performance of Bartók's *Bluebeard* and reading a news account of a young man who held a girl captive in a backyard air raid shelter—but he also allows for the subtler influence of what Fowles calls the "universal" male adolescent fantasy about an isolating event that throws one into contact with an admired but unapproachable female.[34] The inspiration for *The French Lieutenant's Woman,* Fowles writes in "Notes on Writing a Novel," was a persistent image from a hypnopompic dream about a woman standing at the end of the Lyme Regis Cobb, an image which would become his character Sarah but whose origins he could not recall, though he suspected at the time that it had "percolated down to the coast of consciousness" from the "dense hinterland" of his previous reading experience.[35] He further analyzes the dream's significance in his foreword to *Ourika,* in which he describes his later realization that the black cloak worn by the woman was a displacement of the skin color of an African servant he had once read about, named Ourika, who, like Sarah, was educated but exiled from French culture and—consciously, at least—forgotten by Fowles.[36]

Such discussion of half-unconscious origins of his novels takes for granted the insights and methods of depth psychology, and elsewhere Fowles is explicit about his respect for Freud and Jung: "I've often said that if I felt I needed psychiatry I would certainly go to a Freudian. . . . I think for a writer, Jung is actually the best person to read."[37] Fowles has obviously read and thought about psychology. In "Hardy and the Hag," Fowles is forthright about how much he has learned about himself from a Freudian critique of what he had previously written about composing *The French Lieutenant's Woman.* He recognizes himself as one of those who are deeply marked by the passage from infancy to individuated childhood, who spend the rest of their lives "tampering with reality" in art, unconsciously trying to recover that lost sense of oneness with the mother.[38] Fowles exhibits a continuing confidence in that Freudian insight about novel-writing in his foreword to *The Timescapes of John Fowles:* "In my view all novelists share one common, if often largely unconscious, driving force: and that is a sense of loss, or at any rate of insufferable incompleteness, a deprivation we then habitually blame on the real world around us. This world is so wrong, so inadequate and unimaginative, that we must speak, and correct and supplement it."[39]

Not all of Fowles's autobiographical writing is so deeply inward-looking. His foreword to *The French Lieutenant's Woman: A Screenplay* recounts the drawn-out negotiations to film that novel, and the filming itself in Lyme Regis.[40] In "Golding and 'Golding' " Fowles describes how it felt to have a private dinner with novelist William Golding and reflects on ways that famous writers are regarded by others. Fowles tells about his own attitudes toward Golding the man and "Golding" the verbal construct, from the time Fowles was an undergraduate at Oxford and Golding was a university don to the time that he learned that Golding had won the Nobel Prize for literature.[41] Even a potentially dry topic such as "Geology at Lyme Regis" becomes interesting as Fowles personalizes his experiences as a curator of what he begins by calling "the worst-sited museum in Britain"—a reference to the wintertime threat to the Lyme Regis (Philpot) Museum from saltwater dampness.[42] Indeed, most of Fowles's nonfiction writing can be described as personal essays, for even if they are focused on the outer world, most have an autobiographical dimension.

BIOGRAPHY

Some of Fowles's earliest published writing was biographical, but the occasions demanded a limiting adherence to established forms. His profiles of each member of the school's cricket team for the Bedford School magazine *The Ousel* are only several sentences long but contain pithy assessments, including frank descriptions of individual players' limitations as well as their strengths.[43] In an earlier issue, Fowles wrote the customary profile of his predecessor as Head Boy, Angus Mc-Callum. Although the first half is largely factual, the second half is a tribute to McCallum's leadership: "He realised, when he became Head of the School, that the School was suffering from the effects of four years of war and needed a strong hand to restore it to its former efficiency. He determined to provide the strong hand, and by vigorous, sometimes even drastic action, he showed that he had it." The tone of this characterization is respectful, and the profile is a tribute, but the word drastic rather than, say, *dramatic*, hints at dismay; to find Mc-Callum's strong-handed style worthy of remark suggests that Fowles's own leadership style was probably different.

John Fowles once wrote, "I think the first sign that I might one day become a novelist (though I did not then realize it) was the passionate detestation I developed at my own school for all those editions of examination books that began with a long introduction: an anatomy lesson that always reduced the original text to a corpse by the time one got to it."[44] This detestation has not prevented him from writing numerous introductions of his own to works by others, but he avoids giving plot summaries or "anatomy lessons." When he typically does is to offer some personal connection between himself and the writer whose work he is introducing, followed by a short biographical essay on the writer and, usually, some consideration of the cultural context. The writers are almost never the canonized saints of literature (Hardy excepted). Fowles prefers to introduce unclassical, even forgotten, writers he admires—often for their refusal to conform in some way.

Probably Fowles's most familiar introduction is the "Personal Note" to his translation of "Eliduc" in *The Ebony Tower*.[45] He explains the affinity he has felt for the *lais* of Marie de France ever since he read them at Oxford. He describes what is known or not known about Marie and speculates about what Marie the person must have been like from what she has written: "finely educated," "high-spirited," and possibly "an early victim of male chauvinism, sent to Shaftesbury [Abbey] to mend her wicked ways."[46] And he concludes with a discussion of courtly love, related to—of all things—Watergate. Fowles is perfectly willing to imagine the author behind a text because he is a humanist rather than a post-structuralist, and generally indifferent to critics who might find his biographical approach fallacious or naive. Part of his basis for valuing the writings of Marie de France is sympathy for a twelfth-century woman, who would have to be a nonconformist to be a writer of any kind, and another basis for his sympathy involves recognition that she is, like Fowles himself, a writer of fictions. Indeed, in another introduction, to a collection of her *lais,* Fowles begins, "Marie de France is the first woman novelist of our era."[47]

Fowles seems to have long been attracted to writing by or about people who, like himself, are not interested in conforming to social expectations. His "French lieutenant's woman," Sarah, is a characteristic outcast from her immediate culture, as is her forebear Ourika, whose devotion to her own Charles, Fowles suggests, is a triumph for personal freedom by a woman character rejected by white, French, aristocratic society.[48] A further attraction to Fowles, which he discusses in his epilogue to *Ourika,* is the resemblance of Ourika's situation to that of her author, Claire de Durfort, who had her own reasons to feel rejected—in another sense—by Châteaubriand.[49]

The first introduction Fowles wrote was in 1969, to the little known 1880 novel *Mehalah: A Story of the Salt Marshes,* set in Essex, not far from where Fowles grew up. He describes the author, Sabine Baring-Gould, as a candidate for "the strangest Victorian" and recounts several examples of his eccentric behavior, one of which was to teach classes with a tame bat on his shoulder. Baring-Gould went into the clergy, but Fowles observes that "his keenly independent mind must have warned him that he could never really be at home in a Trollopean Church of England."[50] *Mehalah* is not an undiscovered masterpiece, Fowles admits in his discussion of the novel, but he values it as a representation of the 1870s and sees in the character of Mehalah "the 'new woman' of the Late Victorian period."[51] It is clear that part of Fowles's attraction to the book is an appreciation for the author's willingness to be an individual; even though Fowles does not approve of some of Baring-Gould's attitudes, he notes that the man's faults "are redeemed in part by a deliciously sharp sense of humour and the feeling one has that if the prejudices were sometimes misguided, then at least they were sincerely held."[52]

In 1975, Fowles wrote an introduction to *Hawker of Morewenstow,* a biography of another Victorian and "ecclesiastical odd-man-out," as Fowles characterizes him.[53] Hawker, like Baring-Gould, was something of a religious reactionary who liked to flaunt his eccentricity; Fowles remarks that he is unsure why such men attract nonbelievers like himself but imagines that "it must be a blend of two things: their courage and their difference."[54] Hawker was isolated spiritually, psychologically, and physically in Cornwall, Fowles notes, and the situation is not unlike Fowles's own self-described "kind of exile" in Lyme Regis.[55] In a remark worthy of the sarcastic Hawker, Fowles observes of him, "there, but for the grace of godlessness, go I."[56]

Fowles begins his 1981 introduction to *The Book of Ebenezer Le Page,* "There may have been stranger recent literary events than the book you are about to read, but I rather doubt it."[57] The author, Gerald Basil Edwards, had died five years before and left behind the unpublished manuscript of this novel set on Guernsey. Fowles sees the major theme of the book to be the impact of new values on old, with the island a metaphorical self. The novel is "resolutely old fashioned and simple-tongued," Fowles observes, but he respects the provincialism of the islanders, who resist the homogenizing influences of the world outside in something like the cantankerous spirit of Edwards himself, who destroyed almost all his personal documents and urged those who knew him not to cooperate with any future researchers.[58] Fowles compares Edwards's situation with that of Joseph Conrad, "another exile forced to write in an 'acquired' English," and describes Edwards's last six years of his life, living as a lodger in England, as "ascetic outsiderdom,"[59] One senses in Fowles's presentation a felt brotherhood of the spirit between biographer and biographical subject.

In the late 1970s, Fowles took as his subject a much more famous English eccentric, the seventeenth-century antiquarian John Aubrey, in a much more extensive undertaking: the facsimile publication of Aubrey's chaotic notes and drawings for *Monumenta Britannica.* Aubrey is best known for his biographical *Brief Lives* and for having discovered the holes encircling Stonehenge; Fowles's introduction to the work emphasizes the originality of Aubrey's character as much as his discoveries. Having described Aubrey's major at university as "curiosity," Fowles compares Aubrey's methods—like his own—with those of a magpie, "with privilege to raid from" his more orthodox contemporaries.[60] Fowles observes that Aubrey's lateral thinking—called "maggoty headed" by one contemporary—has led others to underestimate Aubrey's originality, which can be seen in his attitudes toward Stonehenge.[61] Aubrey recognized, Fowles points out, that the monument must be observed directly, in the field; that stones and holes must be interpreted as nonverbal evidence; and that the archaeologist must be willing to look " 'behind' the Romans, a brave leap of the imagination in a period deeply imbued with unquestioning respect for ancient Rome."[62] Fowles praises Aubrey for his theory of education, with "its hatred of corporal punishment, its condemnation of any method that tries to bully the child into instant adulthood."[63] And Fowles calls his edition of *Monumenta Britannica* "a conserving homage to a great conservationist."[64] If there were any doubt that Fowles sees in John Aubrey a kindred spirit, his final paragraph describes himself and his collaborator Rodney Legg as "two more amateurs," in the positive, seventeenth-century sense in which they, too, are universally curious.

Other literary works Fowles has introduced tend to have some aspect of personal interest for him also. The first page of his introduction to *The Hound of the Baskervilles* is devoted to a biographical matter—Arthur Conan Doyle's decision to resurrect Sherlock Holmes after an eight-year hiatus—but Fowles devotes the rest of his space to discussion of his beloved Dartmoor and its legends.[65] His introduction of Stefan Zweig's *"The Royal Game" and Other Stories* makes clear Fowles's regard for the fiction, but he also describes Zweig as an author "hopelessly addicted to his own personal liberty," with an internationalist political orientation, a "shy and reserved" temperament, living in self-imposed exile from his Austrian homeland and mother tongue after World War II—attributes similar to ones Fowles has attributed to himself.[66] Fowles's introduction to *Miramar,* by Naguib Mahfouz, seems based more on cultural difference than on similarity, on some sense of familiarity with the setting or the mind of the author. Indeed, Fowles finds it "remarkable" that Egypt's best-selling novelist should believe in using the technique and the subject matter of the nineteenth century. Fowles's attraction to *Miramar* no doubt has something to do with its independent-minded, Sarah Woodruff–like female protagonist, but his larger aim is to teach Europeans about a culture they often misunderstand; as Fowles points out, *"Miramar* allows us the rare privilege of entering a national psychology, in a way that a thousand journalistic articles or television documentaries could not achieve."[67]

Fowles's reasons for writing several other biographical sketches are obviously related to the deep influence on him of the authors involved. Fowles often has mentioned *The Wanderer,* or *Le Grand Meulnes,* as a book that has long affected him and under whose spell he wrote *The Magus.* Most of Fowles's afterword about Alain-Fournier is biographical, and focuses on the effect of Alain-Fournier's one-hour meeting with Yvonne de Quievrecourt, whom he saw only once again but whose image evidently haunted him—like a muse—for the rest of his (short) life. Fowles remarks about this meeting—La Rencontre, as Fournier subsequently called it—that "one has almost to go back to Dante and Beatrice to find its equal."[68] Some of the biographical events in Alain-Fournier's life bear startling resemblances to experiences of Fowles's own. For one, as Fowles seems to have felt at Bedford, away from Ipplepen, Alain-Fournier found himself at a highly competitive school, a *lycée* outside Paris, "in exile from his beloved Sologne" and confused about what he wanted to do with his life.[69] For another, like Fowles after Spetsai, Alain-Fournier came to London after having met a woman elsewhere, has time to reflect on the experience, and "dreams of writing a novel about it."[70] Part of Fowles's fascination with *The Wanderer* is surely with its author's life, with Alain-Fournier's dependence on the physically absent Yvonne de Quievrecourt as a source of psychic energy. Fowles has described such a situation as a source of creativity for the way it displaces a writer's wish to return to some state of unattainable, unindividuated unity with the mother-environment.[71] This biographical attraction notwithstanding, Fowles probably derives many of his feelings of enchantment from the text of *The Wanderer*, not just from identification with the biographical situation of the novelist.

Fowles's introduction to *Round About a Great Estate* does not mention his attachment to another book by the same author, Richard Jefferies, but Fowles considers Jefferies's *Bevis* to be "the best boys' story in the language."[72] In his essay, Fowles discusses biographical details of people and places around Swindon that Jefferies knew and adapted as the "Great Estate of Okebourne Chace." But Fowles likes the fact that there are two sides of Jefferies: "One is the good journalist, the gifted reporter of what he sees; another a much more secret person, aware that he is unable by such objective means to express what he really feels, really *is*."[73] Part of the attraction of *Bevis*, too, for Fowles, must be Jefferies's ability to induct readers into that felt world, convincing in part because it is based on what Jefferies has observed around him.

Convincing representations of life in the countryside form part of Thomas Hardy's attraction for Fowles, too, but Hardy is not, of course, another novelist who needs to be rescued from obscurity. Indeed, *The French Lieutenant's Woman* can be regarded as a kind of homage to Hardy, whose Tess Durbeyfield certainly casts one of the many "shadows" from which the mysterious Sarah is said to come, and which even contains at one point a biographical discussion of Hardy and Tryphena, who Fowles believes was Hardy's inspiration by her absence.[74] Fowles's further biographical writing about Hardy appears in the introduction to *Thomas Hardy's England*, a study of photographs related to Hardy's life and works, edited by Fowles, with a verbal text by Jo Draper.[75] One of Fowles's first observations is of the contrast between Hardy's undistinguished-looking house, Max Gate, and the vivid worlds of Hardy's novels, a discrepancy that leads Fowles to ironize his own biographical authority with the remark "we should give up trying to understand great writers."[76] Fowles goes on to suggest that Hardy's outward successes, like his house, were for Hardy at a mental remove from the part of him that felt more at home in the past; Fowles observes, "The deep sense of loss this self-exile engenders, the guilt, the sense of the wasteful futility of human history, is a very valuable thing for a writer, since it is also a deep source of energy in creation."[77] Hardy, like Fowles, was a local historian, and part of the last half of Fowles's essay is about

"The Great Change" Hardy sometimes writes about, the depopulation of rural England in the last half of the nineteenth century.[78] Fowles ends, however, with additional biography about the photographers, most of it about Hermann Lea, whom Fowles characterizes as "no Boswell," for his discreet silence about Hardy's "confidences."[79]

As a biographer, then, Fowles tends to write about figures who interest him. The fact that they are invariably artists suggests that he is interested in how they have approached the problems he knows firsthand, how to draw on natural life to produce art, and how it feels to discover that the production of art can be more pleasurable than the process of living, even obsessively so. Fowles's biographies may reveal as much about him as they do about the people he writes about.

TRANSLATIONS

Fowles once told a *Times* interviewer, "I enjoy translation simply because it is much like a crossword puzzle—I am a great aficionado. You have before you a number of pleasing problems to solve and your tool is language. You don't have the novelist's guilt of creating something out of blankness."[80] Although Fowles has played with translating haiku poetry, almost all of his work as a translator has been into English from French, which he studied at Oxford and must have developed a reliable ear for during his year as a lecturer at the University of Poitiers.

Fowles's first published translation was an elegant edition of Perrault's *Cinderella,* illustrated by Sheilah Beckett and published by Jonathan Cape. The title page uses the term "adapted" to describe Fowles's role, even though it is a fairly close translation, evidently because Fowles does not strive to preserve the tones of the 1697 original, but renders the story into contemporary English. The proud stepmother is described as "stuck up," for example, and one of Cinderella's stepsisters comments that her diamond brooch "really is rather super."[81] Perhaps part of the attraction of the project for Fowles was his fascination with a strange princess who, like Sarah Woodruff, mysteriously disappears when a male falls in love with her.

Fowles's 1975 collection *The Ebony Tower* contains his prose translation from medieval French of Marie de France's *lai* "Eliduc." In his foreword to a later collection of Marie's *lais,* Fowles remarks, "There are twists and inflections and smiles in Marie's voice that not even the most painstaking and faithful translation . . . can ever quite capture."[82] Nonetheless, Fowles seems to have done considerable justice to "Eliduc," and it is unfortunate that his translation is condemned in Peter Conradi's *John Fowles,* in which Conradi misrepresents an article by Constance B. Hieatt, who, he says, "notes both how biased and partial is Fowles's translation from Old French, and also how easily it subserves male fantasy." Hieatt's quarrel is not with Fowles's translation, however, but with his comment about Marie's "sexual honesty" in his headnote to "Eliduc" and his "lack of sensitivity to a woman's point of view" in the title novella, "The Ebony Tower." About the translation itself, Hieatt finds nothing to blame and much to praise. She cites one passage to show how accurate Fowles's translation is and then goes on to remark that "the tone of Fowles's discussion of the young princess's mental struggles as she becomes intrigued with Eliduc is much truer to Marie's general flavour in these passages than what may be found in other translations"—the verse translations of Patricia Terry and of Eugene Mason.[83] Hieatt's reservations about Fowles's work are not over his skill as a translator.

Of his 1977 translation of *Ourika,* by Claire de Durfort, Fowles has written that he enjoyed the work: "Englishing it has been a labour of love, no labour at all, and publishing it . . . an act of homage to a forgotten writer."[84]

In the early 1980s, Fowles "Englished" three French plays for the National Theatre. The first was Molière's *Dom Juan,* which Fowles says that he "began by making a rough literal translation with the help of one of my old Oxford professors."[85] The version he ended with drew both praise and blame from London reviewers. John Weightman notes that the translation was not called an adaptation and, thus, should be as close as possible to the original, but that Fowles makes the servant figure speak with an inflated pomposity that is not in the original. Weightman also considers "the most striking peculiarity" to be Fowles's "introduction of 'frank' twentieth-century terms in place of seventeenth-century decorum," which he argues are sometimes "psychologically wrong" but do not seriously detract from the pleasure of watching the play.[86] James Fenton likewise notes that Fowles's translation "has pointed out any possibility of sexual innuendo," but he grants that Fowles "must take some credit for the fact that the play works so well."[87] Irving Wardle points out, "In the one passage where Juan can show humanity, the translation rubs it out. Molière's hero gives alms to a beggar 'for love of humanity': Mr. Fowles quietly slices out the love." Despite such departures from what Wardle calls "textual accuracy," he is willing to grant that many speeches "take on a powerful eloquence."[88]

Fowles published a brief essay in the *Times* on the day his adaptation of Alfred de Musset's *Lorenzaccio* was to open in 1983. Not written for stage performance, the play could not be performed as a strict translation, Fowles points out, partly because of crowd scenes and partly because all the speeches are written in "unmediated Romantic prose," which would make all the characters sound like Musset.[89] Robert Hewison's review notes that Fowles's version does allow for "some quite subtle characterisation of Lorenzaccio himself" but that Fowles's "unpoetic diction" led Hewison to feel "a shortage of poetry at the core."[90] David Kelley points out a "jarring mistranslation of 'orgueil' as 'vanity' " but still finds Fowles's decisions on what to cut admirable. "What is most impressive about Fowles's adaptation," Kelley concludes, "is that in spite of the modification of emphasis it retains the rhythm and economy of the original."[91]

Perhaps the most challenging translation Fowles has undertaken is Jacques Bernard's *Martine,* whose practice has been called "theatre of the unexpressed," or the "school of silence," and whose heroine is an inarticulate peasant girl.[92] Reviewers differed about whether the play— and the translation—were successful. Irving Wardle thought that "the power of the play, well preserved in John Fowles's translation, resides in its total grasp of the people and their circumstances and in its ability to convey this with minimal means." Harold Hobson, on the other hand, considered the play a failure for which "practically everyone concerned with the production can claim credit." Hobson called the translation "infelicitous": "Its Anglicisms destroy belief. 'Forget it' is current English slang. 'You've done for me' recalls Eliza Doolittle. It seems unlikely that a French peasant would call himself 'yours truly.' "[93] A contemporary English working-class male might do so, however, and Fowles was probably attempting to find a contemporary English equivalent for the nineteenth-century French rural dialect. The language of English village life will sound incongruous in a London theater if the playgoer refuses to cooperate in the creation of illusion.

BOOK REVIEWS

In his 1971 essay "Ordeal by Income," Fowles describes the plight of the ordinary young novelist in England who, earning little money from fiction, may try "giving up his true calling and [chase] after other literary hackwork . . . , wasting time on reviewing, Sunday journalism and the rest, and all the time losing faith in himself as a novelist."[94] His own case does not fit the profile, but it does seem odd that Fowles, a financially secure novelist who evidently considers reviewing to be an ill-advised drain on the energies of a novelist, should himself have written more than thirty book reviews between 1970 and 1980.

Fowles's 1964 essay "I Write, Therefore I Am" declares what Fowles believes a reviewer of fiction should not do: "posture" until the book under review is obscured, or condescend as if "all novel writing is a more or less reprehensible exhibition of infantilism."[95] In subsequent interviews, as recently as the mid-1980s, Fowles expresses persistent concern that reviewers—particularly in England—too often treat writers like errant pupils who must be scolded for their faults.[96] Fowles implies that a good reviewer provides a sense of what his or her experience of reading the book has been, in a way that will enable the reader of the review to make a tentative judgment rather than have to accept or reject some authoritative pronouncement by the reviewer.

Fowles's first three reviews appeared in American periodicals, in 1970. The earliest appeared in *The New York Times Book Review,* a review of J. Hillis Miller's *Thomas Hardy: Distance and Desire.*[97] Though Fowles finds much to praise about Miller's book, he concludes that "this is not yet the book we need." The pronoun *we* evidently refers to biographers and readers who want to understand Hardy the man as well as Hardy the writer, or even Hardy the textual construct. At one point, Fowles notes that Miller is good at explaining "how Hardy 'worked' as a creative 'machine,' " but not at answering *"why* was Hardy like this?" Fowles's second review was for *Life* magazine, of Angus Wilson's *The World of Charles Dickens.*[98] Fowles spends less time evaluating the author's approach in this book, probably because Wilson is more willing to assume that there is a writer behind the text. Fowles adopts the very mask he disdains, that of the schoolmaster, to give "full marks" to Wilson, based largely on Wilson's recognition of Dickens's shortcomings as a novelist, which Fowles considers to be "sentimentality, facetiousness, prudery, political and social schizophrenia, overproduction, dictatorship of character over plot, and (blackest of crimes) almost complete inability to invent intelligent, independent women." Fowles admits that the list reveals as much about himself and twentieth-century tastes as about Dickens, but he emphasizes Wilson's ability to show convincingly how Dickens's shortcomings as a writer arose from problems in Dickens's life—the biographical considerations he misses in Miller's book on Hardy.

Fowles's third reviews in 1970, for *Saturday Review,* is extremely critical of *From Cliché to Archetype,* by Marshall McLuhan with Wilfred Watson. Fowles's tone borders on the schoolmasterly, when he faults McLuhan for "the graceless style, the barbarously obscuring jargon, the incoherent hopping from one unfinished argument into the middle of the next." But he shows in this review how the inelegant style and organization of the book, even when deliberate, reflects a vision of the world that Fowles does not accept, indeed, that he finds "sick." "What America needs at the moment," Fowles tells his readers, "is much more the democracy of reason than a dubious aristocracy of half-baked antihumanist theory."[99] His harsh judgment of the book is based on a deeply felt sense of moral and social commitment, not on some vain wish to posture for his readers.

Fowles wrote twenty-one reviews between 1973 and 1977, all for *The New Statesman,* and almost all are of nonfiction books, and many are on subjects of interest to Fowles. His review of *Lighthouse* reflects his fascination with isolating environments, including islands and woods.[100] His two reviews of books about standing stones may have started his thinking about writing his own, 1980 book *The Enigma of Stonehenge*, for the title of one review, "Come to Britain?" refers to his suggestion that such monuments served a votive role, an idea he would later claim as a more or less original contribution to Stonehenge lore.[101] Three reviews are of books of social history—two about Victorian scandals and one based on recorded reminiscences about daily life around the turn of the century.[102] Fowles's only review of a novel for *The New Statesman* also turns out to be something of an essay on Victorian rural life, as represented in a modern reissue of Flora Thompson's *Lark Rise to Candleford*.[103] As one might expect from Fowles the self-proclaimed, amateur field biologist, fully half of the *New Statesman* reviews are of books about physical nature, in some respect. The most remarkable one begins with a description of what life would be like if one awoke to discover one had metamorphosed to a creature with radically different senses—a creature Fowles eventually reveals to be a dolphin (he acknowledges the debt to Kafka).[104]

Even though Fowles had written in 1964 that novelists should not review novels, he evidently overcame his scruple between then and 1978, when Fowles took over from Anthony Burgess as fiction reviewer for *The Irish Press*.[105] During the next year, he contributed eight reviews of novels and collections of short stories. Reviewing Samuel Beckett's *Four Novellas*, Fowles acknowledges that Beckett is "a born alchemist with words," but Fowles wonders why Beckett's "downandoutdom" appeals to so many middle-class readers. Fowles decides that Beckett, like Châteaubriand in the previous century, is offering "an emotional scapegoat for an age desperately in search of one." Fowles goes on to explain why he rejects literary nihilism.[106]

More often when he writes for *The Irish Press*, Fowles examines less well-known Irish writers and, typically, he comments on their technique and contribution to the genre—short story or novel. Perhaps in part because Fowles is not Irish, he tends to locate the writers he is reviewing—even Beckett—within the tradition of Irish writers. What he wants to see is writing that is not bound by that tradition, that is "in the best sense of the word, international," as he says of *Lovers of Their Time*, by William Trevor.[107] Fowles locates himself clearly with respect to literary issues in "Mainstream and Sidestream," a review of *Paddy No More: Modern Irish Short Stories*, which begins with Francis Stuart's attack on "The Soft Centre of Irish Writing." Fowles expresses his "intense suspicion of literary manifestos, especially when they are announced beneath national flags," but he goes on to describe why he found many of the stories to his liking. He notes that one of them "is a flagrant piece of traditional Irish fantasy, as soft and green as a moss-cushion." In the course of the review, Fowles clarifies not only what he thinks of various stories, but also what he thinks of "Paddyism" and those who "write to rule under intellectual trend or theory."[108]

Fowles largely gave over writing reviews after 1978. One exception is a 1980 contribution to *Saturday Review* on Truman Capote's *Music for Chameleons*, perhaps because he wanted to call attention to a book he regards highly.[109] Fowles writes that he is not much interested in Capote's notorious revelations about celebrities, which Fowles wittily refers to as "destruction of plastic fig leaves." Rather, Fowles values Capote's consummate technical skills as a writer and as a combiner of fact and fiction. Fowles compares Capote with the masters of French literary tradition, and suggests at the conclusion that Capote deserves comparison with Flaubert, Maupassant, and Proust. There is evidence in advertising blurbs from Atheneum and Delacorte Press that Fowles privately reviewed some fiction for them in the early 1980s. Fowles's 1982 contribution to *Georgia Review* is, in one sense, a review of *Chronicle of a Death Foretold*, by Gabriel García Márquez; however, the piece—about machoism and the Falklands war—is more properly considered an essay than a review.[110]

To a degree, all of Fowles's reviews are personal essays, which he probably enjoys writing. As a writer of books himself, he has special qualifications to review them. Furthermore, he reads widely and sensitively, and values correspondence from his own readers. The virtual cessation of Fowles's review-writing after 1978 corresponds with his assumption of responsibility for the Lyme Regis (Philpot) Museum, after which time he probably felt that reviewing, if not quite the waste of a novelist's time he once called it, took energy he could no longer afford to expend.

LITERARY CRITICISM

As his statements elsewhere have indicated, Fowles is less than enthusiastic about most academic criticism. Sometimes he tells interviewers that he does not mind serious, scholarly work about himself, but he says that he can understand when William Golding shakes his head over having had more books written about him than he has written himself.[111] Later in his essay on Golding, Fowles adds that there is an "unabridgeable abyss that lies between even the most sensitive and knowledgeable critic and exegetist and the creator."[112] Fowles has been generous with interviews and treats academics with politeness, even respect, but he expresses doubts about the value of much that is written. When asked in a 1987 interview what he thought of Simon Loveday's *The Romances of John Fowles*, he replied, "I read [the book] in proof and didn't much like it. It belongs to a school in England I call the fishmonger school. They put you on a cold slab and then filet you and dissect you. . . . You feel dead at the end of it, you see."[113]

What kind of criticism does Fowles approve? He told a different interviewer, "Good criticism must induce a feeling of greater knowledge of himself or herself in the reader." Elsewhere, he has written that "we now need more understanding of the general psychopathology of the novelist . . . that is, less attention to text, and far more to the process" (ellipsis in original).[114] Fowles's statements align him with the strain of psychological criticism that examines authors rather then characters, and the historicist in Fowles would value psychological methods that take into account environmental influences on a particular author. Fowles would want the analysis written in a way that is accessible to readers who are not psychologists, so that they will feel more knowledgeable about a text and its author when they finish, even if there may be a theoretical basis for arguing that readers' feelings are not based on the "realities" they suppose.

Fowles's use of paired opposition in *The Aristos* as a method of social analysis suggests that he might feel at home in the structuralist camp, even if Fowles does abhor being categorized. He seems to grant the importance of distinguishing speech from writing, but he seems uncomfortable with other aspects of post-structuralism, even though his narrator in *The French Lieutenant's Woman* seems to recognize—before it became fashionable to do so—that Roland Barthes is involved with a profound change in how people look at and write about the world.[115] In interviews, with reference to deconstructionists, Fowles acknowledges that he is "probably a little influenced by my own very half-baked ideas of what they are getting at," in particular the idea that readers are creative, but he refuses to accept that an author is "a mere irrelevant detail"—basically what Fowles's quarrel was with J. Hillis Miller's book about Hardy.[116] He also objects to "pseudo-hermeticism," which he notes that he has found "in a number of recent French exponents of structuralism and semiology,"[117] Fowles does seem to be conversant with post-structuralist criticism, even if he dislikes it.

Fowles practices literary criticism, although he does not announce it as such, in some of his essays of introduction. In "My Recollections of Kafka," Fowles uses himself as a case study of influence in which he writes down what little he can remember about an author he admits influences him, partly to show how the important kind of influence is through tone and feeling rather than specifics.[118] He concludes that essay with the assertion that "all writers are obsessives," an idea he would develop in more depth as a discussion of "preoccupation with loss" in "Hardy and the Hag," Fowles's Freudian critique of Hardy, of himself and—by extension—of any novelist.[119] Fowles's introduction to Stefan Zweig's *"The Royal Game" and Other Stories* also involves psychological criticism when Fowles discusses the behavior of the female character in "Letter from an Unknown Woman," who writes to her former lover—who does not even remember her—to describe the ten years she has adored him and suffered without making herself known to him. The terms of Fowles's analysis are stated less directly in this essay, but he observes that "the hidden secret of the self-denial is precisely its endlessness," that there is a level on which the story's male rake and female devotee embody the author's compulsion endlessly to seek—and to lose—the yearning for primal bliss Fowles had described a few years before in "Hardy and the Hag" as "the chief fuel of the imagination." [120]

This kind of criticism is exploration of the creative process, rather than traditional analysis of a text. There is one work, *Islands,* in which Fowles engages in a fairly sustained critical analysis of Homer's *The Odyssey* and of Shakespeare's *The Tempest.* In his discussion of Shakespeare, Fowles borrows from an academic paper about mazes and language, whose thesis is that Prospero's rejection of magic represents Shakespeare's rejection of playwriting, based on his realization that designing a maze—or writing a play—is solipsistic, not the kind of experience one has when finding one's way out of a maze or attending a play. Fowles notes, "It is almost as if Shakespeare foresaw the very recent neo-Freudian theory of language and literature as the prime alienators of self from reality." [121]

Fowles's discussion of Homer is more original even though it, too, picks up an idea formerly promoted by Samuel Butler and Robert Graves—that the author of *The Odyssey* may have been a woman. Fowles works with it for some twenty-four pages, offering various reasons why "Homer's" narrative reflects a feminine sensibility. [122] The evidence ranges from absence of detail about sea-faring (but lots of domestic details) to the sympathy with which female characters are portrayed. As with the *lais* of Marie de France, Fowles points out that "wisdom always lay at home, or quite certainly not in the overt original purpose of the journey," while "the sea and its islands thus become the domain of what cannot be controlled by wisdom and reason." [123] Although it does not advance his argument that Homer was female, Fowles devotes a paragraph to showing a "brilliant antedating of Freud" by Homer in the passage that describes the meeting of Odysseus and his mother in the underworld, where he attempts to embrace her shade. Odysseus reports, "Thrice, like a shadow or a dream, she slipped through my arms and left me harrowed by an even sharper pain." Fowles comments, "In that brief image lies the genesis of all art; the pursuit of the irrecoverable, what the object-relations analysts now call symbolic repair." [124] In Fowles's comment lies an idea central to his thinking as well as to his literary criticism.

VISUAL ART CRITICISM

Fowles seems to feel a deep ambivalence about visual art. The many references to paintings in his novels and his various collaborations with photographers in books indicate familiarity with and interest in visual arts, but he has expressed concern over the way visual art allows a viewer less imaginative freedom than verbal art allows a reader. He puts the matter succinctly in a discussion of how novel reading differs from film viewing: "A film or TV play is the tyranny of the maker's imagination upon those of his passive viewers. You are given no choice—this is, in every (and largely superfluous) detail, how it happened. You are a pair of eyes chained to a seat, forbidden to have an imagination of your own."[125] Fowles is well aware of his ambivalent attitude: in his introductory essay for *Land,* a book of austere, black and white photographs of British landscapes by Fay Godwin—who also photographed the Scillies for *Islands*—Fowles begins, "I really am not the person to be standing before this collection."[126] He confesses to "a considerable dislike of photography as everyman practices it," and confesses to further doubts about landscape photography as it usually is practiced, but he admits later in the essay, "Serious photography does—by that other sort of perversity, perhaps, which draws all of us to contraries—attract and interest me."[127]

Visual art that is not "serious" commonly fails to express a morally responsible vision by the artist, which Fowles would consider an abuse of the considerable power of the image. In a discussion of films and plays, Fowles once commented that "in a sense all art is totalitarian," but the spectacle of those art forms particularly awes an audience, which "has all the moment-to-moment imagining done for it by the visual image."[128] This distinction is one Fowles often makes when he discusses why he prefers to write verbal narratives, which require each reader largely to create what he or she imagines from a private memory stock, in response to cues provided by the writer.[129] A writer can omit to describe a room; a filmmaker must fill the screen, and a film-watcher must accept that version of a room. Even though film-watching also involves creativity, there is less ambiguity and less opportunity for creative response to a movie than to a novel, Fowles believes; so he remains wary of film as a medium. Another problem with film, or any visual art, in Fowles's view, is the way it privileges the pleasures of art over the instructive potential. By inviting an immediate response, any visual spectacle discourages reflection and consideration of social or moral implications. Fowles criticizes rococo art of the late eighteenth century as having provided us with "pretty objects, but only inside a dangerously narrow excerption from reality." Fowles believes that art should provide human consolation, but not irresponsible escape from human problems.[130] When Fowles states that tourists with cameras are "snapping everything into non-existence," he implies that the images do not reproduce the resonances and ambiguities inherent in the various possible relations of the human beholder to the original scene.[131] It is no coincidence that in *The Collector* the character Clegg is interested in photography as well as incapable of socially developed human relations.

Fowles would probably be inclined to endorse a tipping of the balance in the opposite direction, in favor of instruction, having once stated that "judging things on the boring/amusing scale has, all through history, been a prime sign of the sick culture."[132] His statement also implies that art has a socializing, civilizing function, but he probably would want that aim achieved through individuals, by art that encourages creative, moral growth in the beholder by inviting participation in an expressed moral vision by the artist. This last qualification is, for Fowles, the essential aspect of good art, which he states fairly baldly after a discussion of a Pisanello painting: "Art has no special obligation to be realistic and naturalistic, indeed any obligation at all except to say what the artist wants or chooses to say."[133]

Fowles seems to feel a personal, moral relation with some art objects, so his frequent allusion to artworks in his writing is itself expressive of what Fowles has to say, rather than a contrivance or a pretension. Indications of the importance of visual art to him include the final pages of his somewhat autobiographical novel *Daniel Martin,* which takes place in an art museum as the title character contemplates a self-portrait by Rembrandt. Fowles even chose the paintings that illustrate the covers to *The Ebony Tower* and *A Maggot,* from paintings that partially inspired him to write the books. Another artifact he owns figures in one of his early essays, "The Trouble with Starlets," in which Fowles discusses two theories for the abundance of *putti* in paintings of the ancien régime in France, to draw comparisons with the appeal of the seemingly ageless "cover girl" in contemporary culture. At the end of the essay, Fowles devotes a paragraph to reflection on the lime wood *putto* above his desk, which he perversely regards as a reminder of death, cunning in its timeless smile.[134]

His essay for *Connoisseur* on pottery figurines made by the Talbot family over the past four centuries in La Borne, France, is likewise full of social and moral considerations. He likes the fact that the objects were made by peasants. He likes the way the works express the individuality of the artisan. He even seems to like some aspects of the town of La Borne, to which Fowles attributes some of his perennial values such as "outflung," "mocking of outside authority," and tending "to vote socialist."[135]

In "Remembering Cruikshank," it is the moral content of the drawings that leads Fowles to call Cruikshank "by far the greatest . . . Victorian illustrator." Fowles arrives at his judgment by comparisons and contrasts with other artists. Drawings by Gillray lacks Cruikshank's "toleration," Fowles believes. Phiz was less successful at resisting "the schmaltz in Dickens." Fowles compares Cruikshank to Hogarth for seeing through hypocrisy and to Goya for raging against injustice and to Rabelais for openness and humor.[136] The essay is a short testament to liberalism, as well as an introduction to the art of Cruikshank.

Fowles praises the expressive execution rather than the moral content of art by Tom Adams, illustrator for the covers of Fowles's first three novels. In the introduction to a study of other covers by Adams, for Agatha Christie novels, Fowles praises Adams for what he says all good painters do: "infuse their work with their personal life." Adams's "independence of mind" enables him to find "a truly personal solution" to the problem of working as a cover illustrator, having to deal with a publisher, a writer, and a written text. Fowles values the "obliqueness" of Adams's covers, too, which Fowles sees not only as a lure into the fiction, but also as an apt parallel to the teasing quality of his own narrative.[137]

Fowles seems to value photographs by Don McCullin for their personal, expressive dimension, too. In his introduction to *Open Skies*, Fowles points out that McCullin's landscape photographs are not a portrait of East Somerset, where they were taken, but of the photographer's "uneasy" state of mind. McCullin's outlook is not cheerful; indeed, he is formerly a war photographer and sees darks and lights in the sky as symbols of a larger war, what Fowles calls "the most terrible and senseless conflict facing mankind at the moment . . . between man and his own environment, between human and other nature." Fowles compares the book to a sermon and McCullin to a preacher, whose state of mind Fowles shares.[138]

The attraction for Fowles of Paul S. Penrose's photographs of Lyme Regis seems less their expression of Penrose's mood than their expression of the "soul" of the town during its off-season when, according to Fowles, it is a "solitary, primeval town and harbour permanently embattled with the sea, still haunted by the ghost of its illustrious past." Penrose makes artistic choices that reveal himself when he takes a photograph, but Fowles recognizes in Penrose's images some awareness about the town that Fowles himself brings to the photographs, its "mood of exile." Fowles's judgment seems based on his personal, creative response more than on the photographer's creative production.[139]

Despite his concern about the tyrannical nature of visual art, then, Fowles can be enthusiastic about particular works in visual media. His 1967 preface to the opening exhibition catalog for the Fulham Gallery refers to the problem as "a kind of aesthetic fascism" taking control, but Fowles also expresses a hope that balance can be redressed with a restoration of "the formerly happy marriage between the visual arts and the printed word."[140] Tom Adams was doing his part by opening the Fulham Gallery, exhibiting work in diverse media, and catering to a popular rather than an elite clientele.[141] Fowles's own way of proceeding is to write essays and books to accompany photographs.

HISTORY

The text for *Shipwreck* is not long, an introduction to photographs of shipwrecks taken over several generations by the Gibsons of the Scilly Isles. More than Fowles's other introductions, however, this one does not focus on how events in the past relate to one individual, but, rather, how they relate to a social group. He discusses the practice of "wrecking" on the Cornish coast, that is, of supplementing one's livelihood by plundering ships that run aground—and occasionally helping them to do so. Fowles's approach combines methods of the sociologist and the anthropologist with those of the historian. He examines both the law and the popular misunderstanding of the law, both practices and popular misunderstanding of practices with respect to salvaging wrecks and cargoes. He uses psychological analysis as the basis for speculating on the appeal of wrecks as spectacle. And he relies partly on his own reactions as a guide for judging reactions of the wreckers.[142] Fowles does not write traditional history.

Fowles's books about Lyme Regis are also "new" history, with an examination of life at the level of ordinary citizens, as participants in evolving social processes. His foreword to *A Short History of Lyme Regis* announces as much, even as it discounts its status as history: "This little account in no way pretends to vie with the far greater and more scholarly work of Hutchins, Roberts and Wanklyn concerning Lyme, though it does try to present the town rather more as a changing and often precarious community than as a stage for a cavalcade of well-known names and events."[143] This approach leads Fowles to devote little space to writing about the Duke of Monmouth's ill-fated landing in 1685. On the other hand, Fowles does discuss such matters as the plight of wives' begging to raise ransoms for their husbands captured at sea, the interference of shingle-drift with sewage dispersal, and the need to rely on packhorses until the town acquired a road capable of handling wheeled traffic in 1759.[144] Likewise, in *Medieval Lyme Regis*, Fowles tries to imagine—and to help readers imagine—what ordinary life was like during the fourteenth century, from what was eaten and drunk to who probably was fornicating, and where.[145]

Fowles quotes the town charter of 1785 in its entirety, rather than paraphrase it, in *Medieval Lyme Regis*. Perhaps Fowles's awareness that historical texts are less "objective" than traditional historians believe is one basis for his inclination to present original source documents and let them speak for themselves. His edition of *Monumenta Britannica* is the most voluminous case in point, but Fowles has used the same approach with other historical materials. His foreword to *Picture of Lyme-Regis and Environs* accompanies a facsimile of an 1817 report on a two-day visit to Lyme by M. Phillips, a document that Fowles remarks is "so inaccurate in many places that it is not worth correcting," but that he evidently feels is worth reproducing "above all as a curiosity."[146] Like a fiction or an old book, it offers a glimpse of a different world in its own terms—not terms provided by the traditional historian or the historical novelist.

Lyme Regis Camera, published in October 1990, provides 145 historical glimpses of the town, recorded in photographs taken from the 1850s to the recent past. Fowles has arranged the photographs into groups and provides a caption for each, sometimes relating them to one another, sometimes identifying a building or town character, sometimes expressing an attitude. In the longest section, called "The Town," one Victorian photograph shows Summerhill, the building that for a time housed A. S. Neill's school, whose education promoted the liberation of children. The section "Disasters" records landslips, fires, floods, shipwrecks—even a truck loaded with bricks that once crashed into the Guildhall. Together, the photographs constitute a visual history of a particular place. Banal as some of the pictures may seem, Fowles notes in his introduction, "Books of past photographs are a little what graveyards were for the Victorians: where we think of what we are, and meditate on that meditation-spurning thing, the eternal leaping torrent of life."[147]

Fowles's 1980 book *The Enigma of Stonehenge* is not so much a history of that monument as it is a history of attitudes toward it. As the title implies, Fowles is interested in what is *not* known about Stonehenge, and what the questions historians have asked reveal about themselves. The book no doubt grew out of his own attempts to answer questions as he worked with the manuscripts of John Aubrey's *Monumenta Britannica,* the first part of which appeared the same year. In situating himself between the two extremes who offer answers—the scientists with their certainties and the "lunatics" with theirs, Fowles seems pleased to see Stonehenge as an emblem of the mystery he values in existence, in opposition to the explanations that can interfere with meaningful living as an individual.

With its drawings and photographs, *The Enigma of Stonehenge* does provide a helpful introductory survey of the different archaeological states of Stonehenge, from the first neolithic construction at the site around 2800 B.C. to the last work around the end of the second century, to the current situation with cordons, guards, and a sales complex.[148] Fowles rehearses theories about the origins and uses of Stonehenge as well as its uniquenesses—which Fowles prefers to think were the result of some gifted artist rather than a Mediterranean overseer of works.[149] But he is most interested in what he calls "The Stonehenge of the Mind," the various ideas about what the place means. About William Stukeley, who stole John Aubrey's (wrong) notion that Stonehenge was a Druid temple and spent his lifetime obsessively trying to prove that the Druids were a lost tribe of Israel, Fowles remarks that his image of the noble primitive helped to provide a counterimage to various national chauvinisms of the eighteenth century: "Whatever the archaeological foolishness of the Druid theory, whatever its patriarchal narrowness in religious terms, its effect was essentially humanist." Fowles considers Stukeley a "dissenter" in the broad sense in which he pushed an idea that did not conform to habitual thinking; he "helped the eighteenth century question itself in the way it most needed to."[150]

In an article he wrote for the *Telegraph Sunday Magazine*, a few days before *The Enigma of Stonehenge* was to appear, Fowles describes the project and notes that he has "ventured one or two new ideas" in the book. The contributions he considers original include the possibility that the bluestones were brought from Wales because their color was thought magical in the same way it was regarded by the later Celts who painted themselves blue. Fowles also proposes that the monument may have been meant to be seen readily by the gods—not extraterrestrial visitors looking for a landing strip, but the sun and the moon, to whom Stonehenge may have been meant to convey a votive message.[151]

In these books, and even in his *Curator's Reports* for the Lyme Regis Museum, Fowles does not pretend to write history for the specialist. His insightful readings of texts makes him the kind of amateur historian who can repay a specialist's reading, however. For the nonspecialist with a sense of curiosity about the world, Fowles's writing is always interesting because of its provision of significant details and Fowles's willingness to hazard interpretive guesses about those significances.

SOCIAL AND CULTURAL CRITICISM

Much as the *aristos* is the best for a given situation, not exclusive to some class of aristocrats, Fowles sees himself not as a member of one class, but as a participant in any class. He once told the London *Observer* that he identifies with some aspects of all classes: "I like the simplicity, courage and patience of the working class; the style of the aristocracy; and the capacity of the middle class for revolution. But really I dislike the class system violently."[152] By resisting identification with any one class or ideology, Fowles is able to discern his situation as an individual more clearly. This self-awareness, in turn, puts him in a better position to critique more comprehensive social or cultural situations around him.

One of Fowles's early essays, "On Being English But Not British," is a critique of his own situation in terms of two labels that, to Fowles, represent two very different sets of traits.[153] He does not use the term *British* as a code word for patriotism and nostalgia for empire; nor does he indulge himself in cultural chauvinism about how wonderful it is to be English. Indeed, he makes being English sound almost like a curse, but the label conveniently describes what he recognizes in himself as ways of thinking and behaving that are different from the characteristic traits of the other groups that make up the United Kingdom. Fowles explains how the English, descended from the Anglo-Saxons, tend to be subversive or oppositional to authority, morally perceptive to the point of priggishness, and furtive.[154] He illustrates these traits with the story of Robin Hood, which he sees as an expression of the essential English preference for retreat from public exposure into a private green wood. Fowles returns to this reading of Robin Hood in *Daniel Martin* because it also expresses the novel writer's love for Nottingham Forest of the mind, into which he retreats when he writes.[155] The essay "On Being English But Not British" is odd in one respect, however, in that in the very act of writing the essay, Fowles goes against his thesis that to express oneself publicly is *not* "English." Perhaps Fowles's occasional comment that he is in exile from England relates to this feeling that he should not be expressing what he feels and sees from his private vantage point, "in the trees." He feels compelled to write, but at the same time he believes that writing violates a code of behavior he identifies with.

The English temperament helps to account for their liking for cricket, Fowles explains in his essay "Making a Pitch for Cricket." The game does not appeal to the Celtic temperament, Fowles explains, "perhaps because it is so inturned and self-absorbed, so indifferent to pleasing the public. It is almost as if the English decided to invent a national secret instead of a mere game." Baseball, on the other hand, "is a highly extrovert game, very easy to like fast—accessible, in a word, just as Americans themselves are outgoing in comparison with the English."[156] As he describes cricket, often by means of comparisons to baseball, Fowles goes on to find in cricket various revelations of English behavior. Toward the end, as he discusses the contributions of West Indian cricketers to the game, the essay becomes an indirect plea for improved race relations and social equality, a goal consistent with Fowles's valuing of individual freedom in his fiction.

This idea lies behind two of Fowles's other essays in cultural criticism, or what might be called early feminist criticism. "The Trouble with

Starlets," in 1966, is a discussion of the cult of female youth: "Western, or at any rate Anglo-American, society has become girl-besotted, girl-drunk, girl-distorted. Our artificial world sprouts girls as the teeth Cadmus sowed sprouted armed warriors, and regardless of gender we all worship this plague; it has become a ubiquitous folly of our time. There is a word for this condition: nympholepsy."[157] Fowles explains that he is not opposed to pleasure, but he sees this mania for starlets, or *houris*, as a symptom of attitudes Fowles finds "inhuman and outrageous."[158] Fowles's 1970 essay "Jacqueline Kennedy Onassis and Other First (and Last) Ladies" is something of a proposed remedy for the problem identified in the 1966 essay. If women are to be taken seriously rather than treated as pleasure objects, Fowles suggests, then prominent women must act as individuals and not as articles of adornment. First ladies are in particularly powerful positions, and Jacqueline Kennedy missed an opportunity, Fowles believes, to be judged for more than her style, dress, and furniture; she succumbed to what he calls "the Guinevere syndrome," the wish to please the court as an ornament rather than on the basis of deeper matters. Fowles concludes by urging women, as "Queens of smaller courts," to do better.[159]

An essay written in 1982 called "The Falklands, and a Death Foretold" has an even more urgent tone. The title refers to a similarity in the behavior of the British and the Argentines during the 1981 war over the Falkland Islands, and the inevitable and pointlessly violent behavior in a new novel of Gabriel García Márquez, *Chronicle of a Death Foretold*. Both situations should remind us, Fowles argues, of the threat posed by something we lack a word for: "all that nexus of instincts and feelings that we inherit quite as much from our prehistoric past as from our historical one—the antique lumber room of the species mind, choked with totems and fetishes, ignorance and fear, selfishness and unreason."[160] Fowles is morally outraged over the way politicians on both sides manipulated public opinion during the Falklands affair, and depressed over "how quickly a mothballed tribal past and its emotions can still be reactivated" in the general public.[161] Fowles, who would abolish the monarchy, believes that tribelike worship of rank and power is an important part of the problem in England, as are religious institutions and macho ideology in Argentina and Spain. He explains why belief in "untrammeled liberty of the kind extolled by so many British and American backwoods conservatives" contributes to the sinister attitudes, as does a "ubiquitous refusal to face up to what is infinitely our major problem, overpopulation."[162] Fowles manages to weave these various strands of argument into a coherent—if bitterly negative—assessment of human behavior in the late twentieth century.

WRITING ABOUT NATURE

Fowles once told an interviewer that his favorite nonfiction piece of writing is *The Tree*, that "it was a great pleasure to write." His enjoyment of being in nature seems related to his enjoyment of writing, for he derives pleasure from participating in the worlds each provides. Even Fowles's earliest published piece of writing—when he was eleven or twelve—discusses butterfly collecting in terms uncannily like those he would later use to discuss his writing process. He first describes how to attract moths with beer, honey, or light, as he would later say he arranges situations for characters and then watches to see how they behave. He concludes with a warning for someone setting a specimen to "be patient, for it may not be possible to obtain another one"; the advice to lepidopterists recalls his descriptions of waiting for the proper mood for writing to arrive, and his obvious wish to repeat the experience each time he begins a new writing project.[163]

Although his interest in wildlife and rural habitats was longstanding, Fowles did not treat nature as his topic until 1971, when "The Blinded Eye" appeared in the British magazine *Animals* and "Weeds, Bugs, and Americans" appeared in *Sports Illustrated*. Using different rhetorical strategies for the different audiences, Fowles expresses similar concern in the two essays over culturally shaped attitudes toward nature.

"The Blinded Eye" begins with a quotation from a poem by John Clare, from which the title is taken. Fowles describes his boyhood practices of collecting, killing, and rarity-chasing to illustrate what he goes on to call "the hobby attitude to nature," which leads many such hobbyists to behave like Victorian classifers of nature: "It is as if the whole ecological and ethological bias of the new field biology never took place."[164] Fowles explains that he came to understand the limitations of this attitude in the 1950s, when he became interested in Zen Buddhism and became aware that "the lack of a right ordinary *human* attitude to nature has become of far greater moment for effective conservation than accurate scientific knowledge about this or that species."[165] Using a quotation from Keats, Fowles illustrates that "science may understand nature; but it can never understand what nature requires of man." Hoping to teach his readers to see for themselves, Fowles offers two examples of personal responses to nature and shows the process to be largely associative and personal, and only for an initial moment involved with "scientific processing."[166] He concludes with a discussion of his relation with nature as a kind of dialogue that helps him to feel part of the universe of being and reconciles him to the imperfection of things.[167]

Fowles is less philosophical and less literary in "Weeds, Bugs, and Americans," but there, too, he mentions Zen and Byron and Thoreau.

As in "The Blinded Eye," Fowles wants to change his readers' attitudes
to nature, but this essay is less about ways of seeing than about ways of
behaving. Much of what Fowles tells his American readers he does not
expect them to like. For one, he urges people to stop using pesticides
and weed killers in their yards and gardens. For another, he proposes
marksmanship tests before one could obtain a hunting license.[168] In the
course of his essay, Fowles acknowledges some significant differences
between British and American cultures that have led to the different
attitudes toward wildlife in the two countries, but his point is that these
differences do not excuse people from responsibility for the conservation of nature.

Conservation advocacy has increasingly become the emphasis of
Fowles's writings about nature since those 1971 essays. In "The Man
and the Island," in 1978, Fowles points out that understanding and
appreciating nature are not enough, that a love of nature "is empty if
it is not also a will to safeguard and protect it."[169] In 1980, he cautions
readers in his foreword to *The Sunday Times Book of the Countryside* not
to mistake the photograph of nature for nature itself, and in "The Chesil
Bank," written in 1984, Fowles worries that celebrations of beautiful
places can even blind the reader to the threats such places face.[170] In
his 1987 contribution to *Coastline,* his tone is angry: "Nothing can stop
man's worst self, his vicious notion of what freedom, his freedom, means.
Nothing, either creature or landscape, is so good, so innocent, so pure
that it will not be ruined or exterminated if it will bring more money.
In another species, we would call it cancer."[171] In his 1989 introduction
to *Open Skies,* Fowles mentions that Don McCullin talks like "something
of a convert to conservation, to the Green movement."[172] One might
say the same thing about Fowles—although he would avoid the affilia-
tion—that he increasingly sounds like a Green.

Fowles discusses his own attitude to nature most fully in "Seeing Nature Whole," a 1979 essay in *Harper's Magazine* that would constitute
the philosophical core of *The Tree,* published the next year. He discusses the way humans have evolved as "purposive apes," into increasingly urban, "thinking termites," addicted to tools. Fowles argues that
we must get beyond the notion that nature is there for our use, and
"grant it its unconscious alienation from us."[173] Acceptance that nature
is fundamentally different provides the basis for "a way of knowing
and experiencing and enjoying outside the major modes of science and
art proper, a way not concerned with scientific discovery and artifacts,
a way that is internally rather than externally creative, that leaves very
little public trace."[174] There are echoes of existential philosophy in this
orientation to life as art, but Fowles seems genuinely to depend on wild
nature as a source of personal creativity. Fowles refers to "the 'green'

or creating process" of an artist at one point in the essay, as if the processes of nature and of art parallel each other in his mind, and he uses the word *greenness* in a similar, metaphorical way in his introduction to *After London*, in which it refers to whatever "underlying psychic energy, or *élan*, is vital to the species."[175]

Thriving, green nature is important to Fowles's own creative process, not just as a parallel to the process of writing, but also as an integral part of his personal makeup, or identity, that enables him to thrive and work. It is an expression of the importance of nature to him that Fowles so often discusses isolated, green landscapes, or "sacred combes," as he likes to refer to them. In his fiction, they figure as the pine forest of *The Magus*, the Undercliff of the *French Lieutenant's Woman*, the Brittany wood of "The Ebony Tower," and Exmoor in *A Maggot*. In *Daniel Martin*, they include Thorncombe, Tarquinia, Tsankawi, and Kitchener's Island. In *The Tree*, Wistman's Wood on Dartmoor seems to be one of these special places, and Fowles has described Pasvikelven, in northern Norway along the Russian border, as one of Europe's "magic centers."[176] Such places seem to shape Fowles's being, to inspire his fiction, and to provide the impetus for his nonfiction essays on nature.

NOTES

1. Preface, *The Aristos*. 2nd ed. Plume Books (London, 1968; Boston, 1970; reprinted New York: New American Library, Penguin, 1975), p. 7.

2. "Confined Species," review of *The Ark in the Park*, by Wilfred Blunt; *London's Zoo*, by Gwynne Vevers; and *Golden Days*, by Lord Zuckerman, *New Statesman* (7 May 1976), pp. 612–14.

3. As of 1991, Fowles has published seven book-length works of fiction and is author or coauthor of eight nonfiction books: *The Aristos, Poems, Shipwreck, Islands, The Enigma of Stonehenge, The Tree, A Short History of Lyme Regis*, and *Lyme Regis Camera*. In addition, he has edited three nonfiction books: *Steep Holm—A Case Study in Evolution, Monumenta Britannica*, and *Thomas Hardy's England*.

4. "Notes on Writing a Novel," *Harper's Magazine* (July 1968), p. 90.

5. "Of Memoirs and Magpies," *Atlantic Monthly* (June 1975), p. 82.

6. Introduction, *Thomas Hardy's England*, by Jo Draper, ed. John Fowles (Boston: Little, Brown, 1984), p. 12.

7. "Report from Starship 26," *Poems* (New York: Ecco Press, 1973), pp. 111–13.

8. "I Write, Therefore I Am," *Evergreen Review* 8.33 (1964): 16.

9. "Notes on Writing a Novel," p. 96 [italicized in original]. Fowles says that he "came across the sentence in an obscure French novel."

10. "I Write," p. 16.

11. Ibid., p. 17.

12. *The Aristos*, p. 7 note.

13. Ibid., pp. 212–13. Fowles uses this idea in the parable of the prince and the magician in *The Magus: A Revised Version* (1977; reprinted New York: Dell, 1978), pp. 550–60/552–62.

14. *The Aristos,* p. 13.

15. Ibid., 1964 ed., p. 6.

16. Ibid., pp. 5, 14.

17. Ibid., p. 41.

18. Ibid., p. 56.

19. Ibid., p. 80.

20. Ibid., p. 96.

21. Ibid., p. 100.

22. Ibid., p. 113.

23. Ibid., p. 120.

24. Ibid., p. 123.

25. Ibid., p. 177.

26. Ibid., p. 183.

27. *The Bedside "Guardian": A Selection from The "Guardian" 1982–1983.* vol. 32, ed. W. L. Webb (London: Collins, 1983), pp. 5, 8.

28. "When the Bug Bites—Write," *Times* (12 October 1985), p. 8.

29. *Poems,* p. viii.

30. *The Tree* (New York: Ecco Press, 1983), p. 13.

31. *Bookmarks,* ed. Frederic Raphael (London: Jonathan Cape, 1975), pp. 53–57; reprinted in *Atlantic Monthly* (June 1975), pp. 82–84.

32. "Of Memoirs and Magpies," p. 84.

33. *The Tree,* p. 84.

34. "Collector's Item," *New Edinburgh Review* 55 (August 1981):7.

35. "Notes on Writing a Novel," p. 88.

36. *Ourika,* by Claire de Durfort, trans. John Fowles (1824; Austin, Tex.: W. Thomas Taylor, 1977), p. 8.

37. Katherine Tarbox, "Interview with John Fowles," *The Art of John Fowles* (Athens: University of Georgia Press, 1988), p. 188.

38. "Hardy and the Hag," *Thomas Hardy After Fifty Years,* ed. Lance St. John Butler (Totowa, N.J.: Rowman and Littlefield), p. 31.

39. Foreword, *The Timescapes of John Fowles,* by H. W. Fawkner (Cranbury, N.J.: Associated University Presses, 1984), p. 9.

40. Foreword, *The French Lieutenant's Woman: A Screenplay,* by Harold Pinter (Boston: Little, Brown, 1981), pp. vii–xv.

41. *William Golding: The Man and His Books: A Tribute on His 75th Birthday,* ed. John Carey (London: Faber and Faber, 1986), pp. 146–56.

42. "Geology at Lyme Regis—A Museum Curator's View," *Circular of the Geologists Association of London* 829 (1981):23.

43. "Cricket," *The Ousel* (10 November 1944), p. 106.

44. *The Tree,* p. 46.

45. *The Ebony Tower* (1974; reprinted New York: New American Library, 1975), pp. 109–14.

46. Ibid., p. 111.

47. Foreword, *The Lais of Marie de France,* trans. Robert Hanning and Joan Ferrante (New York: E. P. Dutton, 1978), p. ix.

48. Epilogue, *Ourika*, p. 64.

49. Ibid., p. 54.

50. Introduction, *Mehalah: A Story of the Salt Marshes*, Landmark Library 14 (1880; London: Chatto & Windus, 1969), p. viii.

51. Ibid., pp. xi, xiii.

52. Ibid., p. ix.

53. Foreword, *Hawker of Morewenstow: Portrait of a Victorian Eccentric*, by Piers Brendon (London: Jonathan Cape, 1975), p. 16.

54. Ibid., pp. 16–17.

55. Ibid., p. 19; Daniel Halpern "A Sort of Exile in Lyme Regis," *London Magazine* (March 1971), p. 34.

56. *Hawker*, p. 19.

57. Introduction, *The Book of Ebenezer Le Page*, by G. B. Edwards (Mount Kisco, N.Y.: Moyer Bell, 1981), p. vii.

58. Ibid., pp. viii, ix, xi. Several readers of this book have suggested to me that it might actually have been written by Fowles. James Kaplan points out that the description of the origin of the manuscript sounds like part of a *supercherie*, a literary prank (interview with author, 9 February 1991). The text is not at all Fowles-like, however, and for Fowles straightforwardly to "rescue" someone else's obscure work—as he does with *Mehalah* and *Ourika*—would be more consistent with his character than for him to want to deceive everyone.

59. Ibid., pp. x, xiv.

60. *Monumenta Britannica*, by John Aubrey, ed. John Fowles (Boston: Little, Brown, 1980 [published 1982]), p. x.

61. Ibid., p. xv.

62. Ibid., pp. xix, xx.

63. Ibid., p. xxi.

64. Ibid., p. xxii.

65. Introduction, *The Hound of the Baskervilles*, by Arthur Conan Doyle (1902; reprinted London: John Murray and Jonathan Cape, 1974), pp. 7–11.

66. Introduction, *"The Royal Game" and Other Stories*, by Stefan Zweig, trans. Jill Sutcliffe (New York: E. P. Dutton, 1983), pp. viii–xi.

67. Introduction, *Miramar*, by Naguib Mahfouz, trans. Fatma Moussa-Mahmoud, ed. Maged el Kommos and John Rodenbeck, notes by Omar el Qudsy (London: Heinemann, in association with the American University in Cairo Press, 1978), p. xv.

68. Afterword, *The Wanderer, or The End of Youth*, by Alain-Fournier, trans. Lowell Bair (New York: New American Library, 1971), pp. 212–13.

69. Ibid., pp. 211–12.

70. Ibid., p. 216.

71. See "Hardy and the Hag."

72. "Of Memoirs and Magpies," p. 83.

73. Introduction, *Round About a Great Estate*, by Richard Jefferies (Bradford on Avon, U.K.: Ex Libris Press, 1987), p. 11.

74. *The French Lieutenant's Woman* (1969; New York: New American Library, 1970), pp. 80, 215–16.

75. *Thomas Hardy's England*, pp. 7–32.

76. Ibid., p. 9.

77. Ibid., pp. 12–14.

78. Ibid., pp. 15–22; for "local historian," Simon Gatrell, introduction, *Tess of the d'Urbervilles,* The World's Classics (1891; reprinted Oxford: Oxford University Press, 1988), p. xviii.

79. *Thomas Hardy's England,* pp. 25–32.

80. John Wiggins, "A Fresh Mind on Molière's 'Odd Man Out,' " *Times* (6 April 1981), p. 6.

81. Translation of *Cinderella,* by Perrault (London: Jonathan Cape, 1974), pp. 5, 7.

82. *The Lais of Marie de France,* p. xiii.

83. Constance B. Hieatt, *"Eliduc* Revisited: John Fowles and Marie de France," *English Studies in Canada* 3 (1977): 352–53, 357.

84. *Ourika,* p. 8.

85. Higgins, p. 6.

86. "The Don and the Dons," *Times Literary Supplement* (17 April 1981), p. 436.

87. "Don Juan: The Seduction of Heresy," *Times* (12 April 1981), p. 39.

88. Review of *Don Juan, Times* (8 April 1981), p. 12.

89. "Florentine Fowles," *Guardian* (15 March 1983), p. 11.

90. "Goddess with a Glass-Eyed Lover," *Times* (20 March 1983), p. 43.

91. "Collective Responsibility," *Times Literary Supplement* (25 March 1983), p. 297.

92. John Fowles, "Theatre of the Unexpressed," *Times* (15 April 1985), p. 9; Irving Wardle, "Beauty Without Distortion," *Times* (22 April 1985), p. 13.

93. "Rural Reticence," *Times Literary Supplement* (17 May 1985), p. 551.

94. *Public Lending Right: A Matter of Justice,* ed. Richard Findlater (London and Harmondsworth: André Deutsch in association with Penguin Books, 1971), p. 104.

95. "I Write, Therefore I Am," p. 90.

96. Tarbox, p. 180; compare his remarks in Mark Featherstone-Thomas, "Goodbye, Mr. Chips," *Times Educational Supplement* (21 July 1978), p. 16.

97. "The Most Secretive of Victorian Writers, a Kind of Giant Mouse," *New York Times Book Review* (21 July 1970), p. 4.

98. "Guide to a Man-Made Planet," review of *The World of Charles Dickens,* by Angus Wilson, *Life* (4 September 1970), pp. 8–9.

99. Review of *Cliche to Archetype,* by Marshall McCluhan with Wilifred Watson, *Saturday Review* (21 November 1970), pp. 32–33.

100. "Ivory Towers," review of *Lighthouse,* by Tony Parker, *New Statesman* (9 May 1975), pp. 628–29.

101. "Menhirs Maketh Man," review of *Beyond Stonehenge,* by Gerald S. Hawkins, and *The Old Stones of Land's End,* by John Mitchell, *New Statesman* (22 March 1974), pp. 412–413; "Come to Britain?" review of *Cricles and Standing Stones,* by Evan Hadingham, *New Statesman* (5 December 1975), pp. 728–29; "Mystic Message?" *Telegraph Sunday Magazine* (21 September 1980), p. 18.

102. "Bleeding Hearts," review of *The Akenham Burial Case,* by Ronald Fletcher, *New Statesman* (14 June 1974), pp. 842–43; "Royal Stews," review of *The Cleveland Street Scandal,* by H. Montgomery Hyde, *New Statesman* (19 March 1976),

pp. 362–63; "Horse Magic," review of *The Days That We Have Seen*, by George Ewart Evans, *New Statesman* (1 August 1975), p. 148.

103. "A Lost World," review of *Lark Rise to Candleford*, by Flora Thompson, *New Statesman* (3 August 1973), pp. 154–155.

104. "Voices of the Deep," review of *Whales, Dolphins and Seals*, by D. E. Gaskin, and *Man's Place,* by Karl-Erik Fichtelius and Sverre Sjolander, *New Statesman* (15 June 1973), pp. 892–93.

105. "I Write, Therefore I Am," p. 90; Jay L. Halio, review of *John Fowles: A Reference Guide*, by Barry N. Olshen and Toni A. Olshen, *Yearbook of English Studies* 13 (1983): 358.

106. "Downadoutdom," review of *Four Novellas*, by Samuel Beckett, *Irish Press* (16 February 1978), p. 6

107. "Central Values," review of *Lovers of Their Time*, by William Trevor, *Irish Press* (28 September 1978), p. 6.

108. "Mainstream and Sidestream," review of *Paddy No More: Modern Irish Short Stories*, ed. William Vorm, *Irish Press* (28 December 1978), p. 6.

109. "Capote as Maupassant," review of *Music for Chameleons*, byTruman Capote, *Saturday Review* (July 1980), pp. 52–53.

110. Advertisement for *Savage Day*, by Thomas Wiseman, *New York Times Book Review* (18 October 1981), p. 37; advertisement for *Helliconia Spring*, by Brian W. Aldiss, *New York Times Book Review* (9 May 1982), p. 31; "The Falklands, and a Death Foretold," *Georgia Review* 36 (1982): 721–28.

111. Tarbox, p. 206; "Golding and 'Golding,' " p. 149.

112. "Golding and 'Golding,' " p. 155.

113. Carlin Romano, "A Conversation with John Fowles," *Boulevard* (Spring 1987), p. 38.

114. "For the Dark," review of *The Death of Narcissus*, by Morris Fraser, *New Statesman* (18 February 1977), p. 221.

115. *The French Lieutenant's Woman*, p. 80.

116. James R. Baker, "An Interview with John Fowles," *Michigan Quarterly Review* 25 (1986): 669; Tarbox, p. 195; Fowles, "The Most Secretive of Victorian Writers," p. 4.

117. *"Lettre-postface de John Fowles," Études sur "The French Lieutenant's Woman" de John Fowles*, ed. Jean-Louis Chevalier (Caen, France: Centre Régional de Documentation Pédagogique, 1977), p. 55.

118. *New Views of Franz Kafka*, ed. R. G. Collins and Kenneth McRobbie, *Mosaic: A Journal for the Comparative Study of Literature and Ideas* 3.4. New Views: A Mosiac Series in Literature. Winnepeg: University of Manitoba Press, 1970, pp. 37–38.

119. "Hardy and the Hag," pp. 40–41.

120. *"The Royal Game" and Other Stories*, p. xvii; "Hardy and the Hag," p. 37. The psychological critique of Zweig is not included in the version published as "The Man Who Hated Passports," *Times* (21 November 1981), p. 9.

121. *Islands* (Boston: Little, Brown, 1978), pp. 96–101. Fowles acknowledges his debt to Llewellyn Vaughan-Lee and Malcolm Evans on p. 2.

122. Ibid., pp. 51–74.

123. Ibid., pp. 58–59. In his introduction to *The Lais of Marie de France*, p. ix, Fowles nominates Marie as "the first woman novelist of our era. If I cannot

quite simply call her the first woman novelist, that is only because I believe the writer of the *Odyssey* was also a woman."

124. *Islands,* p. 59.

125. "Is the Novel Dead?" *Books* 1 (1970), p. 5.

126. Introductory essay, *Land,* by Faith Godwin (London: Heinemann, 1985; Boston: Little, Brown, 1985), p. ix.

127. Ibid., p. xi.

128. Christopher Bigsby, "Interview with John Fowles," *The Radical Imagination and the Liberal Tradition,* ed. Heide Ziegler and Christopher Bigsby (London: Junction Books, 1982), p. 115.

129. Leslie Garis, "Translating Fowles into Film," *New York Times Magazine* (30 August 1981), p. 50.

130. Richard Yallop, "The Reluctant Guru," *Guardian* (9 June 1977), p. 8. Fowles objects that "art as consolation" has been "stamped out" in "postmodernist theory."

131. *Land,* p. ix.

132. *The Beside Guardian,* p. 6.

133. *The Tree,* p. 66.

134. "The Trouble with Starlets," *Holiday* (June 1966), pp. 18, 20.

135. "Simple Things, Splendid Forms: Peasant Pottery by the Talbots of La Borne," *Connoisseur* (November 1983), p. 113.

136. "Introduction: Remembering Cruikshank," *Princeton University Library Chronicle* 35.1–2 (1973–74): xiv, xvi.

137. *Tom Adams' Agatha Christie Cover Story,* by Julian Symons, Paper Tiger (Limpsfield, U.K.: Dragon's World, 1981), p. 8.

138. Introduction, *Open Skies,* by Don McCullin (London: Jonathan Cape, 1989), pp. vii–ix.

139. Introduction to portfolio, *Fifteen Photographs of Lyme Regis* (Wellingbourgh, U.K.: Skelton's Press, 1982), unpaginated.

140. "Only Connect," introduction to catalogue of opening exhibition of the Fulham Gallery, 361 New King's Road, London, 27 November to 23 December 1967, untitled and unpaginated (1).

141. Edward Lucie-Smith, "Opening Exhibition: The Fulham Gallery," *Arts Review* (9 December 1967), p. 455.

142. *Shipwreck* (Boston: Little, Brown, 1975), unpaginated (3–12).

143. *A Short History of Lyme Regis* (Boston: Little, Brown, 1982), p. 5.

144. Ibid., pp. 7, 13–14, 25.

145. *Medieval Lyme Regis* (Lyme Regis, U.K.: Friends of the Lyme Regis [Philpot] Museum, 1984), pp. 18–19.

146. Foreword, *Picture of Lyme-Regis and Environs* (Lyme Regis, U.K.: Lyme Regis Museum, 1985), unpaginated (1, 3).

147. *Lyme Regis Camera* (Wimborne, Dorset: Dovecote Press, 1990), unpaginated (7).

148. John Fowles and Barry Brukoff (photographer), (Boston: Little, Brown, 1980), p. 6.

149. Ibid., p. 45.

150. Ibid., p. 112.

151. "Mystic Message," *Telegraph Sunday Magazine* (21 September 1980), pp. 18, 22.

152. "What Social Class Do You Identify With?" *Observer Magazine* (19 September 1976), p. 8.

153. "On Being English But Not British," *Texas Quarterly* 7 (1964):154–62.

154. Ibid., pp. 154, 158, 161–62; Fowles uses the word *furtive* to describe the English in "Perfidious Albion," *Poems*, p. 37, but it also describes the behavior under examination in the essay.

155. Ibid., pp. 157–58, 160; *Daniel Martin*, pp. 287–94.

156. "Making a Pitch for Cricket," *Sports Illustrated* (21 May 1973), p. 108.

157. "The Trouble with Starlets," p. 17.

158. Ibid., p. 20.

159. "Jacqueline Kennedy Onassis and Other First (and Last) Ladies," *Cosmopolitan* (October 1970), pp. 147–149.

160. "The Falklands, and a Death Foretold," *Georgia Review* 36 (1982): 723.

161. Ibid., p. 724.

162. Ibid., pp. 724–26,

163. Tarbox, p. 170; Fowles and D. L. Erwood, "Entomology for the Schoolboy," *Alleyn Court Magazine* 9.2 (1938): 11.

164. "The Blinded Eye," *Animals* 13.9 (1971): 390.

165. Ibid., pp. 390–391.

166. Ibid., p. 391.

167. Ibid., p. 392.

168. "Weeds, Bugs, and Americans," *Sports Illustrated* (21 December 1970), pp. 88, 95.

169. *Steep Holm—A Case History in the Study of Evolution*, ed. the Kenneth Allsop Trust and John Fowles (Sherborne, U.K.: Dorset Publishing Co., 1978). p. 22.

170. *The Sunday Times Book of the Countryside*, ed. Philip Clarke et al. (London: Macdonald Futura Publishers), p. 7; "The Chesil Bank," *Britain: A World by Itself* (Boston: Little, Brown, 1984), p. 27.

171. Introduction to "South Cornwell, Devon and Dorset," in *Coastline: Britain's Threatened Heritage*, ed. Kate Baillie (London: Kingfisher Books, 1987), p. 153.

172. *Open Skies*, p. vii.

173. "Seeing Nature Whole," *Harper's Magazine* (November 1979), p. 54.

174. Ibid., p. 56.

175. Ibid.; Richard Jefferies, *After London: Or, Wild England* (New York: Oxford University Press, 1980), p. xviii.

176. *The Tree*, pp. 82–91; Jan Kjaerstad, "Romanens store frihet: Intervju med John Fowles," *Vinduet* 38.4 (1984): 5 (trans. author).

FICTION OF JOHN FOWLES

When a novelist writes an article titled "Is the Novel Dead?" one might expect that the answer will be no, but Fowles's way of defending the novel indicates what he sees himself to be doing when he writes fiction. He does not argue in historical terms but uses the question to launch a defense of the novel against the alternative of film, as a medium whose demands on a reader better provide something "essential to human development and vital to human happiness—the right, the power and the need to exercise the individual imagination."[1]

This liberating virtue of the novel, generally defined, leads Fowles to criticize particular forms of the novel as less worthy of defense. For one, the classic English novel—or the idea that there is such a thing—leads to the writing of fiction Fowles finds "abysmally parochial, and of no conceivable interest to anyone who is not English and middle-class."[2] Fowles regards the "working-class novel" to be a dead end, having been taken as far as it can go.[3] He finds the American idea of "the recipe novel" particularly detestable, no doubt for the way it resists the freedom of the artist.[4] At the opposite extreme, when Fowles was once asked about the experimental fiction of William Burroughs, with cut up and permutative writing, Fowles responded, "I'm glad that one person's done it, and [such experimenters] do add a tiny bit to the whole broad range of literary experience. . . . I don't think there's much future in the way he's doing it."[5] One starts to wonder what Fowles does like.

In 1964, he described the best fiction in terms borrowed from existentialism: "To me, any novel which doesn't have something to say on the subject of whether and why the characters are authentic or inau-

thentic is difficult to take seriously."[6] In 1982, he chose the vocabulary
of liberal humanism to define his preference for the middle ground:
"To the extent that liberalism is a teaching or converting belief, then I
think realism must always hold a powerful attraction to 'liberal' writers;
conversely the always lurking suspicion of elitism in experimental or
highly intellectual writing (in the novel) will repel them. So will strict
'socialist realism,' in another direction."[7] Fowles wants to write within
this liberal tradition of realism. Novels give him sufficient space to explore and develop the verbal illusion of a social world, and entry by
readers into that world can subtly change their social sensibilities. Fowles's
wish to teach or convert his readers, or his hope that they will evolve,
can make his fiction seem didactic; however, he takes issue with that
word in an afterword to a collection of essays about *The French Lieutenant's Woman:* "The true function of the novel, beyond the quite proper
one of pure entertainment, is heuristic, not didactic; not instruction,
but suggestion; not teaching the reader, but helping the reader teach
himself."[8] The phrase *heuristic novels* is not elegant, but it succinctly
expresses Fowles's attitude that fiction is a tool for learning, an art
form that should promote discovery by an individual reader of his or
her self, with an existential, historicized awareness and an ecological
conscience, within a liberal, democratic, supranational social framework.

In the rest of this chapter, Fowles's novels and stories are considered
as heuristic fictions, in the order they were published. Included is per-
tinent information about the composition, the plot, and the reception
of each one, as well as what Fowles considers his aim to have been.
Page references to the fiction (American editions) are incorporated into
the text.

THE COLLECTOR

Composition

Fowles sat down to compose *The Collector* in late 1960, convinced such
a small-scale book would be more marketable as a first novel than his
amorphous draft of *The Magus,* or any of the other manuscripts he had
written in the 1950s. He was thirty-seven, and thought it important "to
prove that I could write well enough to get published."[9] Fowles has
acknowledged that two events influenced his conception of *The Collector.* First, he attended a performance of *Bluebeard's Castle,* by Béla Bartók, whose opera about imprisoned women seemed to relate symboli-
cally, Fowles thought, to the adolescent male daydream of being isolated
with an attractive but unapproachable female.[10] Second, he came across
an account of a young man who had kidnapped a girl and held her for

105 days in a backyard air raid shelter outside London.[11] Fowles went on to draft the novel in one month and then to revise it until the summer of 1962, when he submitted it to an agent for Jonathan Cape. The publisher was able to negotiate film, paperback, and translation rights for the book even before it appeared in the spring of 1963.[12]

Summary

The Collector is the story of the abduction and imprisonment of Miranda Grey by Frederick Clegg, told first from his point of view, and then from hers by means of a diary she has kept, with a return in the last few pages to Clegg's narration of her illness and death.

Clegg's section begins with his recalling how he used to watch Miranda entering and leaving her house, across the street from the town hall in which he worked. He describes keeping an "observation diary" about her, whom he thinks of as "a rarity," and his mention of meetings of the "Bug Section" confirms that he is an amateur lepidopterist. On the first page, then, Clegg reveals himself to possess the mind-set of a collector, one whose attitude leads him to regard Miranda as he would a beautiful butterfly, as an object from which he may derive pleasurable control, even if "collecting" her will deprive her of freedom and life.

Clegg goes on to describe events leading up to his abduction of her, from dreams about Miranda and memories of his stepparents or coworkers to his winning a small fortune in a football pool. When his family emigrates to Australia and Clegg finds himself on his own, he begins to fantasize about how Miranda would like him if only she knew him. He buys a van and a house in the country with an enclosed room in its basement that he remodels to make securable and hideable. When he returns to London, Clegg watches Miranda for ten days. Then, as she is walking home alone from a movie, he captures her, using a rag soaked in chloroform, ties her up in his van, takes her to his house, and locks her in the basement room.

When she awakens, Clegg finds Miranda sharper than "normal people" like himself. She sees through some of his explanations, and recognizes him as the person whose picture was in the paper when he won the pool. Because he is somewhat confused by her unwillingness to be his "guest" and embarrassed by his inadvertent declaration of love, he agrees to let her go in one month. He attributes her resentment to the difference in their social background: "There was always class between us" (39/39).

Clegg tries to please Miranda by providing for her immediate needs. He buys her a Mozart record and thinks, "She liked it and so me for buying it"; he fails to understand human relations except in terms of things. About her appreciation for the music, he comments, "It sounded like all the rest to me but of course she was musical" (48/46). There is indeed a vast difference between them, but he fails to recognize the nature of the difference because of the terms he thinks in. When he shows her his butterfly collection, Miranda tells him that he thinks like a scientist rather than an artist, someone who classifies and names and then forgets about things. She sees a deadening tendency, too, in his photography, his use of cant, and his decoration of the house. As a student of art and a maker of drawings, her values contrast with his: Clegg can judge her work only in terms of its representationalism, or photographic realism. In despair at his insensitivity when he comments that all of her pictures are "nice," she says that his name should be Caliban—the subhuman creature in Shakespeare's *The Tempest* (62/58).

Miranda uses several ploys in attempts to escape. She feigns appendicitis, but Clegg only pretends to leave, and sees her recover immediately. She tries to slip a message into the reassuring note that he says he will send to her parents, but he finds it. When he goes to London, she asks for a number of articles that will be difficult to find, so that she will have time to try to dig her way out with a nail she has found, but that effort also is futile.

When the first month has elapsed, Miranda dresses up for what she hopes will be their last dinner. She looks so beautiful that Clegg has difficulty responding except with clichés and confusion. When she refuses his present of diamonds and offer of marriage, he tells her that he will not release her after all. She tries to escape by kicking a log out of the fire, but he catches her and chloroforms her again, this time taking off her outer clothing while she is unconscious and photographing her in her underwear.

Increasingly desperate, Miranda tries to kill Clegg with an axe he has left out when he is escorting her to take a bath upstairs. She injures him, but he is able to prevent her from escaping. Finally, she tries to seduce him, but he is unable to respond, and leaves, feeling humiliated. He pretends that he will allow her to move upstairs, with the stipulation that she must allow him to take pornographic photographs of her. She reluctantly cooperates, and he immediately develops the pictures, preferring the ones with her face cut off.

Having caught a cold from Clegg, Miranda becomes seriously ill, but Clegg hesitates to bring a doctor to the house. He does get her some pills, but she becomes delirious, and the first section ends with Clegg's recollection: "I thought I was acting for the best and within my rights" (120/108).

The second section is Miranda's diary, which rehearses the same events from her point of view, but includes much autobiographical reflection on her life before her abduction. She begins with her feelings over the first seven days, before she had paper to write on. She observes that she never knew before how much she wanted to live.

Miranda describes her thoughts about Clegg as she tries to understand him. She describes her view of the house and ponders the unfairness of the whole situation. She frequently remembers things said by G. P., who gradually is revealed to be a middle-aged man who is a painter and mentor whom Miranda admires. She re-creates a conversation with Clegg over, among other things, the Campaign for Nuclear Disarmament. She gets him to promise to send a contribution, but he only pretends to. She admits that he is now the only real person in her world.

Miranda describes G. P. as the sort of person she would like to marry, or at any rate the sort of mind. She lists various ways he has changed her thinking, most of which involved precepts about how to live an authentic, committed life. Then she characterizes G. P. by telling of a time that he met her aunt and found her so lacking in discernment and sincerity that he made Miranda feel compelled to choose between him and her aunt. Miranda seems to choose his way of seeing, and he subsequently offers some harsh but honest criticism of her drawing, which seems to help her to become more self-aware and discriminating. Her friends Antoinette and Piers fail to appreciate the art G. P. has produced, and Miranda breaks with her Aunt Caroline over her failure to appreciate Rembrandt. Miranda describes her growing attraction to G. P., despite their age difference and his history of sexual infidelity. In the final episode about him, however, G. P. confesses to being in love with her and, as a consequence, wants to break off their friendship. She is flattered but agrees that doing so would probably be for the best.

Miranda says that G. P. is "one of the few" (163/144). Her aunt—and Clegg—are implicitly among "the many," who lack creativity and authenticity. Indeed, Miranda associates Clegg's shortcomings with "the blindness, deadness, out-of-dateness, stodginess and, yes, sheer jealous malice of the great bulk of England" (172/151), and she begins to lose hope. She gets Clegg to read *Catcher in the Rye,* but he doesn't understand it. Miranda feels more alone and more desperate, and her reflections become more philosophical. She describes her reasons for thinking that seducing Clegg might change him, and does not regret the subsequent failed attempt, but she fears that he now can hope only to keep her prisoner.

Miranda begins to think of what she will do if she ever gets free, including revive her relationship with G. P. on any terms as a commitment to life. At this point, Miranda becomes sick with Clegg's cold, literally as well as metaphorically. As she becomes increasingly ill, her entries in the journal become short, declarative sentences and lamentations.

The third section is Clegg's, and picks up where his first left off. He tells of becoming worried over her symptoms and over her belief that she is dying. When he takes her temperature, Clegg realizes how ill Miranda is and decides to go for a doctor. As he sits in the waiting room, Clegg begins to feel insecure, and he goes to a drugstore instead, where the pharmacist refuses to help him. When he returns and finds Miranda worse, Clegg goes back to town in the middle of the night, to wake a doctor; this time an inquisitive policeman frightens him off. Miranda dies, and Clegg plans to commit suicide.

In final section, less than three pages long, Clegg describes awakening to a new outlook. He decides that he is not responsible for Miranda's death, that his mistake was kidnapping someone too far above him, socially. As the novel ends, Clegg is thinking about how he will have to do things somewhat differently when he abducts a more suitable girl that he has seen working in Woolworth's.

Interpretation

When *The Collector* appeared, Fowles explained to his first American interviewer how he wanted the novel to be read:

"The Collector" is a parable; I don't want it taken as a thriller and reviewed in the crime columns. It's symbolic, it's an allegory. The girl represents good humanity, hope for the future, intelligence and love. The young man represents the opposites—the affluent society in a world where children eat earth they're so hungry. The generous versus the mean. I'm trying to show that our world is sick.[13]

Over the years since then, his comments about the book's meaning to him have become less moralistic-sounding, but not essentially different. He has described the conflict in terms of the Few and the Many, the intelligent and the stupid, them and us—what he sees as "a biological problem with the human race, that is the enormous variety of intelligence and culture that our societies and of course genetics bring about."[14] Fowles does not use this recognition of inequality as a basis for arguing that the Few deserve special status but instead for arguing that society should try to limit or reduce the injustices that oppress the Many and try to enable the Few to live authentically.[15]

The Collector also is a parable, in that the Few and the Many represent aspects in each of us, who sometimes are oppressed and, to some extent, inauthentic. The narrative is a lesson about how to live, and the examples of teaching in the narrative are examples for the reader. After Caroline responds in her "stupid" way to a Rembrandt self-portrait hanging at Kenwood House, G. P. tells Miranda that he must go: "The goodbye was for me. It wrote me off. Or it said—so you can put up with this? I mean (looking back on it) he seemed to be teaching *me* a lesson. I had to choose. Caroline's way, or his" (161/142). When they return to Kenwood with the Cruikshanks some weeks later, G. P. takes Miranda aside and talks to her about Rembrandt and his painting in a way she thinks is an attempt "to get rid of a whole cloud of false ideas I probably had about it" (163/144). When she tells him that it now moves her, too, he grins: "It can't possibly. Not for years yet" (164/145). He has been helping her to see more clearly while trying not to indoctrinate her with the proper ideas and feelings. For G. P., the painting is a heuristic, and the experience is meant to affect Miranda subtly, to help her to develop her ability to appreciate art and to live authentically. Indeed, she declares that she is continuing to grow up, even in captivity.

Miranda's behavior toward Clegg is modeled on G. P.'s behavior toward her. Clegg's collecting of butterflies is a symptom of his uncreative attitude toward life. He values them as rarities or as acquisitions, not as beautiful creatures. A living butterfly represents both life and art, or life as art, and Clegg's killing of them—or Miranda, or the language, with his clichéd speech—represents the uncreative behavior of the Many. At first, Miranda holds out hope for Clegg: "I feel I've got to show him how decent human beings live and behave" (137/122). Her final, desperate attempt to engage him sexually fails, not because he is physically impotent, but because he is metaphorically dead and cannot respond to life, to a potentially creative act. As she tells Clegg in one of their dialogues, "I try to teach you" (198/173), but he is a victim of biological and social forces that make him incapable of responding to her "lesson."

Reading Jane Austen's *Emma,* about the "education" of its title character, leads Miranda to observe, "I *am* Emma Woodhouse" (166/146). Miranda goes on to describe the similarities she sees in their behavior, but the more important analogy, or intertextual relation, is unstated: The Austen novel is about Emma's growth, and *The Collector* is about Miranda's. On another level, *The Collector* is a heuristic novel, an education for the reader, who is meant to grow and to learn by Miranda's example, as she has by the examples of Emma and G. P.

Reception

Not often is a book with a thesis a best-seller, but *The Collector*—to Fowles's surprise—became one.[16] Within six months of its initial publication, *The Collector* was in its fourth printing, 8,000 copies having been sold in England and more than 40,000 in the United States; by 1971, U.S. sales had exceeded 1 million.[17] Evidently, Fowles's ability to compel reading while he promotes ideas is a commercially powerful combination.

Reviews were generally favorable, but judgments ranged from "a first rate novel" to a "pretentious potboiler."[18] Reviewers tended to split over Miranda's section, often on the basis of whether or not they liked her as a youthful idealist or disliked her as a priggish bore. There was widespread comment to the effect that *The Collector* was an extraordinarily promising first novel.

One response to the novel is of biographical interest, the response of Robert Fowles. John Fowles writes of his father in *The Tree*, "It was not the somewhat scandalous—in suburban terms—content of *The Collector* that worried him nearly so much as the thought that it might be a failure," or that his son was being rash to give up his career in teaching to become a full-time writer.[19] Robert was not indifferent to the book's content, however, according to Mrs. Arthur Grindley, a bookseller in Leigh-on-Sea. She recalls that Robert Fowles came into her bookstore early in 1963, pleased to announced, "What do you think? My son has written a book!" After its publication, however, having read *The Collector* for the first time, he returned "deeply upset." He told the bookseller, who had arranged a special display in the shop window, "I wish I'd never told you about that book. I can't believe such things go through his mind."[20] This anecdote reinforces John Fowles's characterization of his father as concerned for appearances and middle class in his outlook, but it also helps to account for his comment in an interview more than twenty years later that, as he was writing *The Collector*, he could feel some of the inhibitions that affect young writers as they work in dread of the reactions of parents or teachers.[21]

Adaptation (stage, film)

The Collector was first adapted for the stage by France Roche as *L'Obsédé (The Obsessed)*, for a 1966 production at the Théâtre des Variétés in Paris.[22] In 1971, Jeremy Young produced an English adaptation of the novel for the King's Head Theatre Club in London.[23] This version, by David Parker, makes Clegg particularly unsympathetic by introducing a bondage motif. The play opens as Clegg straps himself to his own bed and tests the restraints by struggling as if to free himself; it ends with Clegg's strapping Miranda to the bed, ripping open her housecoat, and taking flash photographs of her as she struggles and dies of pneumonia.[24] Parker updates some of the dialogue. The Oxfam charity replaces the Campaign for Nuclear Disarmament as Miranada's cause,

and a conversation about Vietnam reveals Clegg's lack of engagement with the world outside himself. Miranda's responses are initially quite cool, and Parker elaborates other hints from Fowles to develop her dramatically: At different points she tells a story that builds up to a line from a pop song, she tells Clegg a joke about homosexuals, and she plays charades with him—all of which verbal play goes past him because the limits of his language, like those of his world, are considerable. The contrasting language of the characters and their isolated situation provide an effective adaptation for the stage.

The 1965 film adaptation of *The Collector*, directed by William Wyler for Columbia Pictures, seems more realistic than the stage version, in part because the camera is able to leave Clegg's house and to show him chasing butterflies (the opening shot) or driving about in his van (the final shot). Clegg (Terence Stamp) lies to Miranda (Samantha Eggar) about his name and where they are, seems to take pleasure in telling her that she will never be found because no one is looking for *him,* and sounds paranoiac when he accuses her of deceit after she agrees to marry him: "Don't you think I know you need witnesses to get married?" When Clegg shows Miranda his butterfly collection, she attempts to stab him with a mounting pin but fails, and he subdues her again with chloroform—on the same table where he spreads specimens. These touches make Clegg in the film somewhat nastier than Fowles's naive-seeming character.

One scene in the move is "Hollywood" sensationalism. Clegg's inquisitive neighbor, who appears only before the kidnapping in the book, in the film arrives at the door just as Miranda is taking a bath upstairs. Clegg rushes into the bathroom and gags Miranda, who is, of course, naked, and ties her to a pipe. He then runs downstairs to answer the door, where his neighbor wants to find out if Clegg has been tampering with the secret chapel in the basement, which is listed on the historical register and where another neighbor has seen lights on. As Clegg tries to get rid of his visitor, Miranda manages to turn on the water with her foot and the bathroom begins to flood. Suspense builds as the camera cuts back and forth between the conversation downstairs and the over-flowing water upstairs until it starts to cascade into the foyer. Clegg runs up and turns off the water, deftly explaining that the handle had come off the faucet but his girlfriend was too embarrassed to call out for help.

Fowles does not receive screen credit except for having written the novel, but he helped with the screenplay of Stanley Mann and John Kohn, which became somewhat Americanized during the adaptation process.[25] Although the screenwriters and directors received Academy Award Nominations, Fowles was not pleased with the film, which he has described as "just passable. It ought to have been made as we originally intended to make it. That is, as a small, cheap-budget, black-and-white movie."[26] Fowles has never said so, but he probably would like to have seen the story retain more of its fabulistic quality, which black and white values would enhance; Wyler's realistic, Technicolor treatment of the film tends to make *The Collector* a horror story rather than a fable.

THE MAGUS

Composition

Fowles often has pointed out that *The Magus* is his first novel, even though he did not publish it until 1966.[27] He considers it "an apprentice novel," though it remains his personal favorite and the only one he would care to reread.[28] *The Magus* began as a metaphor of his experience in Greece when he returned in 1953, though he says that he "didn't know what frame, what context to put it in or what style to adopt" as he was composing the first draft.[29] He did know that he wanted to write a book that would haunt people the way Alain-Fournier's *The Wanderer* had haunted him.[30] He can see, in retrospect, that he also was under the influence of Richard Jefferies's *Bevis* and Charles Dickens's *Great Expectations*, as well as the writings of psychologist Carl Jung.[31] He has mentioned the use of some fragments of battlefied description written by his father for Chapter 19, and he says that he found the hypnotism scene in Chapter 36 particularly difficult to get written.[32] He believes that he rewrote the book several times before it was published, making it "less Kafkaesque."[33] This kind of change must have better aligned the book with the advice from Alain-Fournier, which Fowles claims served as his "own secret and perpetual motto on the wall during the writing of *The Magus*": "I like the marvelous only when it is strictly enveloped in reality."[34]

After having prepared *The Aristos* for publication in 1964, Fowles worked to get *The Magus* into the form it would take when it appeared in 1966. He never got over the feeling that he had rushed the novel into print before it was ready, so when Jonathan Cape suggested publishing a reprint of *The Magus* in the mid-1970s, Fowles decided to set aside the project he was then working on to produce a new edition, instead, published as *The Magus: A Revised Version* in 1977.[35] As he revised, Fowles further crafted the style, deleted some passages, and extended some of the dialogic and sexual teasing. He has compared the work of revision to reassembling a weak piece of furniture. In one scene, Conchis tells Nicholas, "I travel to other worlds" (106/109); it is easy to imagine that Fowles derived similar pleasure from revisiting—as he was revising—one of his own favorite "other worlds" of the imagination.

Summary

The Magus is told from the point of view of Nicholas Urfe, who is bored with life. Having attended Oxford and taught for a year at a public school, he decides to take a position as the English teacher at the Lord Bryon School in Greece, on the island of Phraxos. Nicholas looks up a former teacher there, and is warned to "Beware of the waiting-room," without explanation (45/47). Nicholas is not deterred, but during the last few weeks before he leaves, he meets Alison Kelly, an Australian girl who is about to begin training as an airline stewardess. They are both sophisticated about sex and somewhat cynical, but each experiences some regret as they go their separate ways.

During his first six months on Phraxos, Nicholas finds the school claustrophobic but the island beautiful. He realizes that he cannot write good poetry and that he is having difficulty forgetting Alison. In a funk, he visits a brothel in Athens and contracts a venereal disease. He seriously contemplates suicide. The first of the novel's three parts ends at this point.

The mysteries begin as Nicholas goes swimming and someone leaves a book of poems, evidently meant for him to find. As he looks in the woods nearby, he finds a gate to a villa with a nearby sign *Salle D'Attente,* French for "waiting room." One of his colleagues at the school explains that the villa is owned by a rich recluse named Maurice Conchis. Nicholas decides to look him up and finds, inexplicably, that he is expected. After some conversation, as Nicholas is leaving, he finds an old-fashioned glove on the path and surmises that someone has been watching them.

Invited back for the next weekend, Nicholas is astonished by Conchis's collection of art and by his claim to be psychic. After dinner, Conchis tells Nicholas about an episode in his boyhood when he was fifteen and met a fourteen-year-old girl named Lily Montgomery, whose image haunted him afterward. They were both musically inclined and fell in love, but in 1914, she led him to feel that he ought to volunteer for the army. Conchis explains that he deserted at the battle of *Neuve Chapelle,* and offers Nicholas a chance to gamble with his own life by rolling a die and promising that he will take a cyanide pill if the die comes up *six.* It does, but Nicholas refuses to take the pill; Conchis seems to approve his decision, and reveals that the die was loaded against the roller—as was World War I against the soldiers. That night, as Nicholas is going to sleep, he hears voices singing a war song and smells a foul stench.

The next day Conchis encourages Nicholas to read a pamphlet by Robert Foulkes, written as he was waiting to be hanged in 1677. Nicholas takes it with him on a walk, falls asleep, and awakes to see a man in seventeenth-century dress staring at him from across a ravine. The man disappears before Nicholas can reach him.

At dinner that night, Conchis tells of his wartime pretense to be on leave so that he could return to England to visit Lily. As Nicholas retires, he hears a harpsichord accompanied by a recorder, and investigates, to find Conchis and a beautiful girl dressed in Edwardian clothes, but he declines to interrupt them.

The next weekend "Lily" joins them after dinner and speaks in the language of the early 1900s. Their conversation is interrupted when a horn sounds, a spotlight illuminates a nymph who runs by, pursued by a satyr, and another woman seems to shoot the satyr with an arrow. Nicholas is bewildered but decides that Conchis must be re-creating masques for his own amusement. Lily refuses to explain, and Conchis talks in parables. He describes an attempt to found a Society for Reason after the war, and he tells the story of a rich collector whose mansion is burned by a resentful servant. Nicholas begins to fall in love with Lily, who professes to be as mystified by what Conchis may be up to as Nicholas is. Conchis explains that she is a schizophrenic whom he indulges by letting her manipulate men in the controlled environment at Bourani, but that Nicholas must not believe what she tells him. For the weekend's culminating experience, Conchis hypnotizes Nicholas, who experiences the separateness of himself from everything else. Nicholas leaves eager to return for more adventures.

Alison has invited Nicholas to Athens the next weekend. Nicholas finds the villa closed up, so he meets her and falsely tells her that he is suffering from syphilis. They have an enjoyable weekend climbing in the mountains, at the end of which, back in Athens, Nicholas confesses his lie and tells her about Bourani—and Lily. Alison is hurt, and gives him an ultimatum: She will quit her job and join him on Phraxos, or she will leave him. When Nicholas hesitates, a violent argument ensues, and she refuses to let him back in their hotel room.

When Nicholas returns to the villa, Conchis drops the pretense that Lily is a schizophrenic and tells him that she and her twin sister are actresses named Julie and June, whom Conchis has hired for a theatrical experiment. The first evening, Conchis tells Nicholas the story of Henrik Nygaard, a blind madman who believes that he talks with God. Afterward, Nicholas goes to a passionate rendezvous with Julie in the woods, where he is shocked to discover that Julie has sent her twin sister instead. June explains that they feel like prisoners, always watched by Conchis's black valet, Joe, repeatedly told to learn lines and to prepare for improvisations, but never told what it all means. The next day the twins tell Nicholas their backgrounds and show him documents to support their statements. After a day of being shadowed by Joe, even while they are inside an empty chapel, the twins leave with Conchis on his yacht, vowing to insist that he begin to be forthright with them all.

The next Wednesday the yacht returns, and Julie meets Nicholas at night to assure him that there will be no more pretense of schizophrenia; however, Nicholas is to join the twins in the improvisation the next weekend, after which all will be explained. Julie again avoids sex with Nicholas, pleading her menstrual period. On his way back to school in the dark, Nicholas is stopped by a patrol of soldiers in Nazi uniforms, who proceed to beat up a captured partisan. To Nicholas's dismay, he receives a letter on Friday that he will not be welcome, after all, at the villa that weekend.

Nicholas receives two letters the next Thursday, one from Julie indicating that Conchis has told her that Nicholas was sick and the other from Alison's roommate telling Nicholas that Alison has committed suicide. He does not reveal this to Conchis the next weekend, but demands to know the truth. Conchis explains that he is experimenting with a new form of theater, without audience, in which everyone is an actor.

Conchis continues the supposed story of his life with the narrative of the German occupation, when he served as mayor of Phraxos. A crucial event, interpreted differently by different characters in the novel, occurred after the killing of three Austrian soldiers by guerrillas. Conchis was told that the lives of eighty villagers about to be executed in reprisal would be spared if he would club the guerrilla leader to death; he refused, and took his place with the hostages, but managed to survive the mass execution.

Conchis then explains that Julie is his mistress and that they are all about to leave. When Nicholas tries to confront Julie, she disappears, playfully demonstrating one of their hiding places in an old bunker. Inside, she denies what Conchis has said, but as she climbs out of the bunker, she is grabbed and Nicholas locked in. When he gets out, he finds the villa shut up and a skull and a doll hanging from a nearby tree. Nicholas does not know what to think and returns to school.

Several nights later, June appears at the school in distress, concerned about Julie. She says that they have lied to Nicholas and falsified documents about who they are. Nicholas explains that their games have cost the life of Alison. She apologizes, and explains that Conchis is really a psychiatrist doing research and that Julie is at his house in the village, to which June offers to take Nicholas. When he arrives, Nicholas and Julie make passionate love, after which she tells him that Julie is not really her name, and walks out. Three men walk in and restrain Nicholas as they administer an injection that makes him lose consciousness.

Some days later, Nicholas revives, is dressed in ritual garb, and is taken to a chamber decorated with symbols, where he is seated on a throne facing twelve figures in bizarre costumes. As they unmask, they are introduced as psychiatrists, including the former Lily as Dr. Vanessa Maxwell, who reads a clinical diagnosis of Nicholas's psychological problems. She is then stripped to the waist and tied to a flogging frame, as Nicholas is handed a cat-o'-nine-tails and invited to judge her—and the others—by choosing to flay her or not. He declines. Then Nicholas is tied to the frame, to watch Lily and Joe make tender love in front of him. Afterward, he is again made unconscious.

Nicholas awakens on the mainland, alone, He returns to the school and gets himself fired. He goes back to the villa and searches for clues. Although he finds a typescript of a story about how a prince learns to become a magician by accepting that life is full of illusion, Nicholas goes on looking for explanations. The second part of the book ends with his discovery that Alison is still alive, her supposed suicide evidently part of the charade.

In the last part, Nicholas continues his research. Nicholas finds no record of Conchis's supposed credentials in psychology. He interviews one of his predecessors at the Lord Byron School, now living as a monk in Italy, but the monk is not interested in helping Nicholas. He finally succeeds in locating a house in which a Montgomery lived during World War I and the inhabitant directs him to one of the Montgomery daughters, a Mrs. Lily de Seitas. At first, she toys with Nicholas, but when he finds out that she has twin daughters of her own, she admits that she is a friend of Conchis—and of Alison. Nicholas is angry, partly over her refusal to tell him where Alison is, but he gradually overcomes his resentment and they meet again.

Nicholas begins to appreciate what has happened, and even declines to discuss it with his immediate predecessor at the Lord Byron School. Finally, Alison appears when he least expects her, and they have a confrontation in Regent's Park, where he at first imagines that they are being watched from Cumberland Terrace. Nicholas issues her an ultimatum—"them or me." She rejects the ultimatum, and Nicholas walks away from her. When she follows him, he slaps her without understanding why. Then he realizes that they are unobserved and asks forgiveness. The novel ends at that point, with their future relationship uncertain.

Interpretation

The ending is meant to be open, so it is unwise to infer a romantic closure from the Latin quotation that concludes the novel: "Whoever has never loved, let that person love tomorrow; whoever has loved, let that person love tomorrow." From the Latin *Vigil of Venus*, the quotation sounds like a prophecy of love, respectively for Nicholas and Ali-

son, but the "tomorrow" could indicate love at another time, with someone else. Or it could indeed refer to their love, the "shattered crystal
waiting to be reborn" that Nicholas sees in Alison (665/667). What is
more important to appreciate is that Nicholas finally has recognized
that he is free, which he could never recognize so long as he believed
that he was being watched and manipulated by Conchis, as if by some
controlling deity. *Freedom* is a key word in *The Magus*, the title (in Greek)
of the only chapter that has a title (414/420) and, probably, the unspecified word that Nicholas tells Alison is "her word," which he "now"
understands—three paragraphs from the end of the novel (665/667).

The elaborately staged events have been designed, evidently, to shock
Nicholas into self-awareness. The various explanations Conchis has offered usually have some basis in truth but are meant to be taken metaphorically. Indeed, Nicholas has to overcome his impulse to understand everything that has happened in a rational, literal way before he
can accept his experience as somehow therapeutic but, at its core, unex-
plainable.

Conchis describes his activities at one point as metatheater, which
blurs the usual distinctions between art and life by removing not only
the stage and the walls but also the audience (406/413). Nicholas finds
himself unwittingly participating in this drama, which is difficult to dis-
tinguish from life and in which the episodes seem designed to represent systems of thought only to show that they are illusory. By turns,
experiences with mythology, religion, and psychology are made to seem
both real and inadequate. The parable of the prince and the magician
(550–52/560–62) suggests that Nicholas would be wise to accept the
illusory nature of all systematic thought and adopt the ironic smile of
one who manipulates such systems without believing that they involve
"truth."

The various guises Conchis has adopted not only have kept Nicholas
feeling uncertain but also serve to lure him back and draw him into an
artistic labyrinth, much as the novel keeps readers turning pages, in
part, by making them feel unsure about what is going on. Indeed, the
metatheater of Conchis (which he says is to be pronounced like the
word *conscious*) seems analogous to the metafiction that Fowles is writing, meant to put readers through a literary experience that parallels
the dramatic experience Conchis is putting Nicholas through. The sur-
prises to Nicholas also surprise the reader, as the slap of a Zen master
may shock the pupil into new awareness.[36] The reader is expected to
judge Nicholas as he is expected to judge Lily and Conchis. Like Conchis, Fowles disappears at the end, leaving the situation unresolved and
his readers "free" to script their own versions of Nicholas's future, as
Nicholas discovers himself free to do in Regents Park.

Fowles has referred to *The Magus* as "a teaching book," and he is probably referring to teaching the reader, but the narrative is about the education of Nicholas Urfe. He describes his affair with Alison in terms of reciprocal teaching (35/37), and their relationship is the closest he comes to loving in the novel. What Conchis says of Julie, when he describes her as a schizophrenic and himself as a therapist, could apply to Nicholas as well: "I wish to bring the poor child to a realization of her own true problem by forcing her to recognize the nature of the artificial situation we are creating together here" (282/287). Like the boy-prince who grows up to become a magician, *The Magus* is about the education of Nicholas Urfe, who grows up as a human being. Mrs. de Seitas calls Conchis "the greatest teacher in the world" (479/487), and Nicholas has much to learn—as Conchis himself tells Nicholas at one point (405/411). Insofar as a reader identifies with Nicholas—as it is hard not to do with a narrator—the novel is a heuristic, or a tool for teaching the reader how to live.

Reception

Whereas *The Collector* surprised Fowles by the degree of its success, he had thought that *The Magus* would be more successful than it turned out to be.[37] When first published, it received particularly harsh reviews in England. *The Spectator* referred to "intellectual vulgarity," *The Times Literary Supplement* to "a silly book and an unhealthy one," and *The Reporter* to "a jumble of vast platitudes."[38] Penelope Mortimer's review in *New Statesman* concludes that some of the bewilderment results because "one cannot understand that there is nothing there."[39] In the United States, on the other hand, *The Magus* was welcomed, called "a civilizing novel" in *The New Republic* and "a marvelous, compelling" one in the *New York Times*.[40] On American college campuses, the book became a cult novel, prompting more letters to the author than any of Fowles's other books.[41] Readers' reactions seemed to reflect what they thought of being taught; those who were put off by Fowles's evidently didactic intentions found the book pretentious, and those who were willing to suspend belief in their own intellectual adulthood found the book exciting.

Adaptation (film)

The 1968 adaptation of the film is directed by Guy Green, and John Fowles is credited with writing the screenplay. Michael Caine plays Nicholas, Anthony Quinn plays Conchis, Anna Karina plays Anne (the novel's Alison), and Candace Bergen plays Lily and Rose. Despite all this talent, the film lost money and even became somewhat notorious as an artistic failure. Woody Allen has remarked that if he had his life to live over again, he would want everything exactly the same with the exception of seeing the film version of *The Magus*.[42]

The movie opens with Nicholas's arrival on Phraxos, where the camera closes in on a man sitting in front of a cafe; recognition of his face later, outside Alison's hotel room in Athens, is meant to convey the extent of Conchis's control. Nicholas finds a copy of *Seven Types of Ambiguity* in his room and Eliot verses on the beach, in a book marked by a lock of blonde hair. When Conchis appears, he seems to be an eccentric, prone to cryptic-sounding pronouncements and odd-looking salutes to the sun. Candace Bergen is suitably stiff and formal as Lily, but less convincing as a seductress, let alone a pornographic movie actress. Nicholas's relationship with Alison is developed in flashbacks, during one of which she shows him a daisy in a paperweight that she found while she was obtaining an abortion and that now represents "something unspoken, unbetrayed at the heart of things." The scenes in which Nicholas rolls the dice and in which the villagers are executed are suspenseful, but the final ordeal of Nicholas is handled clumsily. First, the would-be hallucinatory special effects appear contrived; then, just as the trial scene begins to acquire some momentum, Conchis kicks a psychoanalysis machine to get it functioning again and destroys any seriousness of tone.

In the final scene, the film tries to convey Nicholas's attempts to come to terms with his experience and the open ending of the novel. He returns to the villa and finds it closed up but sees Conchis driving off in his motorboat, accompanied by the supposedly dead Alison. Nicholas then turns to Conchis's Buddhist statue and smiles back at it; a voice-over recital begins of the lines found earlier on the beach—"We shall not cease from exploration"—read at first in the voice of Conchis, which turns into the voice of Nicholas.

A fundamental problem with the film is its attempt to be too faithful to a 600-page novel. Too much is compressed into ninety minutes, so that each shot must convey complex but essential meaning, and every line of dialogue must carry a philosophical burden. Instead of enjoying the strange experiences at Bourani, as one can do in the novel, a viewer feels rushed and jerked about and, finally, baffled.

Although Fowles wrote the screenplay, he calls the film "a disaster all the way down the line."[43] He notes that the director and producers changed the script. He believes that Candace Bergen did not get the direction she needed. He thinks that Anthony Quinn was "absolutely wrong" for the part of Conchis. "Everyone meant well," Fowles admits, but the movie "just didn't come together."[44] Once Fowles referred to *The Magus* and *Justine* as "the two worst films of the Sixties."[45] The experience no doubt helped Fowles to create the character of Daniel Martin, the failed screenwriter of Fowles's 1977 novel.

THE FRENCH LIEUTENANT'S WOMAN

Composition

Fowles has provided unusually detailed, autobiographical insights into the process of composing *The French Lieutenant's Woman* in his often-reprinted essay "Notes on Writing a Novel," based on the journal he was keeping. He describes how the image of a woman standing on the Cobb, staring out to sea, came to him in a waking dream in the fall of 1966 and persisted until he set aside his other projects to work on her story in the spring of 1967.[46] He proceeded to write the first draft "in one go," over a nine-month period, and then spent the next two years revising.[47] During that stage, he worked line by line to create the illusion of Victorian prose and dialogue, lengthening sentences and deleting contractions.[48] He reduced the amount of illusion-breaking commentary by the narrator because he thought that the novel was becoming too intellectual.[49] He added most of the material about life in the nineteenth century.[50] At his wife's urging, he dropped his idea that he should appear on the train as a maniac-murderer instead of as the Fowles-like narrator.[51] And Fowles switched the order of the endings, so that the conventional "happy" ending would not come last (contrary to the narrator's insistence, on page 406/318, that he does not believe in fixing fights).[52] Fowles has compared the whole experience to writing science fiction, in which trying to imagine how a Victorian would behave was like trying to imagine life on an unfamiliar planet, in the past instead of the future.

The more familiar world of Fowles's present also influenced the writing of the novel, in various ways. At the time he felt the complusion to tell this story, he and Elizabeth had been living in Dorset for less than a year. They were living in the farmhouse that would figure as "the Dairy," on the edge of the Undercliff near Lyme Regis, at the time he began to have the persistent vision of the woman standing on the Cobb. He seems even to have taken Sarah's last name from a prominent local landowner and educationist, Alban J. Woodroffe.[53] In his study at Underhill Farm, Fowles was surrounded by old books, many of them Victorian autobiographies, and by *Ourika*, whose influence on his dream he would realize only years later.[54] And he found himself living in Hardy country, which may have cast a certain spell too. Even if Fowles had not called attention to the Thomas Hardy connection in the novel, it would be difficult not to notice the similarities between Tess Durbeyfield and Sarah, both educated beyond their stations and both associated with the natural landscape. Even more specifically, the scene in which Charles knocks on the door of 16 Cheyne Walk appears to have been modeled on the scene in chapter 55 of *Tess of the d'Urbervilles* in which Angel Clare knocks on the door at The Herons, expecting to find Tess lodging there and eager to be rescued, only to discover that she is living with Alec d'Urberville. The attraction of the situation, to Fowles, was more than a regard for Hardy, however; a male character obsessed with an unattainable female had figured in his previous two novels, as well as in that book seemingly always present in Fowles's mind, Alain-Fournier's *The Wanderer*.

Summary

The first chapter describes Lyme Regis and its Cobb, a harbor quay on which three characters are standing: Charles Smithson, Ernestina Freeman, and Sarah Woodruff. The describing narrator has a distinctive voice, all-knowing yet intimate, with a wide-ranging vocabulary and evidently vast knowledge of political and geographical history. In one sentence the narrator sounds like a Victorian, as he remarks that the male character recently "had severely reduced his dundrearies, which the arbiters of the best English male fashion had declared a shade vulgar—that is, risible to the foreigner—a year or two previously." In the next sentence he sounds modern, as he describes how "the colors of the young lady's clothes would strike us today as distinctly strident" (5/10–11). The narrator's double vision and double voice make him as important as the characters in this novel.

Charles is a middle-aged bachelor and amateur paleontologist; Ernestina is his fiancée, who has brought him to spend a few days with her aunt. Out of a chivalric concern for Sarah, Charles advises her to return from the end of the Cobb to a safer position, but she merely stares at him. As he reflects on this curious meeting, the narrator begins to comment on Charles's outlook on life and on the attitudes that were typical of the age in 1867, with occasional comparisons with 1967.

Ernestina is revealed to be a pretty but conventional young woman. Sarah is an outcast who is reputed to be pining for the French lieutenant who has jilted her. Charles is earnest but intelligent enough to be aware of Ernestina's limitations. When he is looking for fossils along the wooded Undercliff, Charles discovers Sarah sleeping, and must apologize when she awakes and sees him observing her. As he returns to Lyme, he inquires about her at a nearby farm, whose owner tells him that the "French Loot'n'nt's Hoer" often walks that way. Sarah's employer, having separately become aware of that fact, forbids her to walk there any more. Sarah spends that night contemplating suicide, and Chapter 12 ends with two questions: "Who is Sarah? Out of what shadows does she come?"

Chapter 13 begins "I do not know," and the narrator proceeds to discuss the difficulty of writing a story when characters behave inde-

pendently rather than do his bidding. Charles, he complains, did not
return to Lyme as the narrator had intended but willfully went down
to the Dairy to ask about Sarah. But, the narrator concedes, times have
changed, and the traditional novel is out of fashion, according to some.
Novels may seem more real if the characters do not behave like mari-
onettes and narrators do not behave like God. So the narrator, in effect, promises to give his characters the free will that people would
want a deity to grant them. Likewise, the narrator will candidly admit
to the artifice of the narration and will thereby treat his readers as
intelligent, independent beings who deserve more than the manipulative illusions of reality provided in a traditional novel.

Subsequent chapters contain representations of domestic life—a quiet
evening with Charles and Ernestina, a morning with Charles and his
valet, a concert at the Assembly Rooms. During this last, Charles reflects on where his life seems to be leading and on the fact that, as he
puts it, he has become "a little obsessed with Sarah . . . or at any rate
with the enigma she presented" (128/106; ellipsis in original). He returns to the Undercliff, again finds Sarah there, and is shocked to be
told by her that she is not pining for her French lieutenant, that he is
married. The next time Charles encounters her in the Undercliff she
offers Charles some fossils she has found and tells him that she thinks
she may be going mad; she asks him to meet her there once more,
when she has more time, so that she can tell him the truth about her
situation and obtain his advice.

Charles decides to seek advice himself and visits Dr. Grogan, an elderly bachelor and an admirer of Darwin, whose theories they discuss.
When the conversation turns to Sarah, Grogan expresses the belief that
she wants to be a victim. Sarah seems to bear out his view when she
explains to Charles that she indeed became infatuated with the French
lieutenant when he was recovering from an injury in the house where
Sarah was governess, and that she followed him when he left to return
to France. She tells Charles that she quickly realized that he had regarded her only as an amusement, but that she "gave" herself to him
nonetheless, doubly dishonoring herself by choice as well as by circumstances. She seems to be proud of her status as outcast, for it differen-
tiates her from a society she considers unjust. Charles accepts her story—
even finds it fascinating.

When Charles returns to his room at the inn, he finds a telegram
from his bachelor uncle Robert, summoning him home to the family
estate he is in line to inherit. To Charles's surprise, Robert has decided
to marry Bella Tomkins, a young widow, whose sons—if she has any—
would displace Charles as heir. On Charles's return to Lyme Regis,
Ernestina mentions that Sarah was seen returning from their last meeting in the Undercliff, where she had been forbidden to walk, and has

been dismissed by Mrs. Poulteney. At his hotel, Charles finds a message from Sarah, urging him to meet her one more time. Charles has Dr. Grogan call off the search for Sarah, who, it was thought, might have killed herself. Grogan again warns Charles against Sarah, this time by offering him a document to read about a case of bizarre behavior by a young woman in France who manages to get one of her father's officers unjustly convicted of attempting to rape her. Charles decides to meet Sarah again, despite the possibility that she may be deranged and trying to destroy him.

When he finds her, she confesses that she deliberately allowed herself to be seen and, hence, dismissed. Charles is unable to resist kissing her but is bewildered. His feelings turn to dismay when they are stumbled on by Sam and Mary, his valet and Ernestina's aunt's servant, who have come to the Undercliff for their own privacy. Embarrassed, he swears them to secrecy.

Now even more of two minds about his marriage, Charles decides to go to London to discuss his altered financial prospects with Ernestina's father, a prosperous merchant there. Mr. Freeman is more concerned for the happiness of his daughter, who evidently loves Charles dearly, so the engagement stands; but Charles is increasingly uncomfortable with, even trapped by, his situation. He goes to his club and drinks too much. He visits a brothel with two of his friends, but finds the entertainment repellant, and leaves. He picks up a Cockney streetwalker and returns to her flat with her; when she tells him her name is, coincidentally, Sarah, Charles becomes ill and, subsequently, returns to his room. The next morning Charles receives a letter from Grogan, and a note from Sarah with the name of a hotel in Exeter.

Because the train station nearest to Lyme Regis is in Exeter, Charles must pass through that town on his way back from London. Having steamed open the note from Sarah, Sam is confident that they will spend the night in Exeter, so that Charles can visit Sarah, but they proceed to Lyme, where Charles and Ernestina are reunited. The narrator recounts that they go on to marry, have seven children, and live well into the twentieth century. In the next chapter, the narrator explains that this traditional ending is just one possibility, a hypothetical future for his characters. Charles recognized his freedom of choice and "actually" did decide to put up at Exeter for the night, precisely as Sam had expected.

As the story resumes and continues to unfold, then, Charles visits Sarah at her hotel. He must see her in her room because she has supposedly injured her ankle, though she has purchased the bandage before the "accident" occurred. Charles is overcome by passion and takes her to bed, only to discover that she is a virgin, despite what she had told him about the French lieutenant. She confesses that she has deceived him, says that she cannot explain why and, furthermore, cannot marry him. Stunned by the whole experience, Charles visits a nearby church and meditates on the human condition. He decides that Sarah has been trying to "unblind" him with her stratagems (368/288), so that he would recognize that he is free to choose. He writes a letter to Sarah, telling her how much she means to him, and then returns to Lyme to call off his engagement.

Sam does not deliver the letter. Ernestina is distraught when Charles tells her that he is unworthy to be her husband, more so when she realizes that the true reason is another woman. Sam correctly surmises that his master's star will wane as the marriage is called off, so determined to protect his prospect of marriage to Mary, he leaves his position as Charles's valet in hope that Ernestina's aunt and her father will help him.

When Charles returns to Exeter, he finds Sarah gone to London, having left no forwarding address. As he follows her, by train, a bearded figure sits opposite Charles and watches him as he dozes. The character is the narrator himself, who professes not to know where Sarah is or what she wants; indeed, he is wondering what exactly to do with Charles. He compares writing a novel to fixing a fight in favor of one boxer or another; to seem less dishonest, he decides to show the "fight" as if "fixed" both ways, with different "victors," or endings. Because the last ending will seem privileged by its final position, he flips a coin to determine which ending to give first.

The narrative resumes the description of Charles's search for Sarah. He checks agencies for governesses, patrols areas frequented by prostitutes, and advertises—all without success. He visits the United States and advertises there. Two years after she disappeared, Charles gets a cable from his solicitor saying that Sarah has been found. Charles hopes that Sarah has decided to answer the ad, but the narrator explains that Mary has seen Sarah enter a house in Chelsea, and that it is Sam who responded to the ad, now that he is a thriving employee of Mr. Freeman as well as a happy father and husband, but still slightly guilt-ridden over his having intercepted the letter at Lyme.

When Charles arrives at Sarah's house, he finds her surprised to see him and not apologetic about having left him in ignorance of her whereabouts. She gradually is revealed to be living in the house of Dante Gabriel Rossetti and several other artists and models of the Pre-Raphaelite Brotherhood. Charles is shocked, partly by the rather notoriously unconventional company she is keeping and partly by her lack of repentance for having deceived him and left him in uncertainty. He accuses her of implanting a dagger in his breast and then twisting it, on page 454/355. She decides not to let Charles leave without revealing that she has had a child by him, named Lalage. Chapter 60 ends with the three of them evidently on the threshold of some kind of future together.

Chapter 61 begins with the bearded narrator in front of Sarah's house with a watch, which he sets back fifteen minutes and drives off. The narrative resumes on page 463/362 with the same piece of dialogue from page 454/355, about twisting the knife. In this version of the conversation, Charles sees that she cannot marry without betraying herself, and that he cannot accept her on more independent terms. He leaves without realizing that the child he notices on the way out is his. The narrator ends the novel by noting that Charles has at least begun to have some faith in himself, despite his not feeling that he understands Sarah, and that the reader should not imagine that the last ending is any less plausible than the one before it.

Interpretation

The epigraph to the novel, from Marx, announces a key theme in the novel: "Every emancipation is a restoration of the human world and of human relationships to man himself." Sarah is already emancipated in that she is willing to live as a social outcast in a highly conformist community, which is a microcosm of English Victorian society. By the end of the novel, she has found a small community of artists who allow her to be herself without feeling like an outcast. The narrator describes Sarah to be dressed "in the full uniform of the New Woman," which Charles has seen in America (347), a country he associates with freedom of speech and emancipation of blacks (339). The narrator implicitly links Sarah with the political emancipation of women that he has seen advance over the succeeding century.

To label Sarah a liberated woman before her time would be a mistake, however, at least in the sense that she is not meant to be understood in terms of labels. The question "Who is Sarah?" is meant not to be answered, for she is an embodiment of mystery. Labeling her "the French lieutenant's woman" is the first mistake the townspeople make, for categorizing her turns her into an object, a stereotypical fallen woman, and destroys what the epigraph calls "human relationships." Other labels, whether generous, like "Tragedy," or uncharitable, like "the French Loot'n't's Hoer," are no better. Grogan's attempts to explain her in terms of nineteenth-century theories of female hysteria also are less than satisfactory, and the association of Sarah with various femmes fatales from the cultural past provides no answers either. To label Sarah is to confine her, just as to write a conventional novel is confining in a way that the narrator will not accept.

Charles's role is similar to that of Nicholas in *The Magus* or Clegg in *The Collector*, that of a male in need of emancipation from stultifying social codes. For reasons never made clear in *The French Lieutenant's Woman*, Sarah manipulates Charles into awareness of his freedom to be himself. Her methods are less extravagant than those of Conchis's metatheater in *The Magus*, but her means is similar to his and her end— called "emancipation" rather than *eleutheria*—is effectually the same. Furthermore, as in *The Magus*, the manipulation of the reader into awareness of his or her freedom seems to be the author's real agenda. Rather than leave this aim tacit, in *The French Lieutenant's Woman* the narrator breaks into the narrative to insist that the reader enter into the game and choose how the narrative will end. He does to the reader what Sarah does to Charles—offers a situation as a heuristic. Providing a dual ending may be the most manipulative act of all, since the narrator pretends that only two (or three) endings are possible, but it enables him to reinforce the novel's theme on a metanovelistic level.

Reception

The French Lieutenant's Woman is by far Fowles's most successful novel, but he never expected it to do well. Indeed, he feared to read the reviews, which he anticipated would take him to task for writing a pastiche. He also imagined that the book would be too cerebral to be popular.[55] In fact, the reviews were generally favorable and, sometimes, ecstatic. A long front-page essay in the *New York Times Book Review* by Ian Watt called the novel "immensely interesting, attractive and human."[56] Joyce Carol Oates called it "an outlandish achievement!"[57] In England, Fowles won the W. H. Smith award for the most outstanding contribution to English literature during the year."[58]

At the same time, the book was popular. In the United States, *The French Lieutenant's Woman* was on the *New York Times* best-seller list for more than a year, at times jockeying with *The Godfather* for the number one position. By 1977, it had sold over more than 3 million copies. There was even a marked increase in tourism in Lyme Regis after the novel was published [59]

More recently, English critic Malcolm Bradbury praised *The French Lieutenant's Woman* as "one of the best books that have come out of Britain since the war," and Fowles as "one of our great writers."[60]

Adaptation (film)

Unhappy with the film adaptations of his two previous novels, Fowles insisted on the power to veto a director he did not want filming *The French Lieutenant's Woman*. Even directors he approved seemed unable to devise a workable approach to adapting the novel, the usual strategies involving a Victorian character representing the author-narrator, half in and half out of the story. By 1971, Fowles was beginning to think that the film would never get made.[61]

In 1978, Karel Reiz agreed to direct the film with Harold Pinter to write the script. It was Reiz who proposed turning the novel about writing a novel into a movie about making a movie, with parallel stories to provide alternate endings. Pinter says that he "grabbed" the idea and went to work.[62] Shooting began in Lyme Regis on May 27, 1980, and United Artists released the film the next September.[63]

The film begins with a shot of Sarah on the Cobb, but as the camera pulls back, she is revealed to be an actress in Victorian dress, making a film. The story of the film within the film is that of Sarah and Charles, who are united at the end, as are their counterparts in the next-to-last ending of the book. That story is interrupted by the parallel story of Anna and Mike, who are the actress and actor playing Sarah and Charles. They are having a casual, adulterous affair away from the set, where they sometimes rehearse lines for the next day's shooting. Mike wants Anna to leave her husband, but she leaves Mike instead, driving off from the wrap party at the end. Mike's last action is to shout after her from the window of the same room that was used to shoot the reunion scene between Charles and Sarah for the movie they were making. A nice blurring of the two stories is introduced as Mike mistakenly shouts Anna's screen name, "Sarah"—an idea reportedly first suggested by Fowles.[64]

Fowles is very satisfied with the results, calling the film "a brilliant metaphor" for the book.[65] He praises Jeremy Irons for being able to act an English, upper-class gentleman without making him seem like an idiot.[66] And the casting of Meryl Streep, an American, to play Sarah, Fowles sees as a successful risk of imagination that also constitutes "historical justice," for he associates Sarah more with America than with Victorian Britain.[67] Fowles evidently hoped that the film would preserve some of the novel's ambiguity; Streep has commented, "I promised John Fowles that I would not try to explain Sarah."[68]

THE EBONY TOWER

Composition

Fowles composed the stories in the same order they appear in the book: "The Ebony Tower," "Poor Koko," "The Enigma," and "The Cloud." Between the first and second stories by Fowles is a translation of "Eliduc," a medieval *lai* by Marie de France, with an introductory note by Fowles (discussed above as nonfiction).

"I thought I would like to have a shot at it," Fowles once explained, when asked why he suddenly took up the short story as a form.[69] He wrote the five pieces in less than three months, sometimes dashing off up to 8,000 words a day when at work on a first draft.[70] Doing so was a relief from work on *Daniel Martin,* he once commented, which had been under way for about four years, since publication of *The French Lieutenant's Woman* in 1969.[71] His working title for this collection of stories was *Variations,* he announces on page 117/109, in part because the stories contain themes he has treated before.

"THE EBONY TOWER"

Summary

David Williams, an English art critic and color-field painter, arrives in northern France to interview an older painter named William Breasley, who is living in self-imposed exile from England and Paris. Away from his wife, David finds himself affected by the atmosphere at Breasley's manor, which is deep in one of the old woods of Brittany, filled with priceless paintings, and inhabited not only by the great painter but also by two young art students, Diana and Anne.

The girls befriend David, and warn him that he can expect to be baited by their host. At dinner, as Breasley becomes increasingly drunk, he attacks the art establishment and, sometimes, Williams himself. Finally, the girls put Breasley to bed, and Diana explains that Breasley's reference to an "ebony tower" was his attempt to denigrate contemporary artists who work with abstraction because they are afraid to be clear; then she encourages David to dismiss what Breasley has said by telling David that an ebony tower is where you dump things you are too old to appreciate.

The next day Breasley is back to his usual cantankerous self. They all go on a picnic in the woods, where Diana and Anne go swimming in the nude as Breasley explains to David that he passed a kind of test the night before. After lunch—an enactment of Manet's *Le Déjeuner sur l'herbe*—Breasley goes to sleep and the women tell David about their lives. The three of them go swimming, and then the four of them return to the house, where David conducts one more interview, about Breasley's politics and his sources.

That night's dinner is friendlier. Afterward, Diana puts Breasley to bed early, and Anne explains that Breasley wants Diana to marry him. The two women take David upstairs to look at Diana's artwork, which he is impressed by. After Anne leaves, Diana tells David more about herself. They then decide to take a walk in the garden, where David kisses Diana and she responds with passion. He hangs back, and she senses that sexual intercourse would be a mistake. "She had broken away; and he had let her, fatal indecision" (107/100). He then tries to persuade her to come to bed with him, but she goes to her room and locks the door. He believes that he has both come alive and been prevented from living, that he has both lost his principles and feared to act against them.

The next day Diana absents herself from the house until David has left. He spends the drive back to Paris thinking about her with regret, feeling that he has been in a dream. At the airport, he meets his wife, who is flying in from England for a holiday. When she asks him how things went, he answers, "I survived" (114/106).

Interpretation

"The Ebony Tower" is about painting as an art versus painting as a science. Breasley paints what he feels, distilling a lifetime of experience into original expression. Williams is more intellectual, methodical as a painter and logical as a critic. Breasley is admirable but so eccentric that he is hard to identify with. Furthermore, Williams's verbal facility and Breasley's inarticulateness, although they reveal that Williams has a logically oriented mind and Breasley an intuitively oriented one, also make Williams easier to understand. On the other hand, Williams's art reflects his life, which is cautious and conventional but not satisfying for him, whereas Breasley just lives and seems happy to be alive and creating.

At the end of the story, the reader is left to identify with Williams but, like him, may feel a disturbing awareness that a comfortable, conventional life may be the result of avoiding risks. "The Ebony Tower" is most obviously a variation on "Eliduc," whose medieval protagonist leaves his wife in Brittany for England, where he falls in love; there is even a dead weasel in both stories. "The Ebony Tower" also is a variation on *The French Lieutenant's Woman,* in which an exotic female is rejected for a domestic one, in the first ending, as Charles shrugs off his experience with Sarah and returns to Ernestina. Finally, "The Ebony Tower" is a variation on *The Magus,* in that the narrative-as-heuristic draws the reader along with the narrator into a mysterious world with a magician and his "twin" daughters (Di-Anne) and then sends him back out, like the reader, a wiser person.

Adaptation (television)

The 1984 adaptation of "The Ebony Tower" for Granada Television's Great Performances is a handsome and thoughtful production.[72] The stage talent includes Sir Laurence Olivier as Breasley, the Royal Shakespeare Company's Roger Rees as David, and Greta Scacci as Diana. The screenplay by John Mortimer is faithful but not slavishly so. For example, the script does not get mired down with attempts to explain the title, but merely has Diana refer to Breasley's remark about an ebony tower as his "artistic rubbish tip." David telephones the house after he has left and talks to Anne, but the purpose of the new scene is to show Diana back at work with Breasley on his painting-in-progress. The implications of David's final line in the story are made clearer in the film by extending it from two words to four: "I survived, as always."

There also are some remarkable visual elements. The story's first paragraph describes David's making parallel stripes with a watercolor brush and neatly annotating them. The film emphasizes David's deliberateness with an opening closeup of an artist's hands using a straightedge to draw several horizontal brushstrokes and then turning the straightedge vertically to deposit lines perpendicular to the strokes. The camera then tilts upward to reveal that the artist has been methodically, abstractly rendering a line of poplars against a landscape.

Another imaginative stroke is the treatment of the narrator's comparison of Diana's expression after the kiss to "the implacably resentful stare of the sacrificial and to-be-saved princess of Trebizond" (99/92). In Fowles's story, this is a reference to Pisanello's *St. George and the Princess,* which Breasley refers to as "the Verona thing" (77/72). In the film, Breasley and David have a final confrontation, as David is leaving, during which David accuses Breasley of keeping Diana there in chains. Breasley tells David that there is a painting of St. George in the National Gallery that shows a knight lancing a dragon while a princess watches, but that the dragon is on a leash that the princess is holding, like a pet. Breasley asks, "Didn't St. George make a tiny bit of a twerp of himself?"[73] Breasley's point is that Diana may not want to leave, a point Fowles makes in a similar way in *The French Lieutenant's Woman* when Charles arrives at 16 Cheyne Walk like a knight in armor, prepared to rescue the damsel, only to find that she is not in distress (445/ 349). The painting Breasley has described, *St. George and the Dragon,* is shown at the very end of the film, under the credits. Its painter, Paolo Uccello, is the same painter David has mentioned early in "The Ebony Tower," as he waits to meet Breasley; Uccello's *Night Hunt* is the work said to have influenced Breasley's *Moon-hunt,* his masterpiece that hangs over the fireplace (18/17). Someone on the film's production team has discovered some wonderfully apt connections that go beyond the written, verbal text of "The Ebony Tower."

"POOR KOKO"

Summary

The story is told in retrospect by the elderly victim of a burglary. This narrator is staying in an isolated cottage belonging to friends and working on a book about nineteenth-century novelist Thomas Love Peaock. When he hears a burglar downstairs, he remains quiet, but the burglar discovers him in bed. As the burglar continues to work, he treats his victim kindly and engages him in conversation about crime, society, even Joseph Conrad. Before the burglar leaves, without explanation, he ties up the narrator and burns his notes and manuscript while the writer watches. Then he gives a thumbs-up gesture as he leaves. The last ten pages of the forty-page story is the narrator's attempt to understand why the burglar destroyed his book.

The narrator rejects his friends' belief that the burglar was a Marxist, like their son, who saw the old man as a parasite on an outmoded, bourgeois novelist-host. He also rejects the explanation that the burglar was schizophrenic. He constructs a theory based partly on the cocked-thumb gesture, that the burglar may have felt that they were in a contest with each other—and that he was the underdog. The burglar burned the book, in part, because he resented and was even afraid of the seemingly magical power of its writer, someone far abler than he to use the language.

Interpretation

The story is a variation on *The Collector*, with an artist imprisoned by a criminal. Like Clegg, the burglar is aware of the insurmountability of the gap between the many and the few, but he seems to understand much better than Clegg does the nature of the gap. The burglar's situation is not just the result of a "wrong" class accent, the narrator concludes, but of an inability to wield language in ways that could empower him. Understanding his situation makes him resentful. Whether the burglar could learn to wield the language powerfully does not seem to be an issue.

As Fowles suggests in his discussion of the Many and the Few in *The Aristos*, the disparate abilities of the two characters may be largely a matter of biological chance, and may represent different sides of any person's nature. The reference to Conrad further invites this kind of reading of the story as a psychological allegory, for Conrad wrote that kind of fiction himself—"The Secret Sharer," whose narrator similarly has conversations in an isolated room with a criminal who can be regarded as an aspect of the narrator's own personality.

"THE ENIGMA"

Summary

This story begins with the mysterious disappearance of John Marcus Fielding, a prominent English businessman, a family man of strict character and habits, and a member of Parliament. He was last seen entering the British Museum, but Scotland Yard can find no further evidence of his whereabouts. When solving the case is beginning to seem hopeless, a young detective named Michael Jennings is assigned to it because his public school accent will better enable him to deal with the upper-class family and friends of Fielding. His interviews turn up little new but solidify the impression that Fielding was a responsible, upstanding person.

The last part of the story is Jennings's interview with the former girlfriend of Fielding's son, Isobel Dodgson, a graduate student in English. They have a long talk in Hampstead Heath, and she decides to reveal that she told Fielding on the night before he disappeared that she would be working in the British Museum the next day. She never got there, so she did not see him, but she also mentions that she sensed someone else behind the father's respectable exterior. She goes on to explain that if she were trying to discover what happened, she would pretend to be an author whose main character had disappeared, but who had to write an ending. She suggests several possibilities but likes to imagine that Fielding walked out to create a mystery and to declare his independence of the oppressive system by which he had lived. He might have drowned himself in the pond near his house, in the woods he knew well, and might have passed through the British Museum just to signal her that he knew that she knew that there was more to him than others had discerned. When Jennings offers this explanation to Scotland yard, no one is interested in such a psychological theory, without evidence.

The story ends with a dinner date and lovemaking between Michael and Isobel, which the narrator observes was caused by an enigma that had walked out.

Interpretation

The idea of walking out has been mentioned earlier in the story, as "God's trick," which Fielding has imitated by writing himself as an open-ended mystery story. Isobel explains that if he is found, he will cease to "write" who he is and start to "be written" by others, be labeled as a victim of "a nervous breakdown. A nut case. Whatever" (242/226). Hampstead Heath is to London what the Undercliff is to Lyme Regis, and Isobel's revelations during her meeting there with Jennings parallel an idea that is implicit in *The French Lieutenant's Woman,* that the "real" Sarah lies somewhere behind the labels that people or the doctors assign to her; like Fielding, Sarah must remain difficult to label—enigmatic—if she is to be herself. Fielding's scrapbook about his life reminds Isobel of the way actors behave, and she guesses that he may have finally overcome the sense that he was on stage, playing some role expected by others instead of writing his own script—the same breakthrough Nicholas experiences at the end of *The Magus* when he realizes that no one is watching him any more. Like Fowles's earlier metanovels, which compare life to a baffling fictional construct, "The Enigma" is a metadetective story.

"THE CLOUD"

Summary

The story's events take place in central France, where a group of English acquaintances are relaxing, on vacation. Paul Rogers is an English writer, a Francophile-Anglophobe. His wife, Annabel, is a placid, nurturing mother to their daughters, Candida and Emma. Annabel's sister Catherine has recently lost her husband to suicide and is subject to bouts of depression. A divorced television producer named Peter has with him his son, Paul, and a girlfriend named Sally. As they converse, their personalities are revealed. The men consider Sally sexy, whereas the sisters consider her vapid. Roger is a would-be intellectual who likes to explain everything, and he delivers a lecture on why he likes the French better than the English. Catherine is taciturn but is drawn into a discussion in which she tells the others about Roland Barthes. Peter, who is always looking for marketable ideas, asks her to give him a script. The children play and argue, see a snake, and then see a kingfisher.

Catherine takes Emma to a secluded spot and makes up a story for her about a princess who falls asleep in the woods and then is awakened by a prince and helped by a magician-owl. The prince's parents, however, reject her as a bride. Catherine refuses to end the story, leaving the princess waiting in the woods for her prince to return. Then Candida finds them.

The last part of the story takes place in the afternoon. As Paul reads "The Scholar Gipsy" to Annabel, Peter goes climbing among the rocks, where he, too, sees a snake. He finds Catherine, who indicates that she would like him to rub suntan lotion on her back. She does not resist his sexual advances. Peter returns to the others and lies about having seen her; one of his remarks suggests that she may be dead. As they prepare to leave, to avoid a thunderstorm that suddenly and mysteriously has started to build up, Catherine does not respond to their calls. They leave, and the story concludes, "The princess calls, but there is no one, now, to hear her" (312/291).

Interpretation

The story is another metafiction, in that one of the characters tells an open-ended story within her open-ended story, evidently as a cue that the reader has a parallel, creative responsibility to finish "writing" the characters. The impromptu sex act, which has ambiguous elements of rape and seduction, is a variation on the crucial episode between Charles and Sarah at Exeter in *The French Lieutenant's Woman*. The discussion of Barthes, too, is an elaboration of a theory of discourse referred to in Chapters 13 and 55 of *The French Lieutenant's Woman* and underlying some of Fowles's rhetorical decisions. Paul's diatribe against the English on holiday constitutes a Barthes-like critique of English behavior, which is a variation on an important theme in *Daniel Martin*, the novel Fowles had been working on for several years before he wrote "The Cloud."

There is an intertextural meaning to the story as well, which contains many literary allusions, several in particular to T. S. Eliot's *The Waste Land*.[74] The storm cloud from which the story takes its title has been read as a bringer of rain, of potential redemption of the "waste land," by analogy to the end of Eliot's poem, which supposedly gives the story an optimistic tone.[75] But France is not a "waste land." France has its "fisher-king"—both human and aviary versions (260/243, 263/246)—but he is not disabled and the land is not infertile.[76] The waste land is elsewhere, as Paul attempts to convey to Peter:

We don't realize the arch-centralist nation of Europe is England, he means who else kow-tows to London notions of life as the British do, catch your Frog doing that, who else conforms so absurdly in the manner we behave and speak and dress, take the way the French only care about the quality of the food and the cooking, whereas all we care about is whether the other diners are dressed properly and the bloody table-setting looks nice and clean. (272/254)

The narrator undercuts Paul's talking, calling it "cultural rhubarb," but the narrator immediately goes on to characterize the fundamental problem in terms that echo Eliot's description of London as an "unreal City": "a tired rush of evening people, work-drained automata" (257). The story implies in various ways that France is a fertile "paradise" (237), and that the English visitors are leaving paradise at the end of the story, returning to the fallen world—the waste land—across the Channel.

Reception

The reviews of *The Ebony Tower* were "terrific," to use Fowles's own description of them.[77] The London *Observer* called the collection "the finest thing Fowles has written."[78] Even reviewers who did not like "The Cloud" found favor with the other stories, and one reviewer singled out "The Could" as "perfection."[79] Another reviewer, who enjoyed the book but found it, at times, "perhaps just a bit shoddy," went on to offer this interesting observation about Fowles's work: "In spite of his endless gruff attacks on the 'modern scene,' he is himself so plugged in to the fantasies and dream-worlds of the present day (and not only the sexual), that he is almost certainly one of those writers—good or bad, usually the most interesting—whose work will be much more fairly judged in a later day than his own."[80]

DANIEL MARTIN

Composition

John Fowles has described *Daniel Martin* as "a personal book," his attempt to achieve a more realistic key than is typical for his fictions.[81] One critic has called Fowles's novels "romances" because of his creation of unrealistic, even far-fetched or metaphorical situations, but *Daniel Martin* is something of an exception to that rule.[82]

Fowles began writing *Daniel Martin* as soon as *The French Lieutenant's Woman* was published in 1969, and wrote that he had "just finished" it in February 1976.[83] Even allowing for time he took off to write *The Ebony Tower* and to revise *The Magus*, Fowles had taken nearly seven years to write *Daniel Martin*—a much slower pace than he was accustomed to. As he had had a dreamlike image of the French lieutenant's woman in mind as he started that novel, Fowles worked this time from a vision of "a woman standing in a desert somewhere, who seemed to be weeping."[84] Fowles has noted that he jumped back and forth as he wrote, for example not having composed the first chapter until very late in the process. In another departure from usual practice, Elizabeth did not read the draft manuscript until it was complete. Fowles once remarked that he "liked living with this book, tinkering with it, changing attitudes."[85] This kind of pleasure must be particularly keen in autobiographical work, for which Fowles had to reimmerse himself in his past to explore alternatives. In any case, he prolonged the writing, and the result is itself long—about 300,000 words—but Fowles once noted that he writes for readers who are willing to spend weeks with a book.[86]

The description of farm labor in the west of England in the book's opening chapter recalls Thomas Hardy, as does the killing of rabbits in a scene that resembles the killing of rats in Chapter 48 of *Tess of the d'Urbervilles*. One critic sees even deeper affinities, between Dan's giving up film and Hardy's giving up the novel, and Fowles has acknowledged that he has been influenced by the "constant sense of loss and failure" in Hardy's novels.[87] But it is *A Sentimental Education* that is the "ghost" behind *Daniel Martin*, according to Fowles.[88] Although he did not see himself to be writing something of a cultural history of his time, as Flaubert did, the characters in *Daniel Martin* do represent, in part, what Fowles thinks about his generation in his country, who experienced a developmental "time lag" during World War II.[89] Fowles cautions however, that his characters are meant to be more than speakers for their age, that Dan and Jane are meant to be finding themselves.[90]

Summary

The novel begins in 1942 as 15-year-old Danny Martin is helping with "The Harvest," title of the first chapter. He is terrified by a low-flying German bomber and repelled by the more localized violence against rabbits that have become trapped in the center of a field as the circles of the reaper grow nearer. The chapter ends with his retreat into a beech wood, "innocent, already in exile" (10).

The second chapter, "Games," takes place in the early 1970s, in Hollywood, when Daniel Martin is now a middle-aged, successful screenwriter who is divorced from Nell, with a daughter named Caro. He is dissatisfied with script-writing as well as with his life, and is thinking of trying to write a novel. He receives encouragement from his girlfriend, a young English actress named Jenny, who proposes that he name his fictionalized self Simon Wolfe. The chapter ends as Dan receives a telephone call from England.

The third chapter, "The Woman in the Reeds," takes place in a third time period, when Dan was attending Oxford University in his early twenties. Dan is on a picnic with Jane, sister of his girlfriend Nell, when they discover a body in one of the canals. Andrew, a baronet's son, helps them recover from the shock while they wait for the police to arrive. Dan uses the word "games" to describe their superficial lives at Oxford.

"An Unbiased View" is written by Jenny as a contribution toward Dan's novel. The chapter describes the world of filmmaking as well as how they met, and how she found him attractive because she could not read him easily. "The Door" picks up with a telephone call from Jane, who tells Dan that her terminally ill husband, Anthony, wants to see Dan before he dies. Dan is stunned, and the next chapter, "Aftermath," helps to account for his reaction. After they had returned from their Oxford outing, Jane proposed that they go to bed together, just once, as a gratuitous, Rabelaisian act. "Passage" switches the scene back to the United States, where Dan is flying from Los Angeles to New York, en route to England, and thinking about what it means to be English.

"The Umbrella" returns to Dan's boyhood in the 1930s, as Dan describes how the son of a vicar grew into an atheist. Allusions to *Citizen Kane* help to emphasize Dan's father's lack of demonstrative love for his son. The next chapter, "Gratuitous Act," describes Dan and Jane's sexual intercourse in Dan's room at Oxford, where they are almost discovered by Barney Dillon, who lives in the room above. "Returns" takes place on the airplane from New York to London, where Dan coincidentally encounters the older Barney, who is now a media critic for a London newspaper. Dan's daughter, Caroline, is his secretary.

"Tarquinia" provides another reminiscence of the Oxford days, on a vacation when Dan, Nell, Jane, and Anthony visited Italy and "played Pagan" in the sea near the Etruscan ruins. In "Petard," while Dan stays over in London with Caro, she tells him that she is having an affair with the still-married Barney. On the subway to Paddington Station, in "Forward Backward," Dan thinks back to a trip he took to Devon with Caro to show her where he grew up and ended up buying a farm he found for sale, named Thorncombe. In "Breaking Silence," while riding the train from London to Oxford, Dan thinks back further to the early years of his marriage to Nell—his successes as a playwright that gained him entrée to the film world, his infidelity with an actress, Nell's acquisitiveness and growing discontent with their marriage, her accusation that Dan must be having an affair with his assistant, and her demand for a divorce.

In "Rencontre," Dan meets Jane for dinner, and in "Crimes and Punishments," he recalls how a play of his with obvious parallels in their lives had led to anger all around and a letter from Anthony that wrote him out of their lives. Now, in "Catastasis," Dan goes to the hospital to meet Anthony and finds that Jane long ago told her husband of her gratuitous act with Dan. Anthony explains that they have had a somewhat bloodless relationship in their marriage, due in part to his religiosity, and he wants Dan to be a friend to Jane when he is gone. After he leaves, in "Jane," Dan takes Jane to dinner, where she explains why she is thinking of joining the Communist Party. When they return to Jane's house, in "Beyond the Door," they learn that Anthony committed suicide shortly after Dan left. In "Webs," Nell arrives with Andrew, whom she has married, and their daughter Rosamund. Dan and Caro drive back to London, where Dan watches an old man on the street and thinks about how separated people are from one another.

Jenny writes "A Second Contribution," which describes her view of Dan's Jewish friends Mildred and Abe and of Dan, whose discussions have enabled her to see that he is in love with loss, and that his seeming untypicality is really what is most typical of the English: their ability to hide their true selves from others. "Interlude" provides a narrator's view of Dan, who does expect to lose women, and illustrates Dan's life with a "fable" about twin sisters, Miriam and Marjory, whom Dan allows to move in with him; they are unsophisticated (except as sexual partners), but Dan genuinely likes them. At the end of the chapter, they have moved away, and Dan is haunted by their loss.

In "Hollow Men," Dan meets Barney for lunch, and they discuss his life, including Caro. At breakfast the next day, in "Solid Daughter," Caro tells Dan that Jane thinks him to be two persons, and Caro suggests that he does not want her to know him either. The topic leads Dan to write "The Sacred Combe," about why Robin Hood is the perfect myth for England because the English love to retreat behind masks, to melt into the trees. Dan notes that his own impulse to write a novel may be evidence of this wish to escape from social responsibility into a self-chosen exile, into a private world of self-indulgence.

In "Rituals," Dan meets with David Malevich, his producer, about their next film project, and David suggests that Dan visit possible shooting locations in Egypt. Dan attends the inquest into the suicide and then takes Rosamund, Jane's oldest daughter, to dinner. Dan spends the weekend at "Compton," the title of the next chapter and country estate of Nell and Andrew, where he ponders the existence of the upper class and discusses the state of England with a cynical ultraconservative named Miles Fenwick.

"Tsankawi" is another reminiscence, of a visit to an archeological site in New Mexico. Dan identifies strongly with the place, and is offended that Jenny wants to make gifts out of potsherds she finds there.

In "Westward," back in England, Dan invites Jane and her teenage son Paul to visit Thorncombe. Paul is somewhat obsessed with medieval agriculture, so he agrees to come along if he can visit some sites of historical interest. Dan recalls how he acquired his gardener and housekeeper, Ben and Phoebe, and then, in "Phillida," how he fell in love as a boy with Nancy Reed, who then lived on the farm Dan has bought, until their parents put an end to the romance. After they have arrived, in "Thorncombe," Dan tells Jane about his wish to try writing a novel, and she tells him about Marxist views of the novel and of culture. On impulse, Dan invites Jane to accompany him to Egypt. That night, "In the Orchard of the Blessed," Dan ponders the devaluation of happy endings in contemporary culture but decides that his novel will have one nonetheless. In "Rain," Jane reluctantly agrees to go along to Egypt, and Dan has two strained transatlantic telephone conversations with Jenny.

In "A Third Contribution," Jenny describes a supposedly fictional but extremely detailed sexual liaison with her costar, Steve. When they talk by telephone again, in "The Shadows of Women," she apologizes for having sent it.

Jane and Dan arrive in Cairo in "Pyramids and Prisons," where Dan discusses the film project with an Egyptian agent and Jane visits the pyramids. They attend a dinner party at which the jokes told by an Egyptian playwright reveal much about Egyptian culture, including, in Dan's view, much it has in common with Jewish culture. In "Barbarians," they start a tour up the Nile at Karnak and reflect on the ancient Egyptian obsession with size, which reminds them of ancient Rome and the modern United States. An old German archaeologist named Otto Kirnberger befriends them and offers suggestions about purchasing artifacts. In "Nile," they encounter other tourists, including an American couple, the Hoopers, who disagree about Vietnam but are enthusiastic about visiting Palmyra, Syria. In "The River Between," Kirnberger tells about himself and offers insights into cultural and biological differences. When they arrive at Aswan and "Kitchener's Island," they find a paradise surrounded by technology run amok. Jane imagines living in a house there and accepts some beads from a little girl. Dan increasingly wants to reveal the growing affection he is feeling toward Jane, but instead, he proposes a side excursion to Palmyra on their trip back to England. Back at the hotel in Aswan, "In the Silence of Other Voices," Dan experiences a mental crisis of anxiety that he must choose himself, and of confidence that he alone can create a world in film or fiction, let alone in life, but he sits down and composes a scene that he believes will work. The chapter title "Flights" refers to the return by air to Cairo and to Jane's demurral when Dan declares that he does not want to leave Jane, that there was something right about their day in Oxford, that they should try living together.

In "North," Dan feels depressed. After they arrive in Beirut, he sits in a bar and feels that he must be condemned to pursue emotional situations that contain the structure of their own destruction, for which his thwarted relationship with Nancy Reed was the seed crystal. The drive to Palmyra in the fog takes them to "The End of the World," a desolate landscape Dan compares to the possibilities Jane has destroyed over the courses of their lives. He persuades her that she should stop conforming to an ideal of nobility and sacrifice, acting as if Anthony is still watching her, and instead join him in movement toward a sympathetic, loving relationship. For the first time on the trip they sleep together. The next day, in "The Bitch," still wary of love but proceeding on instinct like the mother dog of the chapter title, Jane buries her wedding ring in the sand.

In the last chapter, "Future Past," Dan meets Jenny in a London pub to discuss why he is ending their relationship. They walk on Hampstead Heath and part. Dan goes into the Kenwood Museum and looks at the Rembrandt self-portrait there, which seems like a sentinel. Dan will not turn back but will continue to choose and to learn to feel and to write his novel. Indeed, the last sentence of Dan's novel, which exists only as an idea in *Daniel Martin*, John Fowles as Dan's "ill-concealed ghost" has adopted as the first sentence of this novel: "Whole sight; or the rest is desolation" (629/673).

Interpretation

As the summary indicates, *Daniel Martin* is, among other things, a metanovel. Dan's description of himself as "a scriptwriter who isn't a novelist" (391/416)—although he will be—neatly reverses Fowles's situation, that of a novelist who isn't a scriptwriter—although he has been. The name that Daniel Martin uses to create a sense of distance between himself and his somewhat autobiographical but fictional character is S. Wolfe, an anagram for Fowles, who is using the name of Daniel Martin for the same purpose in his novel. Dan's discussion of how he will incorporate a happy ending, even if they are out of intellectual fashion, neatly justifies the happy ending of *Daniel Martin*. And the merging of fiction and metafiction in the first and last sentences of *Daniel Martin* is a subtler version of the would-be confessional move in *The French Lieutenant's Woman*, in which "Fowles" enters the novel as a character to flip a coin; in the last sentence of *Daniel Martin*, the narrator, or "Fowles," whose voice has intruded on various occasions (such as the reference to Dan as "our hero" on page 230/245) and has played with shifting tenses and points of view throughout, acknowledges that his presence has been "ill-concealed" in this book. Indeed, it has been concealed only to be revealed, in a game of metafictional striptease.

The book is a novel about writing a novel in a less elaborate way, as well. Dan is given to describe both living and writing in terms of choices. In the early chapters, a metaphorical representation of such choices is the door. At the end of the second chapter, with the phone call, "as in a fiction, a door in the wall opens" (19/18). As the phone conversation continues in the chapter titled "The Door," Dan recognizes that his decision whether or not to return to England could be crucial: "He sees, already, as he sometimes does at the very early stages of a new script, permutations, forks, openings to exploit" (46/47). To choose one door, or road, or script is to reject the alternatives, and this idea recurs. Anthony's suicide is meant to be like a slap on the face, his way of dramatizing to Jane that their path was a mistake, what he calls "a design failure" (177/188) that he hopes Dan can help to correct. Jane let herself drift into Catholicism as she seems to be drifting into Marxism, and Dan tries to show her, at Palmyra, that she is responsible for choosing her path: "You murdered something in all three of us, Jane. Largely without knowing it, and perhaps murder is an unkind word. But you made certain choices, developments, impossible. We're sitting surrounded by what you did to us. Out there" (590/631). What is "out there" is desolation, a landscape physically opposite to "sacred combes" such as Danny's beech wood in the first chapter, or Nancy's "secret place" (356/379), or Thorncombe, or Sherwood Forest, or Tsankawi, or Kitchener's Island, or the Garden of Eden—the rich, private green places that make life worth living and that are metaphorically the fertile worlds of "multiple promise, endless forked roads" (422/450) to which a novelist escapes when he or she writes.

Describing Jane this way gives her character the status of pupil in yet another Fowles heuristic, the Miranda-Nicholas-Charles figure of Fowles's earlier novels who is being taught to have his or her awareness of freedom expanded. Jenny, too, seems to regard Dan as a teacher and herself as one who is learning from him (333/355). But at the same time Dan is teaching he is learning, exploring, and discovering his own sense of freedom. He regards Jane as a mystery; her one-time seduction of Dan, like Miranda's attempted seduction of Clegg, Lily's of Nicholas, or Sarah's of Charles, is meant somehow to be for his own good. So the teacher in this novel also is the taught, and not only by Jane but also by Professor Kirnberger, by Abe Nathan, by Aly Sabry, by Anthony, and so on. Even Anthony, the Oxford don whose death Dan thinks was meant to be "some kind of lesson" (453/483), has quoted one of his students as having taught him something important (181–82/193). In *Daniel Martin*, more than in Fowles's other novels, the teaching and learning seem reciprocal, and that may be the most important way in which this is Fowles's most realistic novel.

Reception

Reviews of *Daniel Martin* were divided in such a way that *Times* literary editor Leon Trewin wrote a feature on the phenomenon, in which he asked, "How does one explain such a difference in literary attitudes when a novel by one of our leading writers is praised to the heights on one side of the Atlantic, but gets the bird on the other?"[91] Trewin goes on to cite from the hostile British reviews and the favorable American reviews, offering the less than satisfactory explanation that Americans have never objected to long novels and that British critical opinion shifts like a pendulum.

The reviewers were not quite so uniform in their judgments as Trewin suggests, but there was a strong, negative consensus in England that *Daniel Martin* was too long and too preachy.[92] Michael Mason was especially harsh in the *Times Literary Supplement*, in which he wrote that "the jokeless wastes of Fowles's fiction are also gawky and indecorous."[93] Jacky Gillott, writing for the *Times*, however, was willing to grant that much was achieved in a novel "whose occasional flaws are immeasurably more fascinating than the small perfections of many another writer."[94] Fellow novelist John Mortimer went further, calling Fowles "the finest novelist of his generation," whose critics were "always ready to cut any major artistic enterprise down to their own size."[95]

In the United States, reviews were generally favorable and occasionally ecstatic. Novelist John Gardner went so far as to argue in *Saturday Review* that "Fowles is the only novelist now writing in English whose works are likely to stand as literary classics—the only writer in English who has the power, range, knowledge, and wisdom of a Tolstoi or James."[96] Not all American reviewers were enthusiastic, however. *Commentary* objected to the "cozy English domesticization of Lukács" and to Fowles's tendency to offer "big thoughts," and *Newsweek* regretted the presence of so many little bits of information: "What can one say of the squirrel that brings us every nut he has stored, the hazelnuts carefully labeled and distinguished from the beechnuts?"[97] If the objections tended to express annoyance, the praises tended to recognize a significant achievement.

MANTISSA

Composition

In a 1971 interview for *London Magazine*, Fowles was asked about the role of "hazard" in his writing. He responded that the sudden appearance of an unexpected but fertile image can dictate the way he writes: "I almost believe in muses. In fact, I wrote a short story last year that did bring the muses into modern life."[98] This story was evidently the germ of *Mantissa*, which Fowles told an interviewer he had written the first draft of rapidly and then set aside for revision, evidently for more than a decade.[99] Fowles prepared the manuscript for private publication in just 100 copies, by a friend in California, but Jonathan Cape and Little, Brown insisted on the right to publish *Mantissa*, by contract. Somewhat uneasily—"embarrassed" is a word he has used—Fowles delivered the manuscript in early January of 1982.[100]

When asked where *Mantissa* comes from, Fowles has answered variously. He has described Flann O'Brien's *At Swim-Two-Birds*, a self-conscious novel by an author Fowles regards highly, as the "the ghost behind *Mantissa*."[101] Another such "ghost" may be Thomas Hardy's *The Well-Beloved*, whose shifting female presence Fowles sees as "the unattainable muse-figure that haunts every male novelist."[102] With Hardy, however, Fowles is not borrowing so much as exploring the same situation, which Hardy represents with Jocelyn Pierston's pursuit of women and which Fowles represents with Miles Green's relationship with Erato:

I've always had this, I suppose, half-unconscious feeling that when you're writing there's a tease element: that something is always teasing you and making you have pratfalls. . . . If there were such a thing as a Muse, I can't imagine she would be that dreadful, wishy-washy figure of legend. I think it would be . . . it's your anima, obviously. And extremely naughty and unhelpful a lot of the time. (ellipsis in original)[103]

Summary

Part I begins with an attempt by Miles Green to regain consciousness, as a pair of eyes above him gradually takes the form of his wife, Claire— or so she tells him, for Miles seems to be suffering from amnesia. His wife leaves, and the female attendant explains that he has been under sedation, but when Miles asks how long he has been in the hospital, she answers, "Just a few pages." Her name is Dr. A. Delfie, and she introduces her West Indian assistant as Nurse Cory. They explain that he must learn to relax, and as part of his treatment, they begin to massage his penis. Miles is shocked as they encourage him to fondle their bodies, more so as Dr. Delfie mounts his erection. She tells Miles to try to provide a climax from as deep as possible, in the interest of his baby, to keep going "to the very last syllable." After he finishes, Nurse Cory brings him a small sheaf of papers, cradled in her arms, which she refers to as "a lovely little story." He begins to wonder if his lost identity is that of "a mere novelist or something" when a crash interrupts and ends this first part of the book.

The cause of the crash becomes apparent in Part II. A woman appears who looks like a twin of Dr. Delphie but has spikes of hair and black eye-makeup, is dressed in boots and a black leather jacket, and holds an electric guitar. She slashes at the guitar strings and the nurses disappear. Then she turns to Miles and accuses him of antifeminist, bourgeois elitism, among other literary crimes, in what he has just written. He defends himself by saying that it could have been worse, that he at least did not represent her running through the olive groves in a transparent nightie—though she would look terrific that way. She begins to run scales on her guitar and it changes to a lyre, as she changes into a traditional muse, dressed in a white tunic. She warns him that she will not, however, be a brainless female body at his perverted beck and call, and she gives him ten sentences to provide a formal apology. As he does so he begins to play with her. She is not very interested—is still a bit queasy from her flight from Greece—and tells him that it is not easy to be the muse of love poetry, Erato, and find that you have been stuck with fiction as well.

Erato tells Miles to listen to a story for a change, and tells him about
her sexual awakening in ancient Greece, when a satyr discovered her
rubbing herself with olive oil. She tells Miles that he must not repeat
her story, that she's told it to only one other person, a French poet who
blabbed. As she tells her erotic story, Miles undresses her and mounts
her. Erato continues to talk and tells Miles that her point is, that he
should not be a modern satyr, who invents women who are implausible
wish-fulfillments of his diseased mind. In fact, she reminds him, any
witness to what they are doing would think it ridiculous, so he should
get off her. Erato then lectures him on how she has no freedom to be
herself as long as she depends on him to create her as a character, even
to kill her off. At that point, Erato gradually changes into an independent-minded, serious woman who speaks intelligently, even intellectually about the sympathy she feels for Miles as a male, a victim of "the
overwhelming stress the prevailing capitalist hegemony puts on sexuality" (102–03). They discuss fictional possibilities for her, which quickly
degenerate into soft-core romance scenarios with crude symbolism and
exotic trappings. Miles turns and accuses her of exceeding the bounds
of artistic decency, and starts lecturing her on how out of fashion her
ideas about novels are. He tells her that she should not expect to be
able to think and to be a universal girlfriend at the same time. After
having delivered several intellectual parting shots and turning to leave,
Miles cannot find a door in the wall. Erato tells him that he cannot
walk out of his own brain. Miles now accuses her of dictating to him,
and whines that he, as author, feels as "written" as she does as a character. She shows him that there is a door, after all, but when he opens
it, he sees only a reflection of himself and the room behind him. When
he turns around, Erato knocks him out with an uppercut to the jaw.

Part III begins with Miles on the floor and Erato retransformed into
Dr. Delphie. An elderly staff nurse enters and accuses Delphie of letting the ward turn to ruin, if not to a striptease show, and departs.
Delphie turns to Miles and kicks him in the ribs. When he sits up, she
tells him that it was a dirty trick by him to make the elderly nurse look
like her sister, Clio, the muse of history. Delphie reminds him that she
is an archetype and that he has been lucky that she appears to him;
indeed, she says that she is never going to do so again, and disappears.
Her now disembodied voice explains that literature is a manifestation
of mental illness, that he has merely been acting out a primal scene
trauma. She advises him to become a ditchdigger. He attempts to make
her jealous by telling her that he preferred the black nurse. She tells
him that he has never been any good as a writer or lover. Suddenly, a
clock on the wall cuckoos, Dr. Delphie reappears, they make up and
make love, not noticing that the walls of the room have become transparent and that people are watching them.

As Part IV begins, they wake up and begin to discuss how it was—both the sex and their previous dialogues. Miles and Erato discuss how they found each other, were perfect for each other in their desire for endlessly revisable textuality. Miles unwisely remarks that he especially liked her as Nurse Cory, and Erato replies that she has singled him out for her affection because he's such an incompetent writer that she can be sure he will never succeed in telling about her. He retorts that he has lots of readers, and that she does not know what it is like to be a writer. She confesses that she did once write an epic satire revealing how immature men are, called *The Odyssey*. He confesses that he wants Nurse Cory. Erato admits that she is not perfect, indeed gets a lot of facts wrong, but her business is to inspire people. Miles complains that they do too much talking.

As they lie together, Miles reflects that he should not complain about his situation, but that Erato does not appreciate his importance and is becoming "just one more brainwashed, average twentieth-century female." As he begins to imagine a compliant, sexy Japanese woman, he finds that Erato has turned him into a satyr. He threatens to write everything down, but she just smiles. When he tries to jump on her, Erato disappears, and he knocks himself out on the wall above the bed. He returns to the form of Miles Green, and Nurse Cory covers him up. The book ends with the cry of "Cuckoo" from the clock above the oblivious patient.

Interpretation

Fowles has elsewhere described the muses as a trick of the Greek imagination, a way of explaining something for which they lacked words. The twentieth century has words—including *anima*—but the models for understanding the creative process are still somewhat primitive. Fowles understands the models, both Jungian and Freudian, as well as the theory of cognitive hemisphericity applied to his own writings by H. W. Fawkner, but Fowles is offering an unscientific, even comic account of what he has experienced as a writer. The structuring analogy between creation and procreation is not original with Fowles; however, the eroticizing, even pornographic account here brings the metaphor to life even as it dramatizes—more vividly than most authors would want to do—the onanistic pleasures of writing fiction.

The theme of metafiction in Fowles's other work is in *Mantissa* taken to a fantastic extreme. The issue of the status of a character, raised by the narrator in Chapter 13 of *The French Lieutenant's Woman*, is here a matter for discussion by the characters themselves. Erato complains that she is stuck with whatever clumsy set of female emotions Miles concocts for her, and then asks Miles to consider his own dubious status, who may be pulling his strings. When he replies, "I'm me. Don't be ridiculous," she points out that he's "so naive" (88). The remark serves to remind readers, if they have forgotten, that the fiction being created in front of them, in a sense, is not only that of Miles Green but also, on a different level, that of John Fowles.

The theme of paired women is evident, again, in *Mantissa*. The muse manifests herself as a variety of females, including Miles's wife, but the discussion repeatedly turns to Dr. Delphie versus Nurse Cory, white versus black, from the initial treatment to the final conversation. Miles comments at one point, speaking to Erato, "Darling, we agreed. I do need you in just one other shape—if only to remind myself how unconveyably heavenly you are in your own" (166–67). Fowles may be offering an explanation of the recurrence of twins in his fiction: His imagination tends to work by contrasting pairs, just as he thinks of writing decisions in *Daniel Martin* as forks in a road.

Reception

Fowles has observed that there is no way for an author to know how someone is going to read a book: "I basically write what I know is going to please *me*, what *I* am going to enjoy. Sometimes I'm right, and sometimes, as I generally was with *Mantissa*, I'm wrong." Rather than finding him too earnest, readers seem to have found him either frivolous or offensive. The latter objection was not that Fowles had been too naughty, but that his obsessions, as represented in his treatment of his female muse, seemed to have such an antifeminist tone. He may have intended for Miles to be the butt of the story, obsessed with sex and a bit of a fool—a reading invited by Fowles's giving the cuckoo the last word— but his structuring metaphor inevitably makes Erato seem less the source of creativity than the adolescent male's eternal playmate.

One of the few positive reviews of *Mantissa* appeared in *Time* magazine, whose reviewer declared that "the joke is on everyone except Fowles."[104] Others were less amused. *The New Republic* considered it "innocent, dumb horseplay, a satiric review cobbled together by British sixth formers at public school."[105] *The Observer*'s reviewer expressed astonishment: "Few writers have ever blown the whistle on themselves so piercingly."[106] In *The Times*, novelist and critic David Lodge expressed concern that *Mantissa*, although "intriguing," indicated a loss of confidence by Fowles in what he is doing.[107] And the *New York Times Book Review* predicted that *Mantissa* would lead "to a sensible downward revision of Mr. Fowles's reputation."[108] Elizabeth Fowles has expressed the wish that her husband had never published it.[109] Even if it pleased him to write it, Fowles seems to have known how it would be received: "I suppose I wrote the book because I knew it was a book most people would disapprove of. Really, I wanted to give people an opportunity to kick me—which they duly did."[110]

A MAGGOT

Composition

In his prologue to *A Maggot*, John Fowles mentions that the book began with an image of a group of travelers. The image had been with him for ten or fifteen years, he told one interviewer, but he did not begin to write this novel until "a year or two" after he had finished *Daniel Martin*. Indeed, it was on a visit to the United States to promote *Daniel Martin* that Fowles "discovered" the history of Ann Lee and the Shakers, who seem to have resonated with his long interest in the history of English dissent.[111] When close to completing the book in 1984, he told an interviewer that he had once vowed never to write another "historical" novel after *The French Lieutenant's Woman*, but was finding the similar work creating a "slightly mythical language" for *A Maggot* "very enjoyable."[112] Within a year, the novel was published.

Fowles has said that he wanted *A Maggot* to be "Defoe-like," but many other influences are evident as well.[113] One was *The Gentleman's Magazine*, which Fowles even reproduces in facsimile here and there in the book "to remind people what the real language of the time, the printed language, really sounded and looked like."[114] He also drew on Lord Lyttelton's *Persian Letters* of 1735 "extensively" as a source for the way people spoke, and read all of Fielding's plays in preparation for writing the dialogue.[115] Fowles's work with John Aubrey's *Monumenta Britannica* and the writing of his own *The Enigma of Stonehenge*, while he was working on *A Maggot*, must have provided material for the night excursion from Amesbury to "Stonage" and perhaps even helped to inspire the character of the mysterious lord who, like the historical William Stukeley, was obsessed with science, religion, and Stonehenge.

Summary

The story begins with a narrator's description of five characters on horseback in the West Country in April. The party is composed of a Mr. Brown and his nephew, a deaf-mute servant named Dick, a woman called Louise, and a bodyguard named Sergeant Farthing. Their journey began in London and has taken them into Devon, where the nephew is to meet his beloved for an elopement—or so they tell the staff at the Black Hart, an inn near Exmoor. When the narration becomes dialogue, relationships seem different. The uncle is subordinate to the nephew, who is referred to as Lacy, not Brown. The woman seems unperturbed when Dick unbuttons his breeches and stands near her with an exposed erection. She does plead for an explanation, however, when the nephew—whom she refers to as "my lord" and who calls her Fanny—chastises her for having worn a bouquet of violets beneath her nose as they traveled that day.

After fifty pages of this narration, whose dialogue is from the eighteenth century but whose narrator is from the late twentieth, a facsimile page with no immediately evident connection appears, part of the "Historical Chronicle" from *The Gentleman's Magazine,* for April 1736, when the fictional story has been taking place. The next page is fictional but purports to be an item from *The Western Gazette* reporting the discovery of a corpse in the woods near Exmoor, hanging from a tree, with a bouquet of violets growing from its mouth.

The next ten pages are in a different, dramatic mode, an interrogation of the Black Hart's innkeeper, Thomas Puddicombe, with the questions and answers marked by *Q*'s and *A*'s, and the whole transcript signed by one Henry Ayscough. After two more interviews and two more excerpts from *The Gentleman's Magazine*, Ayscough's role becomes clearer with a letter to his employer, addressed as "Your Grace," who is evidently the father of the young lord in the party of travelers. Ayscough is confident that the so-called nephew is indeed "his Lordship," this unidentified duke's younger son, but Ayscough cannot imagine what he was doing in this part of the country or why he brought the extra companions, besides his now-deceased servant.

The next section is narrated, in which Ayscough intimidates the actor Francis Lacy into admitting that he was indeed hired by a man he knew was only pretending to be "Mr. Bartholemew," and agreed to pretend to be his "uncle," Mr. Brown, to help him reach the vicinity of his fiancée undetected. Lacy recounts several of their conversations in which Lord —— revealed an interest in Stonehenge, mathematics, and philosophy. Lacy further reports that Farthing told him that he had once seen the woman in their party entering a London house of prostitution owned by a Mrs. Claiborne, that Dick and "Louise" were having a clandestine sexual relationship as they traveled, and that his lordship had stolen out with Dick and her during the night that they lodged in Amesbury, near Stonehenge—all of which information leads Lacy to suspect that more has been going on than he can now explain to Ayscough. He does point out that he and Farthing separated from the rest of the party on the morning after the night at the Black Hart, so he is unable to account for the disappearances of his lordship and the woman.

The next interview, with Hannah Claiborne, establishes that "Louise" is "Fanny," one of her prize prostitutes, who came to her as Rebecca Hocknell, of a Quaker family in Bristol; her ability to feign religiosity and chastity made her an especially sought-after prostitute, known as "the Quaker maid." Lord ——— had paid Claiborne for Fanny's services for one week, for a party in Oxford he told her, but for a trip abroad he told a friend. His real purpose remains obscure.

Ayscough next interviews Jones, the real name of Farthing, whom his agents have located, and learns that Jones decided to follow the three others after they had parted on the road. He tells Ayscough of having seen them meet a woman dressed in silver trousers near a cave in the woods by Exmoor. Sometime after they all entered the cave, he reports, Dick came running out looking terrified and disappeared into the woods; then Rebecca emerged, naked; his lordship never came out. Jones recounts that he assisted Rebecca in reaching Bideford, from which port he shipped to Wales and she to Bristol, but not before she told him that she had seen witches inside the cave, had been raped by Satan, and had witnessed what appeared to be a mock marriage between his lordship and the younger witch.

Several letters follow, from Ayscough's agents who are searching for Rebecca, who is found in Manchester, married to a blacksmith named John Lee, member of a faction that has broken off from the Quakers. When Ayscough interviews her, Rebecca explains that she has repented her past life and is now a devoted servant of God—as well as a mother-to-be. She tells Ayscough that she lied to Jones about what happened in the cave, first to keep him at a distance, physically, and second because he would not be able to understand what really had happened. First she explains that when they visited Stonehenge at night, she saw a bright, "floating lantern" and observed two men watching them. She then explains that she was told to engage in sexual intercourse with Dick while his lordship watched, and that she accepted Dick's subsequent advances out of pity for him. About the cave, Rebecca explains that inside she saw a large maggot-shaped machine floating in the air, with a door and lights inside. She was taken inside it by a gray-haired woman who had previously been three women of three ages who merged into one. She was shown moving pictures of a green world with large buildings that serve as communal housing, which Rebecca now refers to as "June Eternal." The two men she saw at Stonehenge she recognizes were God the Father and God the Son, and the three women were a female trinity of Christ's daughter, widow, and "Holy Mother Wisdom." Ayscough then interviews one of the leaders of the religious sect and learns that Rebecca's views are largely her own, which she has not revealed to the others, even though they do believe in a female aspect of the Trinity. When he calls Rebecca back, she stands by her bizarre story, claiming that she awoke to find the cave empty and his lordship gone, having left with the spiritual "deities" and left his fallen half—that is, Dick—behind. Before the interview ends, she has apparently seen a vision of his lordship in the room and the narrator has

explained that she and Ayscough have radically different ways of seeing
the world—hers artistic, female, and right-brain hemispheric, and his
scientific, male, and left-brain.

Ayscough does not believe her, and he writes in his last letter to the
duke that probably his son killed himself in the cave, having felt more
and more vile about not being able to accept the world as it is and
himself as impotent. The Stonehenge incident, he concludes, must have
been staged. Dick, in despair over his master's suicide, probably imitated his master. The narration concludes in Manchester, where Rebecca has just given birth to a baby girl, whom she names Ann.

Fowles concludes the book in his own voice, with an essay explaining
that Ann Lee became the founder of the Shakers. Even though Fowles
is, he declares, an atheist, he admires religious dissenters and sees the
year 1736 as a convenient marker between the English Revolution of
1688 and the French Revolution of 1789. He observes, too, that sometimes novelists must use far-fetched tropes to convey truths, and that
Rebecca represents an emotional enlightenment, a "painful breaking of
the seed of the self from the hard soil of an irrational and tradition-
bound society" (451/463).

Interpretation

The characters in *A Maggot* tend to have so many false identities and
so many various explanations for what they are doing or have done
that a reader is at a loss to know what to believe—not unlike Nicholas
Urfe on Phraxos, as explanation after explanation for what Conchis is
doing proves to be an illusion. This rhetorical strategy is one way in
which *A Maggot* is another metafiction, whose readers undergo an ordeal that parallels what some of the characters are experiencing. The
characters offer interpretations of events, from Rebecca's belief that
Dick and his lordship were body and soul in some dualistic twinship, to
Ayscough's characterization of his lordship as a psychological "change-
ling," who had to "break the world which bore him" (442/452). Fowles
enters his story not only at the beginning and the end but also to comment on the age or even to confess that he, as a novelist, sometimes
feels the same sense of bafflement that a mystic like John Lee must
have felt over the real world (385–86/393–94).

A reader also may experience a shock of incredulity when the recognition dawns that his lordship is meeting aliens from space. The idea
is not so un-Fowlesian because it is an elaboration of his favored metaphor that different cultures are like different planets. He has even written
a poem called "Report from Starship 26."[116] But he does seem to be
departing rather far from the conventions of eighteenth-century fiction
and nonfiction, even in his experimental hybrid. Nor does the novel

allow readers to consider the "flying saucer" to be a modern interpretation of some mystical experience in Rebecca's mind, for the text describes physical evidence of the burned earth, which even Ayscough does not speculate was somehow "staged"—as he believes the Stonehenge encounter may have been.

The vision of June Eternal constitutes a seemingly earthbound, socialist utopia more than it does a plausibly alien or supernatural culture. To describe the ideal is never easy, and it may be this section of the novel Fowles has in mind when he calls, in his epilogue, for a degree of "metaphorical understanding from our readers before the truths behind our tropes can be conveyed" (451/463). The "truth" behind June Eternal is not the afterlife promised by religion, but of the just society that may seem conspicuous to a 1985 reader by its absence from English culture of 1736, but that has not arrived by the narrator's English culture of 1985 either, if compared with "June Eternal." Fowles is not some naive idealist, as Conchis's derisive remark about "summerlanders" in *The Magus* suggests (235/240), or as Fowles's own comment about perfectibilism in *The Aristos* makes even clearer: "If life were one long happy summer, we should be without the mysterious truths we learn from our 'winters' of suffering."[117] The vision is a trope meant to enable one to recognize the wintry climate of contemporary England.

The familiar themes of Fowles's fictions are present in *A Maggot*. The struggle of the individual self against conditioning social influences is manifest in both Lord ———— and in Rebecca. The twin motif is this time embodied in two males who are not biological twins, but who were born on the same date, Lord ———— and Dick Thurlow. Mysterious incidents are left unexplained, including not only the self-willed disappearance of Lord ————, which resembles that of Marcus Fielding in "The Enigma," but also the unexplained death of Dick Thurlow, whose death signals the liberation of his twin, as the garrotted woman in the reeds of *Daniel Martin* may similarly signal Jane's rejection of her conventional, engaged self the day she has sex with Dan. The spying of Jones on Rebecca at Exmoor—like Frederick Clegg watching Miranda from his van or Charles Smithson watching Sarah sleeping in the Undercliff or Daniel Martin watching from the trees—represents the Fowlesian theme of author and reader as complicitous voyeurs. Like an author writing or a reader reading, the characters watch to see what will happen, not entirely sure they understand what they are seeing, but enjoying the process. And the "godgame" of Maurice Conchis and Lily de Seitas in *The Magus* is in *A Maggot* almost literalized as a cosmic scheme, at least for readers who think of flying saucers as "chariots of the gods."

A Maggot is, like Fowles's other novels, a narrative that teaches. The lesson may be more overtly political but not much different in its content from that of *The French Lieutenant's Woman*, which advocated personal liberation, using a past culture whose traditions and institutions were emotionally repressive as a trope for the present. Again, as in Fowles's other novels, a character is selected for "improvement" by another character with superior knowledge, but in this novel, for the first time, the character undergoing the heuristic ordeal is a female. Like Fred Clegg, Nicholas Urfe, David Williams, Daniel Martin, or Miles Green, Rebecca Hocknell is helped to discover who she is by the mysterious, unnamed Lord ————. As she tells Ayscough when he accuses her of teasing and riddling, "If I speak riddles, I was set them. If I confuse thee, so was I confused" (333/340). By the time her experience has ended, she is a new person, spiritually evolved and physically pregnant, whose offspring—like some genetic mutation—will be a force in the evolution of the human species toward the more feminized, communal, green ideal that Fowles envisions.

Reception

Although the book's title and the facsimile pages from *The Gentleman's Magazine* were expected to depress sales, *A Maggot* was successful enough, even a best-seller. In the United States it was not as enthusiastically received as some of Fowles's previous novels had been, but in England, the novel "did slightly better," according to Fowles.[118]

The objections were predictable. "Long on atmosphere and short on narrative," wrote a reviewer for the *New York Times*.[119] The London *Times* reviewer was disappointed to read a mystery story that turns out to be going nowhere, even turns into sermonizing in a tone another reviewer described as "deadly earnestness."[120] *Atlantic Magazine* dismissed the book in two sentences, as "foggy nonsense."[121]

Other reviewers were willing to grant Fowles some benefit of doubt. *The Listener's* reviewer was troubled by the politics of the novel, which seem to endorse "a noble but now past (and essentially rural) tradition, that can still teach us but can no longer lead us," but still recognized that *A Maggot* is a book with "wit as well as a majesty."[122] *The Christian Science Monitor* found the solution unworthy of the mystery but noted that "Fowles is attempting something very difficult, and perhaps impossible: to dramatize the experience of transformation, of *transfiguration*."[123]

Those who liked *A Maggot* liked it immensely. *The New Statesman* reviewer liked the political content and thought that the book had "a profound bearing on our understanding of ourselves and our own time."[124] The reviewer for *The Times* effused, "The imaginative power of the novel is astounding, the technical virtuosity and structural daring equally so."[125] And no matter how "devious and experimental his structures," remarks the reviewer for the *London Review of Books,* John Fowles knows how to tell a good story.

NOTES

1. *Book* 1 (1970), pp. 2, 5.

2. "When the Bug Bites—Write," *Times* (12 October 1985), p. 8; Christopher Bigsby, "Interview with John Fowles," *The Radical Imagination and the Liberal Tradition,* ed. Heide Ziegler and Christopher Bigsby (London: Junction Books, 1982), p. 114.

3. James Campbell, "An Interview with John Fowles," *Contemporary Literature* 17 (1976): 462.

4. David North, "Interview with Author John Fowles," *Maclean's* (14 November 1977), p. 4.

5. Campbell, p. 461.

6. Roy Newquist, "John Fowles," *Counterpoint* (New York: Rand McNally, 1964), p. 224.

7. Bigsby, p. 124.

8. *"Lettre-postface de John Fowles," Études sur "The French Lieutenant's Woman" de John Fowles,* ed. Jean-Louis Chevalier (Caen, France: Centre Régional de Documentation Pédagogique, 1977), pp. 54–55.

9. John Fowles, "Collector's Item," *New Edinburgh Review* 55 (August 1981): 7; Campbell, p. 457.

10. "Collector's Item," p. 7. Fowles mentions Bartók on p. 172/151 of the novel.

11. "Caliban Revisited," review of *The Collector, Time* (2 August 1963), p. 68; "Collector's Item," p. 7.

12. Richard Boston, "John Fowles, Alone But Not Lonely," *New York Times Book Review* (9 November 1969), p. 2.

13. Norton Mockridge, "Smell of Success Makes Him Nervous," *New York World Telegram* (19 September 1963), p. 21.

14. *The Aristos,* 2nd ed. (New York: New American Library, Penguin, 1975), p. 10; "I Write Therefore I Am," *Evergreen Review* 8.33 (1964): 17; Roy Plomley, *Desert Island Discs,* No. 1575, 10 January 1981, Radio 4 (London: British Broadcasting Corporation), p. 8.

15. Raman K. Singh, "An Encounter with John Fowles," *Journal of Modern Literature* 8 (1980–81): 183; Newquist, p. 225.

16. Mark Featherstone-Thomas, "Goodbye, Mr. Chips," *Times Educational Supplement* (21 July 1978), p. 16.

17. Newquist, pp. 221–22; Geoffrey Wansell, "The Writer As a Recluse: A Portrait of the Novelist John Fowles," *Times* (12 May 1971), p. 14.

18. Granville Hicks, "A Caliban with Butterflies," *Saturday Review* (27 July 1963), p. 19; Morris Renek, "Worn Elastic," *Nation* 197 (1963): 352.

19. John Fowles, *The Tree* (New York: Ecco Press, 1983), p. 13.

20. Mrs. Arthur Grindley, interview with author, Leigh-on-Sea, Sussex, 24 June 1988.

21. Katherine Tarbox, "Interview with John Fowles," *The Art of John Fowles* (Athens: University of Georgia Press, 1988), p. 175.

22. Genêt, "Letter from Paris: Oct. 25, " *New Yorker* (5 November 1966), p. 162.

23. Irving Wardle, review of *The Collector*, *Times* (9 February 1971), p. 10.

24. Stage adaptation by David Parker of *The Collector* (London: Samuel French, 1973) pp. 1, 34.

25. Singh, p. 198.

26. Daniel Halpern, "A Sort of Exile in Lyme Regis," *London Magazine* (March 1971), p. 44. Samantha Eggar also was nominated as Best Actress.

27. North, p. 6.

28. Singh, p. 187.

29. Halpern, p. 35.

30. Campbell, p. 458.

31. Foreword, *The Magus: A Revised Version* (1977; reprinted New York: Dell, 1979), pp. 6/6–7.

32. *The Tree*, p. 13; Tarbox, p. 172.

33. Campbell, p. 457.

34. Afterword, *The Wanderer: Or The End of Youth (Le Grand Meulnes)*, by Alain-Fournier, trans. Lowell Bair (New York: New American Library, 1971), p. 223.

35. Robert Foulke, "A Conversation with John Fowles," *Salmagundi* 68–69 (1985–86): 375; Richard Yallop, "The Reluctant Guru," *Guardian* (9 June 1977), p. 8; Lorna Sage, "John Fowles," Profile 7, *New Review* (October 1974), p. 33.

36. Fowles tells a Zen parable involving a slap at the end of his book *Islands* (Boston: Little, Brown, 1978), p. 106.

37. Boston, p. 2.

38. Bill Byrom, "Puffing and Blowing," *Spectator* (6 May 1966), p. 574; "No Wise," *Times Literary Supplement* (5 May 1966), p. 381; Glendy Culligan, "The Magician and the Bore," *Reporter* (24 February 1966), p. 58.

39. Penelope Mortimer, "Into the Noösphere," *New Statesman* (6 May 1966), p. 659.

40. Joseph Epstein, "An English Nabokov," *New Republic* (19 February 1966), p. 29; Eliot Fremont-Smith, "Players of the Godgame," *New York Times* (17 January 1966), p. 45.

41. Singh, p. 186.

42. Woody Allen, letter to author, 10 June 1988. He adds that he enjoyed the book extremely. The remark has been misattributed to Peter Sellers, in a review of *A Maggot* by David Edgar, "Prostitute's Apocalypse," *Listener* (7 November 1985), p. 29.

43. Plomley, p. 14.

44. Singh, p. 198; Plomley, p. 14.

45. Halpern, p. 44.

46. "Notes on Writing a Novel," *Harper's Magazine* (July 1968), p. 88.

47. Boston, p. 2; "Notes," p. 97. Fowles has more recently described the drafting period as "seven months," Joshua Gilder, "John Fowles: A Novelist's Dilemma," *Saturday Review* (October 1981), p. 39; but his journal dates (cited in "Notes") should be more reliable.

48. James R. Baker, "An Interview with John Fowles," *Michigan Quarterly Review* 25 (1986): 664.

49. Sage, p. 34.

50. Richard B. Stolley, "The French Lieutenant's Woman's Man: Novelist John Fowles," *Life* (29 May 1970), p. 59.

51. Donald Hall, "John Fowles's Gardens," *Esquire* (October 1982), p. 94.

52. Gilder, p. 40.

53. *The Woodroffe School: General Information,* Boarding Ed. (Lyme Regis: uncopyrighted, 1983).

54. Gilder, p. 96; Singh, pp. 190–91; Fowles, foreword, *Ourika,* by Claire de Durfort (Austin, Tex.: W. Thomas Taylor, 1977), pp. 6–8.

55. North, p. 8.

56. "A traditional Victorian novel? Yes, and yet . . . ," *New York Times Book Review* (9 November 1969), p. 1.

57. Joyce Carol Oates, "A Novelist's World: Ceremonial, Absurd and Real," *Chicago Tribune Book World* (2 November 1969), p. 3.

58. Michael McNay, "Into the City's Iron Heart," *Guardian* (5 December 1970), p. 8.

59. Yallop, p. 8; David McCullough, review of *The Ebony Tower, Book-of-the-Month Club News* (April 1975), p. 7.

60. Malcolm Bradbury, "The Novelist as Impresario: The Fiction of John Fowles," in *No, Not Bloomsbury* (New York: Columbia University Press, 1988), pp. 282, 293.

61. Halpern, p. 45; Gilder, p. 36.

62. Leslie Garis, "Translating Fowles into Film," *New York Times Magazine* (30 August 1981), p. 54.

63. John Fowles, foreword, *The French Lieutenant's Woman: A Screenplay,* by Harold Pinter (Boston: Little, Brown, 1981), p. ix.

64. Richard Corliss, "When Acting Becomes Alchemy," *Time* (7 September 1981), p. 50.

65. Foreword, *A Screenplay,* p. xii.

66. Garis, p. 50.

67. Foreword, *A Screenplay,* p. xii.

68. Ivor Davis, "Meryl Streep has been seizing the headlines . . . ," *Times* (17 September 1981), p. 9.

69. Plomley, p. 16.

70. John F. Baker, "John Fowles," *Publisher's Weekly* (25 November 1974), p. 6.

71. Fred Hauptfuhrer, "His Stories Are Riddles Wrapped Inside an Enigma Named Fowles," *People Weekly* (7 April 1975), p. 58.

72. *The Ebony Tower,* directed by Robert Knights, screenplay by John Mortimer; with Laurence Olivier as Breasley, Roger Rees as David, Greta Scacci as Diana, Toyah Willcox as Anne, and Georgina Melville as Beth; Great Performances (London: Granada Television, 1984).

73. The traditional, allegorical interpretation of the painting would have Satan (the dragon) under control of the church (the princess) even as it is slain (by St. George), but the painting lends itself nicely to the feminist, mock-chivalric reading of the film.

74. The most obvious is from the end of part 2: "Hurry up please it's time. Goonight Bill. Goonight Lou, Goonight. Goonight."

75. Raymond J. Wilson III, "Allusion and Implication in John Fowles's 'The Cloud,'" *Studies in Short Fiction* 20 (1983): 22, offers this reading as an extension of Carol Barnum's argument that "The Cloud" dramatizes the "breakdown of communication in the wasteland world." "The Quest Motif in John Fowles's *The Ebony Tower:* Theme and Variations," *Texas Studies in Literature and Language* 23 (1981): 154.

76. These motifs are discussed in Jessie Weston, *From Ritual to Romance* (1919; reprinted New York: Doubleday, 1957), pp. 117 and 135. Eliot acknowledges a debt to this source in his headnote to *The Waste Land*.

77. John Baker, p. 6.

78. Paul Bailey, "Skilful [sic] Performers," *Observer Review* (6 October 1974), p. 30.

79. Rene Kuhn Bryant, "Skillful Angler," *National Review* (17 January 1975), p. 52; Kay Dick, "Short Stories to Savour," *Times* (4 December 1976), p. 7.

80. Peter Prince, "Real Life," *New Statesman* (11 October 1974), p. 513.

81. Hall, p. 94; Michael Barber, *An Interview with John Fowles,* Audio-Text Cassette No. 38873 (North Hollywood, Calif.: Center for Casette Studies, 1979).

82. Simon Loveday, *The Romances of John Fowles* (New York: St. Martin's, 1985); James Baker, p. 674.

83. Madeleine Kingsley, "John Fowles: Collector's Piece," *Harper's and Queen* (6 October 1977), p. 151; *"Lettre-postface,"* p. 53.

84. Susana Onega, *Form and Meaning in the Novels of John Fowles* (Ann Arbor, Mich.: UMI Research Press, 1989), p. 178.

85. Mel Gussow, "Talk with John Fowles," *New York Times Book Review* (13 November 1977), p. 84.

86. North, p. 8.

87. Peter Casagrande, *Hardy's Influence on the Modern Novel* (Totowa, N.J.: Barnes & Noble, 1987), p. 152; Gussow, p. 84.

88. Gilder, p. 39.

89. Mark Amory, "Tales Out of School," *Sunday Times Magazine* (22 September 1974), p. 36.

90. James Baker, p. 665.

91. "Falling into a Cultural Gap as Wide as the Atlantic," *Times* (15 October 1977), p. 14.

92. Jeremy Treglown, "Generation Game," *New Statesman* (7 October 1977), p. 482, referred to an overwhelming "long-windedness and didacticism."

93. Michael Mason, "Pulling the Wool," *Times Literary Supplement* (7 October 1977), p. 1135.

94. Jacky Gillott, "Home to Make Peace," *Times* (6 October 1977), p. 20.

95. John Mortimer, "Twenty-one Distinguished Contemporaries Select Their Favourite Reading of 1977," *Times* (4 December 1977), p. 33.

96. John Gardner, "In Defense of the Real," *Saturday Review* (1 October 1977), p. 22.

97. Pearl K. Bell, "The English Sickness," *Commentary* (December 1977), p. 82; Richard Boeth, "Soul Search," *Newsweek* (19 September 1977), p. 110.

98. Halpern, p. 39.

99. Hall, p. 92.

100. James Baker, p. 662; Hall, p. 92.

101. Carol Barnum, "An Interview with John Fowles," *Modern Fiction Studies* 31 (1985): 201.

102. Fowles, foreword to *The Lais of Marie de France*, trans. Robert Hanning and Joan Ferrante (New York: E. P. Dutton, 1978), p. xi.

103. Tarbox, p. 190.

104. Paul Gray, "The Prisoners of Gender," *Time* (6 September 1982): 74.

105. Geoffrey Wolff, "Bloodless Porn," *New Republic* (18 October 1982), p. 34.

106. Martin Amis, "The Magus and His Muse," *Observer* (10 October 1982), p. 31.

107. "Bibliosexuality," *Times* (10 October 1982), p. 44.

108. Benjamin DeMott, "The Yarnsmith in Search of Himself," *New York Times Book Review* (29 August 1982), p. 3.

109. Sarah Benton, "Adam & Eve," *New Socialist* (May/June 1983), p. 9.

110. Tarbox, p. 191.

111. "Message from a Maggot," *Times* (14 September 1985), p. 8.

112. Foulke, p. 376.

113. Barnum, p. 202.

114. James Baker, p. 664.

115. David Remnick, "Fowles, Following Form," *Washington Post* (12 September 1985), p. C8. Lord Lyttelton's name is erroneously given as "Littlejohn," and the year as "1736." The full title is *Letters from a Persian in England to his Friend at Istahan* (London, 1735).

116. *Poems* (New York: Ecco Press, 1973), pp. 111–12.

117. Fowles's comment is in a note on p. 220 about Emily Dickinson, who has been quoted on p. 20 to buttress the assertion on p. 19 that "perfectibility is meaningless" and "it is also evil" because "perfect ends tomorrow justify very imperfect means today."

118. James Baker, p. 663.

119. Herbert Mitgang, "Stonehenge Again," *New York Times* (2 September 1985), p. 34.

120. Peter Kemp, "Shakers in Suspense," *Times* (22 September 1985), p. 44; Reid Buckley, *American Spectator* (January 1986), p. 43.

121. *Atlantic Monthly* (October 1985), p. 108.

122. David Edgar, "Prostitute's Apocalypse," *Listener* (7 November 1985), p. 30.

123. Bruce Allen, "Caterpillar-to-Butterfly Tale Never Takes Flight," *Christian Science Monitor* (3 January 1986), p. B4.

124. Anne Smith, "Naught for Your Comfort," *New Statesman* (20 September 1985), p. 30.

125. Stuart Evans, "Shaking History and Mysticism," *London Review of Books* (19 September 1985), p. 12.

CRITICAL APPROACHES TO THE FICTION

The fiction of John Fowles has generated so much commentary from literary critics and scholars that even in the 1970s, he was beginning to grow uncomfortable with the attention. In a 1981 interview, he told listeners to the BBC that "the most horrible and shocking thing that's happened to me recently was to receive not a very small book, a book I suppose must have been half an inch thick, and that is simply a bibliography of work about my work. And three quarters of which I've never read."[1] By 1991, the list had grown much longer. Fifteen books or monographs have been published solely on Fowles's works, and other books contain chapters or discussions. Almost fifty doctoral candidates have written their Ph.D. theses about Fowles. Not counting reviews of his books or interviews, almost 200 articles have appeared in academic journals.

The range of critical approaches is wide, a fact that should surprise no one who is aware that Fowles's career has coincided with a shift of assumptions in literary criticism, a development related to what is sometimes called the poststructuralist reconfiguration of thought. Nonetheless, the large bulk of Fowles criticism has been fairly traditional. Some critical essays have located Fowles within recent literary history. Others have linked his work to Fowles himself, sometimes using biographical information and sometimes using the methods of psychology in attempts to understand his inner life. By far, most of the criticism has been formalist, analyzing the work and bringing to the attention of the reader some unifying characteristic or thread of continuity. A few essays have applied the techniques and assumptions of deconstruction to find such unified meanings illusory or unrecoverable.

Other essays locate Fowles in a sociological context—sometimes using the techniques of Marxist and new historicist inquiry, and sometimes from a feminist perspective. A few essays focus on reader responses and a work's effects on particular communities of readers. Few of the essays are pure examples of one perspective, but most are influenced by the critic's awareness of other interpretations that different critical approaches might generate.

BIOGRAPHICAL CRITICISM

The most traditional kind of biographical criticism compares an author's life and the overt content of his or her work. The first chapter of Robert Huffaker's book *John Fowles* is called "John Fowles, Daniel Martin, and Naturalism," a title that promises attention to similarities between the life of Fowles and the life of his main character in *Daniel Martin.* Although it is an insightful essay, the chapter does not explore the origins of *Daniel Martin* in a systematically biographical way. Huffaker does point out parallels between John Fowles's and Daniel Martin's experiences on a farm in Devon and at Oxford, and he quotes an interesting letter in which Fowles remarks that "Thorncombe is a conflation of several places and families, and much is made up"; however, Huffaker does not try to develop a precise relation between author and character, aware that to do so completely "would, of course, be impossible even for Fowles."[2] The last section of the chapter does discuss *Daniel Martin,* but not in a much more biographical way than do other formalist critics who recognize Fowlesian themes in the novel. As Huffaker discusses the ironies of the novel's ending in the last sentence of the chapter, where Jane laughs at Dan's Irishry, Huffaker notes that the life of the author remains "in still another dimension" besides the fictional one.[3] That dimension remains to be explored by a critical biographer.

Several other essays with a biographical dimension appeared in the 1980s as critics attempted to reconstruct the process by which Fowles composed the "endings" of *The French Lieutenant's Woman.* Paula Sullivan's 1980 essay for the Bibliographical Society of America does little more than describe the typescripts of the novel at the University of Tulsa.[4] In 1984, Elizabeth Mansfield wrote that "the most startling discovery for the reader of these manuscripts is that originally there were no alternate endings." She explains that the earliest extant typescript, which she calls "Draft I," had a single, conventional happy ending, as follows: Charles finds Sarah married and living in Clapham. She tells him that she never loved him, at which Charles angrily departs. Charles happens to learn from a nearby greengrocer that Sarah's husband has left her, and when he returns to her door, Sarah reveals that she has been supporting herself and their child by modeling at the Royal Academy. The draft ends with their tearful reconciliation. According to Mansfield, Elizabeth Fowles and her husband's publisher, Tom Maschler, objected that the ending was pat and too sentimental; their responses led Fowles first to construct the separate, alternative endings of "Draft II" and then to place the "unhappy" alternative last in "Draft III." Mansfield believes that the final arrangement, with its representation of pursuit of an absent woman, better corresponds with the underlying myth John Fowles entertains about himself.[5] Frederick N. Smith subsequently has argued that the typescripts constitute only partial evidence and that Fowles seems to have had the double endings in mind from the beginning: he offers recollections by Fowles and Maschler to support that view. Smith does not explain, however, the countervailing existence of the advanced typescript ending described earlier, which constitutes strong evidence that the double ending was not planned from the start. Nor is Smith certain which draft Maschler saw.[6] It is possible that Maschler and Fowles could be remembering "Draft I" as a version that did contain embedded, alternative endings, since that version first deprives Charles of Sarah and then rewards him with her when he goes back—even if it does not introduce the alternatives as the published novel eventually would, as distinct endings, metanarratively presented by a bearded impresario with a watch and a florin.

PSYCHOLOGICAL CRITICISM

Most of the essays in psychological criticism use a Jungian model to understand the behavior of Fowles's characters, but a few apply more scientific models to his fictions to try to understand the creative processes of Fowles himself. Gilbert J. Rose is a psychoanalyst who finds evidence in *The French Lieutenant's Woman* that when Fowles writes, he is trying temporarily to restore what Freud called the lost unity with the mother that Fowles once knew as a pre-Oedipal infant.[7] Ina Ferris arrives at a similar insight using a different, sometimes philosophical vocabulary when she argues that Fowles instinctively writes from a desire to recapture the Neoplatonic ideal of lost primal unity. Ferris thinks it is unfortunate that Fowles insists on writing against his imaginative strengths in the outward-looking realist tradition rather than in the inward-looking Romantic tradition he seems to identify with at a deeper level of his personality.[8] H. W. Fawkner uses the insights of neuropsychology and brain-hemisphere research to build a "neuropoetic" hypothesis from the novels, claiming that Fowles is extraordinarily sensitive to shifts of consciousness between brain hemispheres and accurate in his perceptions of time associated with each.[9]

More commonly, psychological critics focus on the textual personalities of the fictional characters. Simon Loveday extends Rose's Freudian insights about the composition of *The French Lieutenant's Woman* with some additional connections among Varguennes, Rossetti, and Charles.[10] In discussing the psychology of Daniel Martin, Bruce Woodcock uses a Freudian paradigm to interpret the dead woman in the reeds as a representation of Daniel Martin's "lost mother," and Daniel's father's umbrella as a comic, phallic symbol of patriarchal authority.[11]

The most favored model for understanding Fowles's characters is Jungian psychology. Carol Barnum's book is a systematic study of the quest for psychological wholeness, which can be explained in terms of encounters with Jungian archetypes of the shadow, the anima, and the mandala. Barnum discerns the quest motif in each of Fowles's novels and explores each using the framework of Jungian psychology and the hero-paradigm of Joseph Campbell to show how "each of Fowles's heroes exemplifies the nature of the struggle facing all of us and the pattern we must follow if we are to restore the wasteland to the garden."[12]

The Collector, for Barnum, is an inverted quest, and G. P. is a Jungian *animus* figure for Miranda. Clegg's problem, on the other hand, can be seen as a fixation on Miranda as *anima,* as Katherine Tarbox points out.[13] The cellar in which Clegg imprisons Miranda is, in Jungian terms, "a demonic parody of Eden, the lowest end of the scale on which the representations of the Edenic archetype might be arranged," as Patricia V. Beatty suggests in her essay that reads *The Collector* as a psychological allegory of failed, personal transformation.[14]

The Magus is treated as a Jungian allegory in several critical works. In 1976, Barry N. Olshen proposed the Jungian process of individuation, of becoming one's own self, as a psychological model for explaining the behavior of Nicholas.[15] The next year Simon Loveday described *The Magus* as "so Jungian as to be almost a textbook," explaining that Nicholas needs to have his *anima* made real to him, in the experience of love, before life will grow rich and meaningful.[16] In an essay that applies a neo-Jungian psychological model of Heinz Kohut, Julius Rowan Raper helps to account for Nicholas's "crippled" *anima* as the result of weak parental "selfobjects" who might have provided Nicholas a "mirror" and a "model" for his development of a stronger "core self."[17] In the novel, Nicholas does not understand why Conchis is manipulating him—victimizing him, as Nicholas tends to see it—but Robert Huffaker points out that Conchis is behaving like a Zen master with a pupil, a relationship that Jung considered analogous to that of a psychoanalyst with a patient.[18]

The French Lieutenant's Woman lends itself to similar, Jungian interpretation of Charles's character. Huffaker points out that Sarah plays one of the roles of the *anima,* that of "sensual seductress." He quotes a passage from Jung that neatly fits Sarah's role in Lyme Regis: "By maintaining a passive attitude with an invisible purpose in background, she aids a man towards his realization, and in that way holds him. At the same time she weaves a web of fate for herself."[19] Deborah Guth uses Jung to account for Sarah's motive in seducing Charles, as well, noting that someone who has undergone a traumatic experience, as Sarah's disappointment over the French lieutenant may have been, will try to re-create the emotional constellation of that experience to exorcize it, by living it through to a satisfactory conclusion. Guth sees the Exeter seduction as a psychological liberation for Sarah as well as a turning point for Charles.[20]

A Maggot receives Jungian treatment from Susana Onega at the end of her book's chapter on that novel. She sees his lordship's interest in mathematics and proportions to be an indication that he is on an alchemical quest, "a man in a mortal struggle with his undiscovered *anima* and with his instinctual unconscious, in search of his 'lost four,' " which she has earlier defined as the philosopher's stone or the wisdom of God, hidden in matter. A female aspect of religious deities discussed by Jung helps to give Rebecca's vision an archetypal quality too. Onega concludes that *A Maggot,* more than Fowles's earlier, existential works, affirms "a certain faith in the capacity for progressive improvement, not only of the individual, but of the human species at large."[21]

Jungian criticism tends to be more formalist than Freudian criticism, sometimes content to identify patterns and archetypes that help to account for the behavior of a character without venturing into deeper speculation about the creative process or the audience response. Myth criticism even more has tended to identify and discuss surface allusions to mythological systems in Fowles's fiction. Raymond J. Wilson, for example, has traced Fowles's use of Celtic myths and modern adaptations such as *The Waste Land* in the stories of *The Ebony Tower*, but his work is more formalist than psychological.[22] Fowles's highly allusive writing invites such readings, as well as overreadings; indeed, Fowles may have decided to drop his epigraph to the original version of *The Magus*, from Arthur Edward Waite's *The Key to the Tarot*, because he had received too many letters from would-be astrologers eager to correspond with a presumably kindred spirit. Nevertheless, there are serious ways of reading the pattern of Tarot allusions in the novel, as Marvin Magalaner and Ellen McDaniel have pointed out, for Nicholas's experiences resemble the progress of the Fool of the Tarot cards, read as stages of an archetypal journey or mythic quest.[23] Michael Tatham has offered a reading of *The French Lieutenant's Woman* as Christian myth, in which Charles is a pilgrim on an allegorical journey and Sarah's enigmatic qualities make her not only extranatural but supernatural—indeed he argues that she is a representation of God; "in its climax the story's religious symbolism is entirely convincing, love will not compel even by her presence. The sense of deprivation of which Sarah has made [Charles] aware has become an abyss, an unappeasable longing. The blind can see."[24] This reading, like any allegorical or archetypal reading of a Fowles novel, requires one to systematize in a way that Fowles's writings taken as a whole do not invite. Indeed, *The Magus* seems a kind of attack on all systems such as Christianity or the Tarot as ways of organizing one's life; to imply, for example, that the seventy-eight chapters parallel the seventy-eight cards of the Tarot pack, as Magalaner does, requires one to view *The Magus* in a way that is at cross purposes with the antiessentialist philosophy and theme of freedom advanced by that or any other Fowles novel.

DECONSTRUCTIVE CRITICISM

Even though Fowles seems to invite poststructuralist readings of his fictions with his references to Barthes in *The French Lieutenant's Woman* (95/80) and *The Ebony Tower* (277/259), not many critics have used deconstructive techniques in their criticism of Fowles. At least one who claims to do so, Robert Burden, devotes most of his work to finding "underlying principles of coherence" in such ideas as "the quest"—a critical purpose that seems inconsistent with assumptions of deconstructive critics who find language radically incapable of supporting such findings and who emphasize ways in which works *fail* to cohere in the ways critics usually point to.[25] Jamie Dopp and Barry N. Olshen, on the other hand, never describe what they are doing with *The Tree* as deconstruction, but their approach leads to some surprising insights into ways that Fowles's concept of the "green man" both represents and subtly subverts the very assumptions Fowles seems to be making about autobiography.[26]

Several essays about *The French Lieutenant's Woman* deal with issues of deconstruction. Robert Siegle discusses the concept of the author in that novel, with reference to theories of Barthes and Foucault, to show that Fowles is too readily dismissed as a conventional thinker. Fowles may indeed sound traditional when he defends the concepts of mystery, selfhood, and authorship, but Siegle notes strands in the novels that work differently and allow "Fowles" to be thought of in textual rather than ontological terms. Siegle points to Chapter 35, in which several voices represent an "author" who is sometimes scientific and antiparochial, at other times one who "cheerfully valorizes existential awakenings," and sometimes the voice of external convention, contesting other such voices for dominance. Siegle urges critics not to let the traditional idea of what an author is frustrate the discovery of new readings that emerge when an author is considered a "textual strategy."[27] Gerald Doherty probes even more deeply into the text with his analysis of ways that metaphor takes over narrative in *The French Lieu-tenant's Woman*. Using concepts borrowed from Paul Ricoeur, Doherty argues that "the text enacts, so to speak, the secret plottings of meta-phor" as Charles and Sarah move out of the private, blissful, and unrhetorical world of the Undercliff into English society. As Charles become wiser, he becomes less sure of what he knows about Sarah—in a way like a modern author who recognizes that plots are not valid, epistemological tools or that predication itself is ambivalent. The nov-el's multiple endings are gestures toward indeterminacy, "fragile inti-mations of sequence amidst a randomness which threatens to divide and dissolve them."[28]

Perhaps the most sophisticated reading of "The Cloud," from *The Ebony Tower*, is Arnold E. Davidson's deconstructive essay, which begins with a quotation from Barthes' *Mythologies*, the work discussed by sev-eral of the characters in the story. Davidson sees "The Cloud" as "a grimly comical fictional mythologizing of" *Mythologies* as well as an il-lustration of the way intellectual discourse becomes "sexual gamesman-ship and powerbrokering." Fowles's story is full of ambiguities and in-determinacies, even on the most basic level of understanding what happens, and the embedded fairy tale of Catherine is problematical in its own ways, as Davidson points out. "Catherine's silence epitomizes the story at the heart of the text—her own and Fowles's," notes David-son, so "The Cloud," as a story, "negates the very measures whereby we would delimit it."[29]

Katherine Tarbox uses the language of deconstruction to describe what goes on in *A Maggot*. The unnamed lord who arranges the jour-ney to the West Country "begins by disorienting Rebecca and ends by deconstructing her. This is the typical strategy of all Fowlesian god-games." A few pages later, Tarbox continues to describe Rebecca's sit-uation as a "masque," an "existential adventure whose aim is to decon-struct its subject and force her to disassemble the elaborate gearwork of lies and appearances" because traditional methods of knowing are ineffectual. Words are "walls" that Rebecca must learn to break through. The metaphor implies that there is meaning behind the walls, but this is a more optimistic view than purely deconstructive critics allow them-selves; Tarbox is perhaps more a humanist than a deconstructive critic, for she praises Fowles for "faith in the ability of human minds to meet in the place beyond words." Furthermore, she believes that "this novel, like his others, is an affirmation of the humanizing influence of fic-tion."[30]

Mantissa has been discussed as a parody of deconstructive tenets by Susana Onega and by Drury Pifer. Onega notes that the book "evinces such a thorough knowledge of these theories, and such a concern with the issues they raise, that one is tempted to see there, too, an attempt to come to terms with the overwhelming realization that the contemporary writer comes at the end of a very long and great tradition of writing, what Harold Bloom called the 'anxiety of influence.' " Onega also comments that the different interpretations of the story by Erato, Miles, or Staff Sister—or Fowles's critics—illustrates a "freedom to 'misread' " that subverts more traditional views of literary authors.[31] Drury Pifer undertakes to write a virtual introduction to deconstructive theory in his critique of *Mantissa*, which he, too, reads as parody. The novel is not the self-reflexive text that "author" Miles Green intended to write, but instead a representation of his unnatural relationship with the muse he has attempted to dominate and has found himself written by. "The muse comes to embody 'textuality,' which is, in the words of the deconstructionists, 'the one cultural given,' " but which is also, Pifer points out, itself a metaphor. After discussion of Derrida and Lacan, Pifer notes that philosophy tends to crowd out human interest in *Mantissa*, that Miles Green (or Fowles?) is perhaps too successful in calling attention to the inadequacy of his text: "If the reader persists in his efforts to find meaning, *Mantissa*'s text will both bind him to analysis and subvert its conclusions." Fowles is always one step ahead of his critics, it seems, succeeding in having written a failed novel—for what that is worth. "Like a man who eats a toadstool to demonstrate its deadly properties," Pifer suggests, *Mantissa* "sickens on [the deconstruction] it opposes" until few readers are likely to want to reread the book.[32]

HISTORICIST CRITICISM

A traditional kind of historicist criticism is literary history, and critics have long been interested in locating Fowles in the sequence of evolving literary forms. Writing for *Critique* in 1967–1968, Thomas Churchill observed of *The Magus* that Fowles had "beaten the room," a metaphorical way of describing his novel's break with the Pinteresque "grayish" and cluttered interiors of much fiction from the early 1960s (including *The Collector*).[33] In 1970, Bernard Bergonzi said of *The Magus* that it was more like American fiction with its "impulse to myth" than like English fiction, and might be the harbinger of a trend away from realism.[34] More recently, Theo D'haen has discussed *The French Lieutenant's Woman* as a "problematic novel," David Lodge's phrase describing novels that make explicit an author's hesitation to commit to more traditional strains of fiction, a mode D'haen believes may signal a shift in social consciousness that later historians will recognize.[35] David Leon Higdon has noted that *The French Lieutenant's Woman* "made concrete Alain Robbe-Grillet's call for a new type of reader participation," in 1963, and Philip Cohen considers *The French Lieutenant's Woman* to be an example of the kind of fiction John Barth calls for in his 1980 essay "The Literature of Replenishment"—neither naive illusionism nor anti-illusionism.[36]

Susana Onega's 1989 introduction to *Form and Meaning in the Novels of John Fowles* reviews trends in English fiction since the 1930s, to locate Fowles in recent literary history. She discusses "the Movement," with its working-class characters, and the "social and liberal" novels that include "campus" novels such as *Lucky Jim*. Onega aligns Fowles with "fabulous and experimental" novelists, particularly with Beckett, Lowry, Golding, and Murdoch, who share his "hopeful" existentialism. Onega observes that Fowles's kind of experimentalism places him in the center of the British half of the spectrum, "whose self reflexiveness is limited by the desire to communicate an intelligible message." Fowles uses metafictional mechanisms, especially that of parody, to release tension between experimentalism and realism. By rewriting stories of a quest for maturity and freedom, Onega further suggests, "Fowles is telling us that even if liberty proves to be unattainable, it is at least possible to create the illusion of this freedom."[37]

Other critics see changes in cultural history, the episteme of the twentieth century, to be shaping Fowles's novels. Although he does not argue that Fowles was directly borrowing from Pirandello and Brecht, Silvio Gaggi discerns their influence on *The Magus* and *The French Lieutenant's Woman*.[38] Robert L. Nadeau sees early twentieth-century ideas associated with "the new physics" at work in Fowles's fiction, ideas such as quantum mechanics, Heisenberg's uncertainty principle, and Einstein's theory of relativity.[39] James R. Baker sees the historical Rossetti in Victorian London as a prototype for the modern English *aristos* in exile within England, as Fowles sometimes sees himself.[40]

Several critics have discussed the idea of history itself and its importance as a theme in Fowles's fiction. A sequence of essays in *Victorian Studies* offers differing views of Fowles as a historian in *The French Lieutenant's Woman*. Patrick Brantlinger finds Fowles's treatment of Victorian society trite and superficial. Ian Adam argues to the contrary that, documentable accuracy aside, "there are many places where a sense of history is conveyed implicitly or with minimal explication." Sheldon Rothblatt points out that Fowles tries to do what any historian wants to do, "to explain why his characters are Victorians and why we are not. And by showing us what we are not, he has helped us to see ourselves as we are"; the bearded figure on the railway car is a parody of Fowles as historian—uninvolved in what he sees and, thus, incapable of understanding the human condition.[41]

David Gross extends the discussion of history as a theme in Fowles's fiction by showing that in *The Magus, The French Lieutenant's Woman*, and "The Ebony Tower," Fowles provides two historical perspectives, to show that a proper relationship with history "is neither to pine for a return to some earlier historical epoch, nor to live unthinkingly in the present age," but "to establish a creative, dialectical relationship with the past, allowing its greater *human* qualities to fructify in our imagination and lead us forward toward a better future."[42] Günther Klotz uses some of the same Marxist principles to describe Fowles's view of society as "dialectical" and to historicize Fowles's novels as narratives that reject the tendencies of his age toward celebration of "modernist morbidity" and "fashions of despair" in favor of "social sanity."[43]

FEMINIST CRITICISM

The French Lieutenant's Woman has generated divergent interpretations by feminist critics. Deborah Byrd calls Sarah "a positive role model" for liberating women and the novel itself "close to being an ideal feminist fictional work."[44] Magali Cornier Michael calls Byrd's reading "naive," and argues that even if Fowles was trying to depict Sarah as an emancipated women, "if only feminist or pro-feminist readers can see the novel's feminism, then I think that Fowles' *The French Lieutenant's Woman* falls short of being a feminist novel."[45] The divergent responses result from the novel's presentation of pro-feminist themes in a manner that can seem anti-feminist because Fowles preserves Sarah's mysteriousness by keeping her at a distance, through strategies such as not entering her mind and defining her by means of masculine fictions about women.

Constance Hieatt has noted that "Fowles is almost exclusively concerned with the problems of men."[46] Indeed, his narrators sound masculine, and the point of view usually is that of a male character in a position to be changed by means of his relationship with females. Another critic, Terry Lovell, recalls that Fowles once claimed, in *The Aristos*, that most of the great artists were Eve-men; this idea, Lovell objects, incorporates both a central role for women and a predominant role for men, as do the novels, in which "the Sarahs are . . . catalysts not aristos."[47] John Haegert has argued—not very persuasively—that *Mantissa* is an attempt to portray a female character who is not a mortal woman but merely "a catalyst, a function, an agent, or a muse—a mere 'mantissa' in the life of his hero."[48] Perhaps *A Maggot* is Fowles's more satisfactory answer to feminist critics, for that novel's protagonist is a female who undergoes a profound change of character, and the narrator tends to disappear for much of the dramatized narrative.

One book of criticism, *Male Mythologies,* by Bruce Woodcock, is devoted to exploring and documenting Fowles's patriarchal biases. Prompted no doubt in part by Fowles's claim to be a feminist, Woodcock goes about uncovering various masculine ideas and myths embedded in the novels so that he can conclude that Fowles is not a proper feminist after all. Indeed, at one point Woodcock suggests that "Fowles himself is a kind of Bluebeard."[49] Fowles's liberal agenda for improving the freedom of everyone, and particularly of women, may not be sufficiently feminist to satisfy readers who want to see a more profound shift in cultural attitudes, but *Male Mythologies* is so unrelieved an effort to ferret out ideological incorrectness that Woodcock's readers may forget that Fowles is sympathetic to the women's movement.

READER-RESPONSE CRITICISM

Two essays on *The French Lieutenant's Woman* refer to theoretical work about reader responses in their discussions of the alternate endings of that novel. Joanne V. Creighton sees the creation of such an open-ended novel and the emergence of reader-response criticism to be parallel developments in response to a cultural dynamic of the late 1960s. Creighton notes that theorist Stanley Fish might describe how the replaying of endings would affect the experience of reading as it is going on, whereas Wolfgang Iser might be more interested in whether a reader truly feels free to choose between the endings.[50] Steven G. Kellman notes that all works of literature, according to Iser, are indeterminate to some extent, and that *The French Lieutenant's Woman* is a work that articulates its inconclusiveness in a way that enriches the experience of readers by engaging their imaginations, "to rescue us from paralysis."[51]

Several critiques of *The Magus* focus on reader responses but do not declare any allegiance to poststructuralist theory as they do so. Robert Scholes's 1969 essay on the "orgastic rhythm of the narrative" uses analogies between the sex act and the act of reading to illustrate how Fowles uses surprise, frustration, delay, intensification, climax, and resolution—among other experiences—to shape the responses of a reader who, Scholes suggests, "strives to mate with the writer."[52] Frank G. Novak is interested in the responses of college students to *The Magus,* which he claims "often affects these young readers in unexpected and unsettling ways" because the final view the book offers is of a world whose forces cannot be understood or controlled. The typical response of this community of readers, according to Novak, is "anxiety."[53]

FORMALIST CRITICISM

By far, most of the critical writing about the fiction of John Fowles has been formalist, that is, concerned with descrying meaningful patterns within the fictional text rather than in its relation with some external context. The books about Fowles pay attention to common themes in Fowles's work, but they vary in what aspects of the text they call attention to. William J. Palmer is particularly interested in relations of

Fowles's first three novels to other literary works, including *Clarissa, Lord Jim,* and *Crime and Punishment;* Michael Thorpe, likewise, discusses the relation of *The Magus* to *The Tempest.*[54] Peter Wolfe offers ingenious comments on the names of Fowles's characters, and Robert Huffaker offers perceptive observations about animal and bird imagery.[55] In her 1988 book, Katherine Tarbox generalizes about Fowles's work: "Each novel ultimately tells the same story, and the story of the survival of individual freedom is the *only* story."[56] In a book the next year, Susana Onega makes a similar observation: "By writing symphonic variations of the only conceivable situation—a fictional hero's quest for maturity and freedom—Fowles is telling us that even if liberty proves to be unattainable, it is at least possible to create the illusion of this freedom."[57]

Other writers have generalized about the kind of work Fowles produces, rather than its themes. Ronald Binns pointed out, in 1973, that Fowles is synthesizing the traditions of romance and realism, "manipulating the romance form to effect both a sceptical examination of the romance experience and, more radically, a critique of contemporary realist fiction for its absence of moral responsibility."[58] Variations on this observation have included a description by Patricia Merivale of Fowles as a writer of "gothic" and "eclectic" allegories, and a book by Simon Loveday on Fowles's novels as "romances," based on Northrop Frye's observation that "the romancer does not attempt to create 'real people' so much as stylized figures which expand into psychological archetypes."[59]

The most frequently practiced kind of formalist criticism traces some theme in Fowles's works, either considered separately or as a whole. How many works constitute the "whole" depends, of course, on when the essay was written. Peter Wolfe's 1975 article "John Fowles: The Existential Tension," for example, and Dwight Eddins's 1976 "John Fowles: Existence as Authorship" trace themes of existentialism or metafiction, respectively, but consider only the first three of Fowles's novels.[60] Other articles trace motifs that range from the predictable (collecting or hidden valleys and unattainable princesses) to the surprising (fishing, fathers, and death).[61] The most intellectually insightful essay to date is David H. Walker's "Remorse, Responsibility, and Moral Dilemmas in Fowles's Fiction," which examines the tension between absolute freedom and personal remorse as a theme that can open up a fairly deep understanding of the first five novels. Walker's discussion includes consideration of two motifs that have received little attention previously: watching eyes and physical slaps. In the course of his predominantly formalist analysis, Walker also draws on biography, psychoanalysis, and language theory to argue that responsible, social compromise—between the warring impulses of remorse and freedom—is the core value in Fowles's fiction.[62]

Two other formalist essays draw on the texts of the novels to find serious fault with them. In "John Fowles and His Big Ideas," Bruce Bawer objects that Fowles's wish to be a philosopher prevents him from being a better novelist. Like some of Fowles's reviewers, Bawer sees too much didacticism, polemics, and "sentimental overgeneralization" in his novels, whose characters Bawer would prefer Fowles made more realistic."[63] A different kind of objection by Karen M. Lever is based not on Fowles's way of presenting characters, but on their tendency always to be on the threshhold of a new maturity. In "The Education of John Fowles," her title is deliberately ambiguous, referring both to the theme of education in all of his novels and to Fowles's seeming inability to write anything but "the novel of education with which it is natural to begin a career." Within those novels, Lever sees messages that seem to conflict with the lessons a reader is expected to learn: the implied author is a collector and presenter of textual curios, a person who is easily titillated, sexually, and "a snob whether he is showing off for the professors or talking down to Book-of-the-Month Club members to make them better informed." When Lever traces his career as a novelist and asks, "Why has John Fowles grown so slowly?" she imagines that he has not grown up as a person either.[64] Lever's evident disdain for the author and dislike of what he has written must make his teacherlike stance particularly annoying for her as she reads.

Formalist critiques of *The Collector* tend to show that the novel is more complex than it might seem. Syhamal Bagchee argues that the contrasts of character and theme are not matters of "white-versus-black readings where Miranda can be taken to represent goodness, beauty, and high morality; her captor, Clegg, evil, ugliness, and immorality." Instead, both characters are extraordinary, both change, and, ironically, both are victimized by being themselves.[65] Perry Nodelman points out that Miranda and Clegg share a conception of difference between classes, and her failure to escape may be a dark comment on the prisonhouse of convention that victimizes everyone.[66] John M. Neary admits that he is going far "out on a limb" as he argues that Clegg is heroic, "that there is an irony beneath the irony," and that at this level, Clegg is "downright poetic in his verbal simplicity, a kind of natural Hemingway, who wages a linguistic war against Miranda's verbal pretensions."[67]

Several essays about *The Magus* have compared the original version of 1965 with *The Magus: A Revised Version* in 1977. Cory Wade discusses both versions in general terms, pointing out that certain premises have been made less mysterious, so that the new novel is more believable but still seems mysterious.[68] About the revised ending of the novel, Michael Boccia observes that the shift to third person in the last chapter and the deletion of the reference to Orpheus at the end removes the basis in the original for guessing that Nicholas would be reunited with Alison, his Eurydice; the new ending makes clearer that the conclusion is to be taken as ambiguous or inconclusive.[69] James R. Lindroth focuses on the deleted reference to Alison's smile, which linked her with Conchis in the original and even called into question whether he might still be controlling events. The new version emphasizes the improvised nature of their dialogue, the "abandonment of prepared scripts" in the unbounded, "open performance site" of Regent's Park, which, Lindroth argues, is a structural contrast with the enclosed metatheater at Conchis's villa.[70] Ellen McDaniel suggests that "the smell of burning leaves," the concluding phrase of the novel, refers to leaves of paper, that is, to the "pages of a book burning"—the script Nicholas is no longer following.[71] She might have added that the novel, too, as script for the reader, can now be put aside.

Among the formalist approaches to *The French Lieutenant's Woman,* several critics have discussed what genre the novel belongs to. Fred Kaplan calls the book "an odd kind of historical novel," and Prescott Evarts, Jr., calls it "a mannerist tragedy set in Victorian times."[72] Elizabeth D. Rankin suggests that Fowles's book is a Victorian novel camouflaged to look like a postmodern one, that "his 'digressive' Chapter Thirteen is actually a diversionary chapter in which, tossing a bone to Robbe-Grillet and Barthes, he insures the literary acceptance (survival) of his actually quite conventional novel."[73] Charles Scruggs offers a justification of Sarah's behavior in the next-to-last "ending," which most critics dismiss as inconsistent with her character but he considers to be more consistent with the epigraph to the novel.[74] Narratologist K. R. Ireland analyzes the text and finds "a repertoire" of more than twenty kinds of narrative sequence used in the novel.[75] Examining how two particular narratological systems fail perfectly to describe characteristics of *The French Lieutenant's Woman,* William Nelles proposes "some minor refinements" to the theories.[76] Perhaps the best reading of the novel as a whole, however, is Linda Hutcheon's essay "The 'Real World(s)' of Fiction: *The French Lieutenant's Woman,*" which takes up for discussion the novel's preoccupation with the imaginative process, its narrative devices, its status as parody, and the relations among characters that enable readers to appreciate thematic, moral meanings.[77]

Fowles's original title of *Variations* for *The Ebony Tower* can be taken as an invitation to see the stories as different versions of the same themes. John B. Humma explores the idea of testing and the idea of the green man as motifs in the collection, but his argument takes an odd turn as he discusses "The Cloud" and argues that Catherine's sexual submission to Peter is her passing of a test; his reading requires her reunion with her dead husband and the green world to take place by means of

Peter, "the person of its antithesis, and nemesis."[78] Ellen McDaniel offers a more satisfactory reading of the incident as a "spiritual and moral, not physical" death.[79]

"The Enigma" has been discussed as a contribution to the popular genre of mystery story. David Brownell traces an evolution of prose style in Fowles's story from impersonal to personal, from detective fiction to romance, and notes that the final implication of the "The Enigma" is that its world is irrational, unlike the conventional world of the mystery story: "The magician in full view of the audience has gotten you to watch a beautiful girl when you thought you were watching the disappearing Tory politician."[80] Brownell implies but never quite states that "The Enigma" is a subversion of its own subgenre, detective fiction—or as *Mantissa*'s Miles Green might put it, "The Enigma" is detective fiction about the difficulty of writing serious detective fiction.[81]

Robert Arlett discusses *Daniel Martin* generically, as a contemporary epic novel. He calls it "an elegaic novel" at one point, and he notes that "the tricks and techniques of dissonance and fragmentation in *Daniel Martin* are closely related to the form of its epic stooge, the movie of Kitchener." Although he calls Jane "Dan's epic muse," Arlett never quite claims that Fowles's novel deserves to be called an epic; indeed, he ends his somewhat rambling essay on a note of discontent over the way Fowles works out the final third of the novel.[82] Other formalist critics have explored themes in the novel, including Fowles's use of filmmaking as a metaphor, which Carol Ward discusses as a medium whose limitations represent the shortcomings of Hollywood and America.[83] Susan Strehle Klemtner notes that "The Tensional Nature of Human Reality" is one of Fowles's chapter titles, and argues that a "dualistic scheme" governs the novel. Among the antitheses she discusses are past and present, day and night, country and city, England and America, *ka* and *ba*, fertility and ruins—even male and female, in Dan and Jane. The idea of "whole sight," Klemtner points out, implies union of such counterpoles at the conclusion of the novel.[84]

Ian Gotts has discussed *Mantissa* in a way that points out, indirectly, how difficult that book is to categorize. In the course of his essay, Gotts refers to it as something John Barth might call "another story about a writer writing a story." Gotts refers to *Mantissa* as an "emblem (however comic) of a loss of confidence in contemporary art's ability to imitate reality." He wonders if it is "a literary suicide note." He calls it a parody of a modern novel on one page, "an allegory of literary creation" on another, "a menippean comedy of ideas" on a third, and "splendid farce" on a fourth. In his last paragraph, Gotts refers to *Mantissa* as "reasonably successful entertainment," "serious modern fiction," and "the kind of trickery that properly belongs to the aesthetic self-questionings of the late 1960s and early 1970s." Perhaps Gotts intends for his readers to feel less able to classify the book when they finish his exuberant essay.[85]

A Maggot has proved challenging to critics who wish to locate it in a genre. Susana Onega looks to the history of the novel, and points out that the use of letters and confessions, with a prologue and epilogue by an editor who has supposedly found the documents being presented, was a narrative strategy of the early eighteenth century used to disguise the fictionality of a novel and to differentiate it from romances.[86] Katherine Tarbox, by contrast, points out *A Maggot*'s departures from the conventional form of the novel: "Several plots alternately vie for attention. The question-and-answer depositions are devoid of point of view. Excerpts from the *Gentleman's Magazine* and other topical sources make their way into the text without comment. Fowles gives us a part-time narrator who has neither authority nor irony, whose discoveries are simultaneous with the reader's. The novel has no consistent protagonist, but a shifting one."[87] David Essex observes that part of the problem is a shift in the book's apparent genre, from what starts off as an apparent historical roman à clef but turns into "some sort of Postmodern hybrid, a 'fiction.' " Essex concludes that *A Maggot* is "a very peculiar chimera of a novel," perhaps appropriately labeled in his title as a "kōan," or Zen puzzle.[88]

NOTES

1. Frank Delaney, *Bookshelf* (11 October 1981), Radio 4, British Broadcasting Corporation.

2. Robert Huffaker, *John Fowles*, Twayne English Authors Series 292 (Boston: G. K. Hall, 1980), p. 36.

3. Ibid., p. 43.

4. Paula Sullivan, "The Manuscripts for John Fowles [sic] *The French Lieutenant's Woman*," *Papers of the Bibliographical Society of America* 74 (1980): 272–77.

5. Elizabeth Mansfield, "A Sequence of Endings: The Manuscripts of *The French Lieutenant's Woman*," *Journal of Modern Literature* 8 (1980–81): 277, 286. I have borrowed several details from the summary in David Leon Higdon, "Endgames in John Fowles's *The French Lieutenant's Woman*," *English Studies* 65 (1984): 357.

6. Frederic N. Smith, "The Endings of *The French Lieutenant's Woman:* Another Speculation on the Manuscript," *Journal of Modern Literature* 14 (1987): 579–81.

7. Gilbert J. Rose, "*The French Lieutenant's Woman:* The Unconscious Significance of a Novel to Its Author," *American Imago* 29 (1972):169.

8. Ina Ferris, "Realist Intention and Mythic Impulse in *Daniel Martin*," *Journal of Narrative Technique* 12 (1982):146–47, 152.

9. H. W. Fawkner, *The Timescapes of John Fowles* (Cranbury, N.J.: Associated University Presses, 1984), pp. 35, 144, 148–49.

10. Simon Loveday, *The Romances of John Fowles* (New York: St. Martin's, 1985), pp. 75–77.

11. Bruce Woodcock, *Male Mythologies* (Totowa, N.J.: Barnes & Noble, 1984), pp. 127, 130.

12. Carol Barnum, *The Fiction of John Fowles* (Greenwood, Fla.: Penkevill Publishing, 1988), p. 147.

13. Barnum, p. 45; Katherine Tarbox, *The Art of John Fowles* (Athens: University of Georgia Press, 1988), p. 49.

14. Patricia V. Beatty, "John Fowles' Clegg: Captive Landlord of Eden," *Ariel* 13.3 (1982):73, 75.

15. Barry N. Olshen, "John Fowles's *The Magus:* An Allegory of Self-Realization," *Journal of Popular Culture* 9 (1976): 916.

16. Simon Loveday, "Magus or Midas?" *Oxford Literary Review* 2.3 (1977): 35.

17. Julius Rowan Raper, "John Fowles: The Psychological Complexity of *The Magus,*" *American Imago* 45 (1988): 74–75.

18. Huffaker, p. 63.

19. Ibid., p. 110.

20. Deborah Guth, "Archetypal Worlds Reappraised: *The French Lieutenant's Woman* and *Le Grand Meulnes,*" *Comparative Literature Studies* 22 (1985): 248, 250.

21. Susana Onega, *Form and Meaning in the Novels of John Fowles* (Ann Arbor, Mich.: UMI Research Press, 1989), pp. 152–53, 158, 174.

22. Raymond J. Wilson, "John Fowles's *The Ebony Tower:* Unity and Celtic Myth," *Twentieth Century Literature* 28 (1982): 302–18; "Allusion and Implication in John Fowles's 'The Cloud,' " *Studies in Short Fiction* 20 (1983): 17–22.

23. Marvin Magalaner, "The Fool's Journey: John Fowles's *The Magus* (1966)," in *Old Lines, New Forces: Essays on the Contemporary British Novel, 1960–1970*, ed. Robert K. Morris (London: Associated University Presses; Cranbury, N.J.: Fairleigh Dickinson University Press, 1976), pp. 81–92; Ellen McDaniel, "*The Magus:* Fowles's Tarot Quest," *Journal of Modern Literature* 8 (1980–81): 247–60.

24. Michael Tatham, "Two Novels: Notes on the Work of John Fowles," *New Blackfriars* 52 (1971): 408, 410.

25. Robert Burden, *John Fowles—John Hawkes—Claude Simon: Problems of Self and Form in the Post-Modernist Novel* (Würzburg, Germany: Königshausen & Neumann, 1980), pp. iv, 152.

26. Jamie Dopp and Barry N. Olshen, "Fathers and Sons: Fowles's *The Tree* and Autobiographical Theory," *Mosaic* 22.4 (1989): 32, 43.

27. Robert Siegle, "The Concept of the Author in Barthes, Foucault, and Fowles," *College Literature* 10 (1983): 128, 132, 136–37.

28. Gerald Doherty, "The Secret Plot of Metaphor: Rhetorical Designs in John Fowles's *The French Lieutenant's Woman,*" *Paragraph* 9 (9 March 1987): 50, 52, 58, 65.

29. Arnold E. Davidson, "The Barthesian Configuration of John Fowles's 'The Cloud,' " *Centenniel Review* 28.4–29.1 (1984–85): 80–83, 89, 92–93.

30. Tarbox, pp. 149, 151, 153, 167.

31. Onega, pp. 134, 136.

32. Drury Pifer, "The Muse Abused: Deconstruction in *Mantissa*," in *Critical Essays on John Fowles*, ed. Ellen Pifer (Boston: G. K. Hall, 1986), pp. 163–64, 167, 174–75.

33. Thomas Churchill, "Waterhouse, Storey, and Fowles: Which Way Out of the Room?" *Critique* 10 (1967–68): 73, 87.

34. Bernard Bergonzi, *The Situation of the Novel* (Pittsburgh, Pa.: University of Pittsburgh Press, 1970), p. 75.

35. Theo D'haen, "Fowles, Lodge and the 'Problematic Novel,' " *Dutch Quarterly Review of Anglo-American Letters* 9 (1979): 164–65, 174–75.

36. David Leon Higdon, "Endgames in John Fowles's *The French Lieutenant's Woman*," *English Studies* 65 (1984): 360; Philip Cohen, "Postmodernist Technique in *The French Lieutenant's Woman*," *Western Humanities Review* 38 (1984): 149.

37. Onega, pp. 1–7, 10.

38. Silvio Gaggi, "Pirandellian and Brechtian Aspects of the Fiction of John Fowles," *Comparative Literature Studies* 23 (1986): 326.

39. Robert L. Nadeau, "Fowles and Physics: A Study of *The Magus: A Revised Version*," *Journal of Modern Literature* 8 (1980–81): 261–65.

40. James R. Baker, "Fowles and the Struggle of the English *Aristoi*," *Journal of Modern Literature* 8 (1980–81): 166, 170–73.

41. " 'The French Lieutenant's Woman': A Discussion," *Victorian Studies* 15 (1972): 343, 345, 348, 355.

42. David Gross, "Historical Consciousness and the Modern Novel: The Uses of History in the Fiction of John Fowles," *Studies in the Humanities* 7.1 (1978): 27.

43. Günther Klotz, "Realism and Metafiction in John Fowles's Novels," *Zeitschrift für Anglistik und Amerikanistik* 34 (1986): 300, 307.

44. Deborah Byrd, "The Evolution and Emancipation of Sarah Woodruff: *The French Lieutenant's Woman* as a Feminist Novel," *International Journal of Women's Studies* 7 (1984): 306, 319n.

45. Magali Cornier Michael, " 'Who is Sarah?': A Critique of *The French Lieutenant's Woman*'s Feminism," *Critique* 28 (1987): 228, 235.

46. Constance Hieatt, "*Eliduc* Revisited: John Fowles and Marie de France," *English Studies in Canada* 3 (1977): 357.

47. Terry Lovell, "Feminism and Form in the Literary Adaptation: *The French Lieutenant's Woman*," in *Criticism and Critical Theory*, ed. Jeremy Hawthorn (London: Edward Arnold, 1984), p. 120.

48. John Haegert, "Memoirs of a Deconstructive Angel: The Heroine as Mantissa in the Fiction of John Fowles," *Contemporary Literature* 27 (1986): 181.

49. Woodcock, pp. 27–28.

50. Joanne V. Creighton, "The Reader and Modern and Post-Modern Fiction," *College Literature* 9 (1982): 222.

51. Steven G. Kellman, "Fictive Freedom through *The French Lieutenant's Woman*," *University of Mississippi Studies in English* 4 (1983): 166–67.

52. Robert Scholes, "The Orgastic Fiction of John Fowles," *Hollins Critic* 6.5 (1969): 3, 12. Fowles's *Mantissa* plays further with this idea, which had in the interim been explored by Roland Barthes in *The Pleasure of the Text* (1973).

53. Frank G. Novak, Jr., "The Dialectics of Debasement in *The Magus*," *Modern Fiction Studies* 31 (1985): 71–72, 79.

54. William J. Palmer, *The Fiction of John Fowles* (Columbia: University of Missouri Press, 1974), pp. 13–20; Michael Thorpe, *John Fowles* (Windsor, U.K.: Profile Books, 1982), pp. 21–23.

55. Peter Wolfe, *John Fowles, Magus and Moralist*, 2nd ed. (Lewisburg, Pa.: Bucknell University Press, 1979), pp. 53–54, 93, 101, 143; Huffaker, pp. 170, 145 n. 2.

56. Tarbox, p. 9.

57. Onega, p. 10.

58. Ronald Binns, "John Fowles: Radical Romancer," *Critical Quarterly* 15 (1973): 319.

59. Patricia Merivale, "Learning the Hard Way: Gothic Pedagogy in the Modern Romantic Quest," *Comparative Literature* 36 (1984): 146, 148; Loveday, *Romances*, 9.

60. Peter Wolfe, "John Fowles: The Existential Tension," *Studies in the 20th Century* 16 (1975): 111–45; Dwight Eddins, "John Fowles: Existence as Authorship," *Contemporary Literature* 17 (1976): 204–22.

61. Robert Campbell, "Moral Sense and the Collector: The Novels of John Fowles," *Critical Quarterly* 25 (1983): 45–53; Ishrat Lindblad, " 'La bonne vaux', 'la princesse lointaine': Two Motifs in the Novels of John Fowles," in *Studies in English Philology, Linguistics and Literature*, ed. Mats Ryden and Lennart A. Bjork (Stockholm: Almqvist and Wiksell, 1978), pp. 87–101; Randolph Runyon, "Fowles's Enigma Variations," *Fowles/Irving/Barthes* (Columbus: Ohio State University Press for Miami University, 1981), pp. 3–35.

62. David H. Walker, "Remorse, Responsibility, and Moral Dilemma in Fowles's Fiction," in *Critical Essays on John Fowles*, ed. Ellen Pifer (Boston: G. K. Hall, 1986), pp. 54–76.

63. Bruce Bawer, "John Fowles and His Big Ideas," *New Criterion* 5.8 (April 1987), pp. 21–36.

64. Karen M. Lever, "The Education of John Fowles," *Critique* 21.2 (1979–80): 86, 97.

65. Syhamal Bagchee, *The Collector:* The Paradoxical Imagination of John Fowles," *Journal of Modern Literature* 8 (1980–1981): 219–20, 222–23, 225.

66. Perry Nodelman, "John Fowles's Variations in *The Collector*," *Contemporary Literature* 28 (1987): 339, 344, 346.

67. John M. Neary, "John Fowles's Clegg: A Metaphysical Rebel," *Essays in Literature* 15 (1988): 48, 52, 55, 60.

68. Cory Wade, " 'Mystery Enough at Noon': John Fowles's Revision of *The Magus*," *Southern Review* 15 (1979): 721.

69. Michael Boccia, " 'Visions and Revisions': John Fowles's New Version of *The Magus*," *Journal of Modern Literature* 8 (1980–81): 245–46.

70. James R. Lindroth, "The Architecture of Revision: Fowles and the Agora," *Modern Fiction Studies* 31 (1985): 58, 66–67.

71. Ellen McDaniel, "Games and Godgames in *The Magus* and *The French Lieutenant's Woman*," *Modern Fiction Studies* 31 (1985): 42.

72. Fred Kaplan, "Victorian Modernists: Fowles and Nabokov," *Journal of*

Narrative Technique 3 (1973): 109; Prescott Evarts, Jr., "Fowles' *The French Lieutenant's Woman* as Tragedy," *Critique* 13.3 (1972): 57.

73. Elizabeth D. Rankin, "Cryptic Coloration in *The French Lieutenant's Woman*," *Journal of Narrative Technique* 3 (1974): 195–96.

74. Charles Scruggs, "The Two Endings of *The French Lieutenant's Woman*," *Modern Fiction Studies* 31 (1985): 110–12.

75. K. R. Ireland, "Towards a Grammar of Narrative Sequence: The Model of *The French Lieutenant's Woman*," *Poetics Today* 7 (1986): 397–420.

76. William Nelles, "Problems for Narrative Theory: *The French Lieutenant's Woman*," *Style* 18 (1984): 215.

77. Linda Hutcheon, "The 'Real World(s)' of Fiction: *The French Lieutenant's Woman*," *English Studies in Canada* 4 (1978): 81–94.

78. John B. Humma, "John Fowles' *The Ebony Tower:* In the Celtic Mood," *Southern Humanities Review* 17 (1983): 45.

79. Ellen McDaniel, "Fowles as Collector: The Failed Artists of *The Ebony Tower*," *Papers on Language and Literature* 23 (1987): 82.

80. David Brownell, "John Fowles' Experiments with the Form of the Mystery Story," *Armchair Detective* 10 (1977): 186.

81. *Mantissa*, p. 118.

82. Robert Arlett, "*Daniel Martin* and the Contemporary Epic Novel," *Modern Fiction Studies* 31 (1985): 173–74, 177, 185.

83. Carol Ward, "Movie as Metaphor: Focus on *Daniel Martin*," *Literature/Film Quarterly* 15 (1987): 12.

84. Susan Strehle Klemtner, "The Counterpoles of John Fowles's *Daniel Martin*," *Critique* 21.2 (1979–80): 59–63, 70–71.

85. Ian Gott, "Fowles's *Mantissa:* Funfair in Another Village," *Critique* 26 (1985): 81, 85, 87, 89, 92–93.

86. Onega, p. 138.

87. Tarbox, p. 136.

88. David Essex, "Review of John Fowles' *A Maggot:* The Novel as Kōan," *Eighteenth-Century Life* 10 (1986): 80–81.

Notes to the Fiction

John Fowles expects much from his readers. His novels are full of unusual words and foreign phrases, and he assumes that readers are widely familiar with the arts of Western culture. The dictionary can help to bridge a vocabulary "gap," but few readers have the resources to appreciate the phrases in French, Latin, or Greek. Even ordinary British usage can be an obstacle to an American reader.

These notes are intended for readers who want to meet Fowles on his terms but who sometimes are not well-enough informed to do so. Although most readers will find it unnecessary to be told, for example, who Picasso was, few are likely to know the paintings of Berthe Morisot. I have provided at least some information about most historical figures and works referred to by Fowles. The notes are arranged in reading sequence for easy use, keyed to the American editions (as listed in the bibliography), with hardcover and paperback page numbers separated by a slash. In the case of *Mantissa*, the hardcover and paperback page references are identical, and thus only one set of pages appears. Readers who seldom need such notes are invited to use them sparingly—and to congratulate themselves.

THE COLLECTOR

Unpaginated/[4]. *Que . . . nee.* The epigraph contains a mistake in the paperback edition, *aux* for *aus*. From a thirteenth-century French poem, *La Chatelaine de Vergi* (*The Lady of Vergi*), the quotation means "which nobody but this pair knew" (translation by John Fowles in a letter to Leon Higdon, published in "The Epigraph to John Fowles's *The Collector*," *Modern Fiction Studies* 32 [1986], p. 570).

4/8. public-school type. Student at an expensive and, therefore, exclusive secondary school in England, like an American private school.

5/8. Barclays. The largest chain of banks in England.

6/10. pools. Off-site betting on soccer matches. Clegg's standard bet, "five bob," is slang for five shillings, worth ¼ pound sterling, or about 65 cents in the early 1960s.

6/10. Rates. The office which handles property taxes for borough services.

7/11. spec. Slang for prospect.

7–8/11. Nonconformist. One who belongs to a Protestant denomination other than the Anglican Church.

8/11. pub. Short for public house, a uniquely English combination of an American tavern and social club.

8/12. posh. Expensive and stylish, in a status-affirming way.

9/12. the manner born. English upper-class people are said to be "to the manner born" if their aristocratic behavior seems natural, as if inborn. Clegg's remark reinforces the idea that such characteristics cannot be learned, that his capacity for change is limited.

12/15. fringe. Hairstyle called "bangs" in the United States.

14/17. the National Gallery and the Tate Gallery. Art museums in London.

15/17. FAR FROM THE MADDING CROWD. The advertisement adapts the title of a novel by Thomas Hardy in 1874.

15/17. Lewes. A town about forty miles south of London.

15/18. estate agent. What Americans call a real estate agent.

15/18. mod cons. Real estate jargon for "modern conveniences."

16/18. torch. A flashlight.

17/19. gormless. Slang for stupid.

17/19. lucerne. Alfalfa.

19/21. homely. Homey, cozy.

22/24. tube. Slang for the Underground, that is, the London subway.

26/28. jumper. A pullover sweater.

27/28. biscuits. Crackers or cookies.

34/35. R.A.P.C. Royal Army Pay Corps.

38/38. M. G. Morris Garage, a car manufacturer.

44/42. Mr. Atlas. Charles Atlas, former "Mr. World" whose bodybuilding program used advertisements urging young men not to be "97-pound weaklings" who get sand kicked in their faces.

46/44–45. chemist. Pharmacist.

53/50. muck. What one "mucks out" of a stable when cleaning it, roughly equivalent to the American word *crap*.

54/51. var. Variations.

54/51. N. H. Abbreviation for National History.

56/53. be mother. A conventional expression for "pour the tea."

58/54. with a plum in their throat. To say that someone speaks as if with a plum in the mouth or throat is a common (lower-class) way of describing an upper-class accent.

58/55. scheduled. Listed on a register of historic buildings and, thereby, restricted from being modified by an owner.

61/57. guinea. One pound plus one shilling, worth about $2.85 American dollars in the early 1960s.

61/57. Mozart. Wolfgang Amadeus Mozart (1756–91), whose name evidently means nothing to Clegg, is probably the world's best-known composer of "classical" music.

61/58. Cézanne. Paul Cézanne (1839–1906) was a French Impressionist painter interested in the way geometric forms seem to underlie surface appearances.

62/58. Caliban. A monster in William Shakespeare's *The Tempest* (1611). Half-man and half-fish, Caliban lives on an island with Prospero and his daughter, Miranda, whom Caliban once tried to rape. The shipwrecked sailer who falls in love with her is named Ferdinand.

65/60. together then. This kind of tea is customarily served at about 4:00 P.M.

72/66. Christie. J. R. H. Christie was hanged in 1953 for murdering his wife and three other women, whose bodies he had hidden or buried at his "horror house" in Notting Hill, London.

76/70. sitting-room. Living room.

76/70. ticked off. Told off, chastised.

77/71. "Come thou tortoise." From one of Prospero's first addresses to Caliban in *The Tempest* (Act 1, Scene 2).

91/83. American film. Perhaps *Susan Slept Here* (1954).

98/89. TCP. A mild antiseptic ointment.

106/96. Tantalus. King condemned to suffer in Hades by not quite being able to reach the fruit above his head or the water below.

125/113. M and D. Mummy and Daddy.

137/122. chessgame with death. Miranda is thinking about a scene in Ingmar Bergman's *The Seventh Seal* (1957).

137/123. Piero. Piero della Francesca (about 1420–92) was an Italian Renaissance painter.

137/123. Pollock . . . Matisse. Jackson Pollock (1912–56), Pablo Picasso (1881–1973), and Henri Matisse (1869–1954) were painters who departed from Piero's more "realistic" representations of the world.

138/123. Morisot. Berthe Morisot (1841–95) was a French champion of Impressionist ideals as well as a painter of domestic scenes, marine landscapes, and portraits.

138/123. tachism and cubism. Both are twentieth-century movements that involve abstraction in painting. Cubists introduced an appearance of three-dimensionality during the years 1907–1914, and tachists used irregular dabs or splotches of color in France in the 1940s and 1950s.

141/126. teddy. The teddy boys were a group of socially violent young men in the late 1950s and early 1960s, more educated than their successors, the skinheads, and not necessarily as violent, but similarly racist.

144/128. Major Barbara. Idealistic character in George Bernard Shaw's *Major Barbara* (1905), who is morally distressed to learn that the Salvation Army's greatest benefactor acquired his money from the sale of whiskey.

148/131. guying. Ridiculing, as effigies of Guy Fawkes are made fun of every November 5 at celebrations of his failure to blow up the Houses of Parliament.

156/138. *David.* Freestanding male nude sculpture of the Italian High Renaissance, by Michelangelo Buonarroti (1475–1564), now in the Uffizi Gallery in Florence.

156/138. *The Catcher in the Rye.* J. D. Salinger's 1951 novel about Holden Caulfield's coming of age in a world of people he finds inauthentic, or "phony."

159/140. Robinson Crusoe. Main character in Daniel Defoe's *Robinson Crusoe* (1719), who also is singularly isolated, on a deserted island.

160/142. Rembrandt. The Flemish painter Rembrandt van Rijn (1606–69) did a self-portrait that hangs in Kenwood House at Hampstead Heath. The painting is described in *Daniel Martin,* page 628/672.

164/145. Professor Higgins. Character in Shaw's *My Fair Lady* who similarly undertakes to change a young woman, Eliza Doolittle.

166/146. Emma Woodhouse. Main character in Jane Austen's *Emma* (1814), who also learns much about herself over the course of the novel.

167/147. Kokoschka. Oskar Kokoschka (1886–1980) was a Viennese-born, naturalized-British painter of psychological portraits that attempt to lay bare the soul of the sitter.

169/149. Nicholson. Ben Nicholson (1894–1982) was one of the first painters of abstracts in England, sometimes using flat-white silhouettes on a plane.

169/149. Pasmore. Victor Pasmore (1908–) is an English painter of murals, naturalistic landscapes (often of the Thames), and abstract lines and rectangles later in his career.

169/149. *trompe-l'oeil.* Highly realistic painting meant to trick the eye.

172/151. pantomime. A uniquely English form of popular art composed of a classic story, usually containing topical humor, singing-along, and cross-dressing. "Pantos" are produced during the Christmas season and often attended ritually by families.

172/151. *Hay Fever.* A comedy by Noël Coward in 1925 about an eccentric family named Bliss.

172/151. Picasso. Pablo Picasso (1881–1973) was a Spanish painter and sculptor. As probably the most renowned Modernist painter of the twentieth century, his name here represents "high" art, disdained by Miranda's middle-class parents in favor of mere entertainment.

172/151. Bartók. Béla Bartók (1881–1945) was a Hungarian composer whose work includes *Duke Bluebeard's Castle* (1911), about a woman who marries a man and discovers the bodies of her five predecessors in a secret room.

172/151. Matthew Smith and Augustus John, Gauguin and Matisse. Matthew Smith (1879–1959) lived most of his career in France, and Augustus John (1878–1961) painted social outcasts; both were English. Paul Gauguin (1848–1903) and Henri Matisse (1869–1954) represent the paradigm of success in art by Frenchmen.

172/151. Braque. Georges Braque (1882–1963) was, like Picasso, a painter who helped to shape the movement known as cubism.

172/152. Moore and Sutherland. Henry Moore (1898–1986) was a sculptor best known for his abstract massive forms with holes. Graham Sutherland (1903–80) painted pastorals and portraits, early, and then created a tapestry for Coventry Cathedral.

173/152. Constable and Palmer and Blake. John Constable (1776–1837) painted rustic scenes, usually with some pictorial idea. Samuel Palmer (1805–81) created more expressive, rural scenes. William Blake (1757–1827) was an English original and visionary who produced books of illustrated, engraved poems.

177/156. Beecham. Sir Thomas Beecham (1879–1961) was an English conductor who founded the Beecham Symphony Orchestra in 1909, which toured and played for opera and ballet.

178/156. Bach. Johann Sebastian Bach (1685–1750) composed numerous pieces for keyboard instruments. A later comment by Miranda (p. 219) suggests that they are listening here to Bach's Invention Number Five.

179/157. Shostakovich. Dmitri Shostakovich (1906–75) was a Soviet composer widely regarded as the greatest symphonist of the middle twentieth century.

180/158. Marks and Spencer. A middle-income department store chain that deals mainly in clothing, something like J. C. Penney in the United States.

180/158. the chemist's. The drugstore.

181/159. Ladymont. An exclusive, private school for girls that Miranda later describes (p. 220/190). The sexual pun embedded in the name suggests that this is a fictional school, but it resembles the one Fowles taught in from 1954 to 1963.

183/160. Nash. Paul Nash (1889–1946) was a painter of the English countryside in a visionary manner and a founder of the avant-garde surrealist group Unit One in 1933.

183/160. Pollock. Jackson Pollock (see note to p. 137/123) produced drip paintings and was the leader of the international movement called Abstract Expressionism.

183/160. Mondrian. Piet Mondrian (1872–1944) was a Dutch painter who experimented with patterns of colored rectangles.

185/162. Ashmolean. Museum in Oxford that owns the panel painting by Paolo Uccello (1397–1475) referred to here as *The Hunt* and in "The Ebony Tower" as *Night Hunt* (p. 18/17). The painting depicts Italian noblemen on horseback and other men on foot, with dogs, pursuing deer in a dark forest. The official title is *The Hunt in the Forest*.

185/162. Sheraton. Thomas Sheraton (1751–1806) was a designer of furniture whose books influenced the making of pieces with simple lines and flat decorations.

186/163. Portobello Road. A street in London known for its antiques and silver, on display in the street as well as in the shops.

187/163. Botticelli. Sandro Botticelli (1444–1510) was an Italian painter whose *Birth of Venus* (1480) depicts a nude but innocent-looking female.

187/164. Anadyomene. Literally, "she who rises," referring to the birth of Venus out of the sea.

187/164. Jung. Carl Gustav Jung (1875–1961) was a disciple of Freud and a pioneer in psychoanalysis whose theories hold that psychological health for a male involves acceptance of but not total submission to his *anima*, a projection of his concept of the female onto a woman. The *anima* reflects the male's own mental makeup, so it can be a problem if a male pursues such fantasy-projections unrealistically or obsessively. Although such a "disease" would be in the male, Jungian theory holds that some women are *anima* types, who tend to attract male projections—the idea G.P. seems to refer to.

188/165. *Après . . . pour "une" princess lointaine.* The first word means "after," and the French phrase that follows means "for *one* remote princess," that is, a unique, unattainable woman.

191/167. Shankar. Ravi Shankar is an Indian musician who plays the sitar, whose music is probably what Miranda refers to as "weird" on p. 143.

194/169. scrumpy. Very strong, alcoholic cider.

194/170. A level / O level. Under a system which was phased out in the 1980s, Clegg has passed ordinary-level exams in two subjects, not an impressive accomplishment. O-levels were taken at age fifteen or sixteen, and passing them constituted something like a high school diploma. Results were used as a basis for screening by prospective employers. Rather than leave school at sixteen, Miranda has gone on to pass an unspecified number of advanced-level exams at age seventeen or eighteen, after two years of study in elective subjects. A-level results determine one's prospects for admission to an English university, whose undergraduate programs last for only three years because A-level work is at the college level, by American standards.

195/170. Mrs. Joe and Pip. Mrs. Joe Gargary brings up Philip Pirrip, or "Pip," in Charles Dickens's novel *Great Expectations* (1861).

196/171. charley. A chump, a patsy.

196/172. argy-bargy. Squabbling.

201/175. Goya. Francisco de Goya (1746–1828) produced numerous etchings, including *The Disasters of War,* praised by Fowles in his essay "Remembering Cruikshank."

201/176. *Goldberg Variations.* Composition by Johann Sebastian Bach that uses one theme in many ways, described in *Daniel Martin* as baroque, calculated, and "so European" (p. 600).

205/179. Thomas. Dylan Thomas (1914–53) was a Welsh writer who lived in London from 1934 to 1937.

211/183. Topolskitis. A sneer at the work of Feliks Topolski (1907–   ), a Polish-born painter of large murals, including *The Coronation of Elizabeth II* in Buckingham Palace. Spelled Topolski-itis in British Editions.

211/183. Maillol. Aristide Maillol (1861–1944) was a French sculptor, painter, and graphic artist whose work usually depicts weighty female nudes, often in repose.

213/185. Stowe. Stowe is an eighteenth-century country house and estate in Buckinghamshire that is now used as a private boarding school.

215/187. *Sense and Sensibility.* Jane Austen's first published novel (1811), whose title refers to the calm temperament of Elinor and the volatile temperament of Marianne Dashwood.

217/188. He starts . . . monster. Miranda is probably thinking of the American B movie subgenre of which the title *I Was a Teenage Werewolf* is typical, the prototype for which is Robert Louis Stevenson's *The Strange Case of Doctor Jekyll and Mr. Hyde.*

220/190. Sinbad. Sinbad relates his seven sailing voyages in *The Arabian Nights Entertainments.*

220/191. Boadicea. A teacher has evidently been nicknamed after the tribal queen who led an unsuccessful revolt against Roman colonists in A.D. 62.

221/191. stodge. Heavy food, particularly the hard-to-digest puddings served at boarding schools.

221/191. Van Goghs and Modiglianis. Paintings by Vincent Van Gogh (1853–90) and Amedeo Modigliani (1884–1920), both of whom died in poverty.

228/196. favourite in the harem. Scheherazade, who narrates *The Arabian Nights Entertainments*—like Bluebeard's wife—is in danger of being killed by her consort.

229/196. lameduck. Slang for adopting someone sympathetically, as Miranda will make clear on p. 245/209.

239/204. Anne Frank. Author of the *Diary of a Young Girl,* written by a Jewish girl who was hiding from the Nazis in an attic in Amsterdam.

246/210. Dettol. A common antiseptic.

246/210. "rub out." Erase.

248/211. *Saturday Night . . . Room at the Top. Saturday Night and Sunday Morning* is Alan Sillitoe's 1958 first novel, whose protagonist is a rebellious and self-centered factory worker named Arthur Seaton. *Room at the Top,* by John Braine in 1957, has as its protagonist an opportunistic employee in a Yorkshire town hall. Both characters are associated with the phrase "angry young men" of London art in the 1950s.

248/211. Bratby. John Bratby (1928–) is a British painter who worked in the Tate Gallery in the 1960s.

252/214. Dante and Beatrice. Dante Alighieri (1265–1321), Italian poet of the *Divine Comedy,* was evidently haunted all his life by the image of Beatrice, whom he had encountered on a street in Florence when she was ten and he was nine.

255/217. Vestal Virgin. Keepers of the sacred flame at the altar of Vesta, goddess of the hearth in Ancient Rome.

263/223–24. *The Tempest.* The quotations and the excerpt of dialogue appear in Act 1, Scene 2. The sentence about Stephano, Trinculo, and wine refers to Act 2, Scene 2, in which they get Caliban drunk.

266/226. golliwog. A grotesque black doll still sold in England, based on the children's books by Bertha and Florence Upton.

269/228. *Fiat lux.* Let there be light, Latin for the act of divine creation.

269/228. Modern Jazz Quartet. Sometimes known as the MJQ and popular in the 1950s, especially among Bohemians.

289/242. nosiest parkers. In British slang, a nosy parker is a busybody.

298/249. Aspros. Aspirin tablets.

298/250. Romeo and Juliet. Lovers in Shakespeare's *Romeo and Juliet* (about 1595) who kill themselves and are found together in the Capulet tomb.

304/254. Down Under. In Australia.

THE MAGUS

13/15. *Un . . . pitoyable.* "A professional rake is rarely a man to be pitied," from the Marquis de Sade's *Justine, or the Misfortunes of Virtue* (1791). The statement refers to the hardening of the heart of M. de Bressac, libertine, and suggests that Nicholas, likewise, should not be pitied during his forthcoming ordeal.

15/17. Queen Victoria. Ruler of England from 1837 until her death in 1901.

15/17. *L'Astrée. The Star* (1607–27) is a pastoral romance often regarded to be the first French novel.

15/18. Tom Durfey. Englishman (1653–1723) who wrote many songs and plays, including an adaptation of *Don Quixote.* Also spelled D'Urfey.

16/18. D. H. Lawrence. Novelist and poet (1885–1930) who grew up in a mining community near Nottingham. His frankness about sexuality made him celebrated and notorious. Nicholas's parents would have heard of Lawrence's novel *Lady Chatterley's Lover* because it was banned in England until 1960.

16/18. Magdalen. One of thirty-six colleges that make up Oxford University.

17/19. third-class degree. The lowest achievement level, something like a C minus.

17/19. Socratic. Socrates (469–399 B.C.) sought truth, wherever it was to be found, by means of discussion.

18/20. Redbrick. Less prestigious universities than Oxford or Cambridge, whose older buildings are made of stone rather than of brick.

18/21. *vous . . . voulu.* You asked for it, Georges Danton. You asked for it.

19/21. British Council. English institution roughly equivalent to the U.S. State Department.

19/21. Roedean. A small boarding school for girls, in Brighton.

19/22. Smith. Matthew Smith (1879–1959) was an English painter who lived most of his career in France and worked with brilliant colors.

20/22. public-school lines. In England, public schools are expensive, exclusive private institutions for male boarding students being groomed for positions of social power. The Lord Byron School is named for George Gordon, Lord Byron (1788–1824), English poet and influential figure in European Romanticism, who died while organizing an independence movement in Greece.

21/23. Chesterfieldian. Philip Dormer Stanhope, Fourth Earl of Chesterfield (1694–1773), wrote letters to his son, somewhat cynically advising him about how to behave in public to his advantage.

28/30. Pom. Australian slang for a recent immigrant from England.

29/31. *affaire de peau.* A matter of flesh.

31/33. *sous les toits.* Under the roofs, a phrase referring to the roofs of Paris, in a well-known song by street singer Edith Piaf.

32/34. *Lear. King Lear* is a 1605 tragedy by William Shakespeare.

32/34. Hemingway. Ernest Hemingway (1899–1961) was an American novelist.

32/34. For *monsieur.* For the gentleman.

32/34. *Santé.* Health (a toast).

34/36. *Quai de Brumes. Port of Shadows,* a 1938 film by Marcel Carné about a soldier whose devotion to a girl results in his death.

35/37. never-never land. Where Wendy and her siblings escape to in J. M. Barrie's 1904 play *Peter Pan.*

35/37. Tate. An art gallery in London.

35/37. sweet. A piece of candy.

35/37. Renoir. Pierre-Auguste Renoir (1841–1919), French painter and leader of the Impressionist movement.

36/37. Old Etonian. An alumnus of Eton College, one of England's most prestigious public schools.

36/38. Muscadet. A sweet wine.

36/38. abo. Short for aboriginal, a precolonial inhabitant of Australia.

38/39. Soho. District in London famous for its night life.

40/41. Medes. Ancient people of West Asia who joined with the Persians under Darius I (521–485 B.C.) to invade Greece.

40/42. twopenny-half penny Don Juan. Cheap imitation of the legendary Spanish womanizer.

41/43. Hogarth. Satirical engravings by the English artist William Hogarth (1697–1764) include a series titled *Marriage à la Mode,* which depicts scenes from the lives of an aristocratic couple who become increasingly bored and unfaithful after their arranged marriage. Alison is probably remembering Plate Two, which shows the disheveled rake of a husband sprawled in a chair, weary after a night of debauchery and dueling, while his wife yawns and stretches nearby after a likewise demanding night of card-playing.

43/45. *condottieri.* Soldiers of fortune.

43/45. Viscount Montgomery. Bernard Law, 1st Viscount Montgomery of Alamein (1887–1976), commanded the British Eighth Army in World War II.

43/45. Pasty. A meat pie, usually shaped like a half-circle.

44/46. effing. F-ing, that is, a euphemism for *fucking.*

44/46. beaks. Slang for schoolmasters.

44/46. Frog. Slang term of contempt for a Frenchman or, here, for the French language.

45/46. *retsina* and *aresinato, raki* and *ouzo.* Alcoholic drinks, respectively, wine flavored with pine tar, unresinated wine, spirits of grain or grape, and anise-flavored liquor.

45/46. O.O.B. Out of bounds.

45/47. Trafalgar Square. An intersection in London with a monument to Lord Nelson, victor at the Battle of Trafalgar, 1805.

46/48. Victoria. A major train station in London.

47/49. dingo. An Australian expression for "oh, well."

48/50. Manzanilla. A very dry sherry.

49/50. Circe. Goddess-enchantress-witch who seduces Odysseus and turns his crewmen into swine in Book Ten of Homer's *The Odyssey.*

50/52. Alice in Wonderland. Character who finds herself in a dream world in Lewis Carroll's *Alice's Adventures in Wonderland* (1865).

50/52. hansom cab. A two-wheeled, covered vehicle drawn by a horse, whose driver rides above and behind his passengers.

51/53. Harrow. Like Eton, a famous English boarding school that aims to prepare boys for Oxford or Cambridge University.

51/53. Clytemnestra killed Agamemnon. When King Agamemnon returned from Troy, according to Aeschylus, he was killed by his wife for having sacrificed their daughter to obtain favorable winds. (In Homer's version, Clytemnestra's lover Aegisthus kills Agamemnon.) His city of Mycenae is north of Spetsai, which Fowles's introduction calls "the real Greek island" of Phraxos (p. 7); so the passage would be more consistent with geography if it stated that the school is "a look *south* from where Clytemnestra killed Agamemnon," rather than *north*.

52/54. *kaphenia*. Cafés.

52/54. Balzac in a fez. A fez is a round hat with a tassel, formerly the national headdress of Turkey. Honoré de Balzac (1799–1850) wrote ninety-one novels about French society, including provincial life. To Nicholas, life on Phraxos seems not to have evolved since the early nineteenth century, when it was ruled by the Turks.

52/54. *chevaux de frise*. Frieze-horses, evidently an ornamentation on the wall surrounding the school.

56/58. B.B.C. British Broadcasting Corporation.

56/58. Antwerp blue. A pale Prussian blue used for impermanent painting.

56/58. Hokusai. Katsushika Hokusai (1760–1849) was a Japanese artist whose prints of everyday life in a flat-looking style commonly depicted actors, prostitutes, and bathhouse girls.

56/59. Sciron. In Greek literature, a robber who is thrown off a cliff by Theseus.

57/59. Gide. André Gide (1869–1951) was a French novelist and a homosexual.

57/59. Arnold. Matthew Arnold (1822–88) was an English poet and a social critic.

57/59. Emily Dickinson. An American poet (1830–86).

58/60. Not *cogito*, but *scribo, pingo, ergo sum*. Nicholas redefines the dictum of René Descartes, "I think; therefore, I am," as the less engaged "I write, I paint; therefore, I am."

59/61. *Félicitations . . . prendre*. "Congratulations," he said. "It is . . ." "You see this in Athens. I'll give you an address. It is Athens where you caught this, isn't it?" I nodded. "The whores there. Sick. Particularly the fools who let themselves be taken in."

59/61. "*Je suis maudit*." "I feel terrible."

59/62. *kyrios*. Mister.

60/62. Catullus . . . mercy. Gaius Valerius Catullus (84–54 B.C.) was a Roman whose love poems often were addressed to the character Lesbia.

60/62. *néant*. The French word for nothingness echoes Jean Paul Sartre's existentialist title *L'Être et le néant* (*Being and Nothingness*, 1943), a phrase Nicholas has used to indicate fashionable existentialist talk at Oxford (p. 17/19).

62/64. Mercutio. In Shakespeare's *Romeo and Juliet* (about 1595), the killing of Juliet's brother Mercutio, inadvertently, by Romeo sets important events of the play into motion.

62/65. *gabbia.* Literally "cage" in Italian.

63/65. Kahn test. A procedure for detecting syphilis.

65/67. *Irrités . . . mystères.* "Not content with that first crime, the monsters did not stop there; they spread her out, naked on her belly on a large table; then they lit votive candles; they placed the image of our Savior at her head and dared to consummate this most fearful of our mysteries upon the sides of this unfortunate girl." From Chapter 12 of *Justine* (see note to p. 13/15), the scene depicts the initiation of Florette into sadism by the monk Raphael and other debauchers.

67/70. Crusoe. In Daniel Defoe's *Robinson Crusoe* (1791), the protagonist describes at length his mental agitation at finding a human footprint on the beach of "his" island, about midway through the narrative.

69/71. "Little Gidding." The last of T. S. Eliot's *Four Quartets* (1942), the title refers to the English estate of Nicholas Ferrar, who established a religious community there in 1625.

69/71. "Each . . . cities." The lines are from "Paysage Moralisé," by W. H. Auden (1907–73). This poem is in *A Little Treasury of British Poetry,* edited by Oscar Williams in 1951 and "one of the commonest paperback anthologies of modern English verse," as Nicholas describes his own book on the same page.

69/71. "Come . . . to be." The lines are from Ezra Pound's "The Needle," stanza one and line one of stanza three (of four), published in *Ripostes* (1912).

69–70/72. "Who . . . beasts." From the opening twelve lines of *Canto* 47 by Ezra Pound (1885–1972).

71/73. SALLE D'ATTENTE. French for "Waiting Room," the phrase used on signs in English railway stations for prospective journey-makers.

71/73. Laval. Pierre Laval headed the Vichy government in France from 1942 to 1944 and was executed for treason after World War II.

71/74. Claude. Claude Gelée, a French painter better known as Claude Lorrain (1600–82) depicted tranquil, "picturesque" landscapes, including several scenes of harbors at sunset that fit Fowles's description.

72/74. Corfiot. An inhabitant of the city of Corfu, on Corfu.

72/74. Casanova. Giovanni Jacopo Casanova (1725–98) was an Italian writer with a reputation for seducing women.

72/74. Boswellian. James Boswell (1740–95), extravert Scotsman and biographer of Samuel Johnson, also was a notorious rake.

72/74. "*Ai!*" "Hey!"

73/75. *estiatoras.* A kind of restaurateur, who cooks food brought to him for consumption later, at the customer's home.

74/76. *agogiati.* Mule driver.

74/76. Socrates, Aristotle, Aphrodite. To an English person newly arrived in Greece, these names would be hard not to associate with Greek philosophy and theology. Although Nicholas does not smile to learn that the messenger's name is Hermes, he might have done so because the association with the classical deity Hermes, messenger to the gods, is ironically apt.

77/79. Orestes. Clytemnestra's son, who avenges the death of his father, Agamemnon, by killing his mother and her lover, Aegisthus. Nicholas is pursued by insects as Orestes was pursued for his act by the twelve Furies in *The Eumenides*, by Aeschylus.

80/83. Hermes, Zeus. As the god Hermes was sometimes a spy for Zeus, the donkey man delivers information as well as mail to Conchis.

80/83. T'ang. Dynastic period in Chinese history from 618–907 A.D. marked by invention of the printing press.

81/84. Picasso. Pablo Picasso (1881–1973) was a Spanish, Modernist painter, one of the founders of the cubist movement.

82–83/85. Bach, Telemann. Johann Sebastian Bach (1685–1750) and Georg Philipp Telemann (1681–1767) were both German composers of harpsichord music, so Nicholas's guess is not inept.

83/85. Prospero. The magician in Shakespeare's *The Tempest* who lives in exile with his daughter, Miranda, on an island whose creatures he has dominion over, one of which is the monster Caliban. (*Magician* is one translation of the Latin word *magus*, the title of the novel.)

84/87. Pan. A reasonable guess, since the classical god of woods and pastures often was represented as a lecherous being, part goat, but an erect phallus is generic to statues of Priapus, son of Dionysus and Aphrodite.

89/91. *Mireille, gantière.* Made by a female glover named Mireille.

92/94. *L'Astrée.* A sentimental pastoral narrative published between 1607–27, *L'Astrée* is considered to be the first French novel.

92/94. "*Oui . . . charmes.*" "Yes, a little flat. But not without its charms."

92/94. *le grand siècle.* The seventeenth century, when French culture, especially under Louis XVI, dominated Europe.

92/95. Rameau. Jean-Philippe Rameau (1683–1764) was a French musical theorist and composer.

92/95. Modigliani. Amedeo Modigliani (1884–1920) was an Italian painter and sculptor in France whose portraits were typically abstracted and orthodoxly colored.

92/95. "*Voilà.*" "There you are."

93/96. Rodin. Auguste Rodin (1840–1917) was a French sculptor whose best-known work is *The Thinker*.

93/96. Giacometti. Alberto Giacometti (1901–66) was a Swiss sculptor and painter best known for his constructions of groups of elongated, emaciated people.

94/96. *catalogue raisonné.* Systematic catalogue.

94/97. Fra Angelico's famous "*Annunciation.*" The original *Annunciation* is a fresco in the convent of San Marco in Florence, Italy, made between 1440 and 1445.

94/97. Pleyel. A family of composers, music publishers, and piano makers in France. A Pleyel harpsichord would be particularly rare.

95/98. Icarus. In Greek tradition, the son of Daedalus, the artificer who contrived to fly out of a labyrinth. Icarus is a "fool that falls" when he flies beyond the prescribed limits and the sun melts his wings.

96/99. Dickens, Cervantes, Dostoievsky, Flaubert. Perhaps the four most famous novelists in Europe: Charles Dickens of England (1812–70), Miguel de Cervantes of Spain (1547–1616), Feodor Dostoevsky of Russia (1821–81), and Gustave Flaubert of France (1821–80).

97/99. Isnik. Isnik, or Iznik, is a city in Turkey whose factories produced pottery beginning in 1469–73. The colors Nicholas describes are probably from the sixteenth century.

97/100. Bonnard. Pierre Bonnard (1867–1947) painted the same woman throughout his career. The painting described is called *Nude Before a Mirror* (1933).

98/100. Gibson girl. An 1890s American female type, from illustrations by Charles Dana Gibson.

99/102. lumber room. A storage room.

101/103. *cassone.* A medieval Italian, ornamented chest.

102/104. Webern-like. Anton von Webern (1883–1945) was an Austrian composer who worked with atonality and serial technique.

103/106. Wordsworth, Mae West, Saint-Simon. William Wordsworth (1770–1850) was an English Romantic poet; Mae West (1892–1980) was an American screen actress and sex symbol in the 1930s; the Count de Saint-Simon (1760–1825) was a French philosopher and social critic.

103/106. Boucheresque. François Boucher (1703–70) painted realistic-looking, somewhat eroticized women.

104/107. *curiosa.* Pornographic literature or art.

105/107. Ascot . . . Kew. Ascot's Opening Day horse race requires formal dress, including gloves for the ladies; the gardens at Kew are her object only because of the sound the owl seems to make. As Nicholas suggests, the image is "absurd."

107/109. "*Sas efcharistoume.*" "Come in."

107/109. "*Eis'ygeia . . . Sygeia.*" "To your health, Nicholas." "Health."

107/110. Caravaggio. Michelangelo Merisi da Caravaggio (1571–1609) painted scenes with dramatically lit figures, as if by spotlights.

111/114. "An English novelist." E. M. Forster (1879–1970) used "only connect . . ." as the epigraph to his novel *Howards End*, with reference to the gap between social classes.

112–13/115. *rarissima avis.* Rarest of birds.

113/115. "Rosenthals and Godowskis." Moriz Rosenthal (1862–1946) was a Ukranian pianist, especially skilled in playing Chopin. Leopold Godowsky

(1870–1938) was an American pianist (born in Poland) who composed, transcribed, and performed piano music.

113/115. Haydn and Mozart. Franz Joseph Haydn (1732–1809) and Wolfgang Amadeus Mozart (1756–91) were Austrian composers of diverse musical pieces, including sonatas.

113/116. *des pianistes en costume de bal masqué*. Piano players masquerading as harpsichordists.

113/116. *ça sera pour un autre jour*. We'll take that up another day.

114/116. Chopin. Frédéric Chopin (1810–49) was a Polish-born composer and pianist who lived in Paris.

114/117. Seferis. George Seferis (1900–71) was a Greek poet who served as ambassador to England from 1957 to 1962 and won the Nobel prize for literature in 1963. The "line" is from number nine of "Sixteen Haiku," titled "Young Fate," which reads, "Naked woman/the pomegranate that broke/was full of stars" (from *Collected Poems: 1924–1955*, translated by Edmund Keeley and Philip Sherrard [Princeton, New Jersey: Princeton Univ. Press, 1967], p. 93).

115/118. Dolmetsch. Arnold Dolmetsch (1858–1940) was a pioneer in the use of original instruments. He restored instruments and wrote a book on the interpretation of seventeenth- and eighteenth-century music.

115/118. Fitzwilliam Virginal Book, Arbeau, Frescobaldi, Froberger. The Virginal Book is a book of musical compositions mostly by Byrd, Bull, and Farnaby in the Fitzwilliam Museum at Cambridge. Thoinot Arbeau (1519–95) was a French priest who wrote an illustrated treatise on dance in dialogue form. Girolamo Frescobaldi (1583–1643) was an Italian organist and composer. Johann Froberger (1616–1667) was a student of Frescobaldi who spent time in London destitute but was later appointed court organist.

115/118. Botticelli beauty. The ideal represented in Sandro Botticelli's painting *The Birth of Venus* (about 1480).

115/118. Pre-Raphaelite. A group of mid–nineteenth-century English artists who wished to reestablish values in painting before the Renaissance and who tended to depict women of stunning but occult beauty.

115/118. *sans pareil*. Without equal.

116/119. *La Vie Parisienne. Parisian Life.*

116/119. Chaliapin in Prince Igor. *Prince Igor* is an opera by Alexander Borodin in 1890. Feodor Chaliapin is considered one of the greatest opera singers of the twentieth century.

117/120. Moltke, Bülow, Foch, Haig, French. Respectively, German chief of staff, chancellor of Germany, French marshall, commander of the British Army in France, and English field marshall—all before or during World War I.

117/120. *coup d'archet*. Violent note (literally "blow of the fiddle-stick").

117/120. Kitchener. Horatio Herbert Kitchener (1850–1916) managed the buildup of the English volunteer army after the outbreak of World War I.

117/120. cricket. Fair play.

117/120. *le consentement frémissant à la guerre.* Shuddering consent to war.

120/123. Armagnac. A dry, French brandy.

120/123. Kaiser Bill. English nickname for Kaiser Wilhelm II, king of Prussia and emperor of Germany from 1888 to 1918.

121/124. *Totentanz.* Dance of death, or *danse macabre,* a late-medieval art motif that represented the presence of death in life as a skeleton leading people to the grave.

122/125. Thanatos. Personification of death in ancient Greece.

123/126. Boches. Disparaging term for German soldiers.

127/130. Gurkhas. Nepalese troops.

129/132. Ave's. Repetitions of *Ave Maria,* that is, Hail Mary, the beginning of a Roman Catholic prayer.

131/134. lingua franca. First language.

131/134. *estaminet.* Tavern or coffeehouse.

133/136. "Tipperary." A World War I song about being far from home.

135/138. *"O kyrios?"* "Where is the master?"

136/139. *dominus.* Lord.

136/139. Ariel . . . Caliban. In *The Tempest,* Ariel is a spirit who serves Prospero out of gratitude for his having once set Ariel free.

137/140. *faux pas.* A social blunder.

137/141. Gandhi-like. Mahatma Gandhi (1869–1948) set an example for social reform by living simply.

140/143. *Punch.* An English magazine with humorous pieces, published weekly since 1841.

140/143. The actual short title of the pamphlet is *An Alarme for Sinners: Containing the Confession, Prayers, Letters, and last Words of Robert Foulkes* (London, 1679).

140/143. pre-Dryden. John Dryden (1631–1700) was the foremost English writer of the Restoration and was made poet laureate in 1668.

141/145. Henry James. Author of *The Turn of the Screw* (1898), a novel in which the status of ghostly apparitions to a pair of children is left ambiguous—perhaps real, perhaps imagined by their governness.

144/147. Adonis. A handsome young man. In Greek mythology, he is beloved by Aphrodite but is killed by a wild boar.

146/149. No man is an island. Theme of John Donne's *Meditation 17,* written in 1624.

147/150. *yin* and *yang.* Opposing principles in Tao philosophy.

147/150. Belsen. A Nazi concentration camp in Germany during World War II.

148/151–52. *bien pensant.* Right-thinking.

149/152. sword. Tristan and Isolde were lovers in Irish legend who are discovered sleeping together but with a sword between them; so that King Marc, Isolde's husband, cannot be certain that she has been unfaithful.

150/153. *o Pappous.* Father.

157/160. Ulysses, Theseus, Oedipus. All three heroes of Greek legend confront mysterious, powerful opponents on their journeys—Ulysses (Odysseus) the witch Circe, Theseus the Minotaur, and Oedipus the Sphinx.

160/164. *rentiers.* People living on fixed incomes.

160/164. *kaphenion.* Glass.

161/164. "*Ah pardon . . . monsieur?*" "Pardon me . . . do you speak French, sir?"

161/164. "*Ah, très bien. . . . monsieur.*" "Oh, good. Thanks very much, sir."

161/164. El Greco. Familiar name of a Spanish painter (circa 1547–1614), one of whose best-known paintings shows dark storm clouds over Toledo, Spain.

161/165. *pittoresque . . . Délos.* Picturesque, but less beautiful than (the island of) Délos.

164/168. *De la communication intermondiale. On Communicating Between Worlds.* The last word of the title is misspelled in the paperback edition.

165/168. *Le Masque Français au Dix-huitième Siècle. The French Masque in the Eighteenth Century.*

165 note/169 note. Theocritus, Virgil. Roman poets who lived from circa 308–240 B.C. and 70–19 B.C., respectively.

168/171. *cabine* at Dior. A dressing room at the firm of Christian Dior, French fashion designer.

169/173. Talleyrand. Charles-Maurice de Talleyrand (1754–1838) was a French statesman who managed to hold high office during the French Revolution, under Napoleon, and after the Restoration of Louis Philippe.

173/177. Nefertiti. Queen of Egypt whose likeness, including a slender neck, is preserved in a painted limestone bust at the Berlin Aegyptus Museum.

175/179. Jouvet. Louis Jouvet (1887–1951) was a famous stage actor in the 1930s and 1940s who was known particularly for his role in Molière's *Dom Juan.*

175/179. *salon.* An elegant drawing room intended for social conversation.

176/180. *marennes.* Oysters.

177/181. *mise en paysage.* Placement in the landscape, situation.

177/181. *tatami.* Japanese straw mat.

177/181. *homme sensuel.* A feeling person.

177/181. *objets d'art.* Artifacts.

177/181. Breguets. Abraham-Louis Breguet (1747–1823) was a Swiss watchmaker noted for the elegance of the faces and hands of his timepieces. The case probably contains examples of his pocket watches.

177/181. Hoffman. E.T.A. Hoffmann (1776–1822) wrote tales that sometimes included mechanical-artificial humans, for example the beautiful, lifelike doll Olympia in "The Sandman."

177/181. *La serva padrona. The Servant Mistress* was a light opera by Giovanni Battista Pergolesi in 1733, about a maidservant who marries her master.

177/181. *la Maîtresse-Machine.* The mechanical mistress.

178/182. Millet. Jean-François Millet (1814–75) was a French painter of rural scenes whose painting *The Gleaners* depicts three peasants laboring in a field.

178/182. *nouveau riche.* One who flaunts newly acquired wealth.

179/183. *pâté d'alouettes.* Paste of larks.

179/183. *étui.* Small case.

180/184. Apollo. Important Greek god associated with light, truth, poetry, music, and archery.

181/186. *cache-sexe.* G-string.

182/186. Edwardian. Describes England during the reign of King Edward VII, from 1901 to 1910.

182/186. *coup de théâtre.* Theatrical stroke.

182/187. goddess. Nicholas discusses her as Artemis on p. 243/249.

183/188. *caractère.* Character sketch.

186/190. *pax Americana.* American-imposed peace, analogous to the *pax Romana* or the *pax Britannia,* when domination by the Romans or the British, respectively, prevented wars.

186/191. Dionysus. Greek god of wine and of ecstasy, he sometimes represents emotional values in opposition to the values of thought represented by Apollo.

187/191. *pompiers.* Firefighters.

188/192. heart of darkness. In Joseph Conrad's novel *Heart of Darkness* (1902), human nature is discovered to be corrupt at its center, an idea represented geopolitically as a journey from London to the interior of colonized Africa, the Belgian Congo.

190/194. *Merde.* French for "bullshit," this document recalls a treatise in *Heart of Darkness* (note to p. 188/192) that describes a plan to civilize Africa, at the end of which the author has scrawled, "Exterminate all the brutes."

191/195. *sic itur ad astra.* Thus to the stars.

193/198. *moue.* A pouting expression.

194/198. Neptune. Roman god of the sea.

194/199. Ulysses . . . mast. In *The Odyssey,* Odysseus stops the ears of his crewmen but has himself tied to the mast of his ship so that he can hear the song of the Sirens without being lured to destruction.

195/200. Sherlock Holmes. Main character in detective fiction by Arthur Conan Doyle (1859–1930).

198/202. "It tolls for thee." Lily alludes to Donne's *Meditation 17* (see note to p. 146/149), in which he tells the reader not to ask for whom the bell tolls.

201/205. *Ochi.* No.

204/208. "Be not . . . again." Caliban to Stephano and Trinculo in *The Tempest*, Act 3, Scene 2.

205/209. Mrs. Pankhurst. Emmeline Pankhurst (1858–1928) was a militant worker to obtain British women the right to vote.

205/210. RADA. Royal Academy for Dramatic Arts.

205/210. Astarte. Phoenician goddess of love.

210/215. Ariadne. In Greek legend, she gives Theseus a ball of yarn to help him find his way out of the labyrinth after he slays the Minotaur.

211/215. Poseidon. Greek god of the sea. A fifth-century B.C. bronze statue of Poseidon throwing a trident (a few have argued it is Zeus hurling a lightning bolt) was found in the sea near Cape Artimision (off Euboea) in 1926–28.

211/215. Henry Moore. English sculptor (1898–1986) who worked with abstract forms, solids and voids.

211/216. Baker Street. Sherlock Holmes lived at 221 Baker Street (see note to p. 195/200).

215/220. sent down. Expelled from university. Oxford and Cambridge, sometimes referred to as "Oxbridge," are the two premier universities in England.

215/220. read. Study as a course of work at the university. "What did you read?" is tantamount to asking an American college graduate "What did you major in?"

220/225. *Roi Soleil.* Sun-king, an epithet for Louis XIV, who built the palace of Versailles as a testament to his (unshared) power.

224/229. Jung. Carl Gustav Jung (1875–1961) was a disciple of Freud who founded a rival school of psychiatry based on a somewhat different psychological model.

228/233. *non sequiturs.* Feelings that do not follow logically.

231/236. Marx. Karl Marx (1818–83) theorized about the value of labor in *Capital.*

233/238. *Buai a chi la tocca.* Woe to whoever touches her.

235/240. *galère.* Crowd.

235/240. *La dive bouteille.* Alcohol—literally, "the divine bottle," the object of Pantagruel's journey in Rabelais's *Gargantua and Pantagruel* (Books 4–5).

237/242. Jesus. Jesus College, at Oxford.

240/246. Svengali and Trilby. Svengali is a mesmerizing character and Trilby the female protagonist in *Trilby* (1894), a best-selling French novel by George du Maurier.

243/248. *Il avait . . . ici.* He always seemed a little sad; he never got used to life here.

246/252. Alison . . . thousand. Like Julie, Helen of Troy had a face that launched 1,000 ships, but it did so as a consequence of unfaithfulness to her husband.

247/252. *Toujours.* Always.

247/252. *Vive.* Long live.

250/255. Lautrec-like. Henri de Toulouse-Lautrec (1864–1901) was a French artist who painted scenes from Parisian night life.

251/256. *barbounia.* Fish served at the beginning of a meal.

257/262. *andarte.* Resistance fighters.

262/267. *Huis Clos.* The title means "closed door," though it usually is translated *No Exit,* so the pun is based merely on a spelling resemblance. Sartre's 1945 play is a classic of existential drama, however, with implications for Nicholas's situation in Conchis's "production."

262/267. *consommé à la reine.* Pure consommé or broth.

266/271. crossword clue. Alison's name is a near-anagram, a mixture of letters that make up "the better part," that is, the larger part, of Nicholas's name. As a character, too, Alison is a center of "better" values that Nicholas lacks in the novel.

267/272. Battle of Britain. The battle was fought in the air against Hitler's bombers in the fall of 1940 by pilots of the Royal Air Force, some of whom became pilots for the airlines after World War II.

267/272. *honi soit qui.* From the expression *Honi soit qui mal y pense,"* motto of Order of the Garter meaning "Shame to anyone who thinks evil of it." Alison is expressing dislike for the implication of moral superiority.

269/274. *England's Helicon.* A collection of Elizabethan pastoral poetry by various authors, published in 1600 and revised in 1615.

274/279. tart. A slang noun for prostitute. As a verb, "to be tarted up" means to be decorated to excess, as to resemble a prostitute with too much makeup and jewelry.

279/284. marking. Grading papers.

282/287. *ad absurdum.* To the point of absurdity.

293/298. *tête-à-tête.* Head-to-head, private conversation.

301/307. *surcroît de malheur.* Excess of misfortune.

301/307. Euripidean. Suggestive of a character from a play by Euripides (about 480–406 B.C.), noteworthy for his sympathetic female characters.

301/307. Strindbergian. Suggestive of plays by the Swedish playwright August Strindberg (1849–1912), which are full of sometimes pathological suffering.

304/309. Montaigne. Michel de Montaigne (1533–92), French writer who virtually invented the essay.

304/309. *Pillar of fire.* Exodus 13:22 and 2 Esdras 1:14.

304/309. Pascal. Blaise Pascal (1623–62), French philosopher whose *Pensées* was a model for Fowles's *The Aristos. Feu* means *fire.*

304/309. Savonarola. Fra Girolamo Savonarola (1452–98) led a religious reaction against Renaissance art but was later condemned and burned as a heretic.

305/310. Tutankhamen. King of Egypt from 1334 to 1325 B.C. His tomb, uncovered in 1922, contained two valveless trumpets, one made of silver and one of bronze with gold overlaid.

307/313. *"Hører du mig? Jeg er her."* "Do you hear me? I am here."

311/317. Victorian picture. The painting described is *The Boyhood of Raleigh,* by John Everett Millais (1829–96).

314/320. Beaumarchais. Pierre-Augustin Caron de Beaumarchais (1732–99) was the French playwright of *The Marriage of Figaro* and *The Barber of Seville,* which were later adapted as operas.

314/320. Restoration comedy. After the restoration of King Charles II in 1660, the English stage reopened; many plays were comedies with female actresses in sexual intrigues.

316/322. *permis de séjour.* Visa.

322/328. racialism. Racism.

323/328. *vriki.* A brass pot to boil coffee and grounds.

326/331. *de trop.* In the way.

327/333. Quintus Horatius Flaccus, Parisiis. The first three words are Horace's Latin name; the last means "printed in Paris."

329/334. Girton. A college for women at Cambridge.

329/335. Chaucer. Geoffrey Chaucer (1343–1400) wrote *The Canterbury Tales.*

329/335. Langland. William Langland (1330–1386) wrote the medieval poem *Piers Plowman.*

329/335. *cachet.* Prestige.

330/335. *Lysistrata.* Comedy by Aristophanes in 411 B.C. about Athenian women who take over the Acropolis and refuse to have sex with their husbands, as a protest against the Peloponnesian War.

332/338. Cinderellas. In the Perrault version of the tale (1697), Cinderella also lives poorly and is similarly dazzled by a wealthy male.

334/339. *"Xerete . . . ellenika?"* "Do you understand modern Greek very well?"

338/343. Stanislavski. Konstantin Stanislavski (1863–1938) trained actors to feel the parts they are acting.

340/346. *trac.* Stage fright.

347/353. Pip. In Charles Dickens's *Great Expectations* (1860–61), Philip Pirrip, or "Pip," is a young man similarly mystified by Miss Havisham, who seems to be his benefactress and who has a daughter he falls in love with.

348/354. costume. Bathing suit.

348/354. seven dwarfs. Characters in the tale of Snow White, whose name describes the color of Julie's skin.

350/356. What a cheek. What nerve.

350/356. "We are not amused." Famous understatement by Queen Victoria on seeing an imitation of herself, here quoted ironically in a pretense of humorlessness.

358/365. Maupassant. Guy de Maupassant (1850–93) was a French writer of naturalistic short stories and novels.

362/368. "Fear the Greeks . . ." She does not need to complete the warning of Laocoön to the Trojans, in Virgil's *The Aeneid* (Book 2): "I fear the Greeks, even when they are bearing gifts."

363/369. don. Professor.

367/373. Sophocles. As a student of classics at Cambridge, Julie has read the plays of Sophocles (495–406 B.C.) in ancient Greek.

367/373. Ophelia. In Shakespeare's *Hamlet* (1603), in a misogynistic speech, Hamlet disgustedly tells his girlfriend, Ophelia, to get to a nunnery (Elizabethan slang for a brothel) or, if she marries, to marry a fool (Act 3, Scene 2).

371/377. sleeping princess. A reference to the fairy tale of the sleeping beauty in the wood.

375/381. N.C.O. Noncommissioned officer, or sergeant.

376/382. *"Was sagen Sie?"* "What did you say?"

376/382. "Lili Marlene." Obvious because the song is associated with wartime Germany—unless, Nicholas realizes, Conchis has selected the title for its echo of Lily Montgomery's name.

377/383. *"Gut."* "Good."

378/384. klepht. A Greek or Albanian brigand exalted to the status of guerrilla-patriot during the Greek war for independence from the Turks.

378/384. noble brigand. For example, the hero of George Gordon, Lord Byron's *The Corsair* (1813).

379/385. *"Nicht schiessen!"* "Don't shoot!"

379/385. *"Mon . . . monde."* "My lieutenant, to me that is the most beautiful music in the world.

380/386. *Weltanschauung.* Worldview, outlook.

381/387. *Leipzig dankt euch.* Leipzig thanks you.

383/390. trial of the young usurper. Nicholas refers to the general testing in *The Tempest* of Ferdinand, whom Prospero eventually allows Miranda to marry—not to Caliban's attempted rape of Miranda or to the later insurrection by Caliban, Trinculo, and Stephano.

385/391–92. *immortelles.* Evergreens.

387/394. *ton.* Stature, "class."

389/396. *mezé*. Drinking glass.

390/396. "*Ne . . . ekanon?.*" No, Barba. The foreigners. What did they do?

391/397. *Mia phora*. Once upon a time.

391/397. *paneyiri*. Celebration.

393/399. Blondel. A twelfth-century troubadour who is reputed to have discovered where Richard the Lionhearted was being held captive by roaming Austria and singing a song they had composed together. When Richard heard Blondel under his window, he completed the verse being sung, thus enabling Blondel to report his location.

393//400. Sisyphean. Endless, resembling the situation in Tartarus in which Sisyphus is condemned eternally to push a rock up a hill, only to have it roll down again.

393/400. gone with the wind of 1940. The year when the Nazis took over Greece, with a glance at the analogous situation in the American Civil War, whose antebellum culture was described with the title *Gone with the Wind*, the 1936 novel by Margaret Mitchell, adapted to film in 1939.

394/401. Balliol College. One of the colleges that make up Oxford University (pronounced BAY-lee-oll).

396/403. Randolph, Carfax. The Randolph Hotel is near the center of Oxford, about one-half mile from Carfax Tower.

400/407. Marlowe. Christopher Marlowe (1564–93), poet and playwright.

404/411. Artaud and Pirandello and Brecht. Antonin Artaud (1896–1948) from France, Luigi Pirandello (1867–1936) from Italy, and Bertolt Brecht (1898–1956) from Germany were all dramatic theorists who experimented with the form.

405/411. Othello. The main character—a black man—in Shakespeare's *Othello* (1605).

406/412. Olivia to your Malvolio. In Shakespeare's *Twelfth Night* (1601), Olivia is a wealthy woman who Malvolio foolishly believes is in love with him.

411/418. *Et voilà*. And there it is.

414/420. Ελευθερια. Transliterated as *eleutheria* on page 425/432, the Greek word means *freedom*.

415/421. *bouc émissaire*. Scapegoat.

415/422. Schubert and Wolf. Franz Schubert (1797–1828) and Hugo Wolf (1860–1903) were Austrian composers.

415/422. *lieder*. Songs.

415/422. Goldberg Variations. A composition by Johann Sebastian Bach (1685–1750).

416/422. Bauhaus. German school of design founded by Walter Gropius after World War I.

416/422. *le sept . . . Folie*. June 7, fourth year of the Great Madness.

418/425. *maquis*. Underground.

418/425. ELAS. Acronym for the Hellenic People's Liberation Army—the Greek resistance.

418/425. *à titre d'office*. As an obligation of my position.

419/425. Goethe and Schiller. Johann Wolfgang von Goethe (1748–1832) and Friedrich von Schiller (1759–1805) were major German poets and dramatists.

419/426. *"Schlamperei . . . Sie?"* "Sloppiness, Lieutenant. Do you see?"

420/426. *Unteroffizier*. Subordinate officer.

426/433. Rossellini. Roberto Rossellini (1906–), whose first work after the war was *Open City* (1945), a film that ends with the execution of an Italian resistance worker.

428/435. Nothing is true, everything is permitted. This statement echoes the view of Ivan in Dostoevsky's *The Brothers Karamazov*, who describes an updated "temptation" of Jesus by "the Grand Inquisitor."

430/437. *deus vindicans*. A god who vindicates, a just god.

430/437. Goya. Francisco Goya (1746–1828) was a Spanish painter who produced a series of etchings called *The Disasters of War*.

437/444. *crime passionnel*. Crime of passion.

438/445. "sooner . . . desires." The line is a "proverb from Hell" in William Blake's *The Marriage of Heaven and Hell* (circa 1793).

441/448. Browne, or Hervey. Thomas Browne (1605–82) and John Hervey, (1616–79) a court favorite of Charles II, lived in more credulous times.

441/448. her death . . . life. Thesis of Donne's *Meditation 17* (see notes to p. 146/149).

442/449. Dufy. Raoul Dufy (1877–1953) was a French, early Impressionist painter of exteriors.

442/450. *presto*. Quickly.

444/452. *Les valises . . . Adieu*. "The suitcases?" "Everything is ready." She eyed me. "Well, sir. Good-bye."

446/453. *"Compris?"* "Understand?"

456/464. dekko. Look.

460/467. Alas, poor Yorick. Nicholas is quoting from the gravedigger scene in *Hamlet*, Act 5, Scene 1.

460/467. Frazer . . . *The Golden Bough*. James Frazer's comparative mythology (1890) contains a description of hanging an effigy of Artemis in her sacred grove, in *The New Golden Bough*, Mentor Books (New York: NAL, 1964), p. 379.

460/468. Gulliver . . . Lilliputians. In Book One of Jonathan Swift's *Gulliver's Travels* (1726), Gulliver is tied down by the six-inch-tall inhabitants of Lilliput while he sleeps.

462/470. Greene. Graham Greene (1904–) is one of England's foremost novelists.

467/474. Palmeresque. Suggesting a landscape by the English painter Samuel Palmer (1805–81).

481/489. Ferdinand and Miranda. Ferdinand is the shipwrecked lover of Miranda in *The Tempest* (see notes to pp. 83/85 and 136/139).

489/496. Kafka. Franz Kafka (1883–1924) was an Austrian writer of fictions about situations that seem to lack meaning.

491/499. Proustian. Evocative, as the main character in *Swann's Way* (1914), the first part of *Remembrance of Things Past*, finds that tasting a spoonful of tea and cake can release memories from his unconscious.

499/507. *soutane*. A priest's cassock.

502/510. Crowley. Aleister Crowley (1875–1947) was a diabolist and member of the Order of the Golden Dawn. Nicholas is thinking that he could mock the ceremony by adapting Henry Stanley's famous, understated greeting to Dr. Livingston in the Congo.

503/512. Smuts. Jan Smuts (1870–1950) was a statesman and sometime prime minister of South Africa.

505/513. Ashtaroth the Unseen. Ashtaroth was a Semitic goddess equivalent to Phoenician Astarte; her literary "meaning" would seem to lie in the way she represents the female, the idea of absence, and the gap of meaning between signifier and signified.

507/515. *"Pedicabo . . . Furi?"* "Shall I bugger you, pathetic Aurelius and shameless Furious?" The threat of homosexual rape is in response to their harsh judgments of the speaker's poems. In the original, by Catullus, (84–54 B.C.) these opening lines are a declarative statement rather than a question (Poem 16).

519/527. Flemish Adoration. For example, see Hugo van der Goes's painting of shepherds adoring Christ in the panel of the 1476 *Portinari Altarpiece*, in the Ufizzi Gallery, Florence.

520/528. *Bitte*. Please.

521/530. Io, Isis, Astarte, Kali. Goddesses associated with fertility in Greek, Egyptian, Syrian, and Hindu religions, respectively (as Nicholas will explain on p. 582/593).

523/531. Lady Jane. In *Lady Chatterley's Lover*, the gamekeeper and his aristocratic mistress nickname each other's sex organs "John Thomas" and "Lady Jane."

523/532. de Vere. An aristocratic English name that happens to mean "truthful."

528/537. *Maja Desnuda*. Often translated *The Naked Maja*, the painting by Goya (about 1800) shows a nude female reclining on her side, looking at the viewer with her hands clasped behind her head.

528/537. Récamier. Madame Récamier (1777–1849) was a social leader in Paris.

530/539. Desdemona. Wife of Othello (see note to p. 405/411).

530/540. Iago. Othello's subordinate who, perhaps consumed with jealousy—

or a sense that life is unfair—is undone by his plotting against Othello and Desdemona.

535/544. *Kal' espera.* Good evening.

538/548. Oedipus crossroads. In Sophocles's *Oedipus Tyrranus,* Oedipus kills his father unaware at a place where three roads meet, and in *Oedipus at Colonus,* Oedipus prepares to die at a place with several branching paths. Both locations are sometimes described as crossroads, an image that serves as metaphor for a life-changing decision.

539/549. Coué-method. One tells oneself daily—and persuades oneself—that "every day, in every way, I am getting better and better."

540/550. Lorre. In the film *Casablanca* (1942), Peter Lorre's character, Ugarte, fears being caught with a letter of transit stolen from the Germans.

540/550. Lonsdale. Hugh Cecil Lowther, 5th earl of Lonsdale (1857–1944), instituted Lonsdale belts for boxing champions.

541/550. Oedipus. When Oedipus discovers that he has killed his father and married his mother, he blinds himself.

541/551. *A . . . qui?* In the pay of whom?

543/553. *Je . . . Urfe.* I would like to speak with you, Mister Urfe.

543/553. *Eh bien.* Well?

544/554. *Pas posible.* Not possible.

545/555. *Avant la guerre.* Before the war.

545/555. *Bien.* Good.

547/557. *Lederhosen.* Leather, knee-length trousers.

549/559–60. *ominus . . . ciculus.* Oh-little master / Nicholas / is a little man / ridiculous // accordingly my / little sodomite / wishes to give much / without delay // in that famous anus / ridiculous / Nicholas / colossal sick-ulus. The poem contains several nonce words and ungrammatical constructions. The first and last words may be bilingual puns; they mean nothing in Latin but contain sounds whose English meaning may be relevant—*Oh* and *sick.* The poem Nicholas has found is evidently a nonsense musing, a "clue" that leads nowhere (like much at Bourani).

554/564. *omphalos.* The center of all, as the omphalos in the Temple at Delphi was thought to be the earth's navel.

560/570. Henry Green. English novelist whose "latest" in 1953 would have been *Doting.*

560/570. Leavis. F. R. Leavis (1895–1978) was an influential literary critic at Cambridge.

560/570. Oxbridge. A conflation of Oxford and Cambridge, the two "right" universities.

564/574. Maria. Olivia's servant, who conspires with others to dupe Malvolio in *Twelfth Night.*

566/576. *Alysson . . . miel.* Water-alyssum, with its odor of honey.

567/577. *La triomphe . . . lui.* The triumph of philosophy would be to shed some light on the obscurity clouding the means that providence uses to direct man along the paths she has mapped out for him. This same "philosophy" also might elaborate some plan of conduct whereby man, this unfortunate person constantly tossed to and fro by the capricious and despotic winds of providence, might somehow be led to understand the decrees of providence on his existence. (From the foreword to *Justine, or The Misfortunes of Virtue*)

570/580. *"Oh . . . meditation."* "Oh, if you think that football is a dignified subject for meditation."

570/581. Peruginos. Pietro Perugino (1450–1523) was one of the artists who painted frescoes decorating the Sistine Chapel.

576/586. Dylan Thomas. Welsh poet (1914–53) who lived in London from 1934 to 1937.

576/586. ponce. Pimp.

576/586. M.G. Morris Garage, a manufacturer of automobiles.

583/593. misplaced letter. The letter *p*, in the word *Olympus*, mountain where the classical Greek gods were thought to live.

585/596. Fragonard. Jean-Honoré Fragonard (1732–1806), French painter of aristocratic scenes that would look appropriate in the rococo interior of Mrs. De Seitas's drawing room. His name is misspelled *Gragonard* in the paperback edition.

588/598. *The Wind in the Willows.* Children's book by Kenneth Grahame, one of whose characters is a "Mr. Rat."

592/603. *Mischief.* This painting may be an invention, for no painter named William Blunt has exhibited with the Royal Academy.

592/603. soppy. Sentimental, as in the American slang *mushy.*

593/603. Women's Institute do. A social function of her chapter of the W.I. network of women's clubs in England.

598/609. Demeter, Ceres. The Greek and Roman goddesses of agriculture, also considered the foundresses of order and marriage, in some traditions mother and daughter who live together. Like Mrs. De Seitas, Demeter is shown seated on a throne in a mural painting at Pompeii.

599/610. Winchester. An English public school.

601/613. Place Pigalle. District of Paris famous for its erotic entertainments.

602/613. Queen Anne. Reigned from 1702 to 1714.

606/617. Orphean performance. Orpheus played his lute to obtain Eurydice's freedom from Hades.

607/618. Gorgonlike. Resembling one of the mythical Gorgons, whose look could turn a beholder to stone.

607/618. My fanny. Close to the American "like Hell."

607/619. *Noh.* Highly conventional Japanese theatrical productions that use traditional masks.

611/622. recce. Military jargon for *reconnoiter,* to spy out in advance.

611/622. *Sygeia.* Health (a toast).

611/622. *poly.* Very (Anglo-Greek slang).

612/623. squiffy. Tipsy.

612/624. pissed. Drunk.

612/624. Mosley. Sir Oswald Ernold Mosley was leader of the Union of Fascists in the 1930s.

615/627. Fielding. Xan Fielding was the pen name of Alex Fielding Wallace (1918–   ), a British agent in World War II.

616/627. D.S.O., M.C. Distinguished Service Order, Military Cross.

618/629. Thomas Hood. English writer and illustrator of children's books (1835–74).

620/631. Little Latin, less Greek. A near-quotation of what Ben Jonson said of Shakespeare's abilities in the preface to the *First Folio,* that he knew "small Latin and less Greek."

621/632. snake-goddess of Knossos. A statue of her, holding snakes aloft in each hand, is in the Archaeological Museum in Herakleion, on Crete.

621/632. Electra. Daughter of Agamemnon and Clytemnestra, Electra urged her brother Orestes to kill their mother and her lover, Aegisthus.

623/634. lifts. Elevators.

623/635. Bow. Made by the Bow porcelain factory, one of the first two porcelainware manufactories in England, founded by Thomas Frye (1710–62) and Edward Heylyn (1695–1758).

630/641. Marie Antoinette. Wife of Louis XVI, imprisoned during the French Revolution and executed in 1793.

631/642. Aubusson rug. An ornate, tapestry rug made in France.

634/645. *Italian Straw Hat.* René Clair's 1927 silent movie that critiques social conventions.

634/646. Mayhew. Henry Mayhew (1812–87) was a Victorian journalist and author of the influential book *London Labour and the London Poor* (1861–62).

634/646. packed art in. Given up art.

634/646. kip. Slang for *bed* or *sleep.*

639/650. Sassenach coddies. A derogatory Gaelic term for an Englishman linked with a Scottish slang word for testicles.

644/656. Mother Courage. Title character in *Mother Courage and Her Children,* a 1939 play by Bertolt Brecht.

644/656. Scylla and Charybdis. A devouring monster with six heads, and a whirlpool, both of which simultaneously threaten Odysseus's ship and men in Book 12 of Homer's *The Odyssey*.

645/656. Not all . . . men. Nursery rhyme about Humpty Dumpty's irreparability.

645/657. Benedick kissed Beatrice. The concluding moment of Shakespeare's *Much Ado About Nothing* (circa 1598–99).

668. *cras . . . amet*. Tomorrow let him love, who has never loved; he who has loved, let him love tomorrow. From the opening lines of an anonymous Latin lyric, *The Vigil of Venus* (*Pervigilium Veneris*, A.D. third century).

THE FRENCH LIEUTENANT'S WOMAN

Unpaginated/7. *Zur Judenfrage. On the Jewish Question*, by Karl Marx in 1843.

3/9. what familiarity breeds. Contempt, proverbially.

4/9. Armada. The Spanish Armada was defeated by Queen Elizabeth's navy in 1588.

4/9. Monmouth. James Scott, Duke of Monmouth (1649–85), invaded with a "force" of eighty-two men in 1685, in an assertion of his claim to the English throne. He was quickly defeated at Sedgemoor and subsequently executed.

4/9. Moore. Henry Moore (1898–1986) was a sculptor who worked in abstract forms using voids as well as solids.

4/9–10. Michelangelo. Michelangelo Buonarroti (1475–1564) was a Renaissance artist whose most famous sculpture is *David*, at the Galleria dell' Accademia in Florence, Italy.

4/10. spy. Although this paragraph can be read as a reference to Dr. Grogan, who has a telescope (p. 150/123), or to the narrator as voyeur, it also refers to a drawing in the Lyme Regis Museum by George Cruikshank (1792–1878), who depicts a local gentleman watching female bathers at Lyme through his telescope.

6/11. Neptune. Roman god of the sea.

7/12. Darwinian. Charles Darwin's *The Origin of Species* had appeared in 1859, eight years before the novel opens.

7/12. *Et voilà tout*. And that is all.

8/13. Jane . . . *Persuasion*. This novel by Jane Austen (1775–1817), published posthumously, is set partly in Lyme Regis. The Undercliff is described in chapter 11, and Louisa falls down in Chapter 12.

10/14. boo . . . goose. A timid person is proverbially afraid to say "boo" to a goose.

12/16. *adagio*. Written over musical notes, the word means "play slowly."

12/16. Chartists. Advocates of universal suffrage and other political reforms, around 1837.

12/16. beavered. Victorian slang for *bearded*.

12/16. German Jew. Karl Marx (see note to the epigraph, n.p./7).

12/16. *Kapital. Das Kapital*, in English *Capital*, was Marx's influential work of economics, containing his "labor theory of value," whose "red fruit" is twentieth-century Communism.

13/17. Almack's. A London club.

14/18. classics. Literature of ancient Greece and Rome (in the original languages).

14/18. Thirty-Nine Articles. The basic tenets of the Anglican Church, or Church of England, since Henry VIII broke with Catholicism (six articles were formulated in 1539 and the rest in 1571).

14/18. Oxford Movement. An ecclesiastical effort to bring the Church of England more into alignment with Roman Catholic tradition, begun at Oxford in the 1830s.

14/18. *propria terra*. As one's own.

15/18. *voyant . . . s'assurer*. Seeing too many reasons not to deny God, but not enough of them to be assured that he exists.

15/18. *infra dig*. Beneath one's dignity.

16/19. *conversazioni*. Conversations.

16/19. had interest. Had influence.

16/19. Gladstone. William Ewart Gladstone (1809–98) was prime minister four times between 1868 and 1894, as a member of the Liberal Party.

16/19. Macaulay. Thomas Babington Macaulay (1800–59) published his *History of England* between 1849 and 1855.

16/19. Lyell. Sir Charles Lyell (1797–1875) was an English geologist whose *Principles of Geology* Fowles mentions on p. 130.

16/19. Disraeli. Benjamin Disraeli (1804–81) was a member of Parliament from the Conservative, or Tory Party, who alternated with Gladstone as prime minister from 1868–1885.

16/19. Byronic. Resembling George Gordon, Lord Byron (1788–1824), writer of poetry and influential figure on the Continent, whose liaisons with Lady Caroline Lamb and with his half-sister Augusta were notorious.

18/21. Regency. The period from 1811 to 1820 in England, during which the future George IV ruled as Prince Regent, nicknamed "Prinny" (as mentioned on p. 26/27).

18/21. riddled. To riddle a fire is to shake ashes down through a grate.

19/21. Stygian. Hell-like, after the river Styx in the classical underworld.

20/22. Slut's wool. Dust balls.

20/23. Gestapo. The German Nazi secret police, notorious for brutality.

21/23. nickname. "Poor Tragedy," the name by which Ernestina has referred to Sarah (p. 8/13), is Grecian in the sense that tragedy as a literary genre originated in Hellenic Greece.

21/23. Low Church. Anglican congregations that shun practices they associate with the Roman Catholic church—or with Anglican High Church services.

21/24. Wellington. Arthur Wellesley, First Duke of Wellington, defeated Napoleon at the Battle of Waterloo in 1815 and served as prime minister from 1828 to 1830.

22/24. the widow's mite. Jesus observes that a poor widow who contributes two pennies—all she has—to the church has done more than a rich person who contributes a large but affordable sum (Mark 12:41–44).

22/24. *de haut . . . en haut.* Superior to inferior one moment, inferior to superior the next.

23/25. Magdalen. After Mary Magdalen, a biblical prostitute who reforms.

25/26. Phiz. Pseudonym of book illustrator H. K. Browne (1815–82), some of whose work was with Dickens novels.

25/26. Leech. John Leech (1817–64) was a book illustrator and caricaturist. Many of his cartoons appeared in *Punch,* including the one described on p. 108.

25/27. Becky Sharp. A clever, sometimes ruthlessly pragmatic character in William Makepeace Thackeray's 1847–48 novel *Vanity Fair.*

27/28. *bouderies.* Pouting, sulkiness.

27/28. Harley Street. Address associated with medical doctors in London.

27/28. day. Hitler invaded Poland on September 1, 1939.

28/28. Juliet. Juliet Capulet, title character in Shakespeare's *Romeo and Juliet* (about 1595), has a nurse who is a tolerant, sometimes comic woman.

28/29. *peignoir.* Dressing gown, robe.

28/29. Laocoön. A Greek statue in the Vatican depicts the death of Laocoön and his sons as they are strangled by writhing serpents.

31/30. Tennyson. Alfred, Lord Tennyson (1809–92), succeeded Wordsworth as poet laureate, from 1850 to 1892. The reference to eyes as "homes of silent prayer" is from *In Memoriam,* in which Tennyson describes the sister of Lazarus (part 32, stanza 1).

31. Treitschke. Heinrich von Treitschke (1834–96) was a German historian and anti-Semite.

31. Good Samaritan. A selfless, charitable man who helps a traveler who has been robbed, beaten, and left lying by the road (Luke 10:30–37).

34/33. Patmos. A small island in the Aegean to which St. John was exiled.

37/35. *Dies Irae.* Day of Wrath, or Judgment Day, from the Roman Catholic chant for the dead.

37/35. McLuhan. Marshall McLuhan (1911–80) was a Canadian theorist of communication media who believed that the isolating "Gutenberg Age" of print was coming to an end and being replaced by a "global village."

38/36. Proustian. Referring to Marcel Proust (1871–1922) whose *Remembrance of Things Past* includes a famous description of the feelings evoked by tasting a piece of madeleine cake dipped in tea ("Overture," *Swann's Way*).

39/37. *Quod est demonstrandum.* Which is to be proved.

39/37. *Ergo.* Therefore.

41/39. Weller. Sam Weller is a Cockney, or London East End manservant to Mr. Pickwick in Charles Dickens's novel *The Posthumous Papers of the Pickwick Club*, or *Pickwick Papers* (1836–37).

42/39. Beau Brummell. George Bryan Brummell (1778–1840) was known as "Beau," that is, "beautiful" Brummell because of his fashion-setting dress.

43/40. Sancho Panza. Comic servant to Don Quixote in Miguel de Cervantes's Spanish, satirical novel *Don Quixote* (1605). The village girl worshipped by Don Quixote is named Dulcinea, but Fowles refers to her as Dorothea, the Anglicized name used by Henry Fielding in his play *Don Quixote in England* (1733).

45/42. *Anningii.* The word would attach to a species named after Mary Anning (1799–1847).

47/43. Baedeker. Karl Baedeker (1801–59) was a German publisher of travel guides.

47/43 note. Eliot. George Eliot was the pen name of Mary Ann Evans (1819–80), novelist. In *Century Magazine* (Nov. 1881), F. W. H. Meyers reports of Eliot, "She stirred somewhat beyond her wont, and taking as her text the three words which have been used so often as the inspiring trumpet-calls of men—the words *God, Immortality, Duty*—pronounced, with terrible earnestness, how inconceivable was the *first*, how unbelievable the *second*, and yet how peremptory and absolute the *third*."

48/44. Homer. Ancient Greek poet whose *The Iliad* and *The Odyssey* were considered the most authoritative sources of insight into all aspects of life until well into the eighteenth century.

48/45. *Beagle.* The *The Voyage of the Beagle*, Darwin records his observations as a naturalist around South America between 1831–35; *The Origin of Species* (1859) posits Darwin's theory of evolution.

49/45. *oubliette.* A place of confinement whose only opening is from above.

49/45. *nulla species nova.* No new species, that is, there was once a creation of all species, so new ones are not emerging and disappearing as part of some evolutionary process.

49/45. Linnaeus. Latin name for the Swedish botanist Carl von Linné (1707–78), who devised an orderly system to classify all life into various classes, orders, genera, and species.

49/45. *exemplia gratia.* For example.

50/46. catherine-wheeled. Refers to a firework that spins and throws off sparks, named after its resemblance to the wheel device with which St. Catherine was tortured.

51/46. *milieux.* Social environments.

51/47. Mrs. Sherwood. Mary Martha Sherwood (1775–1851) wrote pious fictions, including *Susan Gray*.

53/48. Walter Scott. Sir Walter Scott (1771–1832) wrote historical novels, based partly on his observations of the Scottish border region.

53/48. ancestry. Sarah's father's obsession is the first of many parallels between Sarah and Tess of Thomas Hardy's *Tess of the d'Urbervilles*.

53/48. Drake. Francis Drake (1540–96) was knighted by Queen Elizabeth for having circumnavigated the world in the *Golden Hind*.

56/50. green sickness. An anemia to which young women were thought particularly susceptible.

56/50. twigged. Caught on to.

57/51. Brechtian. Referring to Bertolt Brecht (1898–1956), who wrote and advocated plays that did not try to create a sense of illusion but, instead, a distance he called the "alienation effect," so that an audience might take his social message more seriously than they would be likely to do in a theater of conventional, illusionistic drama.

57/51. *Lama . . . me.* "My God, my God, why has thou forsaken me?" is the King James translation of these words spoken by Jesus while on the cross, in which he is quoting Psalm 22 (Matthew 27:46 and Mark 15:34).

58/52. on about. Talking about.

61/54. barouche. A four-wheeled open carriage with driver.

61/55. Blue Vinney. A blue-veined cheese.

68/60. Renaissance. Period in European art history during, approximately, the fourteenth through the sixteenth centuries, characterized by an interest in representing the secular world as classical artists had done.

68/60. Botticelli. Sandro Botticelli (1444–1510) used naturalistic details to represent the ground in his *Primavera,* or *Spring* (1477–78), unlike the plain backgrounds typical of earlier, medieval art.

68/60. Ronsard. Pierre de Ronsard (1524–85) was a French poet.

68/60. Rousseau. Jean-Jacques Rousseau (1712–78) was a Swiss-born French novelist and philosopher associated with the phrase "noble savage." His 1755 *Discourse on the Origin of Inequality* argues that primitive man was innocent and content in the "state of nature," before corrupted by civilization, and his novel *Émile* (1762) extends this idea to childrearing and education.

72/63. lost. Used in the sense that paradise was lost after the fall of man in the biblical Garden of Eden, to which England in 1867 has been compared earlier in the chapter (p. 67/59).

74/64. *grisette.* A French working girl.

74/64. Occam's useful razor. A precept for guiding analysis developed by William of Occam (d. 1349), it holds that the best explanation usually is the simplest one, requiring the fewest assumptions.

74/64. Waterloo. Site in Belgium of Wellington's defeat of Napoleon in 1815.

75/64. Flora. Roman goddess of flowers.

76/66. *soubrettes*. Pert and lively young women servants.

77/66. *à la mode*. Fashionable.

77/66. tick. Credit.

78/67. Don Juan. A legendary Spanish nobleman notorious for his sexual conquests.

79/68. solicitor. In England, a lawyer who advises clients but who does not argue cases, as a barrister would do.

79/68. scuttle. A bucket used to carry coal through the house.

79/68. Smithson. Charles's surname recalls an earlier scientist, James Smithson (1765–1829), whose will led to the establishment in 1846 of the Smithsonian Institution in Washington D.C.

79/68. Vere de Vere. "Lady Clara Vere de Vere" (1842) is a poem by Tennyson about a haughty noblewoman.

80/68. vetted. Screened, by means of background investigation.

80/68. *soirées*. Social gatherings in the evening.

81/69. Mayfair. A fashionable section of London.

81/69. Cretaceous. A period from 70–135 million years B.C., in the Mesozoic Era.

85/73. Jeremiah. A biblical prophet with a mournful attitude.

87/75. *Noli me tangere*. "Touch me not" was said by Jesus to Mary Magdalene after the resurrection (John 20:17).

88/75. *déshabille*. State of being dressed in a disorderly way.

88/75. fire shield. A device resembling a fan, held to protect one's face from excessive heat from a fireplace.

88/75. Hercules. Roman demigod who performed twelve tasks requiring superhuman effort.

89/76. Sodom and Gomorrah. Ancient cities in the Middle East, associated with sin and destroyed by Jehovah.

89/76. enclosure acts. Acts of Parliament between 1709 and 1869 that required the fencing off of private land.

89/76. *Anschluss*. A unification, such as the political takeover of Austria by the Nazis in 1939.

90/76. *de facto*. As a matter of fact.

90/77. older than Shakespeare. William Shakespeare wrote *A Midsummer Night's Dream* about 1596.

92/78. valley of the dolls. Jacqueline Susann wrote a novel titled *The Valley of the Dolls* in 1966, which was adapted to film in 1967, about actresses addicted to amphetamines and barbiturates, taken in capsules termed "dolls."

92/78. Coleridge. Samuel Taylor Coleridge (1772–1834) supposedly wrote "Kubla Khan" under the influence of opium.

92/78. Bosch-like. Resembling Hieronymus Bosch's *The Garden of Earthly Delights* (about 1500), which nightmarishly depicts various kinds of depravity.

93/79. paths of righteousness. A literalizing allusion to Psalm 23.

95/80. Barthes. Roland Barthes (1915–80) was a French writer and critic of culture who advanced the ideas that nothing can be understood except as a text, and that novelists do not exist in relation to their novels in the biographical way usually assumed.

95/80. Robbe-Grillet. Alain Robbe-Grillet (1922–   ) is a French writer of experimentalist novels that deliberately oppose conventional ideas about the forms of fiction. His *Toward a New Novel* (1963) may have influenced Fowles's decision to require a different kind of reader participation in *The French Lieutenant's Woman*.

95/81. puppets. The image recalls Thackeray's *Vanity Fair* (1847–48), whose last paragraph refers to putting away the characters as shutting puppets away in a box.

96/81. ˙ I am a novelist. . . . This chapter, with its digression on novel writing, is in part an homage to George Eliot, whose *Adam Bede* (1859) contains a similar chapter "In Which the Story Pauses a Little," where the narrator observes, "I would not, even if I had the choice, be the clever novelist who could create a world so much better than this" (Chapter 17).

97/82. *hypocrite lecteur.* Hypocritical reader, a phrase from Baudelaire's *Fleurs du Mal (Flowers of Evil)*, an 1857 collection of poems. This phrase also appears in T. S. Eliot's *The Waste Land*.

100/84. Periclean. Like Pericles (490–429 B.C.), Athenian statesman especially famed for his speaking ability.

102/86. *Introit.* The opening of a Roman Catholic mass, sometimes recited for a deceased person.

109/91. Fallen One. Lucifer, the fallen angel.

110/92. *Ursa.* Latin for *bear,* which sounds like Sam's Cockney pronunciation of "her, sir."

110/92. *primum mobile.* First mover, a phrase sometimes used by theologians to describe God.

112/93. *de rigeur.* Required clothing, outfit.

112/93. Cupid. Son of Venus, Roman goddess of love, commonly represented with a bow and arrow that pierces hearts, metaphorically and erotically.

112/93. Maid Marian. Female companion of Robin Hood, longbowman of English legend (and wearer of Nottingham Forest green for camouflage).

113/93. *contretemps.* Unfortunate mischance.

114/95. Sheridan. Richard Brinsley Sheridan (1751–1816) was an Irish playwright, best known for *The Rivals* and *The School for Scandal*.

114/95. Melbourne. William Lamb, Second Viscount Melbourne, was prime minister of England from 1835 to 1841.

114/95. *crim. con.* Abbreviation for "criminal conversation," a legal phrase for adultery.

114/95. Nightingale. Florence Nightingale (1820–1910) was an English nurse known as "the lady with the lamp," who reformed nursing practices.

115/95. Mill. John Stuart Mill (1806–73), best known for his *Autobiography* and his association with Utilitarianism, also wrote *The Subjection of Women* in 1860 (published 1869).

119/99. Gibson Girl. A type of female which formed an American ideal in the 1890's, after the illustrations of Charles Dana Gibson.

119/99. Lavater. Johann Kaspar Lavater (1741–1801) argued that one's face indicates one's character.

120/99–100. *Madame Bovary.* Novel by Gustave Flaubert in 1857 whose heroine commits suicide as well as adultery.

123/101. now . . . tread. A play on the line "Fools rush in, where angels fear to tread," from Alexander Pope's *Essay on Criticism* (1711).

127/104. whist. A card game resembling bridge.

127/105. Ramadan. A Muslim holy month during which daylight fasting is required.

127/105. *vert espérance.* Literally, "green hope," words also associated by Dante with the possibility of divine redemption in the *Purgatorio* (Book 3).

127/105. *sotto voce.* Low-voiced.

127/105. John Bull. Figure who represents England at its most patriotic.

129/106. Handel and Parry/Handel and Bach. John Parry (1710–82) played the harp and published a collection of Welsh melodies which led to the popularity of harp airs in the nineteenth century; his name appears only in the American hardcover edition. Georg Friedrich Händel (1685–1759) and Johann Sebastian Bach (1685–1750) composed keyboard music that Charles has been hearing performed during social engagements.

130/107. moue. Pout.

131/108. Seven Dials. An area surrounding Covent Garden in London, a notorious slum in the nineteenth century.

131/108. The world . . . now. An allusion to William Wordsworth's opening lines of the sonnet "The world is too much with us; late and soon, / Getting and spending, we lay waste our powers." Fowles's narrator shifts the meaning of *world* from "materialism" to "the earth's population."

134/110. A demang, madymoselle. Sam's rendition of *Á demain, mademoiselle,* or "until tomorrow, Miss."

134/110. Roman sign of mercy. Thumbs up.

138/113. *déboulis.* A heap of stones.

142/117. siren . . . Calypso. Calypso has detained Odysseus on her island for seven years when Book One of Homer's *The Odyssey* opens. She is the daughter of Atlas, a siren only in the general sense—not one of those creatures Odysseus encounters in Book Twelve. The narrator is observing that

Charles fails to recognize that Sarah is a siren because he thinks about them too conventionally, as inhabitants only of literary worlds.

146/119. owl. Companion of Minerva, Greek goddess of wisdom.

149/122. *comme il faut*. As it should be, proper behavior.

149/122. *souffrante*. Suffering.

149/122. Hoffmann. Olympia in "The Sandman" is an example of such a mechanical girl in a tale by E.T.A. Hoffmann (1776–1822).

150/123. *Dulce est desipere*. The last line of Horace's ode 12, book 24, states, "*Dulce est desipere in loco*," or, "It is sweet to cast aside serious thoughts at the proper place."

150/123. nereids. Sea-nymphs.

150/123. Gregorian. James Gregory (1638–75) invented the reflecting telescope.

151/123. Virgil. Roman poet (70–19 B.C.) who composed *The Aeneid*.

151/124. Bentham. Jeremy Bentham (1748–1832) founded the school of Utilitarian philosophy.

151/124. Parian. Parian marble comes from the Greek island of Paros.

151/124. Voltaire. Pseudonym of François-Marie Arouet (1694–1778), a French philosopher considered to be a universal genius and free-thinker.

152/124. Vital Religion. One based on belief in a metaphysical soul.

152/124. Paddy. A generic, sometimes derisive name for an Irishman.

152/124. Augustan. A label sometimes applied to English culture around the early eighteenth century for its literary emulations of Rome under Caesar Augustus.

153/125. Burke. Edmund Burke (1729–97) usually is thought of as a conservative for his disapproving *Reflections on the Revolution in France* (1790).

153/125. Arnold. Matthew Arnold (1822–88) wrote the social critique *Culture and Anarchy* (1869), as well as poetry.

154/125. German doctor. Edouard von Hartmann (1842–1906) was a German philosopher and proto-psychologist.

154/126. Bedlam. Short for Bethlehem Hospital, formerly an asylum for the insane in London.

154/126. colleen. Irish slang for a young girl.

155/126. jarvey. Irish term for a coach for hire.

155/126. Not-on. Unthinkable, roughly equivalent to the American phrase "Nothing doing."

158/129. Morland. George Morland (1763–1804) was a painter of rural scenes.

158/129. Foster. Birket Foster (1825–1899) sentimentalized the poor in his paintings.

160/130. Ussher. James Ussher's theory was published in Latin (1650–54), then translated into English in 1658 as *The Annals of the World*. In his "Epistle to the Reader," Ussher explains why the first day of the Christian era must have been October 24, 4004 B.C. (not the 26th), the creation having begun six hours before midnight (not at 9:00) on the 23rd.

161/131. *bas-bleus*. Bluestockings.

162/132. Crusoe . . . Friday. They may be isolated, like Crusoe and Friday in Daniel Defoe's *Robinson Crusoe* (1719), but they have companionship.

162/132. *carbonari*. Members of a secret, revolutionary society in early nineteenth-century Italy (usually capitalized).

166/136. *al fresco*. Out of doors.

167/136. *demi-monde*. The world of sexual impropriety.

170/139. defoliate the milkwort. In Thomas Hardy's *Tess of the d'Urbervilles* (1891), Tess similarly peels "lords and ladies" (jack-in-the-pulpit) while she sits on a bank and talks about her past with Angel Clare (Chapter 14).

176/143. Pre-Raphaelite. The Pre-Raphaelite Brotherhood, or PRB, formed in 1848, was revolutionary in its opposition to academic art in the tradition of Renaissance painter Raphael Sanzio (1483–1520). The PRB's painting and poetry aimed at moral seriousness and symbolic spirituality, as pre-Renaissance medieval painting did, yet at the same time they tried to be highly faithful to perceived reality in their representations.

176/143. a Millais or a Ford Madox Brown. John Everett Millais (1829–96) was one of the founders of the Pre-Raphaelite Brotherhood. Ford Madox Brown (1821–93) was not a "brother" but deserved to be, and usually is considered a Pre-Raphaelite painter (see note above).

176/143. a Constable or a Palmer. John Constable (1776–1837) and Samuel Palmer (1805–81) were English painters of representational, less idealized scenes of English landscape.

177/144. Thélème. The Abbey of Thélème is a place in François Rabelais's *Gargantua* (1534), where only those who are naturally virtuous would be admitted.

184/149. *in flagrante delicto*. Caught in the act of passionate crime.

190/153. trap. A two-wheeled carriage.

191/154. Carolean. Period in English history marked by the beginning of the reign of Charles I in 1630 and the death of Charles II in 1685.

191/154. Tudor. Period in English history marked by the reign of members of the House of Tudor, 1485–1603.

191/154. Gobelins. Owners of a tapestry manufactory in fifteenth-century Paris.

191/154. Claudes. Works of Claude Gellée, or Claude Lorrain (1600–82), French painter of tranquil, often pastoral landscapes.

191/154. Tintoretto. Jacopo Rubisti, "Il Tintoretto" (1518–94) was an important Venetian painter of the Italian Renaissance.

192/155. appointed. Decorated.

193/156. Crystal Palace. A structure of iron and glass built to house an exhibition in London in 1851.

194/156. Baucis. Old woman in ancient Greece who, with her husband Philemon, showed warm hospitality to strangers—who turned out to be Zeus and Hermes.

195/157. limes. Linden trees.

196/158. billycock. A soft, round hat.

197/158. Palladian. An architectural style in vogue in England after 1715, when many Whig landowners built country houses in imitation of the style of Renaissance Italian villas of Andreas Palladio (1508–80).

197/158. Wyatt. James Wyatt (1746–1813) was a late-Palladian architect.

207/166. ostler. One who takes care of horses.

208/166. *Je . . . ferme.* I waited for you all day. I pray you—a woman on her knees asks for help in her time of despair. I will pass the night in prayer for your arrival. From daybreak I will be at the small barn near the sea, reached by the first footpath to the left after the farm.

212/169. ring at Newmarket. A London racetrack.

212/170. *imprimatur*—or *ducatur in matrimonium*. Authorization to be printed—or authorization to be led into marriage.

213/170. *faute de mieux*. Lack of any better alternatives.

214/171. bullfinch. A hedge high enough to stop a hunter, unlike the one Charles's uncle has metaphorically jumped, earlier on the page.

216/172. Manton. Joseph Manton (1760–1835) was a gunsmith.

218/174. *rentier*. One who lives on a fixed income.

223/178. *in . . . altis*. At the brink of death and from the depths—or rather the heights.

224/179. "I shall be revenged." Grogan is adapting a statement by Jonah (2:4).

225/179. Socrates. Greek philosopher and tutor of Plato, Socrates was executed for "corrupting the youth," but was probably charged as well because he made so many people uncomfortable in the pursuit of truth. He is associated with the phrase *know thyself,* inscribed at the site of the oracle at Delphi.

225/180. Malthus. Thomas Malthus (1766–1834) theorized that war and famine are necessary to check population increase.

232/185. Hugo. Victor Hugo (1802–85) was a French poet, dramatist, and novelist whose best-known work is *Les Misérables*.

232/185. Balzac. Honoré de Balzac (1799–1850) was a French novelist whose voluminous, collected works are known as *The Human Comedy*.

232/185. George Sand. Pseudonym of Amandine-Aurore-Lucile Dupin, Baronne Dudevant (1804–76), a French novelist and writer of a four-volume autobiography.

232/185. Matthei. Karl Matthei lived from 1770–1847.

235/188. note. *perfide Albion!* Faithless, treacherous England! (Miss Allen's country of birth.)

236/188. Sir Galahad shown Guinevere. In Arthurian legends, Galahad is morally the purest of Arthur's knights, and Guinevere is Arthur's unfaithful wife.

237/189. Pilate. Pontias Pilate was the Roman procurator of Judea who declined to prevent the execution of Jesus Christ (Matthew 27:24).

239/190. adage. "Hung for the lamb, hung for the ewe" provides a criminal the rationale to compound a crime. Fowles cites the proverb in *A Maggot* (p. 212/215).

239/191. Pisanello. Antonio Pisanello (1397–1455) was an Italian painter whose *Vision of St. Eustace* in the National Gallery depicts a conversion in the forest, where the saint is confronted with a stag with a crucifix in his antlers. The same story is told of both St. Eustace and St. Hubert, so the painting could be of either one (the Gallery puts a question mark after the title).

244/194. Parthian. Characteristic of the warriors of ancient Parthia, who would shoot arrows while retreating.

245/195. Jezebel. Biblical wife of Ahab, who drew him away from God, considered the type of a wicked woman (1 Kings 16).

248/197. Hegel. Georg Wilhelm Friedrich Hegel (1770–1831) was a German philosopher who theorized that history can be understood in terms of oppositions and syntheses.

249/199. Catullus . . . Sappho. Sappho (seventh century B.C.), of Lesbos, wrote a love ode in Greek (poem 2 in volume 1 of *Lyra Graeca* in the Loeb Classical Library) which the Roman poet Catullus (84–54 B.C.) translated into Latin (poem 51). Fowles's English translation is of lines 6–12.

252/201. Janus-like. Contradictory, after the Roman god Janus, who had two opposing faces.

261/207. Aphrodite. Greek goddess of love.

263/209. Bloomer. Amelia Jenks Bloomer (1818–94) advocated the wearing of loose trousers, fitted at the ankles, under a short skirt, with a coat and wide hat, in America about 1850.

266–67/211–12. What . . . fundamental. This paragraph of contrasts resembles the opening paragraph of Charles Dickens's *A Tale of Two Cities* (1859), which begins, "It was the best of times, it was the worst of times."

267/211. Sade. Donatien Alphonse François, Marquis de Sade (1740–1814) linked eroticism and pain, including flagellation, in his writings.

267/212. Bowdler. Dr. Thomas Bowdler (1754–1825) edited *Family Shakespeare* (1818), with immodest passages expurgated. Mrs. Poulteney is said to own a "bowdlerized" Bible, with the Song of Solomon removed (p. 77).

267/212. threshold. Queen Victoria assumed the throne in 1837.

270/214. Mayhew. Henry Mayhew (1812–87) was a journalist whose *London*

Labour and the London Poor (1851–62), based on interviews, is an important sociological document.

270/214. Dickens. Charles Dickens (1812–70) evidently lied about his relationship with Ellen Ternan while he was still married to Catherine.

270/214. Hardy. Thomas Hardy (1840–1928) wrote novels set in "Wessex" (roughly, Dorset, which includes Lyme Regis).

270 note/214 note. Martyrdom. The six laborers who banded together in 1834 in an attempt to increase wages were banished to Australia (but later pardoned).

271/215. Pandora. In Greek legend, the first woman, whose curiosity led her to disobey an instruction not to open a particular box and, in doing so, to release evils into the world.

271/215. Atreids. Statues of Agamemnon and Menelaius, the sons of Atreus, whose palace was at Mycenae in ancient Greece. They were forced to flee when Thyestes murdered their father and later found themselves seemingly abandoned by their gods when they tried to set sail for Troy, in pursuit of Paris and Agamemnon's abducted wife, Helen.

271/216. Egdon Heath. Setting for part of Hardy's *The Return of the Native* (1878).

271/216. Tryphena. The argument that Fowles advances here is laid out more completely—some say unconvincingly—in *Providence and Mr. Hardy*, by Lois Deacon and Terry Coleman (1966).

272/216. Sue Bridehead and Tess. Sue is the heroine of *Jude the Obscure* (1895), and Tess is the heroine of *Tess of the d'Urbervilles* (1891). They resemble Sarah as well as Tryphena, of course.

274/218. Shilling. A shilling in 1967 was worth 1/20 pound, which was then worth about $2.40.

275/219. Wesley. Charles Wesley (1707–88) was an English evangelist and writer of hymns.

275/219. Georgian. Dating from the reigns of George I through IV (1714–1830).

276/219. homelier. Cozier.

276/219. half-crown. Two shillings and one-half.

277/220. Toby jug . . . Ralph Wood. A drinking mug made to resemble a man's head in a three-cornered hat, a design invented by potter Ralph Wood (1715–72). A Toby is an official who allocates space, collects rents, and regulates the types of goods sold at an English marketplace.

278/221. sovereigns. Each sovereign was worth almost three pounds.

280/222. Jorrocks. Mr. Jorrocks was a Cockney grocer who pursued the sports of a country gentleman in humorous sketches by Robert Smith Surtees (1805–64).

282/223. Marcus . . . Palmerston. Marcus Aurelius (121–180) was an Emperor of Rome; Henry John Temple, Third Viscount Palmerston (1784–

1865), was a prime minister of England. The narrator's uncertainty indicates that Mr. Freeman may sincerely admire Palmerston or—less sincerely—have decorated his study with the bust of a classical hero.

287/227. Jesus . . . Satan. The temptation in the desert is recounted in Matthew 4:1–11.

288/228. more famous pilgrim. The main character in John Bunyan's *Pilgrim's Progress* (1678), named Christian, makes an allegorical, religious journey through places that represent ideas and modes of behavior.

288/228. *savoir-vivre*. Knowing how to live.

288/229. Corinthian. The most ornate style of column in classical Greek architecture.

289/229. hansom. A two-wheeled covered vehicle drawn by one horse, driven from behind and above.

289/229. Candide. Naive main character in Voltaire's 1759 satire *Candide: Or, Optimism.*

292/231. ironmonger. Hardware dealer.

293/232. *nouveau riche*. Newly rich, trying to impress.

294/233. parfit. Middle English for *perfect*.

294/233. *preux chevalier*. Valiant knights.

295/234. temptation in the wilderness. See Matthew 4:1–11.

298/236. Mytton. John Mytton (1796–1834) performed foolhardy physical feats.

298/236. Casanova. Giovanni Jacopo Casanova (1740–95) was an Italian writer with a reputation for seducing women.

300/237. brougham. A four-wheeled carriage with driver in front and room for four passengers.

300/238. *Metonymia . . . puella. Metonymia* is a rhetorical device by which one term is represented by some other term associated with it. Nathaniel explains to Charles that *Venus* (goddess of erotic love) represents *puella* (Latin for *girl*, sometimes "loose woman") in Tom's remark that they should "worship at the muses' shrine." Although Terpsichore is one of the muses and the bawdy house is owned by "Ma Terpsichore," to worship at the shrine of the muses is not only to visit but also, metonymically, to have sex with the girls there. The implied identity between sexual intercourse with a muse and artistic inspiration by a muse is an idea that Fowles plays with at length in *Mantissa.*

302/239. *Carmina Priapea. Songs to Priapus,* a collection of indecent Latin poems by anonymous authors, in honor of the Roman god of fruitfulness. The song here quoted (in its entirety) is number 43 (not 44) of the eighty "priapics" in *Poetae Latini Minores (Minor Latin Poets)*, edited by Emil Baehrens and Friedrich Vollmer (Leipzig: Teubner, 1913), vol. 2, fascicle 2, pp. 55–56.

302/239. Camargo. Marie Camargo (1710–70) was a French ballerina who introduced calf-length ballet skirts.

303/240. Heliogabalus. Varius Aviatus Bassianus, a profligate Roman emperor from 218–22, elicited support from the Syrians by adopting this, the name of their sun god, as his own name.

303/240. *History of the Human Heart.* The subtitle of this anonymous novel is *Adventures of a Young Gentleman* (1749; reprinted New York: Garland, 1974).

303/240. Cleland. John Cleland's 1748–49 book was originally titled *Memoirs of a Woman of Pleasure.*

305/242. *danseuse.* Female dancer.

314/248. Etty. William Etty (1787–1849) was an English painter who specialized in female nudes, often in mythological contexts. He was considered too voluptuous by many of his contemporaries.

314/248. Pygmalion. In classical legend, a sculptor who falls in love with the statue he has made, which comes to life and bears him a child. The original medium was ivory, rather than marble.

317/250. cry off. Discontinue, in this case Charles's bachelor ways.

319/252. commode. A small cabinet.

320/252. the Sartrean experience. Discomfort with the human condition. In *Nausea,* Sartre's main character feels revulsion at ordinary objects; in *No Exit,* Hell is represented as an enclosed room.

324/255. *éclairissement.* Clarification.

324/255. *sub tegmine fagi.* "Under the shade of a beech tree," a quotation from Virgil's *First Eclogue.*

324/255. *à la lettre.* Literally.

324/255. *Absolvitur.* The first word of the Roman Catholic ritual of absolution, which a priest grants after confession.

328/258. *ante* Stanislavski. Before Konstantin Stanislavski (1863–1938), Russian drama theorist who advocated, among other things, practice of improvisation.

329/259. Uriah Heep. A character in Dickens's *David Copperfield* (1849–50) who pretends to be extremely humble.

340/267. life span. Because Ernestina died when Hitler invaded Poland, in 1939 (p. 27/28) and Charles was 32 in 1867 (p. 11/16), for him to survive her by a decade (p. 337/264), he would have lived to the improbable age of 114 years.

340/267. Delphic. The oracle at Delphi uttered cryptic-sounding prophecies.

342/268. browns. Copper pennies.

358/281. Grünewald. Matthias Grünewald (1480–1528) was a Northern Renaissance painter whose *Isenheim Altarpiece* in Colmar depicts a *"mater dolorosa,"* or sorrowful mother of Christ at the crucifixion.

359/281. Bradlaugh. Charles Bradlaugh (1833–91) was a social reformer.

360/283. "But you must judge." This statement resembles a tenet central to existential philosophy, "It is necessary to choose," from Jean-Paul Sartre's *Being and Nothingness* (1943).

362/284. render unto Caesar. An allusion to Jesus's defense of tax-paying (Matthew 22:21).

365/287. St. Paul. On the road to Damascus, Saul was struck from his horse and temporarily blinded by a light, from which emanated a voice that asked him why he persecuted Christians (Acts 9:1–8). The converted Saul became Saint Paul.

366/287. Uffizi. The Uffizi Gallery in Florence, Italy, is one of the world's foremost art museums.

367/288. *en passage*. Passing through.

367/288. Tractarian schism. An English high church movement toward Roman Catholic practices, named after a series of *Tracts for the Times* between 1833 and 1841.

368/289. Kingsley. Charles Kingsley (1819–75) was a Christian Socialist and author of novels. He became engaged in a controversy with John Henry Cardinal Newman.

369/289. *Dr. Jekyll and Mr. Hyde*. A novel by Robert Louis Stevenson in 1886 about a virtuous physician named Jekyll, who develops a drug that brings forth the evil side of his personality as "Mr. Hyde."

379/296. Cleopatra. Queen of Egypt from 51 to 30 B.C., whose beauty, like Helen's, was so remarkable that it affected international politics.

386/302. Judah . . . Ephialtes. Judah sold his brother Jacob into Egyptian slavery (Genesis 37:26–28). Ephialtes was a son of Poseidon who captured the god Ares and threatened to destroy Olympus, home of the gods.

390/305. *non sequitur*. Statement that does not follow logically from what precedes it.

394/308. Dante . . . Antinomians. Dante Alighieri (1265–1321) assigned sinners to particularly appropriate punishments in Hell in *The Inferno*. Antinomians reject moral law in the belief that grace alone is necessary for salvation; as heretics, they are probably among those condemned to iron tombs, like Pope Anastasius (Canto 11).

397/311. law . . . ass. An echo of Mr. Bumble's statement in Dickens's *Oliver Twist* (1837): "If the law supposes that . . . the law is an ass" (Chapter 51).

398/311. *Jacta alea est* . . . Rubicon. "The die is cast," said Caesar, that is, there was no turning back once he had crossed the Rubicon into Gaul.

403/315. Gorgon. A creature whose stare could turn people to stone.

404/316. Spurgeon. Charles Spurgeon (1834–92) was a popular, extremely zealous Baptist preacher.

405/317. *nouveau roman*. New novel, a phrase used by Alain Robbe-Grillet in his 1963 *Pour un nouveau roman (Toward a New Novel)*, which describes a need for novels that do not create the illusion of order provided by the traditional, omniscient narrator (see note to p. 95/80).

405/317. "What . . . do with you?" This question echoes a refrain about the protagonist of Dickens's *David Copperfield* (see chapters 10 and 14).

406/318. florin. An English coin, no longer in use, formerly worth two shillings.

411/321. *columbarium.* A funeral vault with recesses to hold urns containing ashes.

414/324. *sine die.* Without specifying a day, at any time.

417/326. *prima facie.* On the face of things.

418/327. No. 10 Downing Street. The address of the house occupied by England's prime minister.

418/327. Girton College. The first women's college at Cambridge University.

418/327. *en masse.* In clusters.

423/331. Faust. Faust, or Faustus, contracts with Mephistopheles for knowledge and pleasure in exchange for his soul.

424/332. skivvy. The lowest order of servant.

426/334. khans and *alberghi.* Inns.

426/334. Poet Laureate. Tennyson held the appointment at the time the novel's events are taking place. Excerpts from his *Maud* serve as epigraphs to Chapters 6, 10, 13, 16, 25, 38, 43, 45, 49, and 56.

430/337. Canaan. The Hebrew Promised land, where milk and honey were supposed to flow.

431/337. Pocahontas. Indian girl (1595–1617) who saved John Smith from execution.

431/337. *pour la dot comme pour la figure.* Beautiful for her dowry as well as for her figure.

432/338. Dana. Richard Henry Dana (1787–1879) was a poet and journalist who founded the *North American Review.* In British editions of the novel, the figure Charles shakes hands with is identified, instead, as "Old Nathaniel Lodge, who had heard the cannon on Bunker Hill from his nurse's room on Beacon Street." The ancestor of Boston's famous family was named Giles, son of John Lodge of London; Giles did not arrive from England until 1791. Fowles probably changed the identity of "Nathaniel Lodge" in the American edition to a recognizable figure to improve the novel's historicity—not as a concession to readers.

432–33/338–39. A far . . . the master. The "more famous writer" in the circle of James Russell Lowell (1819–91)—and co-editor of *The North American Review* after 1864—was Henry James (1843–1916). His eventual decision to become a British subject was the reverse of Charles's move to America. The narrator's parenthetical remark, "I must not ape the master," is a mock apology for the rest of the sentence, which is written in the style of Henry James. His novel *The Bostonians* (1886), like *The French Lieutenant's Woman,* is on one level a treatise of women's liberation.

436/341. *Liberté*-besotted. Drunk with the concept of liberty, as opposed to equality and fraternity (which, Fowles argues, are social virtues opposed to untrammeled, individual liberty in "The Falklands and a Death Foretold," p. 725).

439/344. Sphinx. A dangerous creature in Greek legend who posed riddles to travelers (and killed them if they failed to guess the answers). Charles's mistaken assumptions about Sarah's situation as he arrives at the address he has been given resemble those of Angel Clare about Tess's situation as he arrives at The Herons in *Tess of the d'Urbervilles* (Chapter 55).

441/346. monogram. Several artists of the Pre-Raphaelite Brotherhood, or PRB, signed their paintings with monograms. This one is probably that of Dante Gabriel Rossetti (1828–82), the poet and painter whom Charles guesses that the house belongs to on p. 444/348 and whose identity Fowles makes explicit on pp. 458/359 and 461/361. Also see note to p. 176/143.

442/346. Sibylline. The Sibyl of Cumae guides Aeneas through the Underworld in Virgil's *Aeneid* (Book 6).

442/346. a face he knew. Probably that of John Ruskin (1819–1900), art critic who promoted the Pre-Raphaelite Brotherhood.

444/348. the one downstairs. The man with the pen, described on p. 441/345, has the reputation and the occupation of Algernon Charles Swinburne (1837–1909), a poet who lived with Rossetti in the early 1860s and was the subject of much gossip. The man's age corresponds with that of novelist George Meredith (1828–1909), who also lived with Rossetti for a time and would have been "six or seven years older than Charles"; the man's "Jewish air" suggests Simeon Solomon, an artist linked with the PRB. This seeming conflation of identities evokes the Pre-Raphaelites as a group, as Sarah's situation evokes various women associated with them.

445/348. *bas relief*. A sculpture whose figures project from a background rather than stand free.

445/348. "I see." "Sometimes." The order of these two speeches is reversed, erroneously, in paperback editions of the novel published before 1990, when the problem was corrected.

446/349. fancy dress ball. Costume ball.

446/349. "She is dead." Elizabeth Siddal was a shopgirl who became Gabriel Rossetti's model, then mistress, then wife. She died in 1862 but inspired his painting *Beata Beatrix*, painted during the years 1864 to 1870.

446/349. brother. William Michael Rossetti (1829–1919) was a poet, critic, and editor.

446/349. "The libidinous laureate of a pack of satyrs." John Morley (1838–1923) used this phrase to characterize Swinburne in a review of *Poems and Ballads* for *The Saturday Review*, 4 August 1866, p. 147.

446/349. *ménage à quatre—à cinq*. A living arrangement of four—or five. The phrase is an extension of the French phrase *ménage à trois*, or "household of three," which refers to a sharing of one sex partner. The four imagined by Charles at this point would have been the man with the pen, the two

Rossetti brothers, and Sarah. The "girl who showed him up" may be supposed to represent one of the various "stunners" besides Elizabeth Siddal (whose death Sarah has mentioned), someone such as Alexa Wilding or Maria Stillman.

448/351. Ruskin. See note to p. 442/346.

449/351. Humphreys. Henry Noel Humphreys (1810–79) designed and illustrated books.

453/355. *coup de grâce*. Death blow.

458/358. shot silk. The color changes when it is held at various angles, as verbal texts shift their meanings.

459/359. lumber room. Storage room.

461/361. 16 Cheyne Walk. Address of Tudor House, in Chelsea, London, where the historical Rossetti—and others in the PRB—lived.

462/362. *flânerie*. Dawdling.

462/362. Breguet. Abraham Breguet (1747–1823) was a Swiss maker of clocks and watches.

463/362. landau. A horse-drawn carriage with four wheels, facing seats, and a driver in front.

463/362. rug. Blanket.

465/364. *soupirant*. Sighing lover.

467/366. embankment. Cheyne Walk parallels the bank of the Thames River.

THE EBONY TOWER

"The Ebony Tower"

1/1. *"Et par . . . droit."* "And through long and dark forests / By strange and savage places / There occurred many difficult passages / And many perils and many tight spots / Until he found the proper path." The passage is from the story of Gawain by Chrétien de Troyes, circa 1180.

4/4. *voie communale*. Public road.

4/4. *chemin privé*. Private drive.

4/4. *chien méchant*. Beware of dog.

5/5. Tudor. From the period in England from 1485 to 1603, referring to the characteristic style of domestic architecture in England with stucco and half-timbers.

5/5. Ensor. James Ensor (1860–1949) was a Belgian painter whose best-known work is *Entry of Christ into Brussels* (1888), a criticism of contemporary society.

6/5. Marquet. Albert Marquet (1875–1947) was a French painter and fellow student of Matisse, as well as a Fauve, but later in his career he turned to naturalistic landscapes, especially ports and bridges of Paris.

6/5. Derain. André Derain (1880–1954) was a French painter whose later, Fauvist work used intense, exaggerated colors to express a response to the subject. His later work included landscapes.

6/6. wicked . . . afternoons. David implies a comparison between Breasley and the satyr of *Prélude à l'après-midi d'un faune (Prelude to the Afternoon of a Faun)*, by Stéphane Mallarmé about 1865.

7/6. *galabiya.* A Middle Eastern dress, often decorated, resembling a nightgown.

9/8. *comme chez vous.* As if you were at home, that is, "Make yourself comfortable."

9/9. Luce. Maximilien Luce (1858–1941) was a French painter and lithographer, whose style of landscape was influenced first by divisionism and later used broad areas of color.

10/9. Laurencin. Marie Laurencin (1885–1956) was a French painter who exhibited with the early cubists but also painted fairly conventional, sentimentalized young girls.

10/10. Tate. A prominent art museum and gallery in London.

10/10. Smith. Matthew Smith (1879–1959) was an English painter who lived much in France. He worked with brilliant colors in a manner resembling that of Matisse.

11/10. Bacon. Francis Bacon (1909–) is considered by many to be the foremost contemporary British painter, typically depicts distorted or scrambled, human forms.

11/10. Sutherland. Graham Sutherland (1903–1980) was an English painter who did abstract paintings in the 1930s and, later, a tapestry for Coventry Cathedral.

11/11. Goya. Francisco de Goya (1746–1828) etched and painted the "Spanish agony" during the conflict with Napoleon in 1808.

12/11. Fleet Street. A reference to the English press, collectively, from the London street on which many news publishers have their offices.

12/11. van Gogh's ear. A sensational, biographical detail about Vincent van Gogh (1853–90) concerns his attempt to cut off his ear, which has been thought an indication of madness also expressed in his paintings.

12/12. Rabelais. François Rabelais (around 1494–1553) wrote satirical fiction about the giants Gargantua and Pantagruel.

13/12. *enfant terrible.* Bad boy.

13/12. Aubusson *atelier.* Working group at Aubusson, France, which was the ancient center of tapestry art and manufacture. More recently it has become known for floral-patterned carpets.

13/12. Samuel Palmer and Chagall. Samuel Palmer (1805–81) was a painter of English landscapes in a manner sometimes considered visionary. Marc Chagall (1887–1985) was a painter who juxtaposed realistic and fantastic elements, often using Russian folk motifs.

13/12. Nolan. Sidney Nolan (1917–) is an Australian painter, usually of legend and history.

13/12. Celtic. Pertaining to the ancient peoples of Scotland, Ireland, Wales, and Brittany in northern France, where "The Ebony Tower" takes place. They are "British," not the "English," whom Breasley professes to dislike.

13/12. Diaz. Diaz de la Peña (1808–76) was a member of the Barbizon School, a group of landscape and figure painters in mid-nineteenth-century France. He lived in the forest of Fontainebleu, deliberately away from Paris—like Breasley.

13/13. Pisanello . . . Eustace. Antonio Pisanello was an Italian painter whose *Vision of St. Eustace* (1438) depicts a man on horseback in a somewhat flat-looking forest, surrounded by animals, one of which is a stag with a crucified Christ in its antlers.

13/13. Arthurian. Stories pertaining to King Arthur based on a figure from the late fifth century who led a post-Roman rally of the British people against the Anglo-Saxon (English) invaders.

14/13. International Gothic. The term *Gothic* in art history describes the cultures of northern Europe from about 1140 to 1500. The label originated with Renaissance critics who believed that the art that succeeded that of the Romans was inferior and had originated with the Goths.

14/13. *rara avis*. A "rare bird," that is, unusual.

15/14. Op Art. Art that plays with the physiology of seeing, often exploiting the phenomenon of optical illusion.

15/14. Riley. Bridget Riley (1931–) used mathematically disposed lines to create an optically disturbing sense of movement in her paintings.

16/16. Pasmore. Victor Pasmore (1908–) was an English painter of murals, abstractions, and naturalistic landscapes as well as founder of the Euston School of Drawing and Painting.

17/16. Nicholson. Ben Nicholson (1894–1982) was an early abstract painter in England whose *White Relief* used flat, slightly raised white silhouettes on a white background.

17/16. De Stijl. "The Style" refers to a group of artists, including Piet Mondrian of Holland (1872–1944), who founded a journal in 1917 based on principles of equilibrium and harmony.

17/16. Permeke. Constant Permeke (1886–1952) was a Belgian expressionist painter and sculptor best known for his portrayals of sailors and fishermen with their women.

17/16. Bonnard. Pierre Bonnard (1867–1947) was a French painter—often of his mistress—who followed the Impressionists.

17/16. Dufy. Raoul Dufy (1877–1953) was a French painter and decorator, influenced by Matisse, who produced calligraphy-like drawings on bright backgrounds.

17/16. Jawlensky. Alexey Von Jawlensky (1864–1941) was a Russian painter influenced by the French, who did flat, strong-hued portraits.

17/16. Dix. Otto Dix (1891–1969) was a German painter and printmaker who depicted poverty and prostitution.

17/16. Nevinson. Christopher Nevinson (1889–1946) was a painter of geometrically fragmented landscapes, including scenes from World War I.

17/16. Matthew Smith. See note to p. 10.

17/16. Picabia. Francis Picabia (1879–1953) was a French painter of Cuban-Spanish extraction who was influenced by cubism and helped to found the Dadaist magazine.

17/16. Matisse. Henri Matisse (1869–1954) was a leading member of the Fauvists, who were conducting radical experiments with color.

18/17. *oevre*. Collected works.

18/17. Uccello. Paolo Uccello (1397–1475) was an Italian Renaissance painter whose *Night Hunt* (*The Hunt in the Forest*) depicts men on horseback and on foot, with dogs, chasing deer through a dark wood. Fowles refers to the same painting in *The Collector* as *The Hunt* (p. 185/162).

19/18. Lizzie Siddal. Elizabeth Siddal was a shopgirl invited by Dante Gabriel Rossetti to model for paintings by him and others of the Pre-Raphaelite Brotherhood, a bohemian group of revolutionary London artists formed in 1848. She subsequently became Rossetti's mistress and then his wife. She died in 1862.

20/19. golliwog. A child's doll with black skin, wiry hair, and a grotesque face, based on a doll in an English children's book.

22/20. Millais. John Everett Millais (1829–96) was a painter of the Pre-Raphaelite Brotherhood whose 1849 painting *Isabella* depicts a woman who fits this description of The Mouse.

22/21. *arricciato, intonaco, sinopie*. The terms refer to the technique of painting on wet plaster, or fresco painting. *Arricciato* is the rough coating of line and sand plaster to which the final layer of plaster, or *intonaco* is applied. *Sinopie* is a reddish brown chalk for drawing under the fresco.

22/21. gel. Girl, "gal."

24/22. Breughel. Pieter Breughel the Elder, or "Peasant Breughel" (1529–69), painted landscapes and scenes such as *The Wedding Feast*. His sons Jan ("Velvet Breughel") and Pieter the Younger ("Hell Breughel") also were Flemish painters.

24/23. *Kermesse*. The word can mean *fair,* and italics indicate that it is Breasley's working title, which would connect with the narrator's observation at the bottom of p. 26/24.

25/24. John Thomas. Pet name for the gamekeeper's penis in D. H. Lawrence's novel *Lady Chatterley's Lover* (1928).

26/25. *imago*. The painting has become something like an *imago* in psychoanalysis, the idealized concept of a loved one formed in childhood.

26/25. Olympian. Universal, as if viewed from the top of Mount Olympus, home of the Greek gods.

27/25. Braque and Picasso. Georges Braque (1882–1963) and Pablo Picasso (1881–1973) are both considered "cubist" painters. Picasso's "analytical cubism" is more mathematical and logical than Braque's "synthetic cubism," which tends to express feeling more.

28/26. Miró. Joan Miró (1893–1983) was a Spanish painter whose work became highly abstracted rather than representational. A painting from 1915, the year Miró left the Academy Gali to paint on his own, would be extremely early—and valuable.

28/26. Sérusier. Paul Sérusier (1863–1927) was a French painter and art theorist of symbolist painting. He painted Brittany peasants and religious subjects.

28/26. Gauguinesque. In the manner of Paul Gauguin (1848–1903), French painter who exaggerated forms and colors.

28/26. Filiger. Charles Filiger (1863–1928) was a French painter, engraver, and musician who painted landscapes and lived in Brittany for a time.

29/27. *apéritif*. Before-dinner drink.

30/28. Vivaldi. Antonio Vivaldi (1675–1741) was an Italian composer.

31/30. Noilly Prat. A vermouth.

31/30. *armoire*. A cupboard.

32/30. Edwardian. From the reign of Edward VII (1901–10).

32/30. Pre-Raphaelite. David evidently has accepted at face value Breasley's earlier remark about Lizzie Siddal (see note to p. 19/18).

32/30. bit . . . bird. "Bird" is slang for girl, and "bit of" can precede a variety of slang terms for female sexual partners, or parts.

33/31. Dip AD. Diploma in Art and Design.

33/31. jacked in. Quit, folded.

35/33. *"Je . . . aider."* "May I serve [dinner], Miss?" "Yes, Mathilde. I'm coming to help you."

35/33. self-guying. Self-mocking.

36/34. *crudités*. Raw vegetables.

37/34. Chardin. Jean-Baptiste-Siméon Chardin (1699–1779) painted interiors with subdued lighting and mellow colors.

37/34. Tour. Georges de la Tour (1593–1652) depicted calm figures dramatically lit from a single source within the painting.

37/35. Pythagoras. A Greek mathematician (582–500 B.C.) whose name for Breasley, constitutes a form of insult expressing his disapproval of the way mathematics displaces "life" in purely abstract art.

38/35. *Als ich kann*. As I can.

38/36. synthetic cubist nonsense. Breasley prefers Braque's cubism to Picasso's (see note to p. 27/25) but seems to consider all cubism to be nonsense, cold-blooded—a kind of youthful indiscretion that Braque outgrew.

39/36. *quenelles*. Fish balls.

39/36. *beurre blanc*. White butter.

39/36. *pré salé*. Salt marsh.

39/37. *armoire*. A large, movable cupboard.

40/38. Bugger off. Get the hell out.

43/40. mess of scientific pottage. An allusion to the biblical story of Esau, who sold his birthright to Jacob for a mess of pottage (Genesis 25:29–34).

43/40. *Le fairplay*. Breasley sneers at the very "English" concept of "fair play" in games, of what is "cricket"—on or off the playing field.

44/41. *de facto* and *de jure*. In practice and in theory.

44/41. Einstein's famous equation. $E = MC^2$ (energy equals mass times the speed of light squared) is the basic principle of his theory of relativity.

44/41. *In vino* bollocks. Breasley's adaptation of the Latin aphorism *in vino veritas* (drinking brings out the truth) means drinking brings out "balls," or nonsense—roughly, "bullshit." Breasley is in effect challenging Williams, "Do you think I'm too drunk to talk sense?"

45/42. Adolf. Adolf Hitler correctly assumed that the English would accept his annexation of the Czech Sudetenland in 1938.

46/43. *Tachiste. Fautrier*. Artists from the school of Tachism, which included Jean Fautrier (1898–1964), a French painter educated in London whose style involved thick applications of paint.

46/43. Wols. Alfred Otto Wolfgang Schulze-Battman (1913–51) was a German-born photographer who lived in Paris and worked under the name of Wols. He was befriended by Sartre and became known posthumously as an original master of abstract expression, who influenced the Tachistes.

46/43. Yank . . . Jackson Bollock. Jackson Pollock (1912–56) was an American painter who founded the movement called Abstract Expressionism. Breasley scornfully and vulgarly mispronounces Pollack's name (as he has Picasso's on p. 27/25 as "pick-arsehole") because the word *bollocks*, slang for *testicles*, can also mean in England roughly what Americans mean by *bullshit*.

47/44. *Qu' est-ce . . . ici*. What's he doing here?

50/47. jolly. Very.

51/47. having it off. Having an affair.

51/48. pissed. Drunk.

51/48. *déjeuner sur l'herbe*. Luncheon on the grass.

51/48. dekko. Look.

52/49. Rochester. John Wilmot, Second Earl of Rochester (1647–1680) was an English poet and libertine who went to Paris in exile with the future Charles II during the Puritan interregnum. The couplet attributed to him may be by Fowles, however.

54/51. had read . . . up. Had studied.

54/51. *lais*. Lays. A lay is a literary narrative form sometimes waggishly defined as "a short romance." The second story in *The Ebony Tower*, "Eliduc" by Marie de France, is a *lai*.

54/51. Chrétien. Chrétien de Troyes (1170–90) wrote Arthurian romances in Old French, including *Yvain* (see note to p. 1/1). Tristan, Merlin, and Lancelot are figures from Arthurian legend.

55/51. Marie. Marie de France (1160–90) wrote twelve Celtic *lais*, including "Eliduc," probably while living at the Norman court in England. Fowles discusses her life and art on pp. 117–22/110–14.

55/51. Jung. Carl Gustav Jung (1875–1961) developed a theory of psychoanalysis that included the concept of the archetype, images common to human nature that help to constitute the unconscious.

55/51. Coward. Noël Coward (1899–1973) wrote popular comedies about sophisticated middle-class characters.

55/52. wellingtons. Rubber slip-on boots commonly worn in the country.

55/52. Royal Academician. A fellow of the Royal Academy, the English art "establishment."

56/52. *étang*. Pond.

56/53. knickers. Women's underpants.

57/53. codding. Teasing.

59/55. Gauguin. A reference to Gauguin's paintings of women on Tahiti (see note to p. 28/26).

59/55. Manet. Édouard Manet (1832–83) was a French Impressionist painter. David is thinking about Manet's *Le Déjeuner sur l'herbe* (*Luncheon on the Grass*, 1863), which depicts a nude woman with two fully clothed men and another woman, all enjoying a picnic on the grass in a wood. Breasley has used the title phrase to describe their outing on p. 51/48.

59/56. Vichy. Sparkling water, bottled at Vichy.

61/57. Quattrocento. Resembling a figure in fifteenth-century Italian art.

61/57–58. a painting . . . sailor. The painting would be *The Boyhood of Raleigh*, by Millais (see note to p. 22/20).

61/58. *The Magus*. The Freak is reading Fowles's second novel, whose original version contained an epigraph from Arthur Edward Waite's *The Key to the Tarot* and prompted many letters from "freakish" readers interested in the occult. Fowles found the letters annoying and dropped the epigraph from *The Magus: A Revised Version;* David's speculation is a joke at such readers' expense.

65/61. ATD. Art Teacher's Diploma (see note to p. 33/31).

66/62. blokes. Guys.

67/63. Lautrec . . . Guilbert. Henri Toulouse-Lautrec (1864–1901) was a French post-Impressionist painter and lithographer whose 1892 poster of Yvette Guilbert is called *Le Divan Japonais,* after a Paris cabaret that attracted many literary patrons.

68/63. *Death in Venice*. The film is directed by Luchino Visconti (1971), based on the novel by Thomas Mann (1912).

68/64. flics. Cops.

68/64. Douglas . . . Pickford. Douglas Fairbanks Senior and Mary Pickford were stars of silent films even before the 1920s.

69/64. flapper. Independent-minded female type in the 1920s.

69/64. camiknickers. A one-piece undergarment with legs and a bodice, for females.

69/65. bloody. An obscene intensifier, used something like "fuckin' " in America.

70/65. *News of the World*. One of the London daily tabloid newspapers whose "news" tends to be sensational.

71/66. Groucho. The wriggling eyebrows of American comedian Groucho Marx often were accompanied by a leer and a sexually suggestive remark.

72/67. guyed . . . Venus. Mockingly imitated a modest love-goddess.

76/71. *tête-à-tête*. Private, one-to-one conversation.

76/71. Russell. Bertrand Russell (1872–1970) was a pacifist as well as a philosopher.

76/71. white feather. In World War I, a woman might present a white feather to a male who declined to volunteer as a sign of his cowardice.

77/72. Salt . . . game. To try to put salt on a sparrow's tail, like trying to produce art to please an audience instead of oneself, is a game played only by "mugs," that is, by fools.

77/72. fiddle. Deception, cheating.

77/72. *St. George and the Princess*. This fresco by Pisanello in the Museo Civico in Verona shows two men hanging from gibbets in the upper left background (see note to p. 13/13).

77/72. Fox/Foxe. The *Book of Martyrs* is the common short title of a long work of biography and history of Christians who died for their faith, written by John Foxe (1516–87), and first published in 1563. The martyrs include some who were hanged and then burned by the Inquisition. Some early editions contain woodcuts, a few of which (for example, *The Martyrdome of George Wisehart*) show a hanged man. David Copperfield was likewise fascinated as a child by an illustrated edition of Foxe (Charles Dickens, *David Copperfield*, Chapter 10).

78/73. Pickbum. A reference to "pick-arsehole" on p. 27/25, a similar, derogatory reference to Picasso.

78/73. *Fumisterie*. Practical joke.

78/73. cod. Tease.

78/73. *Guernica*. Picasso's work for the Spanish Pavilion at the Paris International Exposition of 1937. A protest against the Fascist bombing of the village of Guernica, the work generated controversy by calling attention to the atrocity.

78/73. *Si jeunesse savait.* . . . If youth knew [what old age knows].

78/73. poor sods. Short for sodomites, the phrase is equivalent to "poor bastards."

79/74. double meaning. She is his muse as well as his sex partner, enabling him to be vitally creative in two ways.

80/74. *ménage à trois.* Living arrangement among three persons, two of whom share a sex partner.

80/74. getting and spending. A phrase from an 1807 sonnet by William Wordsworth that begins, "The world is too much with us; late and soon, / Getting and spending, we lay waste our powers." David echoes its tone of lament.

81/75. Robin Hood. Medieval outlaw who hid in Sherwood Forest according to legend. Fowles suggests that Robin Hood's furtive behavior is characteristically English, in "On Being English But Not British" and *Daniel Martin* (pp. 270–76/287–90).

81/76. *Les Demoiselles d'Avignon.* This 1907 painting by Picasso served to launch the cubist movement and a revolution in art, which is to Breasley a different "planet" from the words of poster paints in art classes.

83/77. *vacances.* Vacations.

83/78. twit. Jerk.

85/79. RCA. Royal College of Art.

85/79. *voulu.* Deliberate.

85/79. Chopin. Frédéric Chopin (1810–49) is considered a "classical" composer and pianist.

85/79–80. John. Gwen John (1876–1939) was a Welch portrait painter who used muted colors, especially pinks and blues, to depict women.

87/81. Georgian. Built between 1714 and 1830.

87/81. posh. High-status.

89/83. Get . . . me. Diana is applying to her own situation the words of Jesus as he rejects the temptation of Satan (Matthew 4:10)

94/88. Rembrandt. Rembrandt van Rijn (1606–69) is here being invoked as the greatest of the "Old Masters."

95/89. Dutch uncle . . . no clothes. The reproving critic suddenly is revealed to be the dupe, with a reminder of the erotic subtext of the conversation in the phrase from Hans Christian Andersen's tale "The Emperor with No Clothes."

96/89. Maud. The main character in Tennyson's 1855 poem *Maud* has a garden of roses and lilies, where her lover sometimes waits for her.

96/89. black wall of the forest. This phrase also could be used to describe Uccello's *Night Hunt* (see note to p. 18/17).

98/91. Fairy tales. In the tale of the sleeping beauty, a prince "turns up" (a phrase used on p. 96/90) and awakens her to a new situation.

99/92. Tristan and Yseult. Man and woman in Celtic legend who are torn between love and duty to King Marc, her husband and his lord. The king discovers them asleep together in a cave but is not sure that his wife has been unfaithful because there is a sword between them.

99/92. Pisanello masterpiece. *St. George and the Princess* (see note to p. 77/72) shows the princess and St. George and his horse, but not the dragon.

103/95. Monsewer. Scatalogical mispronunciation of *Monsieur*.

105/98. dishy. Sexy.

105/98. Parthian shot. A parting remark, usually meant to wound (like the arrows of retreating Parthians), but here only to amuse.

106/99. *route nationale*. French version of an American interstate highway.

109/102. Constable . . . School. John Constable (1776–1837) was an English Romantic landscapist and J. M. W. Turner (1775–1851), a revolutionary in the use of color. The Norwich School was an English regional school of landscape painting from 1803 to 1834, which favored Norfolk scenes done in watercolor.

111/103. *art pompier*. Conventional art.

111/103. *il . . . racine*. You must cut the root off (translated on p. 78/73).

111/103. *Lebensraum*. Living space, a word used by Hitler to justify expansion.

"Eliduc"

115/107. *De . . . dirai*. The *lai* of "Eliduc" begins thus in the original Old French, translated by Fowles on p. 123/115.

117/109. *récit* and *discours*. Narration and discourse.

117/109. dead woman. As will become evident, Fowles refers to Marie de France.

122/114. Watergate. Common name for the political scandal that led Richard Nixon to resign from the presidency in 1974.

126/118. hopping. The British phrase "on the hop" means "off balance," or "off stride."

130/122. cheeky. Sassy.

"Poor Koko"

143/135. "*Byth . . . dyr.*" Translated by Fowles at the end of the story, p. 187/176.

145/137. BBC. British Broadcasting Corporation.

145/137. Pangloss. In Voltaire's *Candide* (1759), Pangloss is a naive tutor who instructs Candide that everything is for the best.

146/138. flat. Apartment.

147/139. swot. A person who studies very hard.

147/139. Peacock. Thomas Love Peacock (1785–1866) wrote novels that Fowles has acknowledged influence him.

148/140. Hardy. Thomas Hardy (1840–1928) wrote novels and poetry and, like Maurice and Jane, lived in Dorset.

149/140. Sabine farm. Country retreat of Horace (65–8 B.C.), located outside Rome.

149/141. *métier*. Profession.

152/143. Pope, Kant and Voltaire. Writers who were small of stature. Pope was especially unprepossessing—constitutionally weak, hunchbacked, and only about 4 feet 6 inches tall.

152/144. wicket gate. An small gate for foot passengers in the enclosure to a field.

153/145. torch. Flashlight.

158/149. Marx. Karl Marx (1818–83) urged the laboring class to unite against the rich.

159/150. Lamerie. Paul de Lamerie (1688–1751) was a silversmith who produced ornate, rococo pieces.

159/150. Cotman. John Sell Cotman (1782–1842) was a professor of drawing at King's College in London and a painter of large watercolors.

159/150. Scotus. John Duns Scotus (1265–1308) was a Scottish theologian who critiqued the philosophy of Thomas Aquinas.

160/151. Alice . . . sequiturs. In Lewis Carroll's *Alice's Adventures in Wonderland* (1865), Alice hears many non sequiturs, or statements that do not follow logically from what has preceded.

160/151. *I am what I am.* "I am who am" is the usual translation of the Hebrew words beginning with the letters JHVH, otherwise Jehovah.

162/153. Conrad. Joseph Conrad (1857–1924) was a writer of novels in English, his third language, including *Heart of Darkness*. The situation in "Poor Koko" resembles that in Conrad's "The Secret Sharer," in which a ship captain confronts a criminal in his cabin.

163/153. *andante . . . prestissimo.* Moderately slow and even when all should have been as rapid as possible.

163/154. Tories. Members of the Conservative Party.

163/154. Blokes. Ordinary guys.

164/154. pseudo-Marcusian. Wanting to sound like Herbert Marcuse (1898–1979), German neo-Marxist philosopher who influenced the New Left in the 1960s.

164/154. cuppa. Cup of tea.

164/155. Raffles. A gentleman burglar in novels by E. W. Hornung (1866–1921).

165/155. A-levels . . . Redbrick. Advanced-level examinations in elective courses after high school are necessary for admission to a university—even those known as redbrick universities, whose degrees are less prestigious than those of Oxford or Cambridge.

165/155. Maoist. A commune modeled on the principles and practices of Mao Tse-tung (1893–1976), Chinese Communist and revolutionary.

166/156. Labour councillor. A member of her London borough council and a member of the Labour Party, on the political left.

166/156. David. Elizabeth David writes English cookbooks.

166/156. *épater la famille.* Shocking the family.

166/156. besotted—or bepotted. *Besotted* means drunk; *bepotted* is a playful coinage meaning "drunk" on "pot," that is, on *cannabis.*

166/156. Little Red Book. A collection of sayings by Chairman Mao Tse-tung, sometimes carried as a sign of leftist sympathy in the 1960s.

167/157. fly. Sharp, crafty.

169/159. daft gits. Crazy bastards.

172/162. tara. So long.

172/162. nick. Shape.

172/162. electric fire. Space heater.

178/168. four had been reached. They added two plus two.

179/169. torn . . . womb. The narrator compares his manuscript to a fetus, still being created. Macduff is similarly said to have been "from his mother's womb / Untimely ripp'd" in *Macbeth* (Act 5, Scene 8).

180/169. Black Power. A movement among black people in the late 1960s and early 1970s to achieve equal status with whites, if necessary by violence.

183/172. lorry. Truck.

183/172. association football. Soccer.

184/174. *parole . . . langue.* Individual instances of speech are inevitably part of a system of language, so the housebreaker may fear that system because he does not feel that his statements exert any power within it, that they are rhetorically meaningless.

185/174. *ab initio.* From the outset.

186/175. closed shop. A workplace that employs only union members.

186/175. Pericles. Athenian statesman and gifted orator during the fifth century B.C.

"The Enigma"

189/177. Tao Te Ching. A book by Chinese philosopher Lao Tzu whose title is sometimes translated *The Classic of the Way and Its Virtue.* The book is a statement of Taoist philosophy, written either in the fourth or the sixth century B.C.

192/180. "surgery." Usually a medical clinic, here a political "clinic" in which he consults with his constituents.

192/180. down. In England, "down" is always away from London, in this case northward toward East Anglia.

194/182. MP. Member of Parliament.

195/183. Black September. A Palestinian political organization that uses violent means to promote its agenda.

195/183. IRA. Irish Republican Army, a political organization that uses violent means to promote independence for Northern Ireland.

200/188. first. The highest grade possible in a British university, very difficult to obtain.

200/188. M.C. Military Cross.

201/188. Tory party. Another name for the Conservative Party.

202/189. *Marie Celeste.* The *Mary Celeste* was an American brigantine found adrift near the Azores in 1872, abandoned by its crew for reasons never subsequently explained with certainty. A story by Arthur Conan Doyle in 1884 led to the popular re-spelling of *Mary* as *Marie.*

202/189. New Scotland Yard. A branch of government comparable to the U.S. Federal Bureau of Investigation.

203/190. Machiavellian. In the manner of Niccolò Macchiavelli (1469–1527), commonly (if not accurately) reputed to have advocated ruthless pursuit of a political end by whatever means likely to achieve it.

205/192. having it off. Having an affair.

205/192. C of E. Church of England.

205/192. FO. Foreign Office.

205/192. two words. Probably "bugger all," which means, "not a damned thing."

206/193. buccaneer . . . side. To arrange for personal profit.

206/193. Lonrho affair. Lonrho, Limited, is a British-owned international conglomerate whose directors were revealed in May of 1973 to be receiving payments into tax-sheltered accounts in the Cayman Islands.

209/195. the Derby and the Grand National. Horse races.

210/196. Powellite. Enoch Powell is a right-wing member of Parliament. In the late 1960s he spoke out against immigration by people of color.

211/197. bunk. To "light out."

212/198. *Cherchez la femme.* Look for a woman, expect one to be involved.

213/199. Heath. Edward Heath was a Conservative Party prime minister from 1970 to 1974.

213/199. Wilson. Harold Wilson was a Labour Party prime minister from 1964 to 1970.

217/203. Oedipus complex. A phrase from psychoanalysis, having to do with father-son conflict during early childhood.

218/203. *De mortuis.* First two words of a Latin proverb, "Of the dead, say nothing unless it is good."

219/205. Downing Street. Residence of the prime minister.

225/210. bit of bird. Sex partner.

226/211. lezzies. Lesbians, that is, homosexual females.

228/213. *en famille.* Among family.

241/225. Waugh. Evelyn Waugh (1903–66) wrote *Brideshead Revisited* and various other novels depicting and satirizing the upper class.

242/226. Churchill. Winston Churchill, a Conservative Party prime minister, was defeated by Labour Party candidate Clement Atlee in the 1945 election.

244/228. Christie. Agatha Christie (1890–1976) was the author of numerous detective novels and of *The Mousetrap*, London's longest-running play.

"The Cloud"

249/233. "O . . . difference." Spoken by Ophelia shortly before her suicide in Shakespeare's *Hamlet* (Act 4, Scene 5).

251/235. *trouvaille.* Find.

251/235. Martini. A brand of Italian vermouth.

251/235. Courbet. Gustave Courbet (1819–77) was a French "Realist" painter of scenes in the provinces.

252/236. sods. Shortening of *sodomites,* roughly equivalent to *bastards.*

253/237. fifty new pence. After the English decimalized their monetary system in 1969, a new penny was worth 1/100 of a pound.

255/238. "Fancy?" "Do you find her sexually attractive?"

255/239. Laclos. Pierre Choderlos de Laclos (1741–1803) was a French novelist who wrote *Les Liaisons Dangereuses (Dangerous Liaisons).*

256/239. "Cheeky bugger." Roughly, "You naughty boy."

261/244. cow. Derisive British slang for a female.

262/245. *distingué.* Distinguished.

262/245. Juno. Wife of Jupiter in Roman mythology.

262/246. Seurat. Georges Seurat (1859–91) was a French painter whose use of small dots of paint to make up a whole image is analogous to atoms making up substances.

263/246. For . . . joy. A line sung by Ophelia during the "madness" that precedes her death in *Hamlet* (Act 4, Scene 5).

263/246. Regency. From the period of English history from 1811 to 1820.

264/247. *"Sieures . . . merci."* "Gentlemen, ladies." "Hello," says Paul. Then, "Good fishing." "Thanks."

264/247. *"Ça ira . . . pendra."* "So it will be—the aristocrats will be hanged." The words come from a popular song of the French Revolution.

264/247. "Hurry up . . . Goonight." From T. S. Eliot's *The Waste Land* (1922; Part 2, lines 166–71).

265/248. *charcuterie.* Cold cuts.

265/248. *sur lie.* Inferior.

267/249. *Moue.* Pout.

267/249. *rilettes.* Pork pâté.

269/252. Micawber. Mr. Micawber utters this sentiment in Charles Dickens's *David Copperfield* (1849–50).

271/253. "brute . . . calf." Line spoken by Hamlet as he mocks Polonius in *Hamlet* (Act 3, scene 2).

271/254. *milord.* Term of respect used on English gentlemen touring the Continent in the eighteenth century.

271/254. *ça va de soi.* By the same token.

273/255. *le sport.* Hunting and fishing.

274/256. *patisserie.* Pastries.

275/257. rhubarb. Meaningless debate.

275/257. afters. Dessert.

276/258. *soi-disant.* So-called.

277/259. Barthes. Roland Barthes (1915–80) was a French semiotician. The book of essays Fowles refers to is his *Mythologies* (1957), in which "The Blue Guide" can be found among other short essays on French culture and a theoretical afterword (translated by Annette Lavers [New York: Noonday Press, 1972]).

277/259. Petrarch. Francesco Petrarch (1304–74) was an Italian poet.

278/260. How . . . fallen. A biblical reference to the death of Saul (2 Samuel 1:25).

279/261. Kraut. Derisive label for a German, here evidently an elliptical reference to deconstructionist critic Paul de Man, whose French-looking name belies his German origins, and whose methods are approximated in Catherine's description.

289/270. rude. Indecent.

292/272. a story they read. Probably Jane Austen's *Emma* (1816), whose protagonist gets into difficulty when she tries to construct conventional endings for other people's lives.

294/274. *The Scholar Gipsy.* An 1853 poem by Matthew Arnold about an Oxford scholar who wanders through the countryside. Lines 82–83 and 211–15 are quoted below (pp. 275–76).

295/275. Hamlet. Bel would not want to be cast as Hamlet because he insists on complicating his situation until he is unable to act. His girlfriend, Ophelia, would be a more attractive role, Bel thinks, and then recalls an actual casting of a woman as Hamlet at Somerville College. Instead of suggesting the French actress Sarah Bernhardt, the casting decision reminded her of a pantomime, an English popular dramatic form in which the male lead is always played by a woman dressed as a man and the female lead by a man dressed as a woman.

297/277. Apollo. Greek god of light, music, poetry, healing, and masculine beauty.

298/278. *ergo*. Therefore.

298/278. death of fiction. Barthes (see note to p. 277/259) wrote an essay titled "The Death of the Author" in 1968 (republished in *Image-Music-Text* in 1977).

298/278. *Il . . . vivre*. In order to live, it is necessary to philosophize.

DANIEL MARTIN

n.p. [epigraph]. Antonio Gramsci (1891–1937) was a cultural theorist who founded the Italian Communist Party. His *Prison Notebooks* were written during the decade between his arrest by Fascists and his death while still in prison.

1/1. Seferis. George Seferis (1900–71) was Greek ambassador to England and a poet who won the Nobel prize for literature in 1963.

6/5. Caught-ey on the hop again. Caught them unprepared (in midstride) again. Rendered as West Country dialect, as is much of the dialogue in this chapter.

8/7. the last piece. This incident resembles a scene in Thomas Hardy's *Tess of the d'Urbervilles* (1891) in which terriers wait for rats to run from the bottom of a wheat-rick as it is dismantled for threshing (Chapter 48).

8/7. Argus-eyed. All-seeing, like Argus, in Greek legend a giant with eyes all over his body, whom Hera sets to watch Io but Zeus kills.

13/11. Biedermeier. A term used to describe German and Austrian art from 1815–1848, which characteristically was sober, realistic, and utilitarian.

14/13. shored fragments . . . cap you. When Dan alludes to one of the concluding lines of T. S. Eliot's *The Waste Land*, "These fragments I have shored against my ruins," Jenny responds as if they are "capping verses," a competition in which two persons take turns trying to come up with the line that follows whatever line the first one has quoted. "Why then Ile fit you. Hieronymo's mad againe" is the next line of *The Waste Land* (Part 5, lines 431–32). Jenny reminds Dan that she is good at this game because she is an actress, even if she also is a "cow"—British derogatory slang for a female.

15/14. *Camelot*. The 1967 movie focuses on the betrayal of King Arthur by Queen Guinevere and Sir Lancelot.

16/15. Robbins. Harold Robbins wrote notoriously "trashy" novels, such as *The Carpetbaggers* (1961).

16/15. Aristotle. Greek philosopher in the fourth century B.C. who wrote *Poetics*, a theory of tragedy along the line of what Dan is mentally trying to do with film.

20/19. punt. A gondola-like boat, popular to rent for picnics along the rivers and canals of Oxford or Cambridge.

20/19. reading. Studying, "majoring in."

20/19. ETC. Perhaps Exeter (College) Theatre Company.

20/19. *Greats.* A course of university study in philosophy, history, and literature in the classical tradition and in the classical languages. This is the track that students with political ambitions often elect.

20/19. Hayworth. Rita Hayworth was an American movie actress and "pin-up girl" during World War II. A later recollection by Dan (p. 54/55) indicates that Jane's role in this revue sketch was to mimic a Rita Hayworth character.

21/19. Aspasia. Athenian courtesan and mistress of Pericles in fifth-century Greece.

21/19. *hetairai.* Concubines in ancient Greece.

21/20. revising. Preparing for exams.

21/20. plough . . . first. "Plough" is slang for fail; a "first" is the highest grade possible.

22/20. Thucydides. Ancient Greek historian (460–395 B.C.) who wrote a history of the Peloponnesian War.

22/22. plebby. Plebian, working-class.

23/22. swotting. Studying hard, "cramming."

23/22. snog. Love-play, "necking" session.

25/25. Roger. Military slang term of affirmation.

26/25. silage. Food, lunch.

26/25. champers. Champagne.

26/26. Sir Andrew Ague-prick. A demeaning reference to Andrew by means of the name of a gentleman-coward, Sir Andrew Aguecheek, in Shakespeare's *Twelfth Night* (circa 1601).

28/27. *"Fais ce que voudras."* "Do what thou wilt," an idea in François Rabelais's *Gargantua* (1532; Chapter 57)

28/27. Abbaie de Thélème. Abbey of Thelema, an ideal place where only the best people live, in *Gargantua* (Book 1, Chapters 52–58).

28/27. Carfax. A medieval tower located in central Oxford.

29/28. *vieux jeu.* Old-fashioned.

29/29. Oedipus complex. Jane suggests that Dan is rejecting the church in a way that is analogous to a male child's rejecting of the father, part of a complex of attitudes Freud named after Oedipus, the Greek king who inadvertently kills his father and marries his mother.

31/31. Hemingway . . . *Volcano.* The characters in fiction by Ernest Hemingway (1899–1961) often are limited in some way, and the alcoholic ex-British consul in Malcolm Lowry's *Under the Volcano* (1947) commits suicide.

33/33. bird. Girl.

34/34. *Citizen Kane.* Film directed by Orson Welles in 1941 in which Rosebud, the sled of Charles Foster Kane that he associates with his childhood, at his death becomes the focus of an attempt to understand his unhappy life.

34/34. Guying. Making fun of.

34/34. Dettol. Scotches, which Dan refers to as Dettols for their similarity in taste to an over-the-counter mouthwash (and antiseptic).

38/38. Brando. Marlon Brando, American actor, became famous by communicating nonverbally as he played inarticulate characters in films such as *Streetcar Named Desire* (1951) and *On the Waterfront* (1954).

38/38. *shtik.* A routine.

38/39. Kitchener. Horatio Herbert Kitchener (1850–1916), English statesman and field marshal, raised an army of soldier-volunteers in 1914. He is the topic of Dan's current project.

45/46. pack it in. Stop, "knock it off."

51/52. bed-sitter. Rented living accommodation with a bedroom and a "sitting-room," like a one-bedroom apartment.

51/52. Art Nouveau. A decorative style of the late nineteenth and early twentieth centuries commonly using curvilinear, flower-and vine motifs, revived in the late 1960s, especially in poster art.

51/52. Anouilh. French playwright Jean Anouilh (1910–   ) wrote a modern version of Sophocles' *Antigone* in 1944. Anouilh's nationality makes Dan's interest "eclectic."

52/52–53. Tolkien . . . *Beowulf.* An Anglo-Saxon epic poem written down in eighth-century England and studied by undergraduates in the original language, perhaps under J.R.R. Tolkien (1892–1973), who was a distinguished scholar of old English at Oxford University as well as author of *The Lord of the Rings* (1954–55).

52/53. OUDS. Oxford Union Dramatic Society.

52/53. La Bruyère. Jean de La Bruyère (1645–96), in *Characters* (1688), drew faces thought to reveal the faults of the person depicted.

53/54. Nadya Constantinovna. Nadya Constantinovna Krupskaya (1869–1939) was the name of Lenin's widow, after whom the tenants have affectionately nicknamed their leftist landlady.

54/55. Webster. John Webster (1578–1632) was an English playwright, one of whose works is *The White Devil,* a (fictional) film adaptation of which is mentioned earlier on the page (see also the note to p. 20/19). "Webster's immortal line" is not the phrase "strange geometric hinges," but rather a pair of lines from *The White Devil* that Fowles does not provide: "But keep the wolf far thence: that's foe to men, / for with his nails he'll dig them up again" (Act 5, Scene 4). The "line" is "immortal" (in part) because T. S. Eliot uses it in *The Waste Land* (Part 1), a poem cited frequently in *Daniel Martin*. Webster's lines apply to Dan's past, which is being "dug up" by the phone call that arrived in the second chapter, which is said to have opened "a door in a wall" (16, 18), as if on "strange geometric hinges."

54/55. Wykehamist. William of Wykeham (1324–1404) was a pluralist in matters of religion, as well as founder of New College, Oxford.

57/58. Marcel. Gabriel Marcel (1889–1973) was a French Catholic existentialist who advocated exploring experience, not categorizing it.

59/60. Trout . . . Rosamund's Bower. The Trout is a popular pub on the Thames River at Wolvercote, just outside Oxford. Rosamund's (or Rosamond's) Bower is the legendary clandestine meeting place of King Henry II and his mistress, Rosamund Clifford, the "fair Rosamund." The Queen discovered Rosamund in her bower at the center of a labyrinth and stabbed her to death. Only Rosamund's Well remains on what is now the Duke of Marlborough's estate of Blenheim. The site is nine miles northwest of The Trout; Fowles may have relocated it near the pub to exploit its romantic associations or because of Dan's parallel situation, that of a male attached to one woman but attracted to another.

60/61. *acte gratuit*. Gratuitous act, an important concept in André Gide's *The Vatican Caves* (1914), in which the character Lafcadio kills a fellow passenger by pushing him off a train, for no reason.

61/62. Delius. Frederick Delius (1862–1934) was an English composer of operas, including *A Village Romeo and Juliet* (1900–01).

61/62. like a medieval bride. Fowles may have in mind Jan van Eyck's painting *Giovanni Arnolfini and His Bride* (1434).

62/63. Isherwood's camera. Christopher Isherwood (1904–   ) is an English novelist whose *Goodbye to Berlin* (1939) was later dramatized as *I Am a Camera* and *Cabaret*.

62/63. *prima facie*. On the face of it.

62/63. *métier*. Profession, in Dan's case, screenwriter.

63/64. "Method." A reference to "method acting," in which the actor tries to identify with his or her character and then to behave as the character would.

64/65. Shrimptons and Twiggies. Jean Shrimpton and Twiggy were top fashion models and cover girls during the latter half of the 1960s.

66/67. *shiksa*. A non-Jewish female.

70/71. Druce. George Claridge Druce (1850–1932) was a botanist who published floras of Oxfordshire and helped to found the Ashmolean Natural History Society.

70/72. Descartes. René Descartes (1596–1650) was a French philosopher.

71/73. Cinderella. Character in a fairy tale, who analogously, is "exploited" by her two stepsisters. Fowles has published an adaptation of the Perrault version.

72/74. Utopian. *Utopia* is Latin for "nowhere" and the title of Sir Thomas More's book about an ideal republic.

74/76. buffer. Fogey.

77/79. Latimer. Hugh Latimer (about 1470–1555) was a Protestant theologian who was martyred in Oxford, along with Cranmer and Ridley, during the reign of Catholic Queen Mary. His famous sermon "Of the Plough" was delivered in 1548.

77/79. Arian heresy. The belief that Christ the Son and God the Father are not consubstantial, taught by Arius (died 336).

78/80. Platonic. From Plato, the Greek philosopher who regarded emotions to be dangerous because they obscure the ideal.

78/80. *de facto*. For practical purposes.

80/83. Coué-like. In the manner of Émile Coué, who believed in chanting self-promotional statements to build confidence, best known of which is "Every day, in every way, I am getting better and better."

81/83. Henty . . . Beano. G. A. Henty (1832–1902) wrote didactic stories for boys. Biggles is an RAF pilot whose adventures are related in novels by W. E. Johns. *Beano* is a comic strip magazine whose fall annual is a popular Christmas gift.

81/83. Bewick. Thomas Bewick (1753–1828) was an English illustrator of books, often of natural history.

81/84. Gay. John Gay (1685–1732) wrote his popular *Fables* in 1727, much earlier than Bewick's illustrations.

82/84. Clare's . . . Thoreau's. John Clare (1793–1864) wrote poems about nature; Samuel Palmer (1805–81) painted landscapes; Henry David Thoreau (1817–62) wrote *Walden*. All of them looked at their natural surroundings in original, un-academic ways.

82/84. Herrick. Robert Herrick (1591–1674) was ordained in 1623, took up duties in south Devon at Dean Priory in 1630, and published *Hesperides* in 1647, after having returned to London. His actual grave is unmarked.

82/85. Jacobean . . . *Ballads*. From the period of 1603 to 1625 in England, when James VI of Scotland succeeded Elizabeth I as ruler of England. *The Shirburn Ballads* were found in an early seventeenth-century manuscript at Sherburn Castle, Oxfordshire.

84/87. Butler. Samuel Butler (1613–80) wrote *Hudibras*, a poem that treats serious subjects—including religion—in a satirical manner.

85/88. Cumaean . . . Eclogue. Virgil's *Fourth Eclogue* (40 B.C.) containing a prophecy by the seer of Cumae about a coming golden age, ruled by a child, often is interpreted to be a classical prediction of the birth of Jesus.

86/89. Flaubert . . . *Simple*. Gustave Flaubert (1821–80) published the long story *A Simple Heart* in 1877.

88/91. oick. An uncultured person of low social standing.

89/92. gamp. A large umbrella.

89/92. council-houses. Public housing.

89/93. *Rosebud.* Charles Foster Kane's sled (see note to p. 34/34).

90/94. Johnson. Dr. Samuel Johnson single-handedly wrote the first *Dictionary of the English Language* from 1746 to 1755. He defined *awful* as "That which strikes with awe, or fills with reverence."

91/94. *id.* Latin word for *it*, adopted by Freud to represent verbally the psychological forces of the unconscious.

91/95. Candide and Cunégonde. The naive lovers in Voltaire's *Candide.*

97/102. *Isis.* Literary magazine at Oxford University.

98/103. blower. Telephone.

100/104. Tynan. Kenneth Tynan (1927–80) was a British drama critic, one year younger than Fowles, who wrote for *The Observer* and helped to promote plays about the working class.

101/106. intimations of mortality. A verbal play on the title of an ode by William Wordsworth, "Intimations of Immortality from Recollections of Early Childhood" (1807).

101/106. fish-and-chip wrapping. English fish and chips (French fries) often are wrapped in newspaper when sold to be taken out.

101/106. Frost. David Frost specializes in television interviews.

102/107. Schmucks. Fools.

104/109. gone . . . sense. The phrase "gone down" can mean to have graduated from university or to have gone home for vacation.

105/110. "If it were done . . . life to come." Jane evidently expects Dan to be able to complete the first sentence of the soliloquy from Shakespeare's *Macbeth* (1606), "then 'twere well / It were done quickly"; he evidently can do so and follows her drift, even though he does not remember the way the speech ends (Act 1, Scene 7).

109/114. Lawrence. D. H. Lawrence wrote *Sea and Sardinia* in 1921.

111/117. fag. To act as another student's personal servant.

112/118. Mitfordian. Nancy Mitford (1904–73) wrote novels about an upper-class family and an essay on the use of university vocabulary among English aristocrats.

113/119. fancy. To find sexually attractive.

113/119. M4. The motorway, or highway, that connects Heathrow Airport to London or to the West.

113/119. Old Etonian. An alumnus of Eton College.

117/123. *façons de vivre.* Ways of life.

117/124. Pound. Ezra Pound (1885–1972) was an American poet who founded the Imagist school of poetry. Pound's "philosophy" is associated with Fascism.

118/124. Regency rake. A sexual libertine during the period 1817–20, before George IV officially assumed the throne.

118/124. Lumpkin. Tony Lumpkin, a character in Oliver Goldsmith's *She Stoops to Conquer* (1773), is the idle, mischievous stepson of Lord Hardcastle.

123/130. Pagliacci. Italian for *clowns*, the adjective here refers to the character of Canio in Leoncavallo's opera *Pagliacci*, who must perform as a clown with a happy face on the outside while crying on the inside because he is upset over having just learned that his wife has been unfaithful. Dan imagines that Caro would find charming such "depth" in Barney's public-private personas.

125/132. Cut. A term used in film directing to indicate the end of a "take" of a shot.

127/134. Portobello Road. A street in London with numerous shops and sidewalk "stalls."

131/138. RAC. Royal Automobile Club, similar to the AAA in the United States.

133/140. Ibsen. Henrik Ibsen (1828–1906) wrote *Ghosts*, a play that Dan "copies" in the sense that Ibsen's play also is about a metaphorical "father's ghost" being visited on his son, as syphilis.

134/141. SW3. Southwest, inner London—specifically, Chelsea. The full postal code, used all over England, would consist of six alphanumerical signs.

135/142. Pinewood. A film studio in London.

136/143. Tartuffe. A hypocritical, scheming character in Molière's play *Tartuffe* (1664).

136/144. *passé*. Declining.

137/144. WAAF. Women's Army Air Forces, in World War II.

137/144. Circe . . . Delilah. Circe is a witch who tries to seduce Ulysses (or Odysseus) after she fails to turn him into a pig, in Homer's *The Odyssey* (Book 10). In the Old Testament, Delilah cuts off Samson's hair for political purposes (Judges 16).

139/147. Brecht. Bertolt Brecht (1898–1956) was a German playwright whose *Galileo* Dan may have been using as a model play about a trial.

141/149. *au pair*. A live-in helper from a foreign country, usually a young girl who wants to visit and improve her English.

142/150. *demi-monde*. Underworld.

147/155. dreaming spires. A now-conventional phrase describing the skyline of Oxford, from Matthew Arnold's *Thyrsis* (1866).

148/156. *belle laide*. A striking, though not pretty girl.

148/157. *femme fatale*. A woman who deliberately destroys men.

149/157. great illusion. Life, as in the French phrase *la grande illusion*.

149/158. Venus-Minerva . . . Elsinore. Classical goddesses, respectively, of love and wisdom, both to be found at Oxford—as love was to be found at Verona and wisdom at Elsinore, respectively, in Shakespeare's *Romeo and Juliet* and *Hamlet*.

150/159. Gestalt. Mental configuration.

151/160. wrong participle. Jane means that she feels stunned, the past participle rather than the present participle *stunning* Dan has just used to describe her.

151/160. Randolph. The large, expensive hotel in downtown Oxford.

152/161. crows. Catholic priests.

153/162. *Chacun á sa mort.* To each his own death, a witty observation that plays on *Chacun á son gout*—to each his own taste.

156/166. "Crimes and Punishments." A play on the title of Fyodor Dostoevsky's novel *Crime and Punishment* (1866).

156/166. *Lebensraum.* Living space, elbow room.

158/168. Murder . . . unsatisfied. Dan is thinking of William Blake's 1790 proverb from *The Marriage of Heaven and Hell:* "Sooner murder an infant in its cradle than nurse unacted desires."

159/169. Preston Sturges, Veronica Lake. She plays the female lead in his *Sullivan's Travels* (1941).

160/170. *en bloc.* As a whole.

162/173. Price. Fanny Price is the heroine of Jane Austen's *Mansfield Park* (1811).

163/173. Taylorian. A library serving Oxford University.

163/174. *"I will . . . God."* In the "Life of Adam and Eve," a novelistic rendering of legend and biblical texts among *The Old Testament Pseudepigrapha* by an unknown writer of A.D. first century, Satan tells Michael that if the Lord becomes wrathful over Satan's refusal to worship Him, "I will set my throne above the stars of heaven and will be like the Most High."

166/177. human . . . reality. The allusion is to "Burnt Norton," one of T. S. Eliot's *Four Quartets* (Part 1). Dan is comparing his playwright-self to humankind in general, as Eliot characterizes it.

167/178. sister. Nurse.

168/179. rug. Blanket.

168/179. Eden. Anthony Eden was British prime minister from 1955 to 1957.

169/180. *Saint Sebastian.* A version of this martyrdom, by Gerrit van Honthorst, in the National Gallery, shows the executed saint with four arrows piercing his body.

170/180. *prima facie.* On the face of it.

172/182. saw. "It's an ill wind that blows no good" is the "homely saw" Anthony assumes that Dan will recognize.

173/184. Madame Sosostris. In T. S. Eliot's *The Waste Land,* she is described as a "famous clairvoyante . . . with a wicked pack of cards" (Part 1). Anthony uses her Tarot card "fortunes" as a metaphor for apparent determinism, "design." Dan's "joker in the pack" requires a shift of metaphor, to a deck of playing cards.

173/184. Aunt Sally. A game played at pubs in which competitors take turns throwing sticks in attempts to knock a figure called "Aunt Sally" off her post. Dan is calling philosophy the favorite—and easy—target of clever writers.

175/186. high table. Formal dinners, with guests, in the dining halls of Oxford colleges.

175/187. Carroll. Lewis Carroll was the pseudonym of Charles Dodgson, an Oxford don in mathematics, who wrote the "nonsense" poem "Jabberwocky" as well as *Alice's Adventures in Wonderland* (1865).

176/187. Casanova. Giovanni Jacopo Casanova (1725–98) describes numerous sexual encounters in his *Memoires* (1826–38).

180/191. glass-bead game. Herman Hesse discusses spiritual, intellectual striving in a Utopia of the future in *The Glass Bead Game* (1943). Anthony seems to believe that one's life of the mind thrives at the expense of one's virility.

181/193. Saint Samuel à-Beckett. Anthony is mockingly comparing the high regard for the nihilistic writings of Samuel Beckett (1906–89) with worship of a saint such as Thomas à Becket (1118–70), the archbishop of Canterbury murdered in his cathedral. Anthony considers Beckett's work "fancy French nonsense" because Beckett composed in French.

181/193. Pascal. Blaise Pascal (1623–62) was a French mathematician and philosopher whose examination of Christianity and the human condition in *Pensées* would influence the existentialists, among others.

181/193. Voltaire. Pseudonym of François-Marie Arouet (1694–1778), a philosopher who was particularly suspicious of easy moralizing.

181/193. *mutatis mutandis*. The necessary changes having been made.

182/194. good Samaritan. Jesus describes a Samaritan who helps the victim of a robbery and beating (Luke 10:30–35).

183/194. Spengler. Oswald Spengler (1880–1936) was a German philosopher who wrote *The Decline of the West*, with whose pessimism Dan associates the "horrors" of his world.

186/198. Rousseau, Châteaubriand. Jean-Jacques Rousseau (1712–78) and François-René, Vicomte de Châteaubriand (1768–1848) are both associated with the valuing of liberal thinking and feeling.

187/199. BBC. British Broadcasting Corporation.

188/200. Maoist. Pertaining to the theory of communism adapted to rural circumstances in China by Mao Tse-tung (1893–1976).

189/201. People . . . houses. Jane assumes that Dan will complete the proverb, "People who live in glass houses shouldn't throw stones," and will recognize that the British are in no position to sneer at the Russians for being unsophisticated.

189/201. Joan-of-Arc. Unlike Jane, St. Joan believed that she had been called by God to save her country.

189/201. SCR. Senior Common Room, that is, intellectual drawing-room Marxists.

192/204. Solzhenitsyn. As Alexander Solzhenitsyn is a vigorous critic of The Soviet Union, with writings that include *The Gulag Archipelago* (1973–75), Jane will be a critic of Britain.

192/205. *Phèdre.* A French play by Jean Racine in 1677.

194/206. Tanagra. The terra-cotta fragments from there would date from the third to the fourth century B.C.

194/207. *"Je . . . non."* "Excuse me, sir. I am . . . ." "No, no."

194/207. Jacobsen. Arne Jacobsen (1902–   ) is a Danish designer of functional flatware, chairs, and desks. His "Egg" is a swivel chair of upholstered plastic with an aluminum frame.

195/208. Scott. Robert Falcon Scott (1868–1912) was a British naval officer who died on his second expedition to Antarctica.

196/209. *je . . . tout.* "I didn't know how . . . ." "Yes, yes. He was fed up with it. That's all."

197/210. Atropos. One of the three goddesses of fate, the one who cuts the thread of life at its end.

198/211. Cézanne. Paul Cézanne (1839–1906) was a French painter whose home, like Gesèle's, was Aix-en-Provence.

202/215. North Oxford. Section of the city where most of the faculty live.

202/215. Jesus . . . adultery. The story, in which Jesus invites him who is without sin to cast the first stone, is an addition to the original Gospel of St. John (8:1–11).

202/216. *Hedda Gabler.* Henrik Ibsen, Norwegian playwright, wrote this play, about a troubled, violent marriage, in 1890.

204/217. Lévi-Strauss. Claude Lévi-Strauss (1908–   ) is a French anthropologist, structuralist, and theorist about culture.

204/218. James. William James (1842–1910) was a psychologist and philosopher associated with American pragmatism.

204/218. Murdoch. Iris Murdoch (1919–   ) has written novels whose "situations" can be described as complicated, sophisticated, sexually charged, and a bit strange.

205/218. Jocasta. As Anthony's former student, Jane's male friend is like a son to Dan and would be even more like Oedipus (who kills his father and marries his mother, Jocasta) if he were to marry Jane.

206/220. Languish. Lydia Languish is a character in Richard Brinsley Sheridan's 1775 play *The Rivals,* which Jane evidently has acted in.

208/221. scholar-gypsy. The phrase aptly describing a creative writer's life is borrowed from Matthew Arnold, who wrote a long poem titled *The Scholar-Gypsy* in 1853.

212/227. Knox. John Knox (1510–72) was a Scottish religious reformer and follower of John Calvin.

213/227. Electra. In Greek legend, she helps Orestes avenge the death of her father. The narrator's comment refers to Jane's—like the sky's—lack of subdued colors, let alone mourning dress, by means of an allusion to the title of a play by Eugene O'Neill, *Mourning Becomes Electra* (1931).

214/228. *en clair*. In the clear, that is, unencrypted.

214/228. Philemon and Baucis. An elderly couple in classical legend who show perfect hospitality to a pair of strangers, who turn out to be Zeus and Hermes in disguise.

218/233. up . . . period. "Up" means attending university. During the Evelyn Waugh period, refers to Oxford of around 1925, described in his *Brideshead Revisited* (1945).

219/233. bloody-minded. Willful, difficult.

224/238. sick it up. Throw it up, get rid of it.

225/240. wasn't on. Just wouldn't be done.

225/240. Freud and Marx. Caro is imagining that they tried to account for her behavior with intellectual models.

226/241. *imprimatur*. Let it be published, that is, Dan gives his approval for her to proceed.

229/243. dustbins. Garbage cans.

229/243. Godot. The man on the street, with his comic appearance and isolation, resembles a character from Samuel Beckett's *Waiting for Godot* (1955).

229/244. Mayhew. Henry Mayhew (1812–87) was a journalist whose *London Labour and the London Poor* (1851) was based partly on interviews.

229/244. Snow. C. P. Snow (1905–80) was a novelist and public administrator whose Roger Quaife in *Corridors of Power* (1964) could be described as an "establishment fixer."

230/244. Bumble. An officious character in Charles Dickens's novel *Oliver Twist* (1837).

230/244. *deus ex machina*. God out of a machine, that is, a clumsy contrivance by which a playwright resolves the problems at the end of a play by lowering an all-powerful god onto the stage by means of machinery.

231/246. Minnesota . . . Newman. Abe and Dan are imitating the two main characters of the 1961 film *The Hustler*: Minnesota Fats (Jackie Gleason) and Fast Eddie Felson (Paul Newman).

231/246. Robinson. Edward G. Robinson (1893–1973), well-known film actor from the 1930s and 40s, had a square face.

232/247. Ray. Nicholas Ray's film credits for direction include *Johnny Guitar* (1954) and *Rebel Without a Cause* (1955).

232/247. limey. Slang for an Englishman, from the old practice of issuing limes to sailors in the British Navy to prevent scurvy.

232/247. orange-horse. Fowles will explain this term on p. 237/252.

232/247. Cagney and Bogart. James Cagney (1904–   ) and Humphrey Bogart

(1899–1957) tended to play roles in which they violated traditional codes of etiquette with women.

233/248. goys. Non-Jewish males (the correct Yiddish plural form is *goyyim*).

233/248. Sidney . . . thing. Sidney Carton, a character in Charles Dickens's *A Tale of Two Cities* (1859), goes to the guillotine in his friend's place, saying at the end of the novel, "It is a far, far better thing that I do, than I have ever done."

234/249. Blethering Heights . . . hair-do. Jenny is mocking the "Romantic" behavior in Emily Brontë's *Wuthering Heights* (1847) and the cult of Byron-worship in Europe in the preceding decades.

234/249. Mr. Knightly to my Emma. Jenny thought of him as a gentleman and of herself as a woman who learns from him, like Emma in Jane Austen's *Emma* (1816).

240/255. *echt.* Pure.

244/259. pissed. Drunk.

244/260. argybargy. Squabbling.

245/261. East End Mycenae. Mycenae was a city-state in ancient Greece where Clytemnestra murdered her husband, Agamemnon, and Orestes murdered his mother and her lover, Aegisthus. The East End is a working-class section of London.

246/261. Laius. Husband of Jocasta, whose venomous retort to Oedipus at the intersection of three roads leads Oedipus to lose his temper and kill Laius, unaware that the man he has slain is his biological father.

246/261. ponce. Pimp.

249/264. *Speculum Amanti. Mirror for Lovers.*

251/266. Brecht. The kind of courage Brecht immortalized was maternal stoicism, in *Mother Courage* (1941).

254/270. "Hollow Men." The chapter title alludes to T. S. Eliot's poem "The Hollow Men" (1925).

253/269. posh. High class.

257/273. *droit-du-seigneur.* Right by rank, that is, the boss's implicit "privilege" of sex with his subordinates.

258/274. Eumenides. Ancient Greek goddesses of vengeance, here, sources of guilt.

258/275. *saeva indignatio.* Savage indignation, a phrase that Juvenal (60–136) used to describe the feeling out of which he wrote satire.

259/275. Junius. Pseudonym of a writer of letters to a London newspaper between 1769 and 1772 that attacked the king and his ministers for abusing their powers.

259/275. Orwellian. Resembling George Orwell (1903–50), whose description of his youth was considered too libelous to print before 1968.

259/275. Beaverbrook. William Maxwell Aitken, 1st Baron Beaverbrook (1879–

1964) was a publisher who championed the cause of British Empire in London's *Daily Express.*

260/276. Lolly. Lollipop, that is, for the immediate gratification.

261/277. *aere perennius.* Perennial honor, that is, fame in the classical sense.

263/280. play. *When We Dead Awaken* is a play written by Henrik Ibsen in 1900.

263/280. interval. Intermission.

268/285. we never really lived. This phrase echoes a conversation in *When We Dead Awaken* (see note to p. 263/280).

268/285. miz. A misery, that is, a person who insists on being miserable.

268/286. grasshopper . . . ant. An allusion to the fable attributed to Aesop (sixth century B.C.).

271/288. Walt Disneys and Errol Flynns. Errol Flynn played Robin of Locksley in the 1938 Warner Brothers film *The Adventures of Robin Hood;* Walt Disney Studios produced *The Story of Robin Hood and His Merrie Men* in 1952.

271/288. *ex nihilo.* Out of nothing.

272/289. Oxford Movement. John Keble (1792–1866) and John Henry Newman (1801–90) advocated a revival of high church tradition within the Church of England. They were widely suspected of wanting reunification of the Anglican with the Roman Catholic Church.

272/289. *Monsieur Nicolas.* Fowles translates an excerpt from the passage summarized in his introduction to *Land* (pp. x-xii).

273/290. Palmer. Samuel Palmer lived with a few friends at Shoreham from 1825 to 1830, withdrawn from the world, reading Milton and Virgil.

273/290. Garden . . . *Shangri-La.* The Garden of Eden is described in Genesis (2:8–9), the Forest of Arden in Shakespeare's *As You Like It* (about 1599), and Shangri-La in James Hilton's *Lost Horizon* (1933).

273/290. Quarlesian. Francis Quarles (1592–1649) was an English poet who published *Emblems* in 1635, which combined visual with verbal texts.

274/291. Bergman . . . Ray. Ingmar Bergman (1918–) is Swedish; Luis Buñuel (1900–) is Spanish; Satyajit Ray (1921–) is Indian.

276/294. James . . . Nabokov. Henry James (1843–1916) lived in exile from America, in England; Virginia Woolf (1882–1941) lived in exile from much of English culture as a woman; Vladimir Nabokov (1899–1977) lived in exile from Russia in the United States and from there, later in life, in Switzerland.

279/297. Lawrence. Commonly known as "Lawrence of Arabia" who, like Kitchener, organized an army.

279/297. finger. Kitchener appeared on a World War I recruiting poster in which he points at the beholder (similar to American "Uncle Sam Wants You!" posters).

279/297. Dombey. A character in Charles Dickens's *Dombey and Son* (1848).

284/302. quality . . . strained. The judge's question and Dan's answer allude to Portia's speech in Shakespeare's *The Merchant of Venice* (about 1597; Act 4, Scene 1).

285/304. Greer. Germaine Greer, author of *The Female Eunuch* (1970), is a British feminist.

292/311. *Country Life.* A magazine about upper-class English stately homes, gardens, living.

297/316. tug . . . forelocks. To nod the head and pull the hair in front, a traditional gesture of respect from villagers to lords of the manor.

297/316. football pools. Betting on soccer matches, which involves predicting draws, or ties.

301/321. daft deb. Silly debutante.

302/322. Bolshie. A mocking abbreviation of Bolshevik, that is, a person of far-left political leaning.

303/323. *Vie de campagne.* Country life.

305/325. haha. A sunken wall, hidden from view in a ditch.

306/326. folly. A structure built to look ancient, invented in the eighteenth century, often to terminate views across a landscape.

309/328. sixty million. Roughly the population of England.

309/329. passée. Behind the times.

310/329. *savoir vivre.* Knowledge of how to live.

310/330. Marmaduke. Fowles quotes "a vulgar ballad" about the adventures of a Lord Marmaduke in *The French Lieutenant's Woman* (291/230).

310/330. Great Wen. Slang for a large crowded city, that is, London.

311/331. Sitwell. Osbert Sitwell (1892–1969) was a poet who served reluctantly in World War I.

311/331. *obiter dictum.* Incidental opinion.

313/333. under the bed. The phrase is a standard gibe at anti-Communists, said to imagine that there is a Communist hiding under every bed.

313/333. Robespierre. French revolutionary who turned autocrat and executed his opponents.

314/334. Nineteen eighty-four. The year refers to George Orwell's novel *1984* (published in 1949), set in what was then a future in which the English people had no personal freedom.

314/334. your party. Fenwick, a Conservative, assumes that Dan is a Social Democrat—and that Labour will be the ascendant party.

314/334. *Titanic.* The supposedly unsinkable ocean liner that struck an iceberg and went down in 1914.

314/334. proles. Proletariat, working class.

315/335. *faux pas.* A serious social blunder.

315/335. *à la grecque.* In the Greek way, that is, by military dictatorship.

318/338. Pilate. Fenwick, like Pontias Pilate, washes his hands of responsibility for events.

322/344. Mumford. Lewis Mumford (1895–   ) is a social scientist and author of books on architecture and urban planning.

323/344. *posada*. Inn.

323/344. piñón. A scrub pine.

326/347. Siddons. Sarah Siddons (1755–1831) was the foremost actress of tragic heroines in the late eighteenth century.

328/349. Edgar Allan/Allen. Jenny has been quoting from Edgar Allan Poe's "The Raven" (1845).

330/351. Olympian. As if viewed from on top of Mount Olympus, legendary home of the Greek gods.

331/352. *Citizen Kane*. The film's narrative of Kane's life is told by means of a biographical newsreel and four reminiscences, as a reporter tries to discover the significance of Kane's last word, "Rosebud" (see note to p. 34/34).

335/357. Ripley. "Ripley's Believe It or Not" featured surprising facts, illustrated in the comic sections of newspapers.

337/359. *en poste*. On equal footing.

338/360. Pythia. The prophetess of Apollo at Delphi was called Pythia. Wytham is the name of the house Jane and Anthony lived in.

339/362. Tess. Tess Durbeyfield is digging up turnips in one scene of Hardy's 1891 novel *Tess of the d'Urbervilles* (Chapter 43).

345/368. Phillida. The epigraph is the first of ten stanzas that make up the anonymous sixteenth-century ballad of "The Disdainful Shepherdess" (*Roxburghe Ballads* 6.460).

345/369. Drake and Raleigh. Sir Francis Drake (1540–96) and Sir Walter Raleigh (1552–1618) were both gentlemen at the court of Queen Elizabeth.

346/369. 1647. The actual date is 1664 on the stone porch of Dornafield Farm (Two Mile Oak, Newton Abbot, Devon) which was Fowles's primary model for Thorncombe, according to an interview with James R. Baker, *Michigan Quarterly Review* 25 (1986) p. 681.

347/370. Wizard. Adolescent slang for *excellent*.

348/371. Portnoy's complaint. An allusion to Philip Roth's 1969 novel *Portnoy's Complaint*, whose title refers to the theme of guilt over masturbation.

348/371. thirty bob. Thirty shillings, worth a pound and a half.

348/371. Grable. Betty Grable's style of hair was fairly short and curly all around.

348/371. Durbin. Deanna Durbin (1921–   ) was a Canadian-born actress and singer for Universal Studios in the late 1930s and early 1940s.

349/372. pasties. Cornish meat pies.

354/377. arsy-varsy. Vice-versa, backwards.

358/381. Je . . . amat. Nancy is conjugating the French verb *to be* and the Latin verb *to love*.

358/382. Gulliver. Lemuel Gulliver is literally tied down by the six-inch-tall Lilliputians in Book One of Jonathan Swift's *Gulliver's Travels* (1726).

358/382. *Wet*. Non-committal, "wishy-washy."

385. Romeo and Julietishness. Shakespeare's Romeo and Juliet were from feuding families; Dan and Nancy are from socially distinct classes.

362/386. pestlery . . . French letter. A pessary (diaphragm) and a condom, respectively.

362/386. spots. Pimples.

365/389. *da capo*. Over again.

368/392. So . . . lesson. The narrator is naughtily echoing the Anglican church service.

377/402. Slough of Despond. An allegorical place in John Bunyan's *Pilgrim's Progress* (1678).

377/402. burke. Suppress.

379/404. grockle. A tourist.

380/404. dekko. A look.

382/407. everso. Very. "Ever so much" is a common English intensifier after "Thanks."

382/407. *I found* . . . me. From "The Disdainful Shepherdess" (see note to p. 345/368).

386/411. PPE. A degree in Philosophy, Politics, and Economics.

388/413. Socratic. Questioning, after the method of Socrates (469–399 B.C.).

389/414. Cultivate your garden. An allusion to the last sentence of Voltaire's *Candide*: "We must cultivate our garden."

389/414. "Get . . . me." Jesus's words to Satan during the temptation in the wilderness. (Matthew 4:10).

389/415. Récamier. The salon of the witty and beautiful Madame Récamier (1777–1849) was the most highly regarded in early-nineteenth-century France.

390/415. Lukács. Georg Lukács (1885–1971) was a Marxist critic and theoretician, in particular of the novel.

390/415. *à la* Solzhenitsyn. Alexander Solzhenitsyn (1918–), Nobel Prize-winning author, spent seven years in a Stalinist labor camp.

391/416. Prometheus . . . stable. For his presumption in helping humanity, Prometheus was punished by Zeus, by means of a vulture which ate his liver. Cleaning the Augean Stables was a labor of Hercules. In his role as novelist, Dan will implicitly resemble both gods.

391/417. "Sartre?" "Marx." Jean Paul Sartre (1905–80) and Karl Marx (1818–83) both theorized about history.

392/417. EEC. European Economic Community, also known as the Common Market.

392/417. CPI. Communist Party of Italy.

393/418. *Geist.* Soul.

403/429. Midas. A legendary king who turned everything he touched to gold.

404/430. *Living.* Also translated as *To Live* or *Doomed to Live,* Akiro Kurosawa's film *Ikuru* is about the pursuit of meaning in life by a man dying of cancer.

404/431. *Zeitgeist.* Spirit of the age.

405/431. Damascus. Saul of Tarsus was converted when struck from his horse and blinded by a light, on his way to Damascus.

410/437. "O Western wind . . . again." The anonymous lyric has been modified slightly by Fowles.

412/439. Albicocci [sic.] Jean-Gabriel Albicocco (born 1936) is the French director who adapted *Le Grand Meulnes (The Wanderer)* to film in 1967.

421/449. *comme it faut.* What is "done."

422/450. Mozart. Wolfgang Amadeus Mozart (1756–91) was an Austrian composer, whose symphony in G-minor is one of those written under severe financial pressure in the summer of 1788.

423/450. *aut Caesar, aut nullus.* Either Caesar or nothing.

427/455. Vermeer. Jan Vermeer (1632–75) was a Dutch "little master," whose painting *Young Woman with Water Jug* (1655) fits Dan's description.

430/458. Fellini. Federico Fellini (1921–) is an Italian film director whose *Amarcord* was released in 1974.

432/460. *sabra.* A person born in Israel.

432/461. Ashkenazy. Vladimir Ashkenazy (1937–) is a Soviet-born pianist who became a citizen of Iceland in 1972.

433/462. The Utrillos and the Klees. The paintings owned by Kate's parents include works by French painter Maurice Utrillo (1883–1955) and Swiss painter Paul Klee (1879–1940).

434/462. Goya. Jenny has adopted the pose of Francisco Goya's *Maja Desnuda (The Maja Nude,* or *The Naked Maja,* 1800), in which the woman reclines on her side with her hands behind her head.

438/467. *De trop.* Too much, overdone.

439/468. MCPs. Male Chauvinist Pigs.

444/473. Dangerous liaisons. Dan borrows this phrase from the usual translation of the title of a novel by Pierre Choderlos de Laclos, *Les liaisons dangereuses* (1782).

445/474. Dreyer. Theodore Dreyer, of Denmark, directed *The Passion of Joan of Arc* (1928), a highly regarded film in which Falconetti played Joan expressively.

454/484. Cheshire Cat. Feline character in *Alice's Adventures in Wonderland* whose smile is more substantial than its body.

457/486. Blue Guide. Hachette World Guides, a series of travel books known as *Guide Bleu* in France, discussed in *The Ebony Tower* (pp. 277–78/259–60).

459/489. *"Merde . . . français."* "Shit?" "Ah, good. You speak French?"

460/489. *Une supidité stupéfiante.* A stupefying act of stupidity.

462/491. baksheesh. Bribe money.

463/492. *chateaux.* Castles.

464/494. Hays Office. The familiar name of the Motion Picture Producers and Distributors of America, Incorporated, founded in 1922 under Will H. Hays and terminated in 1945, whose code of self-censorship shaped the content of U.S. films until 1966.

465/495. Mameluke. The Mamelukes were a military slave class until the early nineteenth century.

465/495. *souk.* Market.

466/496. *déclassé.* Below expectations.

467/497. Matthau. Walter Matthau is an American actor, best known for his role as Oscar in *The Odd Couple* (1968).

468/498. Austen. Jane Austen once compared her novels, with their narrowly circumscribed social situations, to this kind of cameo, a "little bit (two inches wide) of Ivory on which I work with so fine a brush" (16 December 1816 letter to James Edward Austen).

468/498. Shaw. George Bernard Shaw (1856–1950) won the Nobel prize for literature in 1925.

468/498. Pascal. Gabriel Pascal (1894–1954) was a Hungarian producer who persuaded George Bernard Shaw to sell the film rights to his plays and then produced and sometimes directed several adaptations.

468/498. Sahl. Mort Sahl is an American humorist.

470/499. Ustinov. Peter Ustinov is a British actor and director who also is an ebullient impersonator and raconteur.

472/502. *The Entertainer.* A 1960 play by John Osborne, adapted as a film by Tony Richardson, set during the Suez crisis of 1956. The film is about the life of a bankrupt song-and-dance man named Archie Rice.

473/503. more famous Jane. That is, Jane Austen, mentioned on p. 468/498.

475/506. Greene. Graham Greene (1904–   ) wrote novels set in Vietnam, Argentina, and the Congo as well as in England.

476/507. *lingua franca.* Common language.

477/508. *Mrs. Dalloway.* A 1925 novel by Virginia Woolf.

478/509. Barge-borne Queen. The phrase refers also to Queen Cleopatra's procession on the Nile River.

478/510. intimations of mortality. The phrase echoes William Wordsworth's 1807 ode "Intimations of Immortality from the Recollections of Early Childhood."

479/510. Bacon. Francis Bacon (1909–) is a British painter of violent, disquieting scenes.

479/510. *nouveaux riches*. Newly rich.

481/513. *Caveat emptor*. Let the buyer beware.

487/519. Perfidious Albion. Based on an Anglophobic French phrase using an ancient name for Britain.

489/521. Newcastle. Carrying coals to Newcastle (which is a source of coal) is a British expression for doing something unnecessary.

491/524. Ganymede. In Greek legend, a beautiful boy who served Zeus as cup-bearer, here a homosexual lover.

493/526. Heraclitean. Heraclitus (540–470 B.C.) is best known for asserting that one cannot step into the same river twice.

495/528. Tati. Jacques Tati is a French filmmaker and comic actor whose *Playtime* (1968) focuses on American tourists in Paris.

495/528. Cartier-Bressons. Henri Cartier-Bresson (1908–) is a French photographer.

496/529. *rasant*. Boring.

496/529. Cocteau. Jean Cocteau was a French director of films, which include *Beauty and the Beast* (1946).

500/533. *angst*. A feeling of dread, of metaphysical anxiety.

500/534. *Ivanhoe*. Sir Walter Scott's novel *Ivanhoe* (1819) includes the matter of Robin Hood, the legend Dan finds so indicative of the English character.

500/534. Erasmic. In the way of Desiderius Erasmus (1467–1536), Dutch Humanist who urged moderation during the Reformation.

501/534. Mann. Thomas Mann (1875–1955) was a German novelist whose works include *Death in Venice*.

502/536. Flaxman-like. John Flaxman (1755–1826) was an English sculptor and designer of pottery for Wedgwood.

503/537. *horror vacui, horror uni*. Abhorrence of a vacuum, abhorrence of one-ness.

507/541. Virgil, Voltaire. Virgil's young Aeneas and Voltaire's Candide were innocents.

507/541. signal. Admiral Nelson ordered the engagement that would become known as the Battle of Trafalgar with the signal, "England expects every man will do his duty."

517/552. Baudelaire. Charles Baudelaire (1821–67) was a French poet and critic.

518/552. KGB. The Soviet secret police.

519/554. DDR. *Deutsche Demokratische Republik*, what was East Germany.

520/555. *Volk*. Folk, the idea of which was appealed to by Hitler as a romanticized, popular heritage.

528/564. "I read . . . winter." From *The Waste Land* (Part 1).

529/565. *Fais . . . voudras.* Do what you would like.

530/566. Cassandra. Trojan prophetess who was always right and was never believed. Jane is saying that Dan believes his memory and is wrong.

531/567. *boîtes.* Short for *boîtes de nuit,* or nightclubs.

533/569. MiGs. Soviet fighter planes designed by Mikoyan and Gurevitch.

533/569. Damocles. A Syracusan flatterer who was seated at a banquet with a sword suspended over his head by a single hair.

533/570. Lawrence. "Lawrence of Arabia" (1888–1935) was the Englishman who united Arab tribes to drive out the Turks.

534/570. *genius loci.* Spirit of place.

535/571. *sui generis.* One of a kind.

536/572. Rousseau. Henri Rousseau, or "The Douanier" Rousseau (1844–1910) painted jungle scenes of primitive simplicity, tranquility. He was called "Douanier" because he served as a clerk in the customs office.

536/573. a Manet or a Renoir. Édouard Manet (1832–83) and Pierre-Auguste Renoir (1841–1919) were French painters interested in optical effects, in the movement known as Impressionism.

539/575. Ave Maria. Hail Mary, a prayer assigned as part of the Roman Catholic ritual penance, sometimes recited with prayer beads resembling the ones Jane has just been given.

544/581. Valentinoed. Rudolph Valentino played the Sheik of Araby in *The Sheik* (1921); so his name constitutes a better word for *abducted* than *shanghaied*—a metaphor derived from the Far East rather than the Middle East.

549/587. *gloire* and *patrie.* Glory and country.

554/593. Eurydice. Orpheus loses her by looking back as they leave Hades.

554/593. *jardin publique.* Public garden.

556/595. set texts. For national exams, works on which students are tested.

556/595. Racine and Balzac. Jean Baptiste Racine (1639–99) and Honoré de Balzac (1799–1850) are exemplary French writers, of plays and novels, respectively.

560/599. Chopin. Frédéric Chopin (1810–49) was a Polish composer and pianist who lived in France.

560/599. *de trop.* Too much, in the way.

560/599. Mozart. Wolfgang Amadeus Mozart (1756–91) was a gifted composer in various genres.

561/600. Bach. Johann Sebastian Bach's compositions include the Goldberg Variations (1741–42), which are comprehensive surveys of thirty keyboard styles on one original theme.

561/600. Langland. William Langland (1330–86) wrote *Piers Ploughman,* which contains the line cited (Passus 1, line 12).

569/608. Eliot. Possibly a reference to the lines from *The Waste Land* that begin, "Who is the third who walks always beside you"? (Part 5, line 360).

569/609. *terra firma.* Solid ground.

573/613. Gadarene. Associated with swine, from the episode in which Jesus exorcizes demons that subsequently enter the nearby swine (Matthew 8:28–34).

573/614. *couture.* Fashion.

579/619. Thane of Glamis. A Scottish nobleman whose death figures in *Macbeth* (Act 1, Scene 3).

586/627. A loaf . . . thou. Dan is alluding to Edward Fitzgerald's translation (1859) of *The Rubáiyát of Omar Khayyám,* from the twelfth century (stanza 12).

593/634. less *credo . . . absurdum.* Less "I believe" now than "I deny it because it is impossible." Believing because of the very absurdity of doing so, out of wonder, is the position held by Tertullian, whose rule of faith is usually rendered *"Credo quia impossible";* Dan finds Tertullian's rule more a basis for atheism.

593/634. Tiresias. He was given power to descry the truth, like Dan, in compensation for his blindness.

598/640. Eliot . . . *hence.* From *The Waste Land* (Part 1, line 74).

607/649. Oxbridgery. The complex of attitudes promoted by Oxford and Cambridge universities, including the idea that theirs are superior subcultures.

613/655. *Un beau . . . madame?* A beautiful view of the customs house, isn't it, Madame?

614/656. *plus ça change. . . .* The more things change . . . [the more they stay the same].

615/658. her local. Her pub, that is, the public house or tavern that Jenny considers "hers." The landlord is the tavern keeper.

615/658. half pint. A small mug, traditionally ordered by women, whereas men customarily order full pints. Guinness is a brand of dark, Irish stout.

622/665. Monroe. Marilyn Monroe killed herself, according to one theory, because she felt rejected by President John F. Kennedy—the unidentified antecedent of "he" in the preceding sentence.

622/665. Lovelace. Clarissa dies at the end of Samuel Richardson's novel *Clarissa,* after having been raped by Lovelace. Dan is refusing to play the role of the one who ruined Jenny's life.

623/666. Forster's *Only connect.* The phrase is the epigraph to E. M. Forster's novel *Howards End* (1910).

624/667. Constable. John Constable (1776–1837) was an English painter of landscapes, including views of London from the suburbs.

625/668. *ingénue.* An artless, innocent girl.

625/668. Bluebeard. He kills his wives and puts their corpses "together" in a secret room, in Perrault's tale "Bluebeard."

625/669. Darby and Joan. Stock names for a rustic couple.

626/670. vetted. Screened, interviewed.

MANTISSA

n.p. Descartes. René Descartes (1596–1650), French philosopher, is best known for his statement, "I think; therefore, I am." The first epigraph elaborates that idea and its accompanying mind-body dualism.

n.p. Marivaux. Pierre Marivaux (1688–1763) wrote *The Game of Love and Chance* in 1730.

1. Lemprière. John Lemprière (died 1824) wrote a standard classical dictionary, the *Bibliotheca Classica*, whose entry cited here means *Muses*.

3. alpha and omega. The first and last letters of the Greek alphabet, that is, A–Z, or all-encompassing.

7. Dickens. *The Posthumous Papers of the Pickwick Club* (1836–37), known as the *Pickwick Papers*, was the first novel by Charles Dickens and, like *Mantissa*, contains shifting characters and little plot.

7. Bottom, Titania. These two characters in Shakespeare's *A Midsummer Night's Dream* (circa 1595) are, like Miles and his muse, a male fool (whose name is scatalogical) and his female love object.

10. non sequitur. A statement that does not follow logically from what went before.

11. Irish gentleman. Flann O'Brien, pseudonym of Brian O'Nolan (1911–66), wrote the metanovel *At Swim-Two-Birds* (1939), quoted in the epigraph to Part IV (page 157) and again (without identification) on the last page of *Mantissa*. O'Brien's novel includes a scene in which a character with magical powers transforms the walls of a room and levitates its furniture, including a clock, "a token that the free flight of time had also been interfered with" (New York: NAL Penguin, 1976, pp. 252–54).

14. Delfie. Delphi was a seat of prophecy in ancient Greece. Its prophetesses were females who would become inspired by the gods and utter sounds which were interpreted by male priests.

15. sister. British term for *nurse*.

15. Cory. In classical legend, the Corybantes were secondary divinities or priests of the Great Mother.

17. Peacock. One of Fowles's favorite authors is Thomas Love Peacock (1785–1866).

22. It won't bite you. Her remark is both a cliché of reassurance and a glance at male gynophobic fears of the devouring mother or of the toothed vagina (discussed in Joseph Campbell's *Primitive Mythology* [New York: Viking-Penguin, 1969], pp. 73–76).

24. Bugger off. Get the hell out.

24. National Health. The British socialized medicine program.

25. Mrs. Grundy. A character in Thomas Morton's *Speed the Plough* (1798), who has come to represent the voice of rigid propriety.

26. ego, superego, id. These are terms borrowed from Sigmund Freud's model of human psychology.

34. Gladstone. William Gladstone (1809–98) was a member of Parliament and several times prime minister of England.

34. *frisson*. Pleasurable shudder, thrill.

36. cow. A derogatory, British slang term for women.

39–40. Kama . . . Masters. The *Kama Sutra* is an ancient Hindu treatise on sexuality; Pierre Aretino (1492–1556) wrote *The Harlot's Dialogues*; the *Hokuwata Monosaki* I have not been able to identify; Alfred Kinsey published reports on American male and female sexual behavior in 1948 and 1953; William Masters (1915–   ) and Virginia Johnson (1925–   ) conducted experiments and published *Human Sexual Response* in 1966.

41. Lovely. That's right.

41. baby . . . syllable. Fowles is literalizing the traditional metaphor of biological procreation for artistic creation. Roland Barthes uses the metaphor in *Mythologies* to describe the writer on vacation, whose "muse is awake, and gives birth, non-stop."

44. Who's a clever boy. A British parent-to-child expression of congratulations.

47. Erato. One of the nine muses, a fact that the Lemprière epigraph does not make explicit.

50. *Doppelgänger*. Alter ego, sometimes in literature a personification of a character's other self.

51. Nemesis. Greek goddess of divine retribution.

51. massacre. On St. Valentine's Day, February 14, 1929, members of Al Capone's gang disguised as policemen murdered members of the rival Moran gang in a Chicago garage.

51. bleedin'. In England *bleeding* is a strong, obscene intensifier (referring to Christ's blood).

51. sod. Short for *sodomite*, an insult.

51. arse. Ass.

52. piss around. Fool around.

53. sister. A feminist.

53. bugger. A term of opprobrium that labels him a homosexual.

53. Scott. Sir Walter Scott (1771–1832) wrote the *Lay of the Last Minstrel* in 1805.

53. Hogg. James Hogg (1770–1835) wrote *Private Memoirs and Confessions of a Justified Sinner* (1824), a title that also describes *Mantissa*.

54. *kaput*. Dead.

55. takin' the mickey. Making fun of her, a somewhat vicious teasing.

55. Numero Uno. Number one, that is, a prime example.

55. soppily. In a silly, sentimental way.

55. Duncan. Isadora Duncan (1878–1927) was an influential dancer who discarded ballet slippers and conventional dress for bare feet and Greek chitons.

56. Botticelli. The Italian Renaissance painter Sandro Botticelli (1444–1510) painted the first freestanding nude in Western art since before the Middle Ages, *The Birth of Venus,* which depicts her drifting ashore on a half-shell.

56. cock. Slang for *nonsense,* related to the adjectives *daft, wet,* and *dotty* that follow.

56. Lydian. A musical scale from *F* to *F*.

59. bit of bird. Slang for a sexual conquest.

59. *vis-à-vis.* As opposed to.

61. Lesbos. Island where the Greek poetess Sappho wrote her homoerotic love lyrics.

63. *histoire, discours.* A narrative, as opposed to a discursive text, especially in the post-structuralist sense in which everything is a text, the personifying author as well as the personified character.

63. Uncle Tom Cobbleigh and all. This line appears twice at the end of a long list of names in *The Ballad of Widdicombe Fair* and means, roughly, "everybody and his brother."

63. *à deux.* For two.

64. *nouveau roman.* "New novel," an experimental mode of fiction described by Alain Robbe-Grillet in 1962 that, in practice, uses detailed description rather than conventional plot.

65. Euterpe. The muse of lyric song.

65. Cecilia. Saint Cecilia (died A.D. 230) is the patron saint of music.

69. toenail. Satyrs were lecherous, woodland deities with hooves.

69. golliwogs. An English child's doll with black skin and a grotesque face.

72. aunt. Aphrodite, goddess of love, was born at sea and stepped ashore on Cyprus. Both Mnemosyne and Aphrodite are daughters of Zeus, according to one tradition, so Aphrodite would be the sister of Erato's mother and could be considered Erato's aunt on that basis.

73. Thalia. The muse of comedy and bucolic poetry.

73. tweely. In an affectedly arty manner.

73. Musagetes. An epithet meaning "Leader of the Muses" (one of "Aunt Polly's" roles).

75. Pierian Fountain. A spring in Thessaly, where the Greek muses were reputed to have been born.

75. Syrinx. The name of a mountain nymph who was transformed into a reed, from which panpipes are made. Here, of course, his penis.

78. Nefertiti. Queen of Egypt in the fourteenth century B.C. whose funerary bust represents her with an extremely long neck.

80. historians. The muse of history is Erato's sister Clio.

83. *Carmina Priapea. Songs to Priapus*, 83 indecent Latin poems by anonymous authors, in honor of the Roman god of fruitfulness, collected as "Priapics" in *Poetae Latini Minores (Minor Latin Poets)*, edited by Emil Baehrens and Friedrich Vollmer (Leipzig: Teubner, 1909–13), vols. 1 and 2.2. What Erato has "pinched" includes the idea of relating sexual play and play with the alphabet (see numbers 7 and 53, for example).

87. Verlaine. Paul Verlaine (1844–96) was a French poet who also wrote *The Wretched Poets*, one of whom was another "Frog poet," Mallarmé—the name Miles mouths to Erato, but which she misunderstands as "my arms ache." She is remembering Mallarmé's composition of *Prélude to the Afternoon of a Faun* (1865).

87. *Con amore*. With love.

90. *Ad nauseum*. To the point where nausea sets in.

91. on the never-never. On the installment plan.

92. Rokeby. The "Rokeby Venus" also is known as *The Toilette of Venus* or *Venus at Her Mirror*, by Diego Velázquez (1599–1660).

95. Uncle Toms. Uncle Tom is a pious, kindly black character in Harriet Beecher Stowe's *Uncle Tom's Cabin* (1851–52), whose name has come to stand for passive failure to support the liberation of slaves.

95. Bluebeard. A character in French folklore who kills a succession of wives until his seventh finds their bodies in a forbidden room.

98. deus ex machina. An artificial development, like the lowering onto the stage of a "god out of the machinery" to distribute justice and end a play.

98. unities. Deriving from Aristotle, it has been argued that good tragedy embodies a single time, place, and action.

100. Jane Austen. English novelist (1775–1817).

100. wine-dark. A stock phrase used by Homer to describe the sea.

100. Proust. Marcel Proust (1871–1922) wrote *Remembrance of Things Past*.

102. *Angst*. Anxiety over the meaninglessness of life.

104. *voulu*. Obvious.

107. *recherchée*. Farfetched.

107. *deuxième dialogue. Second dialogue*.

108. *de trop*. Too much.

108. Messalina *de nos jours*. A Messalina for our time. The original Messalina was the depraved third wife of Claudius I.

108. Alice-in-Wonderland. *Alice's Adventures in Wonderland* is an 1865 fantasy by Lewis Carroll.

110. Leavises. F. R. Leavis (1895–1978) and his wife, Q. D. Leavis (1906–81), were influential literary critics at Cambridge University.

110. Steiner. George Steiner (1929–   ) is a critic of international culture.

110. *vraisemblable*. Believable.

112. *ex voto*. After the vow.

114. Bara. Theda Bara, film actress who made her debut in 1914, was promoted as a deadly Arabian beauty who devoured men.

114. Dietrich. Marlene Dietrich played a bewitching nightclub singer in the 1930 German film *The Blue Angel*.

116. Todorov. Tzvetan Todorov (1940–   ) is a French structuralist critic who sought to discover the universal syntax of narrative.

116. *facies*. Aspects.

117. stone. A "stone" is an English measurement of weight equal to fourteen pounds.

118. Melpomene. The muse of tragedy.

121. Jong. Erica Jong's first novel, *Fear of Flying* (1973) was controversial for its explicitness about female erotic fantasies. Erato mistakenly believes that Miles has told her to read Jung, the "Swiss psychologist."

123. *Ciao*. Good-bye.

123. *Mann ist was er isst*. You are what you eat.

125. marquis. The Marquis Donatien Alphonse François de Sade (1740–1814) wrote novels that depicted violent eroticism.

127. Joyce and Beckett. James Joyce (1882–1941) and Samuel Beckett (1906–89) were friends and writers of highly serious, modernist fictions.

129. Magritte. René Magritte (1898–1967) was a Belgian painter of startling visions.

134. Dr. Bowdler. The Doctor is named after Dr. Thomas Bowdler (1754–1825), the notorious editor and "purifier" of Shakespeare and the Bible.

135. Bedlam. The familiar name for Bethlehem Hospital for the insane.

135. nappies. Diapers.

135. Thatcher. Matron is named after Margaret Thatcher, prime minister when *Mantissa* was published, whose mother-knows-best manner earned her the nickname "England's Nanny."

139. lead. Leash.

139. Todorov. Tzvetan Todorov (1939–   ) has developed a structuralist theory of narrative.

147. Smith, Holliday. Bessie Smith (1894–1937) was perhaps the greatest singer of blues, and Billie Holliday (1915–59) was the most influential jazz singer.

147. Wasp. Acronym for white, Anglo-Saxon Protestant.

148. Shakespeare . . . Eliot. Erato claims that she has inspired all the famous representations of women, including Milton's (Eve in *Paradise Lost*), Rochester's (in "The Imperfect Enjoyment"), Shelley (in "The Witch of Atlas"), Keats (in "Ode on a Grecian Urn"), Wells (in *The Time Machine*), and T. S.

Eliot (in *The Waste Land*, whose "love" scene in Part 3 Erato goes on to describe).

150. *Times Literary Supplement*. Although the *TLS* has not written about Fowles using the words Miles considers to be a feather in his cap, one *TLS* reviewer has referred to "the jokeless wastes of Fowles' fiction" and the "sickeningly inescapable" presence of "Fowles the sage" in *Daniel Martin* (Michael Mason, "Pulling the Wool," 7 October 1977, p. 1135). The rest of the review suggests that Fowles is a "hack," as Miles's reviewer seems to have characterized him and Fowles may want to convey the tone of this higher-brow detractor without using his actual words.

157. *Deux . . . parler*. "Two beautiful eyes need but to talk," from *The Colony* by French playwright Pierre Marivaux (1688–1763).

163. I grant . . . go. From Shakespeare's Sonnet 130, line 11.

165. *interruptus*. *Coitus interruptus*, the interrupted act of sexual intercourse (she refers to the end of Part 1).

172. *Odyssey*. The *Odyssey* was written down in the eighth century B.C. and attributed to Homer. Fowles rehearses Samuel Butler's argument that Homer was a woman in *Islands* (pp. 51–54).

175. *engouement*. Infatuation.

177–78. Charlie. In Athens, during the late fifth century B.C., Aristophanes wrote the plays alluded to: *The Birds*, *The Frogs*, and *Lysistrata*.

179. didn't know their *phalloi* from their *pyge*. Didn't know their pricks from their asses.

180–81. nose. Virgil's *Aeneid* is about the founding of Rome. Ovid wrote *The Art of Love*. Horace wrote 103 odes. Catullus wrote poems about his love for Lesbia, including two about Lesbia and her sparrow, which she feeds (2) and grieves for after its death (3).

186. Cartlanditis. The "disease" of writing like Barbara Cartland, British novelist who has written numerous popular romances.

186. blessed damozel. *The Blessed Damozel* is the title of a painting by D. G. Rossetti (1828–82).

187. Casanova . . . Harris. All were or are notorious as seducers of women.

189. Trojans. With reference to a large wooden horse, Sinon warned his fellow Trojans to beware of Greeks bearing gifts.

189. *à la japonaise*. Japanese-style.

191. *in extremis*. At a moment of crisis.

196. aestho-autogamous . . . Shanahan. "Aestho-autogamy," or artistic self-fertilization of the kind that occurs at the end of Part 1 of *Mantissa*, is a literary phenomenon of interest to Dermot Trellis, fictional author of the manuscript that constitutes part of *At Swim-Two-Birds* (O'Brien, p. 55; see note to p. 11). The statement by Shanahan is made after one of Trellis's other characters declines to seduce a girl when the author falls asleep and frees the character to make up his own mind (p. 89).

196. dream-babbling . . . fields. When Sir John Falstaff dies in Shakespeare's *Henry V,* he is said to have "babbled of green fields" (Act 2, Scene 3).

A MAGGOT

7/5. Apollo. Greek god of light, purity, and music. He was depicted in art as beardless and handsome, tall but muscular, with long hair.

10/9. C———. Not spelling out the names of places and people was sometimes done in the eighteenth century to protect an author but also was a conventional way to promote the illusion that actual identities were being masked in a fiction.

11/10. *souk.* A market.

11/10. Clio. The muse of history.

17/16. *vacua.* Vacancy, that is, silence.

18/17. *In comoedia vitae.* In the comedy of life.

19/18. Romeo . . . wheel. A history is a story; Shakespeare's *Romeo and Juliet* (about 1595) begins with a choral prologue describing the lovers as "star-cross'd," that is, fated; they are "bound upon destiny's wheel" in the sense that a prisoner would sometimes be tied to a wheel after having his bones broken as a practice of torture, and also in the sense that they are controlled by Fortuna, the allegorical figure whose turn of her wheel could alter one's destiny, especially bring down one who had previously been mounted high. Lacy is arguing that Bartholemew in life is freer than a character in a tragedy.

29/28. Chardin. Jean-Baptiste-Siméon Chardin (1699–1779) painted middle-class, domestic scenes.

30/30. to encourage the others. The narrator's phrase is used by Voltaire in Chapter 23 of *Candide* (1759) to describe the English justification for executing Admiral Byng by firing squad, for having let himself be defeated by the French off Minorca.

34/34. Bedlam. Bethlehem Hospital, an insane asylum.

34/34. Hector. Warrior and champion of Troy during the Trojan War, he was always found where the fighting was heaviest.

34/34. George. The king of England must be George II, from 1727 to 1760, if "the last but one monarch" was Queen Anne (p. 15).

36/36. Muses. In Greek legend, they were nine daughters of Zeus and Mnemosyne, each associated with a different art or mode of "poetry," a term that in the eighteenth century could include various forms of verbal discourse.

37/37. Witch of Endor. King Saul secretly visits a woman necromancer at Endor, who summons the spirit of Samuel, Saul's predecessor (1 Samuel 28).

40/40. *Shandy*-like. In Laurence Sterne's novel *Tristram Shandy* (1759–67), there are deliberately blank pages in Chapters 18 and 19 of volume 9.

43/43. Sade. Donatien Alphonse François Sade (1740–1814), known as the Marquis de Sade, wrote novels representing the inflicting of pain for erotic purposes, from which the word *sadism* derives. *A Maggot* is taking place four years before his birth, so the year must be 1736.

47/47. pox. The great pox was syphilis, distinguished from smallpox.

47/48. *fête galante* by Watteau. An aristocratic holiday such as the one anticipated in *The Embarkation for Cythera* (1717) by French painter Antoine Watteau. The "environment" in the painting is out of doors in a green wood during the daytime.

49/50. Midas-rich. In Greek legend, Dionysus granted Midas's wish that all he touched might turn to gold.

53/53–54. Historical Chronicle. This is a reproduction of an actual feature in the *Gentleman's Magazine,* a compendium of the month's news.

55/55. *Felon de se.* Crime against the self, that is, suicide.

55/55. 10 miles. The actual village of South Molton corresponds geographically with the location of "C———" and the Black Hart in the novel, for South Molton is ten miles from Barnstaple and has a forked road two miles to the west, as well as woods and a stream of the sort described on pp. 211–12/213–14. The narrative shift to a fictional geography at that point marks the movement of the characters into the kind of mysterious domain represented by Bourani in *The Magus.*

65/65. megrims. Migraine headaches.

68/68. *Posse comitatus.* Body of men authorized to assist an officer in the keeping of peace in a county.

70/70. *Jurat . . . me.* She swears, the 31st of July, the year of our Lord 1736, before me.

76/76. *non compredit.* She does not understand.

82/82. mommet. A contemptible, hollow person.

83/83. *Jurat . . . coram.* She swears, the day and year above, before.

89/89. *Rarissimae aves.* The rarest of birds.

89/89. *politesse.* Social politeness, tact.

91/91. Ovid. Roman poet (43 B.C.–A.D. 17) was author of *The Metamorphoses.*

92/92. City is Whig. The City is the financial district of London; Ayscough means that the merchant class as a whole is not Tory and not high Church of England, as Beckford evidently is.

93/93. *Id est.* That is.

95/95. members. Members of Parliament.

97/97. *videlicit.* Namely.

97/97. *Jurat . . . me.* He swears, the 31st of July, the year above, before me.

99/99. *Non est inventus.* It is not discovered.

100/99. *prima facia.* Face value.

100/100. *omne . . . est.* Roughly, what they don't understand they make important.

100/100. *in loco.* In the locale.

100/100. *idem.* Also.

100/100. *auspicium melioris aevi.* Indicating a better age, that is, better luck in the future.

100/100. Mercury to Jupiter. The chief god's messenger.

100/100. *ad captandum vulgum.* To deceive the common people.

101/101. *aitchum non amant.* They don't like to pronounce *h*'s.

101/101. foul-ravelled Boeotian. Terribly confused, barbarian language.

101/101. Sacheverell. A Tory clergyman who preached that the church was in danger from the Whigs. He was impeached for treason but given a light sentence.

101/101. *non obstante.* Notwithstanding.

102/102. instrument. Evidently, a telescope.

102/102. *curiosi.* Inquirers.

102/102. Royal Society. An institution for the advancement of science, founded in 1662.

102/102. Sloane. Hans Sloane was president of the Royal College of Physicians from 1719 to 1735—and a collector of butterflies.

102/103. *in tenebris.* In the shadows, in the dark.

102/103. *primum mobile.* Prime mover, that is, main cause.

103/103. Gay. John Gay died in 1732, having written *The Beggar's Opera* (1728) as well as *The Shepherd's Week* (1714).

103/103. *quo fata trahunt, sequamur.* Where the fates draw us, let us follow.

103/104. Porteus. The fortunes of Captain John Porteus, who fired on one mob and was later hanged by another, is a recurring topic in the excerpts from the *Historical Chronicle* in the novel.

103/104. mobility. Mob.

107/107. Cicero. Marcus Tullius Cicero (106–43 B.C.) was famed for his oratory, appropriate decoration for a lawyer's office.

108/107. Pope or Voltaire. Alexander Pope (1688–1744) and François-Marie Arouet, or "Voltaire" (1694–1778), were less than five feet tall. Pope was slightly deformed as well.

109/109. Thalia, Melpomene. The classical muses of comedy and tragedy, respectively.

109/109. pantomime. A form of light theatrical comedy and burlesque with singing and dancing. John Rich (1692–1761) was a London producer, among other things of *The Beggar's Opera,* and a manager of Covent Garden.

109/109. Ketch. Jack Ketch was the hangman at Tyburn, where criminals were executed in London.

111/111. Fielding. The Little Theatre in the Haymarket was known as "Mr. Fielding's scandal shop," but *Pasquin* was performed in the New Theatre, whose management Fielding had taken over in 1736. After the Licensing Act of 1737, Fielding turned to the writing of fiction, including *Tom Jones.*

111/111. *Beggar's Opera.* John Gay's 1728 *The Beggar's Opera* depicted a gang of thieves in a way that satirized members of Parliament, whose leader resembled the prime minister, Sir Robert Walpole.

113/113. Queensberry . . . Walker. Catherine Hyde, Duchess of Queensberry was Gay's patronness and a great beauty. Mrs. Oldfield was an actress. Thomas Walker (1698–1744) played Macheath in *The Beggar's Opera,* but his constant intemperance led to a decline of his fortunes.

121/121. *The Cit Grown Beau.* Lacy's "Englished" title is today usually translated *The Bourgeois Gentleman,* a play by Molière (1660).

123/123. Topham. Thomas Topham (1710–49) was a performer of strong-man feats.

126/126. *Facile . . . volumus.* We easily believe what we want to believe.

130/130. *Macbeth.* The scene with the drunken porter at the gate is in Act 2, Scene 3 of this play (about 1606).

131/131. *The Recruiting Officer.* This 1706 comedy by George Farquhar contains such a sergeant, named Kite.

136/137. *quieta non movere.* Don't stir up the peaceful, that is, let sleeping dogs lie.

137/138. Saunderson. There was a historical Nicholas Saunderson (1682–1739), who was a professor of mathematics at Cambridge University despite having been blinded by smallpox during infancy.

139/140. title. Probably *Philosophiae Naturalis Principia Mathematica,* or *Mathematical Principles of Natural Philosophy* (1687).

139–40/140–41. monk . . . what. This sequence is made up of so-called Fibonacci numbers; rectangles based on them form what the Greeks called "Golden Sections" and also describe a form of spiral thought to have mystical properties. The sequence was discovered by Leonardo Pisano, a medieval mathematician who wrote *Liber Abaci,* or *The Book of the Abacus* (1202), a work that introduced Europe to the Arabic numeral system (mentioned on p. 188/190).

141/143. Stukeley, William Stukeley spent his life promoting the theory that Stonehenge was built by the Druids, who he believed were a lost tribe of Israel.

142/143. other learned writer. The Druid thesis was first advanced by antiquarian John Aubrey (1626–97), but Stukeley does deserve credit for first pointing out the relation between the heel stone and the summer solstice, as Fowles notes in *The Enigma of Stonehenge* (p. 9).

143/144. Newgate. London prison, setting for *The Beggar's Opera,* which Jonathan Swift referred to as a "Newgate pastoral."

145/146. great work. Lacy is reading *Paradise Lost,* published by John Milton in 1667.

146/147. Morpheus. Greek god of dreams.

147/148. *post facto.* After the fact.

159/161. *Jurat . . . me.* He swears before me the 24th of August 1736.

161/163. *anno praedicto.* Aforementioned year.

170/172. James Stuart. "The Old Pretender," The Catholic son of James II, who claimed to be the rightful heir to the English throne after the Glorious Revolution of 1688 had established that the Monarch must be a Protestant.

178/181. Charke. Charlotte Charke (died 1760) was an actress and writer, the youngest daughter of Colley Cibber. She left her husband, took to the stage, and acted the part of Fopling Fribble, modeled on her father, in Fielding's *Tom Thumb* (1731).

179/182. *Jurat . . . me.* He swears before me the aforementioned day and year.

182/184. *ipsissima verba.* The very words.

182/184. Cyprian rites. Perhaps lovemaking, the "rites" of Venus, who came ashore on Cyprus after having been born at sea, according to tradition.

182/184. Tacitus. Publius Cornelius Tacitus (A.D. 55–120) was a Roman historian.

182/184. *meretricum . . . lenis.* The gentle queen of meretricious beginnings.

186/188. *Quantum . . . illo!* What a change from that!

186/188. *ter-veneficus.* Triple-poisoner.

187/190. *in cathedrâ Lucasianâ.* Occupying the Lucas Chair (a mathematics professorship).

188/191. *phyllotaxis.* Taxonomies of plants, whose leaves sometimes illustrate the form of the Fibonacci spiral (see note to pp. 139–40/140–41).

189/191. *dementia in exsilio.* Madness in exile, that is, ivory-tower syndrome.

189/191. *In delitescentia non est scientia.* There is no knowledge to be gained from concealment.

189/191. *amici amicitiae.* Friends to friendship.

193/195. &c. Abbreviation for *et cetera* (and so forth).

198/200. Faribelly. Carlo Broschi, or Farinelli, was one of the great eighteenth-century *castrati*, who was in London 1734–37.

199/201. nice. Particular.

199/201. Odsocks. By God's (Jesus') hooks (fingernails).

203/205. *Non respondet.* He does not answer.

206/208. *Respondet.* He responds.

207/210. Maunt. Might not.

209/212. fifth of Moses. The Fifth Commandment (Exodus 20:12).

222/225. bumbardo. Bumblebees.

228/232. *Non . . . regredi.* Not to go forward is to go back.

229/233. Defoe. Daniel Defoe's statement, in "The Shortest-Way with the Dissenters: Or Proposals for the Establishment of the Church," appeared on 1 December 1702, not "in 1703."

229/233. *ex parte.* In the interest of one side only, partial.

230/234. *casus belli.* An event that leads to war.

233/237. *die . . . p'dicto.* Day and year aforementioned.

243/248. debosht. Debauched.

246/251. upon the stone. Tess Durbeyfield similarly lies down on the "altar stone" at Stonehenge, in Thomas Hardy's *Tess of the d'Urbervilles* (Chapter 58).

269/275. *Testis . . . nullus.* One witness (is not better than) no witness.

269–70/275. Mars . . . Rome. Mars is the Roman god of war, his sister Bellona the goddess. John O'Groats, in Scotland, is the northernmost point in Britain.

271/277. *viz.* Abbreviation for *videlicit,* Latin for *that is to say.*

271/277. enthusiasm. A common, derogatory term describing the religious attitude of religious sects that "dissented," or did not "conform" to the Church of England (or of Rome).

274/280. Mopsus. Name for a shepherd.

274/280. Arcadian. Resembling an idyllic, pastoral, mountainous area in Greece.

275/281. Egyptians. Travelers, gypsies.

277/283. *id est.* That is.

278/285. *vestigia.* Remaining signs.

279/286. *qualibet.* Wherever.

281/287. *in re.* Regarding this.

281/288. Hales. Stephen Hales (1677–1760) was an inventor and physiologist. One of his inventions was the *orrery,* a model that demonstrated the movement of planets around the sun. He was a friend of William Stukeley (see note to p. 141/143).

282/289. *socius.* A member.

283/289. D.D. R.S.S. Doctor of Divinity, Royal Society Socius.

288/294. Tetrevangelium. Book of the four evangelists—Matthew, Mark, Luke, John—used for readings in church services.

315/321. *idée reçue.* Received idea.

315/321. child. Edward Gibbon, born in 1737, would write *The History of the Decline and Fall of the Roman Empire* (1776–88).

315/322. *abbé mondain.* Secular abbot, that is, clergyman.

317/324. Vapours. Depression.

340/346. *de rigeur.* Required.

347/353. *die . . . praedicte.* Day and year aforementioned.

357/364. lion's . . . within. Rebecca alludes to a story of Samson, who killed a lion and later found honey in its carcass (Judges 14:8).

375/383. *Magna creatrix.* She who creates, the Great Mother.

383/391. Erinnyes. Greek goddesses of vengeance.

385/393. Paine. Thomas Paine (1737–1809), born in England, was a writer of pamphlets and a leader of the American Revolution.

385/393. *cogito, ergo sum.* "I think; therefore, I am" was the founding assertion of identity on which René Descartes (1596–1650) based his philosophical speculations.

385/393. Popes . . . Johnsons. All famous writers of the eighteenth century. Alexander Pope (1688–1744) was the leading poet; Joseph Addison (1672–1719) and Richard Steele (1672–1729) edited *The Spectator;* Samuel Johnson (1709–84) wrote biography, fiction, poetry, and the first dictionary of English.

386/394. Robespierre. M.F.M.I. de Robespierre (1758–94) here represents abuses of power by French revolutionaries after 1789.

401/409. Fox. George Fox (1624–91) was founder of the Society of Friends, or Quakers.

422/431. By faith . . . Rahab. Rahab was a harlot in Jericho who sheltered Hebrew spies before the seige of the city (Joshua 2). Rebecca is quoting an Old Testament passage celebrating her: "By faith Rahab the harlot did not perish with those who were disobedient, because she had given friendly welcome to the spies" (RSV, Hebrews 11:31). Sometimes Rahab's story is cited as an example of works rather than faith alone as a justification of salvation (James 2:18–26), but Rebecca is emphasizing Rahab's faith—like her own. Ayscough's strong, negative reaction to Rebecca's claims parallels a strain of uneasiness among church fathers of Rahab's status as a saved, even a sacred prostitute.

433/442. Herod. Herod Antipas judged Jesus Christ.

435/445. father. Turtullian (A.D. 155–225) first expressed this "rule of faith."

435/445. *non obstante.* Nevertheless.

436/446. *rota fortunae.* Fortune's wheel (see note to p. 19/18).

437/447. *puellae cloacarum.* Women of the sewer, whores.

439/449. *Horresco referens.* I shudder to recall.

439/450. Chimaera. A fantastic creature in Greek myth, here representing madness.

441/451. *Nos . . . nihil.* We knew these things to be nothing.

442/452. *Fiat . . . vili.* Let the experiment be done on the worthless body.

447/459. Blake. William Blake (1757–1827) asks in "The School Boys," "How can the bird that is born for joy, / Sit in a cage and sing?" Perhaps lines from "Infant Sorrow" also helped to shape Fowles's vision: "Struggling in my father's hands: / Striving against my swadling bands" *(Songs of Innocence and of Experience)*.

452/464. *siècle de lumières*. Age of Enlightenment.

452/464. *en masse*. In large numbers.

452/461. Mies. Ludwig Mies van der Rohe (1886–1969) was an architect associated with the International Style glass skyscrapers, but he was influenced by eighteenth-century design.

454/466. Greek . . . Troy. The Greeks hid soldiers inside a wooden horse outside Troy; the Trojans brought the horse inside the city walls, at the "price" of their own destruction.

APPENDIX: CENSUS OF CHARACTERS

This alphabetized list of characters offers refreshment of memory to readers who may lose track of a name as they read, or while a book has been set aside. The census includes most characters who are named, even if they do not have speaking parts in the story. After the surname are given names, when known, and nicknames in parentheses. Several characters who have important roles but who are never named I have included at the end. After each name, in brackets, is an abbreviated title: *Col* for *The Collector, Mgs* for *The Magus, FLW* for *The French Lieutenant's Woman, ET* for *The Ebony Tower, DM* for *Daniel Martin, Mts* for *Mantissa,* and *Mgt* for *A Maggot.* After the title is the page where a character's name is first mentioned (or pages, if the first name is introduced separately from the last name, nickname, etc.); both hardcover and paperback page numbers are provided, in that order, separated by a slash. In several cases, aliases are cross referenced to the name with the strongest claim to be "real."

Abdullam [*DM* 479/510]. The only honest antique dealer in Luxor.

Acland [*Mgt* 68/68]. Apothecary and clerk in the town of C———, helps investigate and writes to the coroner about Dick Thurlow.

Adam [*Mgs* 496/504]. Blonde, crew-cut sailor, assistant to Conchis.

Alain [*DM* 495/529]. Young French journalist working on a magazine article on the cruise up the Nile.

Amanda [*Mgs* 621/633]. Drama student and fiancée of John Briggs.

Ambelas, Hermes [*Mgs* 74/76, 392/399]. Carries food and mail to the Villa Bourani.

Anderson, Steve (The Prick, The P.) [*DM* 13/12, 36/37, 63/64]. Egotistical, married, playboy, acts opposite Jenny in a film under production.

Andrea [*DM* 142/150]. Production secretary, helps Dan with scripts, has an affair with Dan and tours the Nile with him, is killed by her jealous husband.

Andrew [*Mgs* 363/369]. Cambridge professor of mathematics, Julie's bisexual boyfriend.

Anne (The Freak) [*ET* 20/19]. In "The Ebony Tower," former art student and friend of Diana, lives with Breasley, reads *The Magus*.

Annie [*Col* 5/9]. Clegg's aunt, rears Clegg from age two to fifteen with her husband, Dick, and then by herself after he dies.

Antoinette (Toinette) [*Col* 126/113]. Acquaintance of Miranda who first annoys G. P. then becomes his sex partner.

Anton [*Mgs* 415/421, 488/496]. See Mayer, Heinrich.

Aphrodite [*Mts* 72, 78]. Erato's "aunt."

Arbuthnot, Major [*DM* 87/90]. Gouty parishioner visited by Mr. Martin.

Assad, Jimmy [*DM* 459/488]. Tall, balding political cynic who meets Daniel Martin and Jane Mallory in Cairo.

Athanasoulis, Catherine [*Mgs* 444/451, 452]. See Maria.

Aubrey [*FLW* 411/321]. Solicitor for Mr. Freeman.

Ayscough, Henry [*Mgt* 70/70]. Barrister, conducts inquiry into the mysterious disappearance of Lord——— for his father, the Duke of ———.

B———, Lord [*Mgt* 155]. Friend of Lord ———, introduces him to Hannah Claiborne and "Fanny."

Barbara [*DM* 378/402]. Daughter of Daniel Martin's aunt in Carlisle, corresponds with Dan, turns Catholic and becomes a nun.

Barnecott [*Mgt* 66/66]. Discovers the corpse of Dick Thurlow.

Barrow [*Mgt* 134/134]. Russian merchant through whom Lacy is paid.

Bartholemew (Mr. B) [*Mgt* 18/16, 133/133]. See ———, Lord.

Beckford, Sampson [*Mgt* 22/21, 87/87]. Curate in the town of C———, educated at Oxford, conservative and pompous.

Behrens, Dr. [*Mgs* 397/404]. Alison Kelly's doctor.

Ben [*DM* 214/228]. Gardener at Thorncombe, alcoholic, works slowly but thoroughly.

Ben [*FLW* 196/157]. Father of Ebenezer, pensioner at Winsyatt.

Benson [*FLW* 212/170]. Butler at Winsyatt.

Betty [*Mgt* 81/81]. Chambermaid at the Black Hart inn, shares a room with Dorcas Hellyer.

Betty Anne (Betsy Anne) [*FLW* 344/270, 401/314]. Maid at the Endicott Family Hotel.

Bill [*DM* 31/31]. Director, present at the casting interview when Daniel Martin meets Jenny.

Bill [*Mgs* 23/25]. Friend of Pete Spencer-Haigh.

Bob [*Col* 10/13]. Son of Clegg's Aunt Annie, lives in Brisbane, Australia.

Breasley, Henry [*ET* 7/7, 11/10]. Famous artist, temperamental, lives and paints in France as a self-imposed exile from England in "The Ebony Tower."

Briggs, John [*Mgs* 618/629]. American teacher, replaces Nicholas Urfe at the Lord Byron School.

Broughton, Piers [*Col* 40/39]. Student at the Slade School of Art, friend of Miranda, rumored to be her fiancé.

Brown [*Mgt* 22/21]. See Lacy, Francis.

Bruneau, Charles Victor [*Mgs* 112/115]. Music teacher to Maurice Conchis when he was young.

Buchanan, Father [*DM* 213/227]. Catholic priest, discusses funeral arrangements with Daniel Martin.

Bullock [*Mgt* 95/95]. Canon of the Anglican Church at Exeter, Beckford's patron.

Burgh, Sir Thomas (Tom) [*FLW* 298/235–36]. Acquaintance of Charles Smithson's at Cambridge, member of his club in London, generous.

Caroline [*Col* 125/113]. Miranda's aunt, likes modern art, lacks authenticity.

Catesby, Peter [*Col* 38/37]. A middle-class oaf according to Miranda, takes her to a coffee-bar where Clegg sees them.

Catherine (Kate) [*ET* 251/235]. In "The Cloud," silent, recently widowed sister of Annabel, disappears—perhaps dies—at the end.

Charles [*Mgt.* 271/276]. A knighted gentleman who has engaged both Henry Ayscough and Richard Pygge in business unrelated to the disappearance of the son of the unidentified Duke.

Charlie [*Mgs* 23/25]. Friend of Pete Spencer-Haigh, would-be protector of Pete's interest in Alison Kelly.

Charlie [*Mts* 177]. Erato's nickname for Aristophanes, whose plays she inspired.

Ciardi, Mario [*Mgs* 505/513]. Professor from Milan, on the board at the "trial" of Nicholas.

Claiborne, Hannah (Mother Claiborne) [*Mgt* 42/42, 134/135, 151/153]. Keeper of a brothel in London, employs Rebeca Hocknell as Fanny, "the Quaker Maid," hires her out for a supposed "folly" at Oxford.

Clegg, Frederick (Ferdinand) [*Col* 10/13, 37/37]. A collector of various beautiful things, uneducated, insecure, impotent with women.

Conchis, Maurice (Mr. Rat, Gambardello) [*Mgs* 79/81, 169/173, 588/598–99]. Eccentric millionaire and owner of the villa Bourani on Phraxos, a man of many poses, creator of "the godgame," which Nicholas Urfe finds himself "playing."

Cory [*Mts* 15]. West Indian nurse, supposed reincarnation of Shakespeare's "Dark Lady."

Cotton, Lady [*FLW* 23/25]. Philanthropist to whom Mrs. Poulteney is accustomed to compare herself.

Cruikshank, Barber [*Col* 162–63/144]. Friend of G.P.

Cruikshank, Frances [*Col* 162–63/144]. Wife of Barber, friend of G.P.

Crutchley [*Col* 6/10]. Works with Clegg, teases him about girls.

Day, Samuel [*Mgt* 102/102]. Inquirer into natural science.

Delphie, A. [*Mts* 14]. Miles Green's doctor.

Demetriades (Méli) [*Mgs* 52/53]. Friend of Nicholas Urfe at the Lord Byron School, introduces him to Conchis.

Deukans, Count Alphonse de [*Mgs* 175/179]. Wealthy misogynist and art collector, befriends Conchis in Paris, commits suicide when his estate is destroyed.

Devereaux, Henry [*Mgt* 94/94]. The only gentleman living in the neighborhood of C———, according to Parson Beckford.

Diana (Di, The Mouse) [*ET* 8/8, 49/46]. In "The Ebony Tower," former art student, live-in assistant to Henry Breasley, finds herself attracted to David Williams.

Dick [*Col* 5/9]. Clegg's uncle, helps to rear him from age two, dies in 1950 when Clegg is fifteen.

Dimitraki, Barba [*Mgs* 389/396]. Eighty-year-old man, carried mail to Bourani before World War II.

Diffrey, Alderman [*Mgt* 271/277]. Merchant and shipbuilder in Bristol, employs Amos Hocknell, dismisses him for proselytizing.

Dillon, Bernard (Barney, Boring Bernard) [*DM* 92/96, 116/122, 450/480]. Lives above Daniel Martin at Oxford, writes a gossip column for a university magazine, becomes a television "personality," hires Caroline Martin as a secretary and has an affair with her.

Dillon, Margaret [*DM* 103/107]. Wife of Barney Dillon, has an agreement with him that they will live separate lives but will remain married for the sake of the children.

Dodgson, Isobel [*ET* 197/184, 214/200]. In "The Enigma," graduate student in English, sometime girlfriend of Peter Fielding, is considered attractive by Michael Jennings, hypothesizes about the disappearance of Marcus Fielding.

Donald [*Col* 146/129]. Former boyfriend of Miranda, cowardly.

Doodah [*Mts* 178]. Erato's name for Plato.

Drummond [*ET* 193/181]. Agent for Marcus Fielding in his district.

Ebenezer [*FLW* 195/157]. Blacksmith at Winsyatt.

Elaine [*DM* 159/169]. Girl from the Midwest with whom Daniel Martin has an affair in Hollywood.

Eliduc [*ET* 123/115]. In "Eliduc," a knight in Brittany, married to Guildelüec, goes into exile in England, falls in love with Guilliadun.

Endicott, Martha [*FLW* 274/218]. Owner of the Endicott Family Hotel, in Exeter.

Erato [*Mts* 84]. Muse of love poetry, sex partner of Miles Green.

Ercole [*Mgs* 585/595]. Italian houseboy at the Allitsen Road house of Mr. and Mrs. Simon Marks.

Evans, David [*Col* 153/135]. Friend of Miranda Grey, is affected by George Paston's scorn for the working class.

Ezekiel [*Mgt* 66/66]. Stableboy at the Black Hart Inn.

Fairley, Mrs. Frederick [*FLW* 19/22]. Housekeeper for Mrs. Poulteney, an incipient sadist and spy.

Fairwether, Lady [*FLW* 81/69]. Dowager who attends one of Mrs. Freeman's soirées.

Fane [*Mgt* 95/95]. Member of Parliament from the borough of C———.

Fanny (The Quaker Maid) [*Mgt* 42, 135]. See Lee, Rebecca.

Farrow, Sam [*FLW* 38/36, 43/40]. Manservant to Charles Smithson, marries Mrs. Tranter's servant Mary.

Farthing, Timothy/Jones, David (Tim, Sergeant Cut and Come Again) [*Mgt* 30/29, 31/30, 63/63, 130/130]. Bit actor from Wales, hired as a braggart soldier by Lord ——— and Francis Lacy, spies on "Louise" at Exmoor, is told a story of a Satanic ceremony in the cave.

Fearn, P. J. [*Mgs* 328/334]. Supposed manager of a bank in London.

Fenwick, Miles [*DM* 296/315]. An older, Conservative barrister and member of Parliament, invited to dinner at Compton, content to watch Britain fall apart because he "has his."

Fenwick, Elizabeth [*DM* 296/315]. American "Wasp," attends dinner at Compton with her husband.

Fielding, Caroline [*ET* 195/183]. In "The Enigma," younger daughter of John Marcus, is abroad when her father disappears.

Fielding, Francesca [*ET* 195/183]. In "The Enigma," older daughter of John Marcus, is abroad when her father disappears.

Fielding, John Marcus [*ET* 191/179]. In "The Enigma," rich, happily married Conservative member of Parliament who mysteriously disappears.

Fielding, Mrs. [*ET* 192/180]. In "The Enigma," wife of John Marcus Fielding, concerned with appearances.

Forsythe [*FLW* 24/26]. Vicar of Lyme Regis, spiritual advisor to Mrs. Poulteney, leads search for Sarah after her dismissal.

Fotheringay [*Mgt* 403/412]. Magistrate in Manchester borough where Rebecca Lee is interrogated.

Freak. See Anne.

Fredriksen, Johnan [*Mgs* 578/588]. Schoolmaster in Kirkenes, answers Nicholas's inquiry about the Nygaards.

Freeman [*FLW* 132/109]. Owner of a chain of stores, believes in profits and earnestness.

Freeman, Emily [*FLW* 390/305]. Sister of Mrs. Tranter, wife of Mr. Freeman.

Freeman, Ernestina (Tina) [*FLW* 6/11, 10/14]. Conventional girl, engaged to Charles Smithson, jilted for Sarah Woodruff.

Fursey-Harris [*FLW* 33/34]. Vicar of Charmouth, where Sarah meets the French Lieutenant.

Georgiou [*Mgs* 388/394]. Tavern keeper on Phraxos.

Gertie [*Col* 197/172]. Wife of Clegg's Uncle Steve in Melbourne, Australia.

Gisèle [*DM* 193/206]. French maid of Jane and Anthony Mallory, hosted Anne Mallory in France.

Gold [*DM* 31/31]. Film producer, attends casting interview when Jenny meets Dan.

Green, Claire [*Mts* 4, 6]. Wife of Miles, anxious about his amnesia.

Green, David [*Mts* 9]. Son of Miles and Claire Green.

Green, Jane [*Mts* 9]. Daughter of Miles and Claire Green.

Green, Miles [*Mts* 6]. Married novelist inside whose brain the stories inspired by Erato take place.

Green, Tom [*Mts* 9]. Son of Miles and Claire Green.

Grey, Carmen (Minny) [*Col* 214/185]. Sister of Miranda, addressed in the journal, clever.

Grey, Dr. [*Col* 174/153]. Father of Miranda, weak and alcoholic, a failed surgeon.

Grey, Mrs. [*Col* 150/133]. Miranda'a mother, bitchy and alcoholic.

Grey, Miranda [*Col* 4/8]. A student at the Slade School of Art in London, well educated, matures during her imprisonment by Clegg.

Grillet, Susan [*Col* 235/201]. Acquaintance of Miranda who marries a baronet three times her age.

Grogan, Doctor [*FLW* 59/53]. Early admirer of Darwin, advisor to Charles Smithson, believes Sarah to be a hysteric.

Guildelüec [*ET* 123/115]. In "Eliduc," lives in Brittany, married to Eliduc, asks for a separation to become a nun.

Guilliadun [*ET* 123/115]. In "Eliduc," princess in England, elopes with Eliduc to Brittany, "dies" but revives, marries Eliduc, later joins Guildelüec in a convent.

Gunhild [*Mgs* 588/599]. Norwegian au pair in the house of Lily de Seitas.

Halberstadt, Arne [*Mgs* 505/513]. Director of Conchis' metatheater, on the board at the "trial" of Nicholas.

Hales, Stephen [*Mgt* 283/289]. A theologian and amateur chemist who examines a soil sample from outside the Exmoor cave (based on a historical figure).

Hannacott, Bill [*DM* 350/373]. Neighbor of Nancy Reed who humiliates Dan with a crosscut saw—and infuriates Nancy.

Harold [*DM* 35/35]. Ex-boyfriend of Jenny when she was in Birmingham.

Harriet [*FLW* 420/329]. Servant of Mary and Sam Farrow, helps with the baby.

Harrison, Joseph (Joe) [*Mgs* 342/347, 445/452]. Black psychiatrist from the University of Idaho, plays a mute valet to Conchis or an American actor at various stages of the novel.

Harry [*DM* 381/406]. Nancy Reed's husband, a foreman at Dagenham.

Harvey, Henry [*Mgt* 272/278]. Son in the house where Rebecca Hocknell first worked, is discovered "in sin" with her.

Hawkins [*FLW* 194/156]. Son of Mrs. Hawkins, greets Charles Smithson at the gate of Winsyatt.

Hawkins, Mrs. [*FLW* 194/156]. Head laundrymaid at Winsyatt.

Hellyer, Dorcas [*Mgt* 30/29, 73/73]. Maid of all work at the Black Hart Inn, seventeen years old, resists sexual advances by Farthing.

Hocknell, Amos [*Mgt* 239/244]. Bristol Quaker, carpenter and joiner by trade, dismissed for religious proselytizing, father of Rebecca Hocknell Lee.

Hocknell, John [*Mgt* 298/304]. Prophet among the Quakers, uncle of Rebecca Hocknell.

Hocknell, Martha Bradling/Bradlynch [*Mgt* 271/277]. Wife of Amos, mother of Rebecca Hocknell Lee.

Hocknell, Rebecca [*Mgt* 151/153]. See Lee, Rebecca.

Holmes, Constance [*Mgs* 464/471]. Supposed mother of Julie Holmes.

Holmes, June [*Mgs* 211/216]. Supposed actress, and sister of Julie, played by Rose, twin sister of Lily and daughter of William and Lily de Seitas.

Holmes, Julie Neilson [*Mgs* 211/216, 329/334]. Supposed schizophrenic and sister of June, played by Lily, twin sister of Rose and daughter of William and Lily de Seitas.

Hooper, Marcia [*DM* 486/518]. American touring Egypt, likes movies and books.

Hooper, Mitchell [*DM* 486/518]. American touring Egypt, scientist, from Joliet, Illinois.

Hughes, William A. [*Mgs* 394/401, 596/607]. See Seitas, William de.

Hunnicut, Mrs. [*FLW* 202/162]. Acquaintance of Mrs. Tranter.

Jane [*Col* 7/10]. Crutchley's girlfriend, works in sanitation, thought by Clegg to be vulgar.

Jane [*ET* 148/140]. In "Poor Koko," married to Maurice, owns Holly Cottage, where the events of the story take place.

Janet [*Mgs* 21/24]. Girlfriend of Nicholas Urfe when he is teaching in East Anglia, after Oxford.

Jean-Louis [*Col* 212/184]. Shy French boy who meets Miranda at Collioure.

Jean-Pierre [*ET* 28/26]. In "The Ebony Tower," Breasley's cook and gardener.

Jem [*FLW* 121/100]. A poacher.

Jennings, Michael (Mike) [*ET* 203/190]. In "The Enigma," public school graduate, investigator for Scotland Yard, holds the rank of sergeant, assigned to investigate the disappearance of Fielding.

Jenny [*Col* 13/16]. Bartender at the coffeehouse Miranda visits.

Jojo [*Mgs* 634/645]. Scottish girl, befriended by Nicholas in London.

Jorgensen, Thorvald [*Mgs* 506/514]. From Aalborg University in Denmark, plays the colonel who captures Nicholas in the woods.

Karazoglou [*Mgs* 75/77]. Biology master at the Lord Byron School.

Katherine (Kate) [*DM* 430/458]. Steve's American girlfriend, invites Jenny to join them in a ménage à trois.

Kazanian, Annette [*Mgs* 506/514]. See Maria.

Kelly, Alison (Allie) [*Mgs* 20/23, 23/26, 30/32]. From Australia, airline stewardess, formerly promiscuous, is undervalued by Nicholas Urfe, is protected by Lily de Seitas, meets Nicholas in Regent's Park at the end of the novel.

Kelly, Mary [*Mgs* 398/404]. Mother of Alison.

Kemp, Joan [*Mgs* 576/586]. Landlady of Nicholas in Charlotte Street, London.

Kirnberger, Hans [*DM* 522/557]. Son of Otto Kirnberger, escaped to the West in 1939 to become an archaeologist in the United States.

Kirnberger, Otto [*DM* 485/516]. Old German expert on the pharoahs, a guide at Luxor.

Kluber, Anton [*Mgs* 415/421]. Lieutenant in the *Wehrmacht*, first German commandant of Phraxos during the Nazi occupation.

Knight, Jimmy [*DM* 296/315]. Film producer, involved in a deal with Miles Fenwick.

Kottopoulos, Yanni [*Mgs* 505/513]. Stage manager of Conchis' metatheater, sits on the board at the trial of Nicholas Urfe.

Kretschmer, Friedrich [*Mgs* 505/513]. Doctor of psychology and director of the Institute of Experimental Psychology at the University of Idaho, chairs the board at the trial.

Krupskaya, Nadya Constantinovna [*DM* 53/54, 259/276]. Nickname (after Lenin's widow) of Dan's Marxist landlady in Oxford.

Labib [*DM* 578/618]. Drives Dan and Jane through Lebanon and Syria, loves his Chevrolet.

Lacy, Francis/Brown [*Mgt* 17/16, 22/21, 119/119]. Middle-aged member of the traveling group, an actor in London, hired to act the part of "Mr. Brown," the uncle of "Mr. Bartholemew," goes to Exeter so does not see any of the events at Exmoor.

Lalage [*FLW* 458/359]. Daughter of Sarah and Charles, conceived in Exeter, being brought up in Chelsea, London.

Lee, Ann (Mary) [447/459]. Historical founder of the Shakers, biological daughter of Rebecca Lee and Dick Thurlow.

Lee, John [281/288]. Blacksmith and preacher in Manchester, marries Rebecca Hocknell.

Lee, Rebecca/Rebecca Hocknell/Louise/Fanny (The Quaker Maid) [*Mgt* 32/32, 41/42, 135/135, 151/153, 281/288]. Daughter of Quakers, becomes a London prostitute known as "Fanny," at age twenty-three journeys to Devon as "Louise," engages in sexual intercourse with Dick Thurlow, is introduced to mysterious strangers by Lord ———, has a religious vision and joins a sect of Dissenters, marries John Lee, gives birth to Ann Lee.

Lee-Jones, Arthur [*Mgs* 578/588]. Major who answers Nicholas's inquiry about the Battle of Neuve Chapelle.

Lester, Penny [*Col* 124/112]. Dormitory mate of Miranda.

Leverrier, John [*Mgs* 75/77, 87/89]. English schoolmaster at the Lord Byron School before Mitford and Nicholas.

Lewis [*DM* 3/1]. Drives the reaper-binder during the harvest.

Lily [*Mgs* 406/412]. See Seitas, Lily de.

Locke, Colonel [*FLW* 420/329]. Lives at Jericho House, hires Sam after he quits Charles's employ.

Louise [*Col* 152/135]. Friend of Miranda, girlfriend of a Welsh miner's son, person Miranda asks about when she is ill.

Louise [*Mgt* 32/32]. See Lee, Rebecca.

Luck, Robert [*Mgt* 103/103]. Master of the grammar school at C———, former teacher of John Gay, interviewed by Ayscough.

Luscombe, Bill [*DM* 4/2]. Son of a farmworker.

Luscombe, Mr. [*DM* 4/2]. Farmworker during the harvest.

Luscombe, Mrs. [*DM* 9/8]. Feels no sympathy for the rabbits during the harvest.

Mabel [*Col* 5/9]. Crippled daughter of Dick and Annie, five years older than Clegg when he is informally adopted.

McNeil, Jenny [*DM* 12/11, 39/40]. Actress, Anglo-Scottish girlfriend of Daniel who encourages him to write a novel.

McDonald, Bill [*Col* 224/194]. One of Miranda's artist-acquaintances who do not worry about making money.

Malevich, David [*DM* 95/99]. American producer whom Daniel considers "good" at his job, acts as Jenny's agent at the novel's end.

Mallory, Anne [*DM* 187/199]. Middle child of Anthony and Jane, is in Florence when her father commits suicide.

Mallory, Anthony [*DM* 21/20, 101/105]. Roman Catholic, "Greats" scholar at Oxford, marries Jane and lives at Wytham, is dying of cancer when he calls Daniel back to England for a conversation before committing suicide.

Mallory, Jane [*DM* 22/21, 101/105]. Has a one-time affair with Daniel at Oxford, marries Anthony, politically Marxist, travels to the Middle East with Daniel in the latter part of the novel.

Mallory, Paul [*DM* 187/200]. Fifteen-year-old youngest son of Jane and Anthony, quiet and sullen, interested in history.

Mallory, Rosamund (Roz) [*DM* 134/141, 216/230]. Oldest child of Jane and Anthony, goddaughter of Daniel, is happy working for the BBC.

Marcus, Mary [*Mgs* 505/513]. Doctor of psychology from Edinburgh, on the board at the trial of Nicholas.

Margaret (Squinty Four-eyes) [*DM* 88/91]. Ten-year-old schoolmate of eleven-year-old Daniel.

Margaret (Maggie) [*Mgs* 22/24, 23/25]. London University student from Australia who lodges below Nicholas and introduces him to Alison.

Margison, Sally [*Col* 245/209]. Fellow student of Miranda at Ladymont School, whom Miranda manipulates to show a clique that she is cleverer than they are.

Maria [*Mgs* 80/82, 506/514]. Housekeeper at Bourani who Nicholas concludes was probably "really" a peasant rather than Dr. Annette Kazanian (and Madame Maurice Conchis) or Catherine Athanasoulis.

Marian [*Col* 305/255]. Clegg's prospective second victim at the end of the novel.

Marjory (the Drag) [*DM* 242/257]. Younger and prettier of the "fairy sisters" with whom Daniel gets involved casually in London.

Mark [*DM* 22/21]. Older, fellow student of Daniel at Oxford, landed at Anzio, chum of Andrew, moves to New Zealand in the 1950s.

Marks, Mrs. Simon [*Mgs* 586/597]. Lives in the house where Lily Montgomery de Seitas was born, provides Nicholas with her current address.

Martha [*DM* 38/39]. Jenny's cleaning woman.

Martin, Parson [*DM* 75/77]. Daniel's father, vicar of a parish in Devon.

Martin, Caroline (Caro) [*DM* 34/34, 43/44]. Daniel's daughter by Nell, described by him as a poor little rich girl.

Martin, Daniel H. (Dan, Danny) [*DM* 10/8, 11/10]. Main character of the novel, grows up in Devon, attends Oxford, becomes a playwright, then a screenwriter, and, finally, a novelist.

Martin, Millie (Miz Martin) [*DM* 11/9, 75/77]. Sister of Daniel's father, dowdy and simple-hearted.

Mary [*FLW* 73/63]. Mrs. Tranter's servant, marries Sam Farrow, recognizes Sarah in Chelsea.

Mary [*FLW* 312/246]. Baby daughter of Sarah the London street prostitute.

Mathilde [*ET* 35/33]. In "The Ebony Tower," Breasley's cook and gardener, with Jean-Pierre.

Maurice [*ET* 148/140]. In "Poor Koko," married to Jane, owns Holly Cottage, where the narrator is working on his book.

Mavromichalis [*Mgs* 542/552]. Deputy headmaster of the Lord Byron School, tries to persuade Nicholas to resign.

Maxwell, Margaret [*Mgs* 505/513]. Costume designer for Conchis's metatheater, "really" Rose De Seitas.

Maxwell, Vanessa [*Mgs* 506/514]. Doctor of psychiatry and member of the board at the trial of Nicholas, "really" the younger Lily de Seitas.

Mayer, Heinrich [*Mgs* 505/514]. Swiss doctor, head of a faculty in Vienna, plays Anton in the metadrama.

Michel [*Mgs* 33/35]. A man Alison Kelly is trying to forget.

Miles [*DM* 296/315]. Member of Parliament, engaged to marry a daughter of Fenwick, investing in a film of Jimmy Knight's.

Millie [*FLW* 55/50]. Servant of Mrs. Poulteney, is ministered to by Sarah after she faints.

Miriam [*DM* 240/255]. Darker-skinned of the two "fairy sisters" with whom Daniel becomes involved in London, sentimental.

Mitford, Alexander (Sandy) [*Mgs* 43/44, 581/591, 608/620]. Nicholas's predecessor at the Lord Byron School, meets him in London.

Mitchell, Col. [*Mgt* 95/95]. Member of Parliament from C————.

Montague, Harry [*FLW* 261/208, 410/321]. Charles's solicitor in London.

Montague, Captain [*Mgs* 120/123]. Regular officer for whom Conchis was batman during World War I.

Montgomery, Charles Penn [*Mgs* 584/594]. Surgeon in St. John's Wood, father of Lily Montgomery de Seitas.

Montgomery, Florence [*Mgs* 584/594]. Wife of Charles Penn Montgomery, mother of Lily Montgomery de Seitas.

Montgomery, Lily [*Mgs* 114/116, 168/171]. See Seitas, Lily Montgomery de.

Montgomery, May [*Mgs* 590/601]. Eldest sister of Lily Montgomery de Seitas, lives in Chile.

Montgomery, Rose [*Mgs* 590/601]. Sister of Lily Montgomery de Seitas, died in 1916.

Mopsus [*Mts* 72]. Young shepherd, seen masturbating by Erato, later banished from Mount Olympus for bestiality.

Mouse. See Diana.

Murphy, Mr. Sergeant [*FLW* 411/321]. Top counsel, employed by Mr. Freeman in the proceeding against Charles for breach of contract.

Musagetes, Apollo (Aunt Polly) [*Mts* 73]. Manager of Mnemosyne's traveling freak show.

Nathan, Abe [*DM* 37/38, 65/66]. Movie script "doctor," married to Mildred, friend of Daniel who lets him live in "the cabin."

Nathan, Mildred [*DM* 37/38]. Lives in Bel-Air, married to Abe.

Nathaniel (Nat) [*FLW* 298/236]. Member of Charles's club, son of a bishop.

Nevinson, Douglas P. R. [*Mgs* 394/401, 580/590]. Former English master at the Lord Byron School, corresponds with Mrs. De Seitas.

Nielsen [*Col* 183/161]. Wife of a Dane, bed partner of G.P., condescending.

Nobby [*Col* 34/35]. Acquaintance of Clegg, advises him about how to treat women.

Nygaard, Gustav [*Mgs* 298/303]. Formerly a doctor, manages his brother's farm at Seidevarre, Norway.

Nygaard, Henrik [*Mgs* 300/306]. Sits on a promontory in northern Norway waiting for revelations from God.

Nygaard, Ragna [*Mgs* 301/306]. Wife of Henrik Nygaard, is rearing two children and working the farm of her mad husband in Norway.

Omar [*DM* 533/570]. Boatman who takes Dan and Jane to Kitchener's Island.

Parsons, Miss (P) [*ET* 192/180, 206/193]. In "The Enigma," elderly secretary to Marcus Fielding.

Paston, George (G.P.) [*Col* 125/113, 208/181]. Painter, mentor to Miranda, dislikes collectors, doesn't suffer fools, respects makers, bisexual, teaches Miranda to see with more awareness.

Paterescu [*Mgs* 59/61]. Village doctor on Phraxos, treats Nicholas for venereal disease.

Pete [*Mgs* 23/25]. Boorish, Australian airline pilot and former boyfriend of Alison Kelly.

Peter [*DM* 291/309]. Lover of Jane Mallory, divorced and studying at Harvard, terminates their relationship the night after Anthony's suicide.

Peter [*ET* 251/235]. In "The Cloud," a television producer, recently widowed, egotistical, sexually attracted to various women.

Pettigrew [*Mgt* 68/68]. Coroner at Barnstaple.

Phoebe [*DM* 214/228]. Housekeeper at Thorncombe, a Methodist, cleans compulsively and overcooks green vegetables.

Poulteney, Frederick [*FLW* 22/25]. Deceased head of Marlborough House.

Poulteney, Mrs. [*FLW* 18/21]. Owner of Marlborough House, obsessively opposed to dirt and immorality, hires Sarah as companion.

Pruszynski, Ignaz [*Mgs* 580/590]. Former Polish resistance fighter who plays the Nazi colonel who detains Nicholas.

Puddicombe, Thomas [*Mgt* 15/14, 34/34]. Landlord at the Black Hart Inn, burgess of the town of C———.

Pygge, Richard [*Mgt* 279/279]. Attorney who serves as agent for Henry Ayscough in the search for Rebecca Hocknell in Bristol and Manchester.

Queenie [*DM* 4/2]. Cleaning woman at the vicarage.

Randall, Andrew, Baronet [*DM* 24/23, 25/24, 119/125]. Rich undergraduate contemporary of Daniel at Oxford, sees him punting with Jane, marries Nell, and lives at Compton. An English aristocrat.

Randall, Andrew (The Runt) [*DM* 112/118, 295/314]. Ten-year-old son and heir of his namesake.

Randall, Nell (Lady Randall, previously Nell Martin) [*DM* 27/27, 119/125]. One of the "heavenly twins" at Oxford, somewhat shallow, marries Daniel, mother of Caro, divorces Daniel and marries Andrew Randall.

Randall, Penelope (Penny) [*DM* 295/314]. Dumpy-looking schoolgirl of fifteen, half-sister of Caroline Martin.

Reed, Louise [*DM* 346/369]. Twin sister of Mary, older sister of Nancy, lets Dan drive the tractor.

Reed, Mary [*DM* 346/369]. Twin sister of Louise, older sister of Nancy, engaged to a man from Totnes.

Reed, Nancy (Nan) [*DM* 88/91, 346/369, 367/391]. Admired in Sunday school, pet of her family, adolescent first-love with Daniel.

Reed, Mr. [*DM* 348/371]. Father of Nancy, provides black market food to his village during the war.

Reed, Mr. (Old Mr. Reed) [*DM* 345/368]. An educated yeoman and "natural gentleman," widowed grandfather of the Reed girls, veteran of World War I.

Reed, Mrs. [*DM* 346/369]. Active in the Mother's Union, tells Daniel's father to keep Daniel and her daughter Nancy apart.

Richard [*DM* 113/119]. Etonian ex-boyfriend of Caroline Martin, fawns over Andrew.

Richard [*ET* 165/156] In "Poor Koko," the younger son of Maurice and Jane, has dropped out of Cambridge and lives in a commune.

Robert [*Col* 186/163]. G.P.'s older son.

Rogers, Annabel (Bel) [*ET* 251/235, 257/240]. In "The Cloud," the thirty-one-year-old mother of Candida and sister of Catherine.

Rogers, Candida (Candy) [*ET* 253/237, 257/240]. In "The Cloud," the elder daughter of Peter and Annabel, a pseudo-adult, sees a kingfisher.

Rogers, Emma [*ET* 262/245]. In "The Cloud," the younger daughter of Peter and Annabel, takes Catherine to the woods and hears a story about a princess named Emma.

Rogers, Mrs. (Mrs. R.) (*FLW* 316/249, 317/250]. Portly cook in the house of Mrs. Tranter.

Rogers, Paul [*ET* 251/235]. In "The Cloud," a Francophile and Anglophobe writer of novels who likes to explain everything.

Rose [*Mgs* 406/412]. See Seitas, Rose de.

Roughwood, Mrs. [*FLW* 438/343]. See Woodruff, Sarah.

Sabry, Ahmed [*DM* 467/497]. Egyptian satirical playwright, admirer of Shaw and of Arab socialism, meets Daniel and Jane in Cairo.

Sally [*ET* 251/235]. In "The Cloud," a vapid, sexy, bad actress; companion of Peter.

Sam (Old Sam) [*DM* 4/2]. Farmworker in Devon, helps with the harvest.

Sarah [*FLW* 315/249]. London streetwalker, picked up by Charles when drunk.

Saunderson, Anne [*Mgt* 189/192]. Amanuensis to her blind father, Nicholas, writes his letter to Ayscough.

Saunderson, Nicholas [*Mgt* 139/138, 189/192]. Blind mathematician at Christ's

College, Cambridge University, former tutor of Lord ——— in mathematics (a historical Cambridge don).

Sarantopoulous [*Mgs* 73/75]. Café owner on Phraxos, tells Nicholas Urfe about Conchis.

Seitas, Benjie de [*Mgs* 587/598]. Ten-year-old son of Lily Montgomery de Seitas, lives in Much Hadham.

Seitas, Lily de [406/412, 596/607]. Unmarried daughter of Lily Montgomery de Seitas, "real" name of the twin who has a scar on her wrist and plays the roles of Julie Holmes, Dr. Vanessa Maxwell, and Lady Jane.

Seitas, Lily Montgomery de [*Mgs* 585/596, 596–97/607]. Born Lily Montgomery; married William Hughes; mother of May, Lily, Rose, and Benjie de Seitas; friend of Maurice Conchis and, later, Alison Kelly.

Seitas, Rose de [*Mgs* 406/412, 596/607]. Daughter of Lily de Seitas (the former Lily Montgomery), twin sister of the younger Lily de Seitas, plays the roles of June Holmes and Margaret Maxwell, probably named after her mother's sister.

Seitas, William A. [596–97/607-08]. Born William Hughes, first English master at the Lord Byron School in the 1930s; marries Lily Montgomery; later changes his name to her mother's maiden name of de Seitas; father of May, Lily, Rose, and Benjie de Seitas.

Sidney [*DM* 146/155]. Daniel Martin's agent during his career as a writer of film scripts.

Simpson, Mr. [*FLW* 422/330]. Superintendent at Mr. Freeman's store.

Singleton, Mr. [*Col* 30/31]. Manager of Clegg's bank.

Skinner, Arkles [*Mgt* 301/307]. Strong-man and bully of Mrs. Claiborne, has to be physically prevented from abducting Rebecca.

Skinner, Digory [*Mgt* 68/68]. Sergeant at mace and constable at C———, helps to investigate the discovered chest.

Smith [*Mgt* 155/157]. See Lord ———.

Smithson, Charles Algernon Henry (Charley) [*FLW* 7/12, 15/19, 298/236, 413/323]. Born in 1835, amateur paleontologist, heir to Winsyatt and fiancé of Ernestina Freeman as the narrative begins in 1867, discovers a more independent self from his experiences with—and without—Sarah Woodruff.

Smithson, Sir Robert (Bob) [*FLW* 190/153, 192/155]. Owner of Winsyatt, uncle of Charles Smithson, becomes engaged to Bella Tomkins.

Smithson, Sir Charles [*FLW* 15/19]. Grandfather of Charles Smithson, pioneer archaeologist.

Sotiriades [*Mgs* 546/556]. Head of a family of tourists from Athens who visit Phraxos.

Soula [*Mgs* 391/397]. Housekeeper for Conchis before World War II.

Spencer [*FLW* 227/182]. Friend of Grogan, runs an asylum.

Spencer-Haigh, Miss [*Mgs* 22/24]. Personnel agent for the British Council, interviews Nicholas Urfe for a teaching position.

Stefan [*Col* 224/194]. One of Miranda's artist-acquaintances who do not worry about making money.

Steve [*Col* 10/13]. Younger brother of Clegg's Aunt Annie.

Sugden, Geoffrey [*Mgs* 579/590]. English master at the Lord Byron School before World War II.

Talbot, John [*FLW* 32/31]. Captain in the Navy, employer of Sarah Woodruff in Charmouth.

Talbot, Mrs. [FLW 33/32]. Wife of John Talbot, unwisely lets Sarah go to Weymouth.

Talbot, Paul [*FLW* 52/47]. One of Sarah Woodruff's charges in Charmouth.

Talbot, Virginia [*FLW* 52/47]. One of Sarah Woodruff's charges in Charmouth.

Taylor [*Mgt* 208/211]. Coachman to an admiral, previously to Sir Henry W———.

Taylor, Ann [*Mgs* 31/33, 397/403]. Apartment-mate of Margaret.

Terpsichore, "Ma" [*FLW* 300/238]. Brothel keeper in London, about fifty.

Thalia [*Mts* 73]. Muse of comedy and bucolic poetry.

Thurlow, Dick [*Mgt* 28/28, 100/99]. Deaf-mute and half-witted servant to Lord ———, grows to adore "Louise" as they engage in sexual intercourse for Lord ———, flees from the cave on Exmoor, is found hanged in the nearby woods.

Timothy (Tim) [*DM* 35/35]. Ex-boyfriend of Jenny.

Tom (Old Tom) [*Col* 6/10]. Co-worker of Clegg's in the Town Hall.

Tom [*ET* 63/59]. Diane's first boyfriend.

Tom [*ET* 253/237]. In "The Cloud," is a difficult four-year-old boy, son of Peter.

Tomkins, Bella [*FLW* 196/158, 216/173]. Young widow, engaged to marry Charles's uncle.

Tony [*DM* 142/150]. Film director, has had an affair with Andrea.

Tony [*ET* 222/208]. In "The Enigma," manages the Fielding farm at Tetbury Hall in East Anglia.

Tranter [*FLW* 11/15]. Lives in Lyme Regis, sister of Mrs. Freeman, likable and innocent, has never married, is visited annually by Ernestina.

Trimble, Miss. [*FLW* 203/163]. Shopkeeper and town gossip.

Trotter, Mrs. [*FLW* 212/170]. Housekeeper at Winsyatt.

Tucker [*Mgt* 68/68]. Mayor of C———.

Tudor, John [*Mgt* 343/349]. Ayscough's clerk and recorder, shares lunch with Rebecca Hocknell during her interview.

Urfe, Nicholas (Nicko) [*Mgs* 16/18, 23/25]. Narrator, born to a military family in 1927, seducer of girls, pseudo-existentialist, elected by Conchis to discover himself by way of the "godgame."

Vanbrugh-Jones, Miss C. [*Col* 40/39]. Miranda's aunt, whom she lives with.

Varguennes, M. [*FLW* 35/34]. French lieutenant, injured in a wreck off Charmouth, recovers in the Talbot house, plays with the affections of Sarah Woodruff.

Vassili, Barba [*Mgs* 465/473]. Gatekeeper at the Lord Byron School.

Vladislav [*DM* 148/156]. Andrea's jealous, deranged husband.

Wardley, James [*Mgt* 298/304]. Elder and teacher of the Shakers, waits for Rebecca Lee outside Ayscough's office, based on a historical figure.

Whyte, Billy [*Mgs* 36/37]. Snobbish acquaintance of Nicholas Urfe's from Oxford, described as "rich."

Williams [*Col* 6/10]. Borough treasurer, superintends Clegg's office.

Williams [*Mgt* 202/204]. Employs Jones as a clerk in Cardiff after the Exmoor incident.

Williams, Alexandra (Sandy) [*ET* 7/7, 15/14]. In "The Ebony Tower," the older daughter of David and Beth, has chicken pox.

Williams, Beth [*ET* 3/3, 7/7]. In "The Ebony Tower," the wife of the protagonist, David, stays behind to nurse Beth, meets David in Paris at the end of the story.

Williams, David [*ET* 3/3, 7/7]. In "The Ebony Tower," an abstract artist and art critic, travels to Coëtminais in Normandy to interview Breasley, finds himself attracted to Breasley's assistant Diana.

Williams, Louise [*ET* 28/30]. In "The Ebony Tower," the younger daughter of David and Beth.

Wimmel, Dietrich [*Mgs* 418/424]. Nazi colonel in the S.S., methodically tortures and executes Greek partisans.

Wisdom, Holy Mother [*Mgt* 375/382]. Female embodiment of a divine trinity, appears to Rebecca Hocknell outside the Exmoor cave as a young woman in silver trousers and a smock and inside as a gray-haired woman.

Wishbourne, Mrs. [*Mgt* 155/158]. Hannah Claiborne's rival in brothel-keeping.

Woodbury, Miss [*FLW* 416/325]. Teacher at a girls' academy, resembles Sarah Woodruff.

Woodruff, Sarah Emily [*FLW* 24/26, 414/324]. Known as "the French lieutenant's woman" or as "the French lieutenant's whore," hired by Mrs. Poulteney as a woman supposedly seduced, abandoned, and in need of charity, lies to and seduces Charles Smithson but remains sympathetic and enigmatic, becomes a member of the Rossetti household of Pre-Raphaelite artists in London, may or may not marry Charles in the end(ings).

Wolfe, Simon J. [*DM* 18/17]. Main character in the autobiographical novel Daniel Martin talks about intending to write.

——Unnamed burglar [*ET* 154/145]. In "Poor Koko," robs cottages used only on weekends, likes Joseph Conrad but burns the book-length manuscript of the narrator for reasons that remain uncertain.

———Unnamed constable [*ET* 178/167]. In "Poor Koko," a police sergeant who discovers the narrator at Holly Cottage.

———Unnamed scholar [*ET* 145/137]. In "Poor Koko," narrator with poor eyesight, is writing an academic book on Thomas Love Peacock.

———Unnamed lord (Poor John, his Lordship)/Bartholemew (Mr. B.) (Philocomoedia)/Smith [*Mgt* 18/16, 120/120, 133/133, 155/157, 409/417]. Younger son of the Duke of ———, in his late twenties, bald, sexually impotent, mathematically inclined, hires companions for a trip to Exmoor, introduces Rebecca Hocknell to mysterious strangers—and disappears.

———Unnamed duke (Your Grace) [*Mgt* 99/99, 155/157]. Father of the unnamed lord who disappears, appears at Rebecca Hocknell's interview, fears that his son may be homosexual, carries a staff like a bishop's crozier.

———Unnamed nurse (staff sister) [*Mts* 137]. Elderly nurse, argumentative and hot-tempered, "real sister" of Dr. Delphie.

BIBLIOGRAPHY

To indicate the nature of John Fowles's less familiar works, I have grouped primary sources by type: Narrative Fiction, Poetry, Drawing, Screenwriting, Expository Books and Pamphlets, Expository Essays, Book Reviews, Published Letters, Advertising Copy, Translating and Adapting, Editing, and Isolated Quotations. Within these groups, I have arranged works in the order published, to indicate how Fowles's career has evolved, through 1990. When he has provided a date of composition different from the publication year, I have included it in brackets. Secondary sources, about John Fowles and his works rather than by him, are in alphabetical order by author within the following categories: Interviews and Interview-based Articles, Books, Essays in English, Unpublished Doctoral Dissertations, Selected Reviews, and Bibliographic Studies.

WORKS BY JOHN FOWLES

Narrative Fiction

The Collector. London: Jonathan Cape, 1963; Boston: Little, Brown, 1963; reprinted New York: Dell, 1964.

The Magus, Boston: Little, Brown, 1965; London: Jonathan Cape, 1966; reprinted New York: Dell, 1967.

The French Lieutenant's Woman. London: Jonathan Cape, 1969; Boston: Little, Brown, 1969; reprinted New York: New American Library, 1970; Franklin Center, Pa.: Franklin Library, 1979 (limited edition, leather bound, illustrated, signed by the author); London: Jonathan Cape, 1980 (limited edition, calf-bound and gilt-edged, signed by the author and the principals of the film production).

The Ebony Tower. London: Jonathan Cape, 1974; Boston: Little, Brown, 1974; reprinted New York: New American Library, 1975.

"The Ebony Tower." *Cosmopolitan,* October 1977, pp. 147, 149, 151, 153, 155, 157, 159, 163–64, 166, 168, 170, 172, 174, 176, 178, 180, 182, 184, 186, 188, 190, 192, 195, 197, 199, 200–201, 203, 205, 206–7. Reprinted from *The Ebony Tower,* pp. 1–114/1–114.

The Magus: A Revised Version. London: Jonathan Cape, 1977; Boston: Little, Brown, 1978; reprinted New York: Dell, 1979.

"The Treasure of Tsankawi." *Times,* 1 October 1977, p. 6. Excerpt from *Daniel Martin,* "Tsankawi" chapter, pp. 343–52/322–31.

Daniel Martin. London: Jonathan Cape, 1977; Boston: Little, Brown, 1977; reprinted New York: New American Library, 1978.

"On the Undercliff." In *The West Country Book,* edited by J. C. Trewin, pp. 103–8. Exeter, U.K.: Webb & Bower, 1981. Excerpt from *The French Lieutenant's Woman,* Chap. 10.

"Mantissa." *Antaeus* 40/41 (1981): 105–21. Excerpt from *Mantissa,* Chap. 1, pp. 1–25 (slightly modified).

"The French Lieutenant's Woman." *Cosmopolitan,* November 1981, pp. 209, 212, 216, 218, 220, 223, 225–26, 228. Excerpt from *The French Lieutenant's Woman,* Chap. 29, 31 (minus the last sentence), 33, and 34.

Mantissa. London: Jonathan Cape, 1982; Boston: Little, Brown, 1982; reprinted New York: New American Library, 1983.

A Maggot. London: Jonathan Cape, 1985; Boston: Little, Brown, 1985; reprinted New York: New American Library, 1986.

"The Enigma." *The Penguin Book of Modern Short Stories.* Edited by Malcolm Bradbury, pp. 189–233. New York: Viking, 1987. Reprinted from *The Ebony Tower,* pp. 177–231/189–247.

Poetry

"In Paradise." *Translantic Review* 14 (Autumn 1963): 9–15.

"A Village Between," "Unasked," "Villagers." *Transatlantic Review* 16 (Summer 1964): 36–37.

"By the Appian Way," "At Ostia" (presented as "Two Roman Poems"); "Mirage," "Barbarians," "The Fascists' Best Friend," "On the Upper Terrace." *Antaeus* 1 (Summer 1970): 20–24.

"Crusoe," "Aboulia." *Mademoiselle,* May 1973, p. 160.

"Amor Vacui," "It Is a Lie." *Antaeus* 9 (Spring 1973): 68–69. *Poems.* New York: Ecco Press, 1973.

"Conditional." *Labrys* 2 (June 1978): unpaginated (5–7).

Conditional (broadside). Northridge, Calif. Lord John Press, 1979.

"Tourists at the Erectheion," "Julia's Child," "John Clare," "Crabbing." *Occasional Poets: An Anthology,* edited by Richard Adams, pp. 58–63. New York: Viking, 1986.

"Barbarians," "Amor Vacui," "It Is a Lie." *The Antaeus Anthology,* edited by Daniel Halpern, pp. 132–34. New York: Bantam, 1986.

Drawing

"De Loin." In *Self-Portrait: Book People Picture Themselves,* by Burt Britton, p. 215. New York: Random House, 1976.

Screenwriting

The Enigma of Stonehenge. Writers and Places 3, 29 January 1981. British Broadcasting Corporation. Also narrated by Fowles, with a photograph of him as a boy, about twelve.

The Magus. Directed by Guy Green. With Michael Caine, Anthony Quinn, Candice Bergen, and Anna Karina. Twentieth-Century Fox, 1968. (A mimeographed copy of the 122-page shooting script, dated 26 August 1966, is owned by the Lilly Library, University of Indiana.)

Expository Books and Pamphlets

The Aristos: A Self-Portrait in Ideas. London: Jonathan Cape, 1964; Boston: Little, Brown, 1964.

The Aristos. 2nd ed. London: Jonathan Cape, 1968; Boston: Little, Brown, 1970.

Shipwreck. Photographs by the Gibsons of Scilly. London: Jonathan Cape, 1974; Boston: Little, Brown, 1975.

Islands. Photographs by Fay Godwin. London: Jonathan Cape, 1978; Boston: Little, Brown, 1978.

Curator's Report 1978. Lyme Regis, U.K.: The Philpot Museum, 1979.

Tree. Preface and photographs by Frank Horvat. London: Auram Press, 1979. Boston: Little, Brown, 1979. Reprinted (without preface or photographs) New York: Ecco Press, 1983.

Lyme Regis Museum Curator's Report: With Notes on Recent Discoveries and New Acquisitions: 1979. Lyme Regis, U.K.: Lyme Regis (Philpot) Museum, no date [1980, uncopyrighted].

The Enigma of Stonehenge. Co-author Barry Brukoff. London: Jonathan Cape, 1980. New York: Summit Books, 1980.

Lyme Regis Museum Curator's Report: With Notes on Recent Research and New Acquisitions: 1980. Lyme Regis, U.K.: Lyme Regis (Philpot) Museum, 1981.

Lyme Regis Museum Curator's Report: With Notes on Recent Research and New Acquisitions: 1981. Lyme Regis, U.K.: Lyme Regis (Philpot) Museum, 1982.

A Short History of Lyme Regis. Wimborne, U.K.: Dovecote Press, 1982. Boston: Little, Brown, 1982.

Lyme Regis Museum Curator's Report: With Notes on Recent Research and New Acquisitions: 1982. Lyme Regis, U.K.: Lyme Regis (Philpot) Museum, 1983.

Of Memoirs and Magpies. Austin, Tex.: W. Thomas Taylor, 1983.

Lyme Regis: Three Town Walks. Lyme Regis, U.K.: Friends of the Lyme Regis Museum, 1983.

Lyme Regis Museum Curator's Report: With Notes on Recent Research and New Acquisitions: 1983. Lyme Regis, U.K.: Lyme Regis (Philpot) Museum, 1984.

Medieval Lyme Regis. Lyme Regis: Lyme Regis (Philpot) Museum, 1984.

Lyme Regis Museum Curator's Report: With Notes on Recent Discoveries and New Acquisitions: 1984. Lyme Regis, U.K.: Lyme Regis (Philpot) Museum, 1985.
A Brief History of Lyme. Lyme Regis, U.K.: Friends of the Museum, 1985.
Lyme Regis Museum Curator's Report: With Notes on Recent Discoveries, Research and New Acquisitions: 1985. Lyme Regis, U.K.: Lyme Regis (Philpot) Museum, 1986.
Lyme Regis Museum Curator's Report: With Notes on Recent Discoveries, Research and New Acquisitions: 1986. Lyme Regis, U.K.: Lyme Regis (Philpot) Museum, 1987.
Poor Koko. Helsinki: Eurographica, 1987.
The Enigma. Helsinki: Eurographica, 1987.
Lyme Regis Museum Curator's Report: With Notes on Recent Discoveries, Research, and New Acquisitions: 1987–88. Co-author Liz-Anne Bawden. Lyme Regis, U.K.: Friends of the Lyme Regis (Philpot) Museum, 1989.
Lyme Regis Camera. Wimborne, U.K.: Dovecote Press, 1990.

Essays

Erwood, D. L., co-author. "Entomology for the Schoolboy." *Alleyn Court Magazine* 9.2 (1938): 11.
Biographical profile of Angus Bruce McCallum. *Ousel: The Journal of Bedford School,* 28 June 1944, p. 52.
"The School *v.* Oundle School," "The School *v.* R.A.F., Little Staughton," "R.A.F., Cardington, *v.* The School," "House Cricket," in "Cricket." *The Ousel: The Journal of Bedford School,* 27 July 1944, pp. 77–81 passim.
"Cricket." *The Ousel: The Journal of Bedford School,* 10 November 1944, pp. 106–7.
"On Being English But Not British." *Texas Quarterly* 7 (1964): 154–62.
"I Write, Therefore I Am." *Evergreen Review* 8.33 (1964): 16–17, 89–91.
"Marriage, Passion, Love . . . : 'My Side of the Dialogue.'" *Vogue,* 15 November 1964, pp. 114–15. Excerpts from *The Aristos,* pp. 95–101, 210–11, 215–19.
"The Trouble with Starlets." *Holiday,* June 1966, pp. 12, 15–18, 20.
Untitled. *Authors Take Sides on Vietnam: Two Questions on the War in Vietnam Answered by the Authors of Several Nations,* edited by Cecil Woolf and John Bagguley, p. 35. New York: Simon and Schuster, 1967.
"Only Connect." Introduction to catalogue of opening exhibition of the Fulham Gallery, London, 27 November–23 December 1967, untitled and unpaginated (1).
"Notes on Writing a Novel." *Harper's Magazine,* July 1968, pp. 88–97. Reprinted without the final paragraph but with five new ones as "On Writing a Novel," in *Cornhill Magazine* 1060 (1969): 281–95. Reprinted three more times with the new paragraphs and the final paragraph restored as "Notes on an Unfinished Novel." In *Afterwords: Novelists on their Novels,* edited by Thomas McCormack, pp. 161–75. New York: Harper & Row, 1969. In *The Writer's Craft,* edited by John Hersey, pp. 411–22. New York: Alfred A. Knopf, 1974. In *The Novel Today: Contemporary Writers on Modern Fiction,* edited by Malcolm Bradbury, pp. 136–50. Manches-

ter: Manchester University Press, 1977; Totowa, N.J.: Rowman and Littlefield, 1977.

Introduction, glossary, and appendix titled "Sabine Baring-Gould and East
Mersea." *Mehalah: A Story of the Salt Marshes,* by S. Baring-Gould, pp. vii–
xiv, 307–8, 309–13. Landmark Library 14. 1880; reprinted London:
Chatto & Windus, 1969.

Preface (3rd version, revised for American publication). *The Aristos,* by John
Fowles, pp. 7–12. 1964; 2nd ed. London: Jonathan Cape, 1968; reprinted Boston: Little, Brown, 1970.

"My Recollections of Kafka." *New Views of Franz Kafka,* edited by R. G. Collins
and Kenneth McRobbie. *Mosaic: A Journal for the Comparative Study of
Literature and Ideas* 3.4: 31–41. New Views: A Mosaic Series in Literature. Winnepeg: University of Manitoba Press, 1970.

"Is the Novel Dead?" *Books* 1 (1970): 2–5.

"Jacqueline Kennedy Onassis and Other First (and Last) Ladies." *Cosmopolitan,*
October 1970, pp. 144–49.

"Weeds, Bugs, Americans." *Sports Illustrated,* 21 December 1970, pp. 84–88, 90,
95–96, 99–100, 102.

Afterword [dated 1970]. *The Wanderer, or The End of Youth (Le Grand Meulnes),*
by Alain-Fournier, translated by Lowell Bair, pp. 208–23. New York:
New American Library, 1971.

"The Blinded Eye." *Animals* 13.9 (1971): 388–92. Reprinted in *Second Nature,*
edited by Richard Mabey, pp. 77–78, 83–89. London: Jonathan Cape, 1984.

"Ordeal by Income." *Public Lending Right: A Matter of Justice,* edited by Richard
Findlater, pp. 99–108. London and Harmondsworth, U.K.: André
Deutsch in association with Penguin Books, 1971.

Untitled advice for young readers. In *Attacks of Taste,* edited by Evelyn B. Byrne
and Otto M. Penzler, pp. 22–23. New York: Gotham Book Mart, 1971.

"Making a Pitch for Cricket." *Sports Illustrated,* 21 May 1973, pp. 100–103, 106,
108, 111–12, 115–16. Reprinted as "Baseball's Other Self: Cricket," in
A Baseball Album, edited by Gerald Secor Couzens, pp. 21–24, 26–33,
35–36. New York: Lippincott & Crowell, 1980.

"The Magus." New Fiction Society Magazine, October 1974, p. 8.

"On the Rocks." *Observer,* 27 October 1974, p. 23. Abridgment of the introduction to *Shipwreck,* unpaginated (3–12).

"Introduction: Remembering Cruikshank." *Princeton University Library Chronicle*
35.1–2 (1973–74): xiii–xvi and Fig. 5 (opposite p. 46).

Foreword and afterword [dated 1973]. *The Hound of the Baskervilles,* by Arthur
Conan Doyle, pp. 7–11, 186–96. 1902; reprinted London: John Murray
and Jonathan Cape, 1974.

"A Personal Note." In *The Ebony Tower,* by John Fowles, pp. 117–22. London:
Jonathan Cape, 1974; Boston: Little, Brown, 1974.

Untitled. In *Bookmarks,* edited by Frederic Raphael, pp. 53–57. London: Jona-
than Cape, 1975. Reprinted as "Of Memoirs and Magpies," in *Atlantic
Monthly,* June 1975, pp. 82–84, and as a limited edition book in Austin,
Tex.: W. Thomas Taylor, 1983.

Foreword. In *Hawker of Morewenstow: Portrait of a Victorian Eccentric,* by Piers
Brendon, pp. 15–21. London: Jonathan Cape, 1975.

"Why I Belong." *New Fiction Society Magazine,* April 1975, p. 3.

"What Social Class Do You Identify With?" *Observer Magazine,* 19 September 1976, p. 8.

"Hardy and the Hag." In *Thomas Hardy After Fifty Years,* edited by Lance St. John Butler, pp. 28–42. Totowa, N.J.: Rowman and Littlefield, 1977.

"The Magus Revisited." *Times,* 28 May 1977, p. 7. Reprinted with minor changes as "Why I Rewrote *The Magus,"* in *Saturday Review,* 18 February 1978, pp. 25–30, and in *Critical Essays on John Fowles,* pp. 93–99. Six paragraphs are deleted in Fowles's foreword to *The Magus: A Revised Version,* pp. 5–11/5–10.

Foreword, epilogue, and notes to the epilogue. *Ourika,* by Claire de Durfort, translated by John Fowles, pp. 5–9, 50–65. 1824; reprinted Austin, Tex.: W. Thomas Taylor, 1977.

"I do not like. . . ." In "Amis on ***, Drabble on **x, Aldiss, Nye & Fowles on *ex, Thwaite & Tennant on Sex, Weldon o." *New Fiction,* October 1977, p. 13.

Foreword. *The Lais of Marie de France,* translated by Robert Hanning and Joan Ferrante, pp. ix-xiii. New York: E. P. Dutton, 1978.

Introduction. *Miramar,* by Naguib Mahfouz, translated by Fatma Moussa-Mahmoud, edited by Maged el Kommos and John Rodenbeck, notes by Omar el Qudsy, pp. vii–xv. 1967; London: Heinemann, in association with the American University in Cairo Press, 1978. Reprinted in *Naguib Mahfouz,* pp. 411–21. New York: Book-of-the-Month Club, 1989.

"The Man and the Island." In *Steep Holm—A Case History in the Study of Evolution,* edited by the Kenneth Allsop Trust and John Fowles, pp. 14–22 (Fowles also is quoted at length on p. 44, about the importance of herbal medicine to monasteries). Sherborne, U.K.: Dorset Publishing Co., 1978.

"A Special Message to Subscribers from John Fowles" and acknowledgments [dated 1978]. In *The French Lieutenant's Woman,* unpaginated (i–iii, viii). Franklin Center, Pa.: Franklin Library, 1979.

"Transposition: Marriage as Model." *A Book of Men: Visions of the Male Experience,* pp. 278–84. Edited by Ross Firestone. Edinburgh: Mainstream Publishing, 1979. Excerpt from *The Aristos,* 1st ed., pp. 95–99.

"Islanders." *The Bedside Book,* pp. 16–17. Edited by Julian Shuckburgh. London: W. H. Smith, 1979. Excerpt from *Islands,* pp. 105–6.

Queries number 66, 67 in "Collections and Information Sought." *GCG: Newsletter of the Geological Curators Group* 2.5 (April 1979): 263.

"Seeing Nature Whole." *Harper's Magazine,* November 1979, pp. 49–68. Excerpt from *The Tree,* pp. 24–79.

"In Absentia: Some Books of the Year," *Times Literary Supplement,* 23 November 1979, p. 4.

Introduction and acknowledgments [dated 1978]. *After London: or, Wild England,* by Richard Jefferies, pp. vii–xxii. World's Classics. 1885; reprinted Oxford: Oxford University Press, 1980.

Preface [4th version, newly revised for British re-publication, dated 1979]. *The Aristos,* by John Fowles, pp. 7–12. 2nd ed. 1968; reprinted Boston: Little, Brown, 1970; reprinted London: Jonathan Cape, 1980.

"Mystic Message." *Telegraph Sunday Magazine,* 21 September 1980, pp. 15, 18, 22.

Broadsheet transcription of and commentary on a facsimile letter from Charles I, giving orders for the seige of Lyme Regis in 1644. Wincanton, U.K.: Dorset Publishing Co., 1980.

Foreword. *The Sunday Times Book of the Countryside: Including One Thousand Days Out in Great Britain and Ireland,* edited by Philip Clarke, Brian Jackman, and Derrik Mercer, p. 7. London: Macdonald Futura Publishers, 1980.

"John Aubrey and the Genesis of *Monumenta Britannica.*" In *Monumenta Britannica: John Aubrey (1626–97),* edited by John Fowles, annotated by Rodney Legg, vol. 2, pp. 605–16. 2 volumes. Sherborne, U.K.: Dorset Publishing Co., 1980–82. Slightly modified for publication in the United States as a foreword to the single volume *Monumenta Britannica: Or, A Miscellany of British Antiquities,* pp. ix–xxii. Boston: Little, Brown, 1980 [published in 1982 with a 1980 copyright date].

Introduction [dated 1979]. *Tom Adams' Agatha Christie Cover Story,* by Julian Symons, pp. 7–8. Paper Tiger. Limpsfield, U.K.: Dragon's World, 1981. Published in the United States as *Agatha Christie: The Art of Her Crimes: The Paintings of Tom Adams,* pp. 7–8. New York: Everest House, 1981.

Introduction [dated 1980]. *The Book of Ebenezer Le Page,* by G. B. Edwards, pp. vii–xiv, 398n, 399–400. London: Hamish Hamilton; Mount Kisco, N.Y.: Moyer Bell, 1981.

"Collector's Item." *New Edinburgh Review* 55 (August 1981): p. 7.

Foreword. *The French Lieutenant's Woman: A Screenplay,* by Harold Pinter, pp. vii–xv. Boston: Little, Brown 1981.

Introduction. *"The Royal Game" and Other Stories,* by Stefan Zweig, translated by Jill Sutcliffe, vi–xviii. London: Jonathan Cape, 1981; New York: E. P. Dutton, 1983. Reissued by Dutton in 1989 as *"The Burning Secret" and Other Stories.* Abridged as "The Man Who Hated Passports." *Times,* 21 November 1981, p. 9.

"Geology at Lyme Regis—A Museum Curator's View." *Circular of the Geologists Association of London* 829 (1981): 23–24.

Introduction to portfolio. In *Fifteen Photographs of Lyme Regis,* by Paul S. Penrose, unpaginated. Wellingborough, U.K.: Skelton's Press, 1982.

"The Falklands and a Death Foretold." *Guardian,* 14 August 1982, p. 7. Reprinted as "The Falklands, and a Death Foretold." *Georgia Review* 36 (1982): 721–28.

"Wistman's Wood." *Antaeus* 45/46 (1982): 88–93. Headnote and excerpt from *The Tree,* unpaginated (98–112).

"Voices of the Deep." *Whales: A Celebration,* pp. 200–201. Edited by Greg Gatenby. Boston, Little, Brown, 1983. Excerpted from a 1973 review in *The New Statesman,* 15 June 1973, pp. 892–93.

Introduction. *The Bedside "Guardian": A Selection from the "Guardian" 1982–83,* vol. 32, edited by William Webb, pp. 5–8. London: Collins, 1983.

"Florentine Fowles." *Guardian,* 15 March 1983, p. 11.

"Simple Things, Splendid Forms: Peasant Pottery by the Talbots of La Borne." *Connoisseur,* November 1983, pp. 113–17.

Introduction. *Thomas Hardy's England,* by Jo Draper, pp. 7–32. London: Jonathan Cape, 1984. Boston: Little, Brown, 1984.

"The Chesil Bank." *Britain: A World by Itself: Reflections on the Landscape by Eminent British Writers: With Commentaries by Dr. Franklyn Perring,* pp. 18–31. London: Aurum, 1984; Boston: Little, Brown, 1984.

Foreword [dated 1982]. *The Timescapes of John Fowles,* by H. W. Fawkner, pp. 9–16. Cranbury, N.J.: Associated University Presses, 1984.

M. A. Taylor, co-author. Note. *GCG: The Geological Curator* 4.3 (1984): 174.

Introductory essay. *Land,* by Fay Godwin, pp. ix–xx. London: Heinemann, 1985; Boston: Little, Brown, 1985.

"The Theater of the Unexpressed." *Times,* 15 April 1985, p. 9.

Foreword. *Picture of Lyme-Regis and Environs,* by M. Phillips, unpaginated (i–iv). 1817; reprinted [facsimile] Lyme Regis, U.K.: Lyme Regis Museum, 1985.

"When the Bug Bites—Write." *Times,* 12 October 1985, p. 8.

"Fossil Collecting and Conservation in West Dorset: A Personal View" [dated 1985]. *GCG: The Geological Curator* 4.6 (1986): 325–29.

"Golding and 'Golding.' " *William Golding: The Man and His Books: A Tribute on His 75th Birthday,* edited by John Carey, pp. 146–56. London: Faber and Faber, 1986.

"Vain Memories." In *Quick Singles: Memories of Summer Days and Cricket Heroes,* edited by Christopher Martin-Jenkins and Mike Seabrook, pp. 118–22. London: Dent, 1986.

"The Green Man." *Antaeus* 57 (Autumn 1986): 244–51. Reprinted in *On Nature: Nature, Landscape, and Natural History,* edited by Daniel Halpern, pp. 244–51. San Francisco: Northpoint Press, 1987. Excerpt from *The Tree,* pp. 38–53.

Introduction, glossary [dated 1986]. *Round About a Great Estate,* by Richard Jefferies, pp. 9–14, 117–18. 1880; reprinted Bradford on Avon: Ex Libris Press, 1987.

Introduction to "South Cornwall, Devon and Dorset." *Coastline: Britain's Threatened Heritage,* edited by Kate Baillie, p. 153. London: Kingfisher Books, 1987.

Introduction [dated 1987]. *Oradour: Massacre and Aftermath,* by Robin Mackness, pp. v–viii. London: Bloomsbury, 1988. Reprinted Corgi, 1989; *Massacre at Oradour,* pp. v–viii. New York: Random House, 1988.

Dedication. Book of signatures gathered in appreciation of Miss Sybil Lister for giving Slopes Farm to the Woodland Trust. Lyme Regis: Town Council and Lyme Regis Society, [1988]. Quoted in its entirety in the *Lyme Regis Museum Curator's Report* for 1987–88, p. 13 (cited below).

Items 1, 2, 4, 6, 7, 9, 10, 11 of "Research, Gifts, Acquisitions," "An Apology and Some Notes." In *Lyme Regis Museum Curator's Report: 1987–88: With Notes on Recent Discoveries, Research, and New Acquisitions,* edited by John Fowles and Liz-Anne Bawden, pp. 7–12, 16. Lyme Regis, U.K.: Lyme Regis (Philpot) Museum, 1989.

Foreword. *The Undercliff: A Sketchbook of the Axmouth-Lyme Regis Nature Reserve,* by Elaine Franks, pp. 7–9. London: J. M. Dent, 1989.

Introduction. *Open Skies,* by Don McCullin, pp. v–ix. London, Jonathan Cape, 1989; New York: Harmony Books, 1989.

Notes 1–11. In *Lyme Regis Museum Curator's Report: 1989: With Notes on Recent Discoveries, Research, and New Acquisitions,* by Liz-Anne Bawden, pp. 21–28. Lyme Regis, U.K.: Lyme Regis (Philpot) Museum, 1990.

Notes 1–7. [dated January 1991]. In *Lyme Regis Museum Curator's Report: 1990: With Notes on Recent Discoveries, Research, and New Acquisitions,* by Liz-Anne Bawden, pp. 29–31. Lyme Regis, U.K.: Lyme Regis (Philpot) Museum, 1991.

Book Reviews

"The Most Secretive of Victorian Writers, a Kind of Great Mouse." Of *Thomas Hardy: Distance and Desire,* by J. Hillis Miller. *New York Times Book Review,* 21 June 1970, p. 4.

"Guide to a Man-Made Planet." Of *The World of Charles Dickens,* by Angus Wilson. *Life,* 4 September 1970, pp. 8–9.

Of *From Cliché to Archetype,* by Marshall McLuhan, with Wilfred Watson. *Saturday Review,* 21 November 1970, pp. 32–33.

"Gory Details." Of *Blood: The Paramount Humour,* by Earl Hackett. *New Statesman,* 9 March 1973, pp. 345–46.

"Country Matters." Of *Finches,* by Ian Newton; and *The Pollination of Flowers,* by Michael Proctor and Peter Yeo. *New Statesman,* 27 April 1973, pp. 620–21.

"Voices of the Deep." Of *Whales, Dolphins and Seals,* by D. E. Gaskin; and *Man's Place,* by Karl-Erik Fichtelius and Sverre Sjolander, translated by Thomas Teal. *New Statesman,* 15 June 1973, pp. 892–93.

"All Too Human." Of *Birds, Beasts, and Men,* by H. R. Hays. *New Statesman,* 20 July 1973, pp. 90–91.

"A Lost World." Of *Lark Rise to Candleford,* by Flora Thompson. *New Statesman,* 3 August 1973, pp. 154–55.

"Other Edens." Of *Landscapes and Seasons of the Medieval World,* by Derek Pearsall and Elizabeth Salter. *New Statesman,* 12 October 1973, pp. 524–25.

"Late Harvest." Of *The Worm Forgives the Plough,* by John Stewart Collis. *New Statesman,* 26 October 1973, pp. 612–13.

"Unnatural Habitats." Of *The Unofficial Countryside,* by Richard Mabey; *Insects of Britain and Northern Europe,* by Michael Chinery; and *The Book of Flowers,* by Alice M. Coats. *New Statesman,* 14 December 1973, p. 912.

"Menhirs Maketh Man." Of *Beyond Stonehenge,* by Gerald S. Hawkins; and *The Old Stones of Land's End,* by John Michell. *New Statesman,* 22 March 1974, pp. 412–13.

"Softer Than Beef." Of *Alive,* by Piers Paul Read. *New Statesman,* 10 May 1974, pp. 664–65.

"Bleeding Hearts." Of *The Akenham Burial Case,* by Ronald Fletcher. *New Statesman,* 14 June 1974, pp. 842–43.

"Missing Beats." Of *Autobiography,* by Margiad Evans. *New Statesman,* 13 September 1974, p. 352.

"Ivory Towers." Of *Lighthouse,* by Tony Parker. *New Statesman,* 9 May 1975, pp. 628–29.

"Death on the Ocean Wave." Of *Supership,* by Noel Mostert; and *Death Raft,* by Alexander McKee. *New Statesman,* 4 July 1975, pp. 22–24.

"Horse Magic." Of *The Days That We Have Seen,* by George Ewart Evans. *New Statesman,* 1 August 1975, p. 148.

"Come to Britain?" Of *Circles and Standing Stones,* by Evan Hadingham. *New Statesman,* 5 December 1975, pp. 728–29.

"Royal Stews." Of *The Cleveland Street Scandal,* by H. Montgomery Hyde. *New Statesman,* 19 March 1976, pp. 362–63.

"Confined Species." Of *The Ark in the Park,* by Wilfred Blunt; *London's Zoo,* by Gwynne Vevers; and *Golden Days,* by Lord Zuckerman. *New Statesman,* 7 May 1976, pp. 612–14.

"Apéritifs." Of *Companion Guide to Devon and Cornwall,* by Darrell Bates. *New Statesman,* 11 June 1976, pp. 785–86.

"The Rambler." Of *The Naturalist in Britain,* by David Elliston Allen. *New Statesman,* 6 August 1976, pp. 183–84.

"A Study in Scarlet." Of *The Adventures of Conan Doyle,* by Charles Higham. *New Statesman,* 26 November 1976, pp. 751–52.

"For the Dark." Of *The Death of Narcissus,* by Morris Fraser. *New Statesman,* 18 February 1977, pp. 221–22.

"On Target." Of *Out of Focus,* by Alf MacLochlian. *Irish Press,* 12 January 1978, p. 6.

"Downandoutdom." Of *Four Novellas,* by Samuel Beckett. *Irish Press,* 16 February 1978, p. 6.

"The Nature of Irishness." Of *Selected Stories of Sean O'Faolain. Irish Press,* 13 April 1978, p. 6.

"Sidesteps." Of *The Destinies of Darcy Dancer, Gentleman,* by J. P. Donleavy. *Irish Press,* 1 June 1978, p. 6.

"Irish Keys." Of *Getting Through,* by John McGahern; and *Mrs. Reinhardt and Other Stories,* by Edna O'Brien. *Irish Press,* 15 June 1978, p. 6.

"Central Values." Of *Lovers of Their Time,* by William Trevor. *Irish Press,* 28 September 1978, p. 6.

"Crime and Punishment." Of *Bognail,* by Patrick McGinley. *Irish Press,* 19 October 1978, p. 6.

"Mainstream and Sidestream." Of *Paddy No More: Modern Irish Short Stories,* edited by William Vorm. *Irish Press,* 28 December 1978, p. 6.

"Capote as Maupassant." Of *Music for Chameleons,* by Truman Capote. *Saturday Review,* July 1980, pp. 52–53.

Unpublished review of *Savage Day,* by Thomas Wiseman. Quoted in a publisher's advertisement in the *New York Times Book Review,* 18 October 1981, p. 37.

"The Falklands, and a Death Foretold." Essay-review of *The Chronicle of a Death Foretold,* by Gabriel García Márquez. *Georgia Review* 36 (1982): 721–28.

Unpublished review of *Helliconia Spring,* by Brian W. Aldiss. Quoted in publisher's advertisement in the *New York Times Book Review,* 9 May 1982, p. 31.

Unpublished review of *Flaubert's Parrot,* by Julian Barnes. Quoted on the cover of the British paperback edition. 1984; reprinted London: Pan, 1985.

Unpublished review of *The Chymical Wedding,* by Lindsay Clarke. Quoted on the cover of the American paperback edition. 1989; reprinted New York: Ballantine, 1991.

Published Letters

"Lyme Regis Sewage Plant." *Times,* 23 August 1973, p. 15.

"Hyperbole on the High Seas." *New Statesman,* 18 July 1975, p. 82.

"Lettre-postface de John Fowles." In *Études sur "The French Lieutenant's Woman" de John Fowles,* edited by Jean-Louis Chevalier, pp. 51–65. Caen, France: Centre Régional de Documentation Pédagogique, 1977. In English, dated 10 February 1976.

"Preserving Peonies." *Times,* 20 April 1977, p. 17.

Fowles and 374 others. "A Petition: To the Right Reverend Fathers-in-God, the Clergy, and Laity of the General Synod of the Church of England." *PN Review* 6.5 (1979): 51–56.

Queries 66, 67 in *GCG: Newsletter of the Geological Curator Group* 2.5 (April 1979): 263. Fowles requests information about the letters of James Harrison, a pioneer paleontologist of Charmouth, or the fossil collection of Francis Rawlins.

"The Enigma of Stonehenge." *Times Literary Supplement,* 3 October 1980, p. 1101.

"British Novelist Answers." *Humanist,* May/June 1981, p. 4.

Fowles and 69 others. "The Strike at Foyle's." *Bookseller,* 3 April 1982, p. 1323.

"Fossil Collecting." *Times,* 30 September 1982, p. 11.

Fowles and 152 others. "Authors Say End Low Pay in Book Publishing." *Bookseller,* 9 April 1983, p. 1322.

Advertising Copy

"Join Me, John Fowles, in the New Fiction Society. . . ." *Observer,* 26 October 1980, p. 29.

Note in *Ware Cliffs Appeal,* a form letter requesting contributions, from the Lyme Regis Society, 29 October 1987.

Form letter appealing for membership in the Friends of the Lyme Regis Museum, with tear-off application, undated [1989 membership rates], signed "John Fowles, Hon. Curator."

Translating and Adapting (from French)

Cinderella, by Charles Perrault. Illustrated by Sheilah Beckett. 1697; reprinted London: Jonathan Cape, 1974.

"Eliduc," by Marie de France. In *The Ebony Tower,* pp. 123–42. Circa 1200; reprinted London: Jonathan Cape, 1974: Boston, Little, Brown, 1974.

Ourika, by Claire de Durfort. 1824; reprinted Austin, Tex.: W. Thomas Taylor, 1977.

Preface by Frank Horvat. In *The Tree,* by John Fowles and Frank Horvat, unpaginated (i–v). Boston: Little, Brown, 1979.

Don Juan, by Molière. Directed by Peter Gill. National Theatre Company. 1665;

produced London: Cottesloe Theatre, 7 April 1981 (opening performance).

Lorenzaccio, by Alfred de Musset. Directed by Michael Bogdanov. National Theatre Company. 1834; produced London: Olivier Theatre, 15 March 1981
(opening performance).

Martine, by Jean-Jacques Bernard. Directed by Peter Hall. National Theatre
Company. 1922; produced London: Lyttleton Theatre, 20 April 1985
(opening performance).

Editing

The Kenneth Allsop Memorial Trust, co-editors. *Steep-Holm—A Case History in
the Study of Evolution.* London: Kenneth Allsop Memorial Trust, 1978.

King's Order for Lyme Siege [and] A Letter from Charles I Concerning Lyme (transcribed, with background notes). Lyme Regis, U.K.: Friends of the Lyme
Regis (Philpot) Museum, 1980.

Monumenta Britannica, by John Aubrey. Annotated by Rodney Legg. In England subtitled *John Aubrey (1626–97),* 2 volumes. Sherborne, U.K.: Dorset Publishing Company, 1980–82. In the United States subtitled *A Miscellany of British Antiquities,* 1 volume. Boston: Little, Brown, 1980
[published 1982, with earlier copyright date].

Thomas Hardy's England, by Jo Draper. London: Jonathan Cape; Boston: Little,
Brown, 1984. Reprinted London: Bloomsbury Publishing, 1989.

Isolated Quotations

"The newspapers are full of what we would like to happen to us and what we
hope will never happen to us" (from *The Aristos,* 1st edition, p. 87). In
Great Words of Our Time, compiled by Dee Danner Barwick, p. 42. Kansas
City, Mo.: Hallmark Cards, 1970.

"Doing nothing—that's hard work" (from Mel Gussow, "Talk with John Fowles,"
New York Times Book Review, 13 November 1977, p. 85). In *The Quotable
Quotations Book.* Compiled by Alec Lewis. New York: Thomas Y. Crowell,
1980, p. 128.

"I saw my first film when I was six; I suppose I've seen on average—and dis-
counting television—a film a week ever since: let's say some two and a
half thousand films up to now. How can so frequently repeated an experience not have indelibly stamped itself on the *mode* of imagination?
At one time I analyzed my dreams in detail; again and again I recalled
purely cinematic effects . . . panning shots, close shots, tracking, jump
cuts, and the like. In short, this mode of imagination is far too deep in
me to eradicate—not only in me, in all my generation" (quoted with one
emendation, of *rest* to *like,* from "Notes on Writing a Novel," *Harper's
Magazine,* July 1968, p. 92). Epigraph to *Some Time in the Sun,* by Tom
Dardis, unpaginated (x). New York: Charles Scribner's Sons, 1976.

WORKS ABOUT JOHN FOWLES

Interviews and Interview-based Articles

Amory, Mark. "Tales Out of School." *Sunday Times Magazine,* 22 September 1974, pp. 33–34, 36.

Arkwright, Dominic. [Lyme Regis could be destroyed, say residents, because of proposed sea front development]. *Today* 7 June 1989. Radio 4. London: British Broadcasting Corporation.

Baker, James R. "The Art of Fiction CIX: John Fowles." *Paris Review* 111 (1989): 40–63. Reproduces a page from a typescript draft of *The French Lieutenant's Woman,* with many revisions by Fowles, on p. 40.

———. "An Interview with John Fowles." *Michigan Quarterly Review* 25 (1986): 661–83.

Baker, John F. "John Fowles." *Publisher's Weekly,* 25 November 1974, pp. 6–7. Reprinted in *The Author Speaks: Selected PW Interviews 1967–1976,* pp. 50–53. New York: Bowker, 1977.

Barber, Michael. *An Interview with John Fowles.* Audio-Text Cassette No. 38873. North Hollywood, Calif.: Center for Cassette Studies, 1979. Mailing address: 8110 Webb Avenue, 91605.

Barnum, Carol M. "An Interview with John Fowles." *Modern Fiction Studies* 31 (1985): 187–203.

———. Otherwise unpublished interview 16 March 1984, cited in *The Fiction of John Fowles,* pp. 86 and 99, note 6. Greenwood, Fla.: Penkevill Publishing, 1988.

Benton, Sarah. "Adam and Eve." *New Socialist,* May/June 1983, pp. 18–19.

Bigsby, Christopher. "Interview with John Fowles." *The Radical Imagination and the Liberal Tradition: Interviews with English and American Novelists,* edited by Heide Ziegler and Christopher Bigsby, pp. 111–25. London: Junction Books, 1982.

Boston, Richard. "John Fowles, Alone But Not Lonely." *New York Times Book Review,* 9 November 1969, pp. 2, 52, 54.

Bragg, Melvyn. "Dorset." *The Literary Island,* 2 July 1991. London Weekend Television.

———. "The French Lieutenant's Woman." *South Bank Show,* 1 November 1981. London Weekend Television.

———. *The Lively Arts,* 23 October 1977. British Broadcasting Corporation.

Cameron, James. *Cameron Country,* 3 April 1971. British Broadcasting Corporation.

Campbell, James. "An Interview with John Fowles." *Contemporary Literature* 17 (1976): 455–69.

Cartano, Tony. "John Fowles à la recherche de soi-même." *Magazine Littéraire,* June 1981, pp. 54–56.

Conradi, Peter. Otherwise unpublished interview at the University of East Anglia, 1976, cited on pp. 30, 43, 52, 91 of *John Fowles* (New York: Methuen, 1982).

Critchfield, Richard. *An American Looks at Britain,* pp. 10, 153, 235, 244, 253, 323, 451, 457–58. New York: Doubleday, 1990.

Davies, Tom. "Moods in a Wood." *Observer,* 14 October 1979, p. 52.

Davis, Douglas M. "He Is Like a Lion with Painted Nails." *National Observer,* 24 January 1966, p. 21.

Delaney, Frank. Interview. *Bookshelf,* 11 October 1981. Radio 4. London: British Broadcasting Corporation.

———. *Frank Delaney Programme,* 13 November 1982. Television 2. London: British Broadcasting Corporation.

DeVries, Hilary. "Searching for a Moral Perspective: John Fowles Scans Past for That Which He Can't Find in the 'Amoral' Present." *Christian Science Monitor,* 8 October 1985, pp. 23–24.

Ezard, John. "Author Joins Fight to Restore Ancient Water Mill." *Guardian,* 22 April 1991, p. 2.

Featherstone-Thomas, Mark. "Goodbye, Mr. Chips: Once a Teacher, Always a Teacher? Mark Featherstone-Thomas Talks to Some Ex-Teacher Writers." *Times Educational Supplement,* 21 July 1978, p. 16.

Foulke, Robert. "A Conversation with John Fowles." *Salmagundi* 68–69 (1985–86): 367–84.

Freeman, David. Interview, 7 October 1982. Oxford, U.K.: Radio Oxford.

A Future for the Past? [teleconference on museums] 26 June 1986. Radio 4. London: British Broadcasting Corporation.

Garis, Leslie. "Translating Fowles into Film" (contains interviews with Karel Reiz and Harold Pinter also). *New York Times Magazine,* 30 August 1981, pp. 24–25, 48, 50, 52, 54, 69.

Gilder, Joshua. "John Fowles: A Novelist's Dilemma." *Saturday Review,* October 1981, pp. 36, 39–40.

Gussow, Mel. "Talk with John Fowles." *New York Times Book Review,* 13 November 1977, pp. 3, 84–85.

Hall, Donald. "John Fowles's Gardens." *Esquire,* October 1982, pp. 90–102.

Halpern, Daniel. "A Sort of Exile in Lyme Regis." *London Magazine,* March 1971, pp. 34–46.

Hauptfuhrer, Fred. "His Stories Are Riddles Wrapped Inside an Enigma Named Fowles." *People Weekly,* 7 April 1975, pp. 56–59.

Higgins, John. "A Fresh Mind on Molière's 'Odd Man Out.' " *Times,* 6 April 1981, p. 6.

"Imminent Victorians." *Time,* 7 November 1969, p. 108.

Kingsley, Madeleine. "John Fowles: Collector's Piece." *Harper's and Queen,* 6 October 1977, pp. 150–51, 235.

Kjaerstad, Jan. "Romanens store frihet: Intervju med John Fowles" ("The Novel's Great Freedom: Interview with John Fowles"). *Vinduet* 38.4 (1984): 3–9.

Latham, Aaron. "John Fowles on Islands and . . . Hidden Valleys." *Washington Post,* 10 October 1977, pp. E1, E4.

Loveday, Simon. Otherwise unpublished interview, cited in *The Romances of John Fowles* (New York: St. Martin's, 1985), pp. 148–49, 111 (n. 3), 163 (n. 11).

McCullough, David. "Eye on Books." *Book-of-the-Month Club News,* April 1975, pp. 6–7.

McDaniel, Ellen. Otherwise unpublished, 1977 interview cited in "Fowles as

Collector: The Failed Artists of *The Ebony Tower*," *Papers on Language and Literature* 23 (1987): 79.

McNay, Michael. "Into the City's Iron Heart." *Guardian,* 5 December 1970, p. 8.

"Message from a Maggot." *Times,* 14 September 1985, p. 8.

Mockridge, Norton. "Smell of Success Makes Him Nervous." *New York World Telegram,* 19 September 1963, p. 21.

Molony, Rowland. "John Fowles: The Magus." *Dorset: The County Magazine,* 30 November 1973, pp. 19–23.

Monaghan, Charles. "Portrait of a Man Reading." *Washington Post Book World,* 4 January 1970, p. 2.

Munro, J. Richard. "Letter from the Publisher." *Sports Illustrated,* 21 December 1970, p. 5.

Newquist, Roy. "John Fowles." *Counterpoint,* pp. 217–25. New York: Rand McNally, 1964.

Nichols, Lewis. "Mr. Fowles." *New York Times Book Review,* 30 January 1966, p. 8.

North, David. "Interview with Author John Fowles." *Maclean's,* 14 November 1977, pp. 4, 6, 8.

O'Conner, Patricia T. "Mystery and Faith." *New York Times Book Review,* 8 September 1985, p. 11.

Olshen, Barry N. Otherwise unpublished interview cited in *John Fowles* (New York: Frederick Ungar, 1978), p. 34 and n. 6.

Onega, Susana. "Fowles on Fowles." Actas del X Congreso Nacional de A.E.D.E.A.N., pp. 57–76. Zaragoza, Spain: Libreria General, 1988. Reprinted as an appendix to *Form and Meaning in the Novels of John Fowles,* pp. 175–90. Ann Arbor, Mich.: UMI Research Press, 1989.

Parker, Bruce. *Mainstream,* 4 December 1979. British Broadcasting Corporation.

Plomley, Roy. *Desert Island Discs* No. 1575, 10 January 1981. Radio 4. London: British Broadcasting Corporation.

Porterfield, Christopher. "Mysterious Movers and Shakers." *Time,* 9 September 1985, pp. 67–68.

Remnick, David. "Fowles, Following Form." *Washington Post,* 12 September 1985, pp. C1, C8.

Robinson, Robert. "Giving the Reader a Choice—A Conversation with John Fowles." *Listener,* 31 October 1974, p. 584.

Romano, Carlin. "A Conversation with John Fowles." *Boulevard,* Spring 1987, pp. 37–52.

Sage, Lorna. "John Fowles." Profile 7. *New Review,* October 1974, pp. 31–37.

Scott, Gavin. *Newsnight,* 21 September 1981. British Broadcasting Corporation.

"A Short Break." *Kaleidoscope* 4 June 1986. Radio 4. London: British Broadcasting Corporation.

Singh, Raman K. "An Encounter with John Fowles." *Journal of Modern Literature* 8 (1980–81): 181–202.

Somerville, Christopher. *Literary Walks,* 8 September 1985. Radio 4. British Broadcasting Corporation (exploration of Lyme Regis and nearby countryside, with discussion of *The French Lieutenant's Woman*).

Stolley, Richard B. "The French Lieutenant's Woman's Man: Novelist John Fowles." *Life,* 29 May 1970, pp. 55–60.

Tarbox, Katherine M. "Fowles Has the Last Word." *A Critical Study of the Novels of John Fowles.* Dissertation, University of New Hampshire, 1986. Reprinted, slightly edited, as an appendix to *The Art of John Fowles.*

Timpson, John. *Tonight,* 7 April 1978. British Broadcasting Corporation.

Today Show, 11 November 1974. New York: National Broadcasting Corporation.

"The Unknown Victorians." *Times,* 3 November 1967, p. 10.

Wansell, Geoffrey. "The Writer As a Recluse: A Portrait of the Novelist John Fowles." *Times,* 12 May 1971, p. 14.

Yallop, Richard. "The Reluctant Guru." *Guardian,* 9 June 1977, p. 8.

Biographical Essays about John Fowles

Barnum, Carol M. "John Fowles." In *Critical Survey of Long Fiction,* edited by Frank N. Magill, vol. 3, pp. 1008–22. Englewood Cliffs, N.J.: Salem Press, 1983.

Dixon, Ronald C. "John Fowles." *Postmodern Fiction: A Bio-Bibliographical Guide,* edited by Larry McCaffrey, pp. 363–66. Movements in the Arts 2. Westport, Conn.: Greenwood Press, 1986.

Edwards, C. W. "School Notes." *The Ousel: The Journal of Bedford School* 48 (1944): 95–98. Contains a photograph of Fowles, age eighteen, p. 96.

"Fowles, John." *Contemporary Authors* 5–8, First Revision, pp. 396–97. Detroit: Gale Research Company, 1963, 1969.

"Fowles, John." *Current Biography Yearbook: 1977,* edited by Charles Moritz, pp. 159–63. New York: H. W. Wilson, 1977.

"Fowles, John." *200 Contemporary Authors,* edited by Barbara Harte and Caroline Rile, pp. 117–18. Detroit: Gale Research Co., 1969.

"Fowles, John." *Who's Who 1988,* pp. 613–14. New York: St. Martin's, 1988.

Gindon, James. "Fowles, John (Robert)." *Contemporary Novelists,* edited by James Vinson, pp. 222–23. 3rd ed. New York: St. Martin's, 1982.

"John Fowles." *World Authors 1950–1970,* edited by John Wakeman, pp. 485–87. New York: Wilson, 1975.

Legg, Rodney. "John Fowles: Belmont House, *The French Lieutenant's Woman,* and 'Allsop Island.' " In *Literary Dorset,* pp. 20–21, 116. Wincanton, U.K.: Dorset Publishing Company, 1990.

Pifer, Ellen. "John Fowles." *British Novelists Since 1960,* part 1, edited by Jay L. Halio, pp. 309–36. Vol. 14 of *Dictionary of Literary Biography.* Detroit: Gale Research Company, 1983. Contains a reproduction of an unidentified typescript by Fowles, with numerous authorial revisions, p. 315.

Thorpe, Michael. "John Fowles." *British Writers,* Supplement, vol. 1, edited by Ian Scott-Kilvert, pp. 291–311. New York: Charles Scribner's Sons, 1987.

Books and Monographs About Works by John Fowles

Barnum, Carol M. *The Fiction of John Fowles: A Myth for Our Time.* Greenwood, Fla.: Penkevill Publishing, 1988.

Bellman, James F. and Kathryn. *The French Lieutenant's Woman: Notes.* Lincoln, Neb.: Cliffs Notes, 1979.

Borch, Kirsten, and Kurt Mikkelsen. *Identitet og frihed i John Fowles' romaner [Identity and Freedom in John Fowles's Novels].* Udgivelsesudvalgets samling af studenterafhandlinger 23. Odense, Denmark: Odense Universitets Konsistorium, 1983.

Conradi, Peter. *John Fowles.* Contemporary Writers. London; New York: Methuen, 1982.

Fawkner, H. W. *The Timescapes of John Fowles.* London; Cranbury, N.J.: Associated University Presses, 1984.

Huffaker, Robert. *John Fowles.* Twayne's English Authors Series 292. Boston: Twayne, 1980.

Loveday, Simon. *The Romances of John Fowles.* London: Macmillan; New York: St. Martin's, 1985.

Olshen, Barry N. *John Fowles.* Modern Literature Monographs. New York: Ungar, 1978.

Olshen, Barry N., and Toni A. Olshen. *John Fowles: A Reference Guide.* Boston: G. K. Hall, 1980.

Onega, Susana. *Form and Meaning in the Novels of John Fowles.* Ann Arbor, Mich.: UMI Research Press, 1989.

Palmer, William J. *The Fiction of John Fowles: Tradition, Art, and the Loneliness of Selfhood.* Columbia: University of Missouri Press, 1974.

Pifer, Ellen, ed. *Critical Essays on John Fowles.* Critical Essays on Modern British Literature. Boston: G. K. Hall, 1986.

Speer, Hilda. *York Notes on The French Lieutenant's Woman.* Burnt Mill, Harlow, U.K.: Longman, 1990.

Tarbox, Katherine. *The Art of John Fowles.* Athens: University of Georgia Press, 1988.

Thorpe, Michael. *John Fowles.* Writers and Their Work. Windsor, U.K.: Profile Books, 1982.

Wolfe, Peter. *John Fowles, Magus and Moralist.* 1976; 2nd ed. London: Associated University Presses; Lewisburg, Pa.: Bucknell University Press, 1979.

Woodcock, Bruce. *Male Mythologies: John Fowles and Masculinity.* Brighton, U.K.: Harvester; Totowa, N.J.: Barnes & Noble, 1984.

Essays in English about Works by John Fowles

Alderman, Timothy C. "The Enigma of *The Ebony Tower:* A Genre Study." *Modern Fiction Studies* 31 (1985): 135–47.

Allen, Walter. "The Achievement of John Fowles." *Encounter,* August 1970, pp. 64–67.

Alter, Robert. "*Daniel Martin* and the Mimetic Task." *Genre* 14.1 (1981): 65–78. Reprinted in *Motives for Fiction,* pp. 144–56. Cambridge, Mass.: Harvard University Press, 1984. Reprinted in *Critical Essays on John Fowles,* pp. 150–62.

Andrews, Maureen Gillespie. "Nature in John Fowles's *Daniel Martin* and *The Tree.*" *Modern Fiction Studies* 31 (1985): 149–55.

Arlett, Robert. "*Daniel Martin* and the Contemporary Epic Novel." *Modern Fiction Studies* 31 (1985): 173–85.

Aubrey, James R. "The Pre-Raphaelite 'pack of satyrs' in John Fowles's *The French Lieutenant's Woman*." *Nineteenth-Century Prose* 18.1 (1990–91): 32–36.

Bagchee, Syhamal. "*The Collector:* The Paradoxical Imagination of John Fowles." *Journal of Modern Literature* 8 (1980–81): 219–34.

———. "*The Great Gatsby* and John Fowles's *The Collector*." *Notes on Contemporary Literature* 10.4 (1980): 7–8.

Baker, James R. "Fowles and the Struggle of the English *Aristoi*." *Journal of Modern Literature* 8 (1980–81): 163–80.

Barnum, Carol. "John Fowles's *Daniel Martin:* A Vision of Whole Sight." *Literary Review: An International Journal of Contemporary Writing* 25.1 (1981): 64–79.

———. "The Quest Motif in John Fowles's *The Ebony Tower*." *Texas Studies in Language and Literature* 23.2 (1981): 138–57. Reprinted in *Critical Essays on John Fowles,* pp. 133–50.

Bawer, Bruce. "John Fowles and His Big Ideas." *New Criterion* 5.8 (April 1987): 21–36.

Beatty, Patricia V. "John Fowles' Clegg: Captive Landlord of Eden." *Ariel: A Review of International English Literature* 13.3 (1982): 73–81.

———. "John Fowles's *Daniel Martin:* Poetics of the Now." *South Atlantic Quarterly* 81 (1982): 78–86.

Begiebung, Robert J. "John Fowles: The Magician as Teacher." Chap. 2 of *Toward a New Synthesis: John Fowles, John Gardner, Norman Mailer,* pp. 17–49, 137–40 (notes). Ann Arbor, Mich.: UMI Research Press, 1989.

Begnal, Michael H. "A View of John Fowles' *The Magus*." *Modern British Literature* 3 (1978): 67–72.

Bellamy, Michael O. "John Fowles's Version of Pastoral: Private Valleys and the Parity of Existence." *Critique* 21.2 (1979): 72–84.

Berets, Ralph. "*The Magus:* A Study in the Creation of a Personal Myth." *Twentieth Century Literature* 19 (1973): 89–98.

Bernstein, John. "John Fowles' Use of Ibsen in *Daniel Martin*." *Notes on Contemporary Literature* 9.4 (1979): 10.

Billy, Ted. "*Homo Solitarius:* Isolation and Estrangement in *The Magus*." *Research Studies* 48 (1980): 129–41.

Binns, Ronald. "John Fowles: Radical Romancer." *Critical Quarterly* 15 (1973): 317–34. Reprinted in *Critical Essays on John Fowles,* pp. 19–37.

———. "A New Version of *The Magus*." *Critical Quarterly* 19.4 (1977): 79–84. Reprinted in *Critical Essays on John Fowles,* pp. 100–105.

Boccia, Michael. "Feminism in *The Magus* by John Fowles." *New Hampshire College Journal* 6 (1989): 59–70.

———. " 'Visions and Revisions': John Fowles's New Version of *The Magus*." *Journal of Modern Literature* 8 (1980–81): 235–46.

Boomsma, Patricia J. " 'Whole Sight': Fowles, Lukács and *Daniel Martin*." *Journal of Modern Literature* 8 (1980–81): 325–36.

Bradbury, Malcolm. "John Fowles's *The Magus*." In *Sense and Sensibility in Twentieth-Century Writing: A Gathering in Memory of William Van O'Connor,* edited by Brom Weber, pp. 26–38. Carbondale and Edwardsville, Ill.: Southern Illinois University Press, 1970. Substantially revised and reprinted as "The Novelist as Impresario: John Fowles and His Magus," in *Possibilities: Essays on the State of the Novel*, pp. 256–71. New York: Oxford University Press, 1973.

———. "The Novelist as Impresario: The Fiction of John Fowles." In *No, Not Bloomsbury*, pp. 279–93. New York: Columbia University Press, 1988. This essay retains bits of Bradbury's earlier essay on *The Magus* but is much expanded and thoroughly revised into a comprehensive assessment of Fowles's "place" in twentieth-century literature.

Brandt, Peter. "In Search of the Eighth Man: A Study of John Fowles." *Revista Canaria de Estudios Ingleses* 7 (November 1983): 39–59.

Brantlinger, Patrick, Ian Adam, and Sheldon Rothblatt. *"The French Lieutenant's Woman:* A Discussion." *Victorian Studies* 15 (1972): 339–56.

Brown, Ruth Christiani. *"The French Lieutenant's Woman* and *Pierre:* Echo and Answer." *Modern Fiction Studies* 31 (1985): 115–32.

Brownell, David. "John Fowles' Experiments with the Form of the Mystery Story." *Armchair Detective* 10 (1977): 184–86.

Bump, Jerome. "The Narrator as Protoreader in *The French Lieutenant's Woman."* *Victorian Newsletter* 74 (Fall 1988): 16–18.

Burden, Robert. "The Analysis of Identity in the Novels and Stories of John Fowles." In *John Fowles-John Hawkes-Claude Simon: Problems of Self and Form in the Post-Modernist Novel: A Comparative Study*, pp. 28–55. Epistemata: Würzburger Wissenschaftliche Schriften: Reike Litteraturwissenschaft 5. Würzburg: Konighausen & Newmann, 1980.

———. "Structure and Interpretation in the Narrative Fiction of John Fowles." Ibid., pp. 150–81.

———. "John Fowles: *The French Lieutenant's Woman.*" Ibid., pp. 271–84.

Byrd, Deborah. "The Evolution and Emancipation of Sarah Woodruff: *The French Lieutenant's Woman* as a Feminist Novel." *International Journal of Women's Studies* 7 (1984): 306–21.

Campbell, Robert. "Moral Sense and the Collector: The Novels of John Fowles." *Critical Quarterly* 25 (1983): 45–53.

Carter, Steven R. "Freedom and Mystery in John Fowles' 'The Enigma.' " *Mystery Fancier* 3.5 (1979): 14–16.

Casagrande, Peter J. " 'The Immortal Puzzle': Hardy and John Fowles." In *Hardy's Influence on the Modern Novel*, pp. 150–72 and 227–28. Totowa, N.J.: Barnes & Noble, 1987.

Chittick, K. A. "The Laboratory of Narrative and John Fowles's *Daniel Martin.*" *English Studies in Canada* 11.1 (1985): 70–81.

Churchill, Thomas. "Waterhouse, Storey, and Fowles: Which Way Out of the Room?" *Critique* 10 (1967–68): 72–87.

Cohen, Philip. "Postmodernist Technique in *The French Lieutenant's Woman.*" *Western Humanities Review* 38 (1984): 148–61.

Costa, Richard Hauer. "Trickery's Mixed Bag: The Perils of Fowles' *French Lieutenant's Woman.*" *Rocky Mountain Review of Language and Literature* 29 (1975): 1–9.

Creighton, Joanne V. "The Reader and Modern and Post-Modern Fiction." *College Literature* 9 (1982): 216–30.

Davidson, Arnold E. "The Barthesian Configuration of John Fowles's 'The Cloud.' " *Centennial Review* 28.4–29.1 (1984–85): 80–93.

———. "Caliban and the Captive Maiden: John Fowles' *The Collector* and Irving Wallace's *The Fan Club*." *Studies in the Humanities* 8.2 (1981): 28–33.

———. "*Eliduc* and 'The Ebony Tower': John Fowles's Variation on a Medieval Lay." *International Fiction Review* 11.1 (1984): 31–36.

Davies, Hunter. "Professional Fowles." *Times*, 2 October 1977, pp. 64–65.

Delbaere-Garant, Jeanne. "Prospero To-Day: Magus, Monster, or Patriarch?" In *Communiquer et traduir: Hommages à Jean Dierickx/Communicating and Translating Essays in Honour of Jean Dierickx*, edited by G. Debusscher and J. P. van Noppen, pp. 293–302. Faculté de Philosophie et Lettres 96. Brussels: Editions de l'Université de Bruxelles, 1985.

Detweiler, Robert. "The Unity of John Fowles' Fiction." *Notes on Contemporary Literature* 1.2 (1971): 3–4.

DeVitis, A. A., and William J. Palmer. "A Pair of Blue Eyes Flash at *The French Lieutenant's Woman*." *Contemporary Literature* 15 (1974): 90–101.

DeVitis, A. A., and Lisa M. Schwerdt. "*The French Lieutenant's Woman* and 'Las Meninas': Correspondences of Art." *International Fiction Review* 12.2 (1985): 102–4.

D'haen, Theo. "Fowles, Lodge and the 'Problematic Novel.' " *Dutch Quarterly Review of Anglo-American Letters* 9 (1979): 162–75.

———. "John Fowles's *The French Lieutenant's Woman*." In *Text to Reader: A Communicative Approach to Fowles, Barth, Cortázar, and Boon*, pp. 25–42, 133–37 (notes). Utrecht Publications in General and Comparative Literature 16. Amsterdam/Philadelphia: John Benjamins, 1983.

Ditsky, John. "The Watch and Chain of Henry James." *University of Windsor Review* 6.1 (1970): 91–101.

Dixon, Terrell F. "Expostulation and a Reply: The Character of Clegg in Fowles and Sillitoe." *Notes on Contemporary Literature* 4.2 (1974): 7–9.

Docherty, Thomas. "A Constant Reality: The Presentation of Character in the Fiction of John Fowles." *Novel* 14 (1981): 118–34.

Doherty, Gerald. "The Secret Plot of Metaphor: Rhetorical Designs in John Fowles's *The French Lieutenant's Woman*." *Paragraph: The Journal of the Modern Critical Theory Group* 9 (9 March 1987): 49–68.

Dopp, Jamie, and Barry N. Olshen. "Fathers and Sons: Fowles's *The Tree* and Autobiographical Theory." *Mosaic: A Journal for the Interdisciplinary Study of Literature* 22.4 (1989): 31–44.

Duriez, Colin. "The Creation of Meaning: An Appraisal of John Fowles' Novels." *Third Way*, 9 February 1978, pp. 7–9.

Eddins, Dwight. "John Fowles: Existence as Authorship." *Contemporary Literature* 17 (1976): 204–22. Reprinted in *Critical Essays on John Fowles*, pp. 38–54.

Evarts, Prescott, Jr. "Fowles' *The French Lieutenant's Woman* as Tragedy." *Critique* 13.3 (1972): 57–69.

Fawkner, H. W. "The Neurocognitive Significance of John Fowles's *Mantissa*." *Studia Neuphilologica* 56 (1984): 51–59.

Ferris, Ina. "Realist Intention and Mythic Impulse in *Daniel Martin*." *Journal of Narrative Technique* 12 (1982): 146–53.

Fleishman, Avrom. *"The Magus* of the Wizard of the West." *Journal of Modern Literature* 5 (1976): 297–314. Reprinted in *Critical Essays on John Fowles*, pp. 77–93.

Fossa, John A. "Through Seeking to Mystery: A Reappraisal of John Fowles' *The Magus*." *Orbis Litterarum: International Review of Literary Studies* 44 (1989): 161–80.

Gaggi, Silvio. "Pirandellian and Brechtian Aspects of the Fiction of John Fowles." *Comparative Literature Studies* 23 (1986): 324–34.

Gilmore, Robin. "The Art of John Fowles." *Dorset: The County Magazine*, 30 November 1973, pp. 25–27.

Gindin, James. "Three Recent British Novels and an American Response." *Michigan Quarterly Review* 17 (1978): 223–46.

Gotts, Ian. "Fowles' *Mantissa:* Funfair in Another Village." *Critique* 26 (1985): 81–95.

Grace, Sherrill E. "Courting Bluebeard with Bartók, Atwood, and Fowles: Modern Treatment of the Bluebeard Theme." *Journal of Modern Literature* 11 (1984): 245–62.

Gross, David. "Historical Consciousness and the Modern Novel: The Uses of History in the Fiction of John Fowles." *Studies in the Humanities* 7.1 (1978): 19–27.

Guth, Deborah. "Archetypal Worlds Reappraised: *The French Lieutenant's Woman* and *Le Grand Meulnes*." *Comparative Literature Studies* 22 (1985): 244–51.

Haegert, John. "Memoirs of a Deconstructive Angel: The Heroine as Mantissa in the Fiction of John Fowles." *Contemporary Literature* 27 (1986): 160–81.

Hagiopan, John V. "Bad Faith in *The French Lieutenant's Woman*." *Contemporary Literature* 23 (1982): 190–201.

Hagen, Patricia. "Revision Revisited: Reading (and) *The French Lieutenant's Woman*." *College English* 53 (1991): 439–51.

Harnack, William. "The Greening of John Fowles." *Humanist*, March/April 1982, pp. 52–53.

Harris, Richard L. " 'The Magus' and 'The Miller's Tale': John Fowles on the Courtly Mode." *Ariel: A Review of International English Literature* 14.2 (1983): 3–17.

Hieatt, Constance B. *"Eliduc* Revisited: John Fowles and Marie de France." *English Studies in Canada* 3 (1977): 351–58.

Higdon, David Leon. "Endgames in John Fowles's *The French Lieutenant's Woman*." *English Studies* 65 (1984): 350–61.

———. "The Epigraph to John Fowles's *The Collector*." *Modern Fiction Studies* 32 (1986): 568–72.

Hill, Roy Mack. "Power and Hazard: John Fowles's Theory of Play." *Journal of Modern Literature* 3 (1980–81): 211–18.

Hogan, Ken. "Fowles' Narrative Style in *The French Lieutenant's Woman*." *CCTE Proceedings* 48 (September 1983): 54–63.

Holloway, Watson L. "The Killing of the Weasel: Hermetism in the Fiction of John Fowles." *ELN* 22.3 (1985): 69–71.

Holmes, Frederick M. "Art, Truth, and John Fowles's *The Magus.*" *Modern Fiction Studies* 3 (1985): 45–56.

———. "Fictions, Reality, and the Authority of the Novelist: Barth's *The Sot-Weed Factor* and Fowles's *The Magus.*" *English Studies in Canada* 11 (1985): 346–60.

———. "Fictional Self-Consciousness in John Fowles's *The Ebony Tower.*" *Ariel: A Review of International English Literature* 16.3 (1985): 21–38.

———. "John Fowles's Variation on Angus Wilson's Variation on E. M. Forster: 'The Cloud,' 'Et Dona Ferentes,' and 'The Story of a Panic.' " *Ariel: A Review of International English Literature* 20.3 (1989): 39–52.

———. "The Novel, Illusion and Reality: The Paradox of Omniscience in *The French Lieutenant's Woman.*" *Journal of Narrative Technique* 11.3 (1981): 184–98.

———. "The Novelist as Magus: John Fowles and the Function of Narrative." *Dalhousie Review* 68 (1988): 288–301.

Humma, John B. "James and Fowles: Tradition and Influence." *University of Toronto Quarterly* 54.1 (1984): 79–100.

———. "John Fowles' *The Ebony Tower:* In the Celtic Mood." *Southern Humanities Review* 17 (1983): 33–47.

Hussey, Barbara L. "John Fowles's *The Magus:* The Book and the World." *International Fiction Review* 10.1 (1983): 19–26.

Hutcheon, Linda. "Parody Without Ridicule: Observations on Modern Literary Parody." *Canadian Review of Comparative Literature/Revue Canadienne de littérature comparée* 5 (1978): 201–11.

———. "The 'Real World(s)' of Fiction: *The French Lieutenant's Woman.*" *English Studies in Canada* 4 (1978): 81–94. Reprinted in *Critical Essays on John Fowles,* pp. 118–32.

Ireland, K. R. "Towards a Grammar of Narrative Sequence: The Model of *The French Lieutenant's Woman.*" *Poetics Today* 7 (1986): 397–420.

Jacobson, Wendy. "Freedom and Women in John Fowles's *The French Lieutenant's Woman.*" *Opus* 2 (1977): 1–18.

Johnson, A.J.B. "Realism in *The French Lieutenant's Woman.*" *Journal of Modern Literature* 8 (1980–81): 287–302.

Johnstone, Douglas B. "The 'Unplumb'd Salt Estranging' Tragedy of *The French Lieutenant's Woman.*" *American Imago* 42 (1985): 69–83.

Kane, Patricia. "The Fallen Woman as Free-Thinker in *The French Lieutenant's Woman* and *The Scarlet Letter.*" *Notes on Contemporary Literature* 2.1 (1972): 8–10.

Kane, Richard C. "Greek Gothic: *The Magus.*" In his *Iris Murdoch, Muriel Spark, and John Fowles,* pp. 120–49, 156–57 (notes). Cranbury, N.J.: Fairleigh Dickenson University Press, 1988.

———. "A Room Without a View: *The Collector.*" Ibid., pp. 105–19, 155–56 (notes).

Kaplan, Fred. "Victorian Modernists: Fowles and Nabokov." *Journal of Narrative Technique* 3 (1973): 108–20.

Kellman, Steven G. "Fictive Freedom through *The French Lieutenant's Woman.*" *University of Mississippi Studies in English* 4 (1983): 159–67.

Kennedy, Alan. "John Fowles's Sense of an Ending." In *The Protean Self: Dra-*

matic Action in Contemporary Fiction, pp. 251–60. New York: Columbia University Press, 1974.

Kersnowski, Frank. "John Fowles's 'The Ebony Tower': A Discourse with Critics." *Journal of the Short Story in English* 13 (1989): 57–65.

Klemtner, Susan Strehle. "The Counterpoles of John Fowles's *Daniel Martin*." *Critique* 21.2 (1979–80): 59–71.

Klotz, Günther. "Realism and Metafiction in John Fowles's Novels." *Zeitschrift für Anglistik und Amerikanistik* 34 (1986): 299–308.

Laughlin, Rosemary M. "Faces of Power in the Novels of John Fowles." *Critique* 13.3 (1970–72): 71–88.

Le Bouille, Lucian. "John Fowles: Looking for Guidelines." *Journal of Modern Literature* 8.2 (1980–81): 203–10.

Lemos, Brunilda Reichmann. "Fowles' Godgame: Characters and Conclusions in *The French Lieutenant's Woman*." *Revista Letras* 32 (1983): 85–93.

Lever, Karen M. "The Education of John Fowles." *Critique* 21.2 (1979–80): 85–99.

Lewis, Janet E., and Barry N. Olshen. "John Fowles and the Medieval Romance Tradition." *Modern Fiction Studies* 31 (1985): 15–30.

Lindblad, Ishrat. " 'La bonne vaux,' 'la princess lointaine': Two Motifs in the Novels of John Fowles." In *Studies in English Philology, Linguistics and Literature: Presented to Alarik Rynell, 7 March 1978*, edited by Mats Ryden and Lennart A. Bjork, pp. 87–101. Stockholm Studies in English 46. Stockholm: Almqvist and Wiksell, 1978.

Lindroth, James R. "The Architecture of Revision: Fowles and the Agora." *Modern Fiction Studies* 31 (1985): 57–69.

Loveday, Simon. "Magus or Midas?" *Oxford Literary Review* 2.3 (1977): 34–35.

———. "The Style of John Fowles: Tense and Person in the First Chapter of *Daniel Martin*." *Journal of Narrative Technique* 10 (1980): 198–204.

Lovell, Terry. "Feminism and Form in the Literary Adaptation: *The French Lieutenant's Woman*." In *Criticism and Critical Theory*, edited by Jeremy Hawthorn, pp. 112–26. London: Edward Arnold, 1984.

McDaniel, Ellen. "Fowles as Collector: The Failed Artists of *The Ebony Tower*." *Papers on Language and Literature* 23 (1987): 70–83.

———. "Games and Godgames in *The Magus* and *The French Lieutenant's Woman*." *Modern Fiction Studies* 31 (1985): 31–42.

———. "John Fowles' Sense of an Ending." *Notes on Contemporary Literature* 13.5 (1983): 6–7.

———. "*The Magus:* Fowles's Tarot Quest." *Journal of Modern Literature* 8 (1980–81): 247–60. Reprinted in *Critical Essays on John Fowles*, pp. 106–17.

McGregor, Barbara R. "Existentialism in *The French Lieutenant's Woman*." *RE: Artes Liberales* 1.2 (1975): 39–46.

McSweeney, Kerry. "John Fowles's Variations." *Four Contemporary Novelists: Angus Wilson, Brian Moore, John Fowles, V. S. Naipaul*. Kingston and Montreal: McGill-Queens University Press; London: Scolar Press, 1983.

———. "John Fowles's Variations in *The Ebony Tower*." *Journal of Modern Literature* 8 (1980–81): 303–24.

———. "Withering into the Truth: John Fowles and *Daniel Martin*." *Critical Quarterly* 20.4 (1978): 31–38.

Magalaner, Marvin. "The Fool's Journey: John Fowles' *The Magus* (1966)." In *Old Lines, New Forces: Essays on the Contemporary British Novel, 1960–1970*, edited by Robert K. Morris, pp. 81–92. London: Associated University Presses; Cranbury, N.J.: Farleigh Dickinson University Press, 1976.

Mansfield, Elizabeth. "A Sequence of Endings: The Manuscripts of *The French Lieutenant's Woman*." *Journal of Modern Literature* 8 (1980–81): 275–86.

Mathews, James W. "Fowles's Artistic Freedom: Another Stone from James's House." *Notes on Contemporary Literature* 4.2 (1974): 2–4.

Mazis, Glen A. "The 'Riteful' Play of Time in *The French Lieutenant's Woman*." *Soundings* 66 (1983): 296–318.

Mellors, John. "Collectors and Creators: The Novels of John Fowles." *London Magazine*, February/March 1975, pp. 65–72.

Merivale, Patricia. "Learning the Hard Way: Gothic Pedagogy in the Modern Romantic Quest." *Comparative Literature* 36 (1984): 146–61.

Michael, Magali Cornier. " 'Who Is Sarah?' A Critique of *The French Lieutenant's Woman*'s Feminism." *Critique* 28 (1987): 225–36.

Michel-Michot, Paulette. "Fowles's 'Poor Koko': A Metaphor of the Quest." In *Multiple Worlds, Multiple Words*, edited by Hena Maes-Jelinek and others, pp. 203–11. Liège: University de Liège, 1987.

Miller, Nan. "Christina Rossetti and Sarah Woodruff: Two Remedies for a Divided Self." *Journal of Pre-Raphaelite Studies* 3.1 (1982): 68–77.

Mills, John. "Fowles' Indeterminacy: An Art of Alternatives." *West Coast Review* 10 (1975): 32–36.

Morse, Ruth. "John Fowles, Marie de France, and the Man with Two Wives." *Philological Quarterly* 63 (1984): 17–30.

Munro, J. Richard. "Letter from the Publisher." *Sports Illustrated*, 21 December 1970, p. 5.

Myers, Karen Magee. "John Fowles: An Annotated Bibliography, 1963–1976." *Bulletin of Bibliography* 33 (1976): 162–69.

Nadeau, Robert L. "Fowles and Physics: A Study of *The Magus: A Revised Version*." *Journal of Modern Literature* 8 (1980–81): 261–74.

Neary, John M. "John Fowles' Clegg: A Metaphysical Rebel." *Essays in Literature* 15 (1988): 45–61.

Nelles, William. "Problems for Narrative Theory: *The French Lieutenant's Woman*." *Style* 18 (1984): 207–17.

Newman, Robert D. " 'An Anagram Made Flesh': The Transformation of Nicholas Urfe in Fowles' *The Magus*." *Notes on Contemporary Literature* 12.4 (1982): 9.

Nodelman, Perry. "John Fowles's Variations in *The Collector*." *Contemporary Literature* 28 (1987): 332–46.

Novak, Frank G., Jr. "The Dialectics of Debasement in *The Magus*." *Modern Fiction Studies* 31 (1985): 71–82.

Occhiogrosso, Frank. "Threats to Rationalism: John Fowles, Stanislaw Lem, and the Detective Story." *Armchair Detective* 13 (1980): 4–7.

Olshen, Barry N. "John Fowles's *The Magus*: An Allegory of Self-Realization." *Journal of Popular Culture* 9 (1976): 916–25.

Onega Jaen, Susana. "Form and Meaning in *The French Lieutenant's Woman*." *Revista canaria de estudios Ingleses*, April 1987, pp. 13–14, 77–107.

Orr, John. "Offstage Tragedy: The New Narrative Strategies of John Fowles, Saul Bellow and William Styron." *New Edinburgh Review* 59 (1982): 21–23.

Palmer, William J. "Fowles' *The Magus:* The Vortex as Myth, Metaphor, and Masque." *The Power of Myth in Literature and Film,* edited by Victor Carrabino, pp. 66–76. Tallahassee: University Presses of Florida, 1980.

———. "John Fowles and the Crickets." *Modern Fiction Studies* 31 (1985): 3–13.

Park, Sue [S]. "John Fowles, Daniel Martin, and Simon Wolfe." *Modern Fiction Studies* 31 (1985); 165–71.

———. "John Fowles's *The Magus:* The Godgame as Word Game." *Proceedings of the Conference of College Teachers of English in Texas* 45 (1980): 45–52.

———. "Time and Ruins in John Fowles's *Daniel Martin." Modern Fiction Studies* 31 (1985): 157–63.

Pifer, Drury. "The Muse Abused: Deconstruction in *Mantissa." In Critical Essays on John Fowles,* edited by Ellen Pifer, pp. 162–76. Boston: G. K. Hall, 1986.

Pifer, Ellen. Introduction. In *Critical Essays on John Fowles,* edited by Ellen Pifer, pp. 1–18. Boston: G. K. Hall, 1986.

Poirier, Suzanne. *"L'Astrée* Revisited: A 17th Century Model for *The Magus." Comparative Literary Studies* 17 (1980): 269–86.

Pollock, John J. "Conchis as an Allegorical Figure in *The Magus." Notes on Contemporary Literature* 10.1 (1980): 10.

Presley, Delma E. "The Quest of the Bourgeois Hero: An Approach to John Fowles' *The Magus." Journal of Popular Culture* 6 (1972): 394–98.

Rackham, Jeff. "John Fowles: The Existential Labyrinth." *Critique* 13.3 (1972): 89–103.

Rankin, Elizabeth D. "Cryptic Coloration in *The French Lieutenant's Woman." Journal of Narrative Technique* 3 (1974): 193–207.

Raper, Julius Rowan. "John Fowles: The Psychological Complexity of *The Magus." American Imago* 45 (1988): 61–83.

Rose, Gilbert J. *"The French Lieutenant's Woman:* The Unconscious Significance of a Novel to Its Author." *American Imago* 29 (1972): 165–76.

Rothschild, Judith Rice. "John Fowles and *The Ebony Tower:* 'Marie de France in the Twentieth Century.'" In *Selected Proceedings of the Twenty-Seventh Annual Mountain Interstate Foreign Language Conference,* edited by Eduardo Zayas-Bazan and Manuel Laurentino Suarez, pp. 129–35. Johnson City: Research Council of East Tennessee State University, 1978.

Rubenstein, Roberta. "Myth, Mystery, and Irony: John Fowles's *The Magus." Contemporary Literature* 16 (1975): 328–39.

Runyan, Randolph. "Fowles's Enigma Variations." In his *Fowles/Irving/Barthes: Canonical Variations on an Apocryphal Theme,* pp. 3–35. Columbus: Ohio State University Press for Miami University, 1981.

Sabre, Jeannette Mercer. "The Sacred Wood in Three Twentieth-Century Narratives." *Christian Scholar's Review* 13 (1983): 34–47.

Salys, Rimgaila. "The Medieval Context of John Fowles's *The Ebony Tower." Critique* 25.1 (1983): 11–24.

Scholes, Robert. "The Orgastic Fiction of John Fowles." *Hollins Critic* 6.5 (1969): 1–12. Reprinted with a revised opening in *Fabulation and Metafiction*, pp. 37–45. Urbana: University of Illinois Press, 1979.

Scruggs, Charles. "The Two Endings of *The French Lieutenant's Woman*." *Modern Fiction Studies* 31 (1985): 95–113.

Siegle, Robert. "The Concept of the Author in Barthes, Foucault, and Fowles." *College Literature* 10.2 (1983): 126–38. Revised and extended as Chap. 5, "Fowles, Contemporary Fiction, and the Poetics of the Author," in *The Politics of Reflexivity: Narrative and the Constitutive Poetics of Culture*, pp. 169–261. Baltimore: Johns Hopkins University Press, 1986.

Smith, Frederick N. "The Endings of *The French Lieutenant's Woman*: Another Speculation on the Manuscript." *Journal of Modern Literature* 14 (1987): 579–84.

———. "Revision and the Style of Revision in *The French Lieutenant's Woman*." *Modern Fiction Studies* 31 (1985): 85–94.

Sofinskaya, Irina. "Myth and Reality: Points of Contact: A Soviet Literary Critic Looks at John Fowles's Short Stories." *Soviet Literature* 1 (1979): 160–66.

Sollisch, James W. "The Passion of Existence: John Fowles's *The Ebony Tower*." *Critique* 25.1 (1983): 1–9.

Sullivan, Paula. "The Manuscripts for John Fowles [sic] *The French Lieutenant's Woman*." *Papers of the Bibliographical Society of America* 74 (1980): 272–77.

Sweet-Hurd, Evelyn. "Victorian Echoes in John Fowles's *The French Lieutenant's Woman*." *Notes on Contemporary Literature* 13.2 (1983): 2–5.

Tatham, Michael. "Two Novels: Notes on the Work of John Fowles." *New Blackfriar's* 52 (1971): 404–11.

Temple-Thurston, Barbara. "Time: The Tensional Nature of Reality in John Fowles' *Daniel Martin*." *Anglo-American Studies* 4: (1984): 51–57.

Turner, Katherine C. "To the Heart of Oakley and Woodruff." *Southern Humanities Review* 10 (1976): 353–61.

Twerski, Yocheved. *A Study of Mystery: The Black Paradox: John Fowles' The Magus* [pamphlet]. 1975 Prize Essay in English. Denver: University of Denver, uncopyrighted.

Wade, Cory. " 'Mystery Enough at Noon': John Fowles's Revision of *The Magus*." *Southern Review* 15 (1979): 717–23.

Wainwright, J. A. "The Illusion of 'Things as they are': *The Magus* versus *The Magus A Revised Version*." *Dalhousie Review* 63 (1983): 107–19.

Walker, David H. "Remorse, Responsibility, and Moral Dilemmas in Fowles's Fiction." In *Critical Essays on John Fowles*, edited by Ellen Pifer, pp. 54–76. Boston: G. K. Hall, 1986.

———. "Subversion of Narrative in the Work of André Gide and John Fowles." *Comparative Criticism: A Yearbook* 2 (1980): 187–212.

Ward, Carol. "Movie as Metaphor: Focus on *Daniel Martin*." *Literature/Film Quarterly* 15 (1987): 8–14.

Wight, Douglas A., and Kenneth B. Grant. "Theatrical Deception: Shakespearean Allusion in John Fowles's *The Magus: A Revised Version*. University of Dayton Review* 18.3 (1987): 85–93.

Wilson, Raymond J., III. "Allusion and Implication in John Fowles's 'The Cloud.' " *Studies in Short Fiction* 20 (1983): 17–22.

————. "Ambiguity in John Fowles' 'The Ebony Tower.' " *Notes on Contemporary Literature* 12.5 (1982): 6–8.

————. "John Fowles's *The Ebony Tower:* Unity and Celtic Myth." *Twentieth Century Literature* 28 (1982): 302–18.

Wolfe, Peter. "John Fowles: The Existential Tension." *Studies in the Twentieth Century* 16 (1975): 111–45.

Wymard, Eleanor B. " 'A New Version of the Midas Touch': *Daniel Martin* and *The World According to Garp*." *Modern Fiction Studies* 27 (1981): 284–86.

Essays on Adaptations of Works by John Fowles

Barber, Susanna, and Richard Messer. *"The French Lieutenant's Woman* and Individualization." *Literature/Film Quarterly* 12 (1984): 225–29.

Conradi, Peter J. *"The French Lieutenant's Woman: Novel, Screenplay, Film."* *Critical Quarterly* 24.1 (1982): 41–57.

Corbett, Thomas. "The Film and the Book: A Case Study of *The Collector*." *English Journal* 57 (1968): 328–33.

Garis, Leslie. "Translating Fowles into Film." *New York Times Magazine*, 30 August 1981, pp. 24–25, 48, 50, 52, 54, 69.

Genêt [Janet Flanner]. "Letter from Paris: Oct. 25." Review of *L'Obsédé (The Collector)*, adapted and directed by France Roche, Théâtre des Variétés. *New Yorker*, 5 November 1966, pp. 162, 165.

Knapp, Shoshana. "The Transformation of a Pinter Screenplay: Freedom and Calculators in *The French Lieutenant's Woman*." *Modern Drama* 28.1 (1985): 55–70.

————. "Story and Discourse: *The French Lieutenant's Woman*." In *Purdue University Seventh Annual Conference on Film*, pp. 87–93. West Lafayette, Ind.: Department of English, Purdue University, 1983.

Man, Glenn K. S. "The Intertextual Discourses of *The French Lieutenant's Woman*." *New Orleans Review* 15 (1988): 54–61.

Mazis, Glen A. "The 'Riteful' Play of Time in *The French Lieutenant's Woman*." *Soundings* 66 (1983): 296–318.

Perry, George. "The Film with Two Endings." *Times*, 20 September 1981, pp. 41, 46–47.

Scruggs, Charles. "Ethical Freedom and Visual Space: Filming *The French Lieutenant's Woman*." *Mosaic: A Journal for the Interdisciplinary Study of Literature* 20.2 (1987): 13–28.

Simmons, Kenith L. *"The French Lieutenant's Woman* as Metaphor: Karel Reisz's Non-Plot Centered Editing." *New Orleans Review* 11.2 (1984): 17–21.

Spitz, Ellen Handler. "On Interpretation of Film as Dream: *The French Lieutenant's Woman*." *Post Script: Essays in Film and the Humanities* 2.1 (1982): 13–29.

Wardle, Irving. Review of *The Collector*, adapted by David Parker, directed by Jeremy Young, King's Head Theatre Club. *Times*, 9 February 1971, p. 10.

Whall, Tony. "Karel Reisz's *The French Lieutenant's Woman: Only the Name Remains the Same*." *Literature/Film Quarterly* 10.2 (1982): 75–81.

Unpublished Doctoral Dissertations

Appleby, Thomas Conrad. "Benevolent Manipulation in the Fiction of John Fowles. *Dissertation Abstracts International (DAI)* 39 (1978): 3591A. University of Michigan.

Asadullah, Saeeda, Khan [misrepresented as "Khan, Saeeda Asadullah"]. "Progressive Integration of Self in John Fowles [sic] Fiction." *DAI* 43 (1983): 2354A. Bowling Green State University.

Bagchee, Syhamal [misspelled as "Shyamal"]. "Modernism, Post-Modernism, and the Novels of John Fowles." *DAI* 42 (1982): 4446A. York University [Canada].

Bailey, Dennis Lee. "The Modern Novel in the Presence of Myth." *DAI* 35 (1975): 7292A–93A. Purdue University.

Beatty, Patricia V. " 'The Geography of the Mind's Total Being': The Edenic Archetype in the Fiction of John Fowles." *DAI* 46 (1985): 976A. University of Alabama.

Bell, Marie Oliver Kiely. "The Personified Author in Fiction: Hawthorne, Warren, and Fowles." *DAI* 40 (1979): 2659A–60A. University of North Carolina.

Bonser, Dennis. "Romance Genres and Realistic Techniques in the Major Fiction of John Fowles." *DAI* 48 (1988): 3114A. Indiana University of Pennsylvania.

Carlson, Joanne Carol. "Women and Men in John Fowles's Fiction." *DAI* 48 (1987): 1208A. University of Minnesota.

Carpenter, Barbara. "Epoch and Archetype: Metaphors of Transcendence in the Fiction of John Fowles." *DAI* 44 (1983): 165A. Tulane University.

Cherry, Roger Dennis. *"Ethos* in Written Discourse: A Study of Literary and Persuasive Texts." *DAI* 46 (1986): 3015A. University of Texas.

Cooper, Pamela Ann. "Creativity and Femininity in the Fiction of John Fowles." *DAI* 50 (1990): 2904A. University of Toronto.

Costello, Jacqueline Anne. "The Facts of Fiction in the Novels of John Fowles." *DAI* 43 (1983): 2343A. New York University.

Cromwell, Lucy Switowy. " 'Whole Sight': A Structural Study of John Fowles's *Daniel Martin." DAI* 41 (1981): 4718A. University of Wisconsin.

Daw, Frederick John Laurence. "Us and Them: Technological Hierarchies in Fowles and Pynchon." *DAI* 44 (1984): 3070A. University of Western Ontario.

Dechert, Donald A., Jr. "John Fowles: The Craft of His Fiction: A Critical Study of Technique in Four Novels." *DAI* 47 (1987): 2592A. Florida State University.

Dixon, Ronald Craig. "Whole Sight: Process in the Fiction of John Fowles." *DAI* 44 (1983): 1450A. State University of New York at Binghamton.

Downing, Richard. "John Fowles: Deconstructor of Literary Convention." *DAI* 43 (1983): 3907A. University of South Florida.

Eldred, Janet M. "Gender and Creativity: Female Artist Subplots from Hawthorne to Fowles." *DAI* 49 (1989): 2648A. University of Illinois at Urbana-Champaign.

Froeb, Jeanne Riley. "The Fiction of David Storey, John Fowles and Iris Murdoch." *DAI* 38 (1977): 1378A–79A. University of Tulsa.

Gardener, Adrienne Kuulei. "John Fowles: The Inward Journey." *DAI* 48 (1987): 12120A. University of Texas at Austin.

Gersten, Irene Fandel. "Captivity and Freedom in Four Novels by John Fowles." *DAI* 41 (1980): 1586A. State University of New York at Binghamton.

Grine, Fakhri Ahmed. "From Isolation to Whole Sight: A Study of Humanist Existentialism in John Fowles, Albert Camus, and Jean-Paul Sartre." *DAI* 49 (1988): 810A. Pennsylvania State University.

Haberhern, Margot Anne. "Imitation with a Twist: The Literature of Exhaustion and Beyond." *DAI* 41 (1981): 4705A. Florida State University.

Helgeson, Susan Louise. "Readers Reading John Fowles' *Daniel Martin:* An Experimental Study of Reading as a Composing Process." *DAI* 43 (1982): 440A. University of Louisville.

Hightower, Sallie Turner. "Moral and Ego Development Stages in the Characters of Doris Lessing, Margaret Drabble, and John Fowles: An Analytical Evaluation Based on Theories of Erik Erikson, Jane Loevinger, and Lawrence Kohlberg." *DAI* 39 (1979): 7340A–41A. University of Houston.

Hill, Roy Mack. "Play in the Fiction of John Fowles." *DAI* 39 (1978): 1550A. University of Houston.

Holmes, Frederick Michael. "Fictional Self-Consciousness in the Works of John Barth and John Fowles." *DAI* 42 (1982): 3595A. Queens University at Kingston.

Hutcheon, Linda Ann Marie. "Narcissistic Narrative: The Paradoxical Status of Self-Conscious Fiction." *DAI* 38 (1977): 3483A. University of Toronto.

Kocher-Lindgren, Gray Meredith. "Narcissus Transformed: Textuality and the Self in Psychoanalysis and Literature." *DAI* 51 (1990): 1608A. Emory University.

Kraft, Ines A. "Choice: Moral Dilemma in the Fiction of John Fowles and Siegfried Lenz." *DAI* 42 (1982): 3589A. Indiana University.

Lorenz, Paul Howard. "Paths to Metamorphosis: The Quest for Whole Sight in Contemporary British Fiction." *DAI* 50 (1989): 450A. University of Houston.

Loughton, Scott Alfred. "The Low Mimetic Hero in Three Novels by John Fowles." *DAI* 47 (1987): 3434A. Brigham Young University.

McDaniel, Ellen. "Dark Towers, Godgames, and the Evolution Toward Humanism in the Fiction of John Fowles." *DAI* 40 (1980): 5049A–50A. Purdue University.

Madachy, James Lee. "The Aesthetic Theory of John Fowles." *DAI* 35 (1975): 5414A–15A. Ohio University.

Mercer, Jeanette Edna. "The Sacred Wood in Four Twentieth-Century Fictional Narratives. *DAI* 42 (1981): 204A. Pennsylvania State University.

Oppermann, Serpil (Tunc). "John Fowles as a Postmodernist; An Analysis of Fowles's Fiction Within Metafictional Theories." *DAI* 49 (1988): 828A. Hacettepe University (Turkey).

Pace, Stephanie Fish. "Expanding Horizons: Character in the Contemporary Novel." *DAI* 41 (1980): 2105A. University of Utah.

Rivenberg, Peter Sterling. "Beyond Enchantment: Character and Power in the

Novels of Iris Murdoch and John Fowles." *DAI* 45 (1984): 1123A. University of Rochester.

Romans, Morgan Dennis. "The Adam and Eve Archetypes in Four Novels by John Fowles." *DAI* 44 (1984): 3698A. Miami University.

Saari, Jon Howard. "Freedom and the Nemo in the Fiction of John Fowles." *DAI* 35 (1975): 4552A. Bowling Green State University.

Shahan, Richard Mark. "The Moral Art of John Fowles: Freedom Through Paradox." *DAI* 46 (1986): 2303A. University of Colorado.

Spoerl, Linda Bell. "The Methods of Madness: Insanity as Metaphor in Five Modern Novels." *DAI* 44 (1984): 3379A. University of Washington.

Sullivan, Karen Lever. "The Muse of Fiction: Fatal Women in the Novels of W. M. Thackeray, Thomas Hardy, and John Fowles." *DAI* 36 (1976): 7447A. Johns Hopkins University.

Tapp, Gary Wesley. "The Story and the Game: Recent Fiction and the Theology of Play." *DAI* 36 (1975): 2814A. Emory University.

Vander Weele, Michael J. "Presence and Judgment in Literary Knowing: A Study of Augustine, Fowles, Fielding and Eliot." *DAI* 42 (1982): 4821A. University of Iowa.

Warburton, Edna Eileen Hand. "John Fowles and the Vision of the Dead Woman: The Theme of Carnal Knowledge and the Technique of Source Inversion in John Fowles's Fiction." *DAI* 41 (1980): 1055A. University of Pennsylvania.

Ward, Carol Marie. "Movie as Metaphor in Contemporary Fiction: A Study of Walker Percy, Larry McMurtry, and John Fowles." *DAI* 42 (1982): 3996A. University of Tennessee.

Wilson, Joan Margaret. "Time as the Organizing Principle in the Romances of John Fowles." *DAI* 50 (1989): 1671A. Southern Illinois University at Carbondale.

Zimmerman, James Richard. "John Fowles on Film: A Study of *The Collector, The Magus,* and *The French Lieutenant's Woman." DAI* 44 (1983): 1095A. Ohio State University.

Zinman, Jane Ann. "Readers, Writers, and the Grounds for a Textual Divorce." *DAI* 49 (1989): 2206A. Ohio State University.

Selected Reviews of Works by John Fowles

The Collector

Auchincloss, Eve. "Pop Art." *New York Review of Books,* 14 November 1963, pp. 17–18.

Balliett, Whitney. "Beauty and the Beast." *New Yorker,* 28 September 1963, pp. 192–93.

Bellis, Jack De. *Sewanee Review* 72 (1964): 532.

Brooke, Jocelyn. "New Fiction." *Listener* 69 (1963): 883.

Brophy, Brigid. "Solitaries." *New Statesman* 65 (1963): 942.

"Caliban Revisited." *Time,* 2 August 1963, p. 68.

Davenport, Basil. *Book-of-the-Month-Club News,* August 1963, p. 8.

Davenport, Guy. "Eros Aped." *National Review,* 5 November 1963, pp. 401–2.

Fuller, Edmund. "Horror Tale of Poignant Originality." *Chicago Tribune Magazine of Books,* 28 July 1963, p. 3.

Gardiner, Harold C. "Some Summer Fiction." *America*, 27 July 1963, p. 99.

Halio, Jay L. *Southern Review* 2 (1966): 962–63.

Hicks, Granville. "A Caliban with Butterflies." *Saturday Review*, 27 July 1963, pp. 19–20.

McGuinness, Frank. *London Magazine*, August 1963, p. 86.

"Miranda Removed." *Times Literary Supplement*, 17 May 1963, p. 353.

Murray, Michele. "Twentieth-Century Parable." *Commonweal*, November 1963, pp. 172–73.

"New Fiction." *Times* 23 May 1963: 15. Reprinted 30 May 1963: 13.

Ochs, Maxwell David. *Minnesota Review* 4 (1964): 460–61.

Phelps, Robert. "The Meek Grub." *New York Herald Tribune Books*, 28 July 1963, p. 9.

Pickerel, Paul. "Love, Irony, and a Bit of Vitriol," in "Novels Wrenched by Ideas." *Harper's Magazine*, August 1963, pp. 95–96.

Prescott, Orville. "The Prisoner in the Cellar." *New York Times*, 24 July 1963, p. 29.

Pryce-Jones, Alan. "Obsession's Prisoners." *New York Times Book Review*, 28 July 1963, pp. 4, 12.

Renek, Morris. "Worn Elastic." *Nation* 197 (1963): 352–53.

Sale, Roger. "The Newness of the Novel." *Hudson Review* 16 (1963–64): 604.

Tracy, Honor. "Love Under Chloroform." *New Republic*, 3 August 1963, pp. 20–21.

Vanderbilt, Gloria. "The Calm, Cool Logic of Insanity." *Cosmopolitan*, July 1963, p. 26.

The Aristos (original and revised versions)

Holmes, Richard. "A Personal Myth." *Times*, 1 August 1981, p. 9.

"Misery in Eden." *Time*, 20 November 1964, pp. 110, 113.

Mortimer, John. "Contra Clegg." *New Statesman*, 2 July 1965, p. 16.

Times Literary Supplement, 8 July 1965, p. 585.

Scholes, Robert. *Saturday Review*, 17 October 1970, pp. 36–37.

The Magus (original and revised versions)

Bergonzi, Bernard. "Bouillabaisse." *New York Review of Books*, 17 March 1966, p. 21.

Burgess, Anthony. *Listener* 75 (1966): 659.

Byrom, Bill. "Puffing and Blowing." *Spectator*, 6 May 1966, pp. 574.

Culligan, Glendy. "The Magician and the Bore." *Reporter*, 24 February 1966, pp. 56, 58.

Davenport, G. *National Review*, 12 July 1966, p. 696.

Donohue, H.E.F. "Collecting John Fowles." *Holiday*, February 1966, pp. 124, 126–27.

Epstein, Joseph. "An English Nabokov." *New Republic*, 19 February 1966, pp. 26–27, 29.

Fremont-Smith, Eliot. "Players of the Godgame," *New York Times*, 17 January 1966, p. 45.

Glaserfield, Ernst von. "Reflections on John Fowles's *The Magus* and the Construction of Reality." *Georgia Review* 33 (1979): 444–48.

Holmes, Richard. "Crystallizing Powers." *Times*, 9 June 1977, p. 12.

Lynch, William J. *Best Sellers,* 15 January 1966, pp. 402–3.

"Man on a String." *Newsweek,* 17 January 1966, p. 86A.

Moore, Brian. "Too Much Hocus in the Pocus." *New York Herald Tribune Book Week,* 9 January 1966, pp. 4, 12.

Mortimer, Penelope. "Into the Noösphere." *New Statesman,* 6 May 1966, p. 659.

Mudrick, Marvin. "Evelyn, Get the Horseradish." *Hudson Review* 19 (1966): 305–7.

Mulvey, Christopher E. *Commonweal,* 1 April 1966, pp. 60–61.

"No Wise." *Times Literary Supplement,* 5 May 1966, p. 381.

Pritchard, William H. "Early Fowles." *New York Times Book Review,* 19 March 1978, pp. 7–8.

Sage, Lorna. "Return to the Island." *Observer,* 12 June 1977, p. 24.

Samstag, Nicholas. "Down to His Last Illusion." *Saturday Review,* 15 January 1966, p. 40.

Scott, J. D. "Seeing Things on Phraxos." *New York Times Book Review,* 9 January 1966, pp. 4–5.

Shuttleworth, Martin. *Punch,* 4 May 1966, p. 668.

"Spidery Spirit." *Time,* 14 January 1966, pp. 92, 94.

Times, 5 May 1966, p. 18.

Wilson, Angus. "Making with the Metaphysics." *Observer,* 1 May 1966, p. 27. Reprinted as "Fowles's Foul Fantasy," in *Critic,* August–September 1966, pp. 50–51.

Wolfe, Peter. *Contemporary Poetry* 1 (1973): 69–72.

The French Lieutenant's Woman

Bell, Pearl K. "The Double World of John Fowles." *New Leader,* 5 January 1970, pp. 19–20.

Chase, Edward T. "Delectable Novel." *New Republic,* 15 November 1969, pp. 23–24.

Conroy, Mary. "A Novelist on the Knowledge." *Times,* 14 June 1969, p. 22.

Davenport, Guy. "Lulu in Bombazeen." *National Review,* 2 December 1969, pp. 122, 125–26.

Edwards, Lee R. "Changing Our Imaginations." *Massachusetts Review* 11 (1970): 604–8.

Fuller, Edmund. "Victorians, Dr. Jekyll & Mr. Hyde." *Wall Street Journal,* 19 November 1969, p. 22.

Gordon, Jan B. "Prisons of Consciousness in Contemporary European Fiction." *Southern Review* 9 (1973): 222–27.

Grant, Annette. "Idle Transcendental Chatter." *Nation* 209 (1969): 667–68.

Gray, Paul Edward. *Yale Review* 59 (1970): 430–32.

Hamilton, Ian. "Errant Apostles." *Listener* 82 (1969): 24.

"Imminent Victorians." *Time,* 7 November 1969, p. 108.

Lehmann-Haupt, Christopher. "On the Third Try, John Fowles Connects." *New York Times,* 10 November 1969, p. 45.

McDowell, Frederick P. W. *Contemporary Literature* 11 (1970): 428–31.

Oates, Joyce Carol. *Chicago Tribune Book World,* 2 November 1969, pp. 1, 3.

Price, James. "Self-Dependence." *New Statesman,* 13 June 1969, p. 850.

Sale, Roger. "Its Discontent." *Hudson Review* 22 (1969–70): 711–12.
"Victorian Author." *Times Literary Supplement,* 12 June 1969, p. 629.
Watt, Ian. "A Traditional Victorian Novel? Yes, and Yet . . ." *New York Times Book Review,* 9 November 1969, pp. 1, 74–75.
Wolfe, Peter. *Saturday Review,* 22 November 1969, p. 85.
Yale Review 59 (1970): 430–32.

Poems

Booklist, 15 September 1973, p. 77.
Kirkus Reviews, 15 March 1973, p. 353.
Portis, Rowe. *Library Journal,* 1 May 1973, p. 1493.
Wolfe, Peter. *Contemporary Poetry* 1 (1973): 69–72.

Cinderella

Times, 1 December 1974, p. 43.

The Ebony Tower

Baily, Paul. *Observer,* 6 October 1974, p. 30.
Barras, Leonard. *Times,* 13 October 1974, p. 36.
Bryant, Rene Kuhn. "Skillful Angler." *National Review,* 17 January 1975, pp. 51–53.
Dick, Kay. "Short Stories to Savour." *Times,* 4 December 1976, p. 7.
Faber, Roderick M. "Three Fowles." *Village Voice,* 14 November 1974, p. 47.
Hill, William B. *Best Sellers,* 15 December 1974, p. 421.
Hirsch, Foster. *America,* 11 January 1975, pp. 18–19.
Lehmann-Haupt, Christopher. "More Magic from John Fowles." *New York Times,* 4 November 1974, p. 35.
Morris, Robert K. "A Forest of Fictions." *Nation* 221 (1975): 214–15.
Morrow, Lance. "Shimmering Perversity." *Time,* 2 December 1979, p. 110.
New Yorker, 23 December 1974, pp. 83–84.
"Ordeals of Our Time." *Times Literary Supplement,* 4 October 1974, p. 1061.
Prince, Peter. "Real Life." *New Statesman* 88 (1974): 513.
Solotaroff, Theodore. "John Fowles's Linear Art." *New York Times Book Review,* 10 November 1974, pp. 2–3, 20.
Tinniswood, Peter. *Times,* 3 October 1974, p. 15.

Ourika

Lingeman, Richard R. "The French Lieutenant's Women." *New York Times Book Review,* 9 October 1977, p. 51.
Lyons, Gene. "Good Fiction, Plain and Fancy." *Nation* 225 (1977): 406–08.

Daniel Martin

Bell, Pearl K. "The English Sickness." *Commentary,* December 1977, pp. 80–83.
Boeth, Richard. "Soul Search." *Newsweek,* 19 September 1977, p. 110.
Burgess, Anthony. *Irish Press,* 13 October 1977.
Curtis, Anthony. "Gut Reactions." *Financial Times,* 7 July 1977, p. 37.
Donoghue, Denis. "Only Disconnect." *New York Review of Books,* 8 December 1977, pp. 45–46.

Duvall, E. S. *Atlantic Monthly,* October 1977, pp. 104–5.

Feo, Ronald De. *National Review* 30 (1978): 288–89.

Gardner, John. "In Defense of the Real." *Saturday Review,* 1 October 1977, pp. 22–24.

Gillot, Jacky. "Home to Make Peace." *Times,* 6 October 1977, p. 20.

Gray, Paul. "The Toughest Question." *Time,* 12 September 1977, p. 75.

Lehmann-Haupt, Christopher. "Un-Inventing the Novel." *New York Times,* 13 September 1977, p. 29.

Lyon, Paul. "Editorial." *Brushfire* 27.2 (1977): 3.

Mason, Michael. "Pulling the Wool." *Times Literary Supplement,* 7 October 1977, p. 1135.

Mathewson, Ruth. "John Fowles, Ghostwriter." *New Leader,* 21 November 1977, pp. 16–17.

Mortimer, John. "Twenty-one Distinguished Contemporaries Select Their Favourite Reading of 1977," *Times,* 4 December 1977, p. 33.

Palliser, Charles. "John Fowles: The Ambivalent Virtues?" *Library Review* 29 (1980): 36–38.

Playboy, October 1977, p. 26.

Pritchard, William H. "An English Hero." *New York Times Book Review,* 25 September 1977, 1, 42.

Raphael, Frederic. "Mr. Fowles Shoots His Bolt." *Times,* 9 October 1977, p. 41.

Rubenstein, Roberta. *Progressive,* November 1977, pp. 55–56.

Sage, Lorna. *Observer,* 9 October 1977, p. 27.

Treglown, Jeremy. "Generation Game." *New Statesman,* 7 October 1977, p. 482.

Trewin, Ion. "Falling into a Cultural Gap as Wide as the Atlantic." *Times,* 15 October 1977, p. 14.

Vansittart, Peter. "Sick Men of Europe." *London Magazine,* December 1977, pp. 92–96.

Islands

Holloway, David. "The World in View." *Daily Telegraph,* 7 December 1978, p. 12.

Times, 24 November 1978, p. xxiii.

Times, 17 December 1978, p. 15.

The Tree

Holmes, Richard. "Illuminated Manuscripts." *Times,* 20 December 1979, p. 10.

Monumenta Britannica

Hunter, Michael. "Laying the Foundations." *Times Literary Supplement,* 28 November 1980, p. 1362.

Trevor-Roper, Hugh. "A Visit to Avebury." *Times,* 16 May 1982, p. 43.

Williams, David. *Times,* 2 December 1980, p. 9.

The Enigma of Stonehenge

Coles, J. M. "Early Expansion." *Times Literary Supplement,* 17 April 1981, p. 440.

Mantissa

Amis, Martin. "The Magus and His Muse." *Observer*, 10 October 1982, p. 31.

Atlantic Monthly, November 1982, p. 170.

Campbell, Robert. *Critical Quarterly* 25.3 (1986): 84–86.

DeMott, Benjamin. "The Yarnsmith in Search of Himself." *New York Times Book Review*, 29 August 1982, p. 3.

Gray, Paul. "The Prisoners of Gender." *Time*, 6 September 1982, p. 74.

Leonard, John. *New York Times*, 31 August 1982, p. C12.

Lodge, David. "Bibliosexuality." *Times*, 10 October 1982, p. 44.

Lyons, Gene. "We Are Not Amused." *Newsweek*, 27 September 1982, p. 72.

Wolff, Geoffrey. "Bloodless Porn." *New Republic*, 18 October 1982, pp. 34–35.

A Maggot

Allen, Bruce. "Caterpillar-to-Butterfly Tale Never Takes Flight." *Christian Science Monitor*, 3 January 1986, p. B4.

Buckley, Reid. *American Spectator*, January 1986, pp. 43–44.

Earight, D. J. "Depositions." *New York Review of Books*, 5 December 1985, pp. 35–36.

Edgar, David. "Prostitute's Apocalypse." *Listener*, 7 November 1985, pp. 29–30.

Emerson, Sally. "A Tale of Five Travellers." *Illustrated London News*, November 1985, p. 106.

Essex, David. "The Novel as Kōan." *Eighteenth-Century Life* 10 (1986): 80–81.

Evans, Stuart. "Shaking History and Mysticism." *Times*, 19 September 1985, p. 12.

Fuller, Jack. "Defoe Haunts Fowles' Dazzling Tour de Force." *Chicago Tribune*, 18 August 1985, Sec. 14: 37, 41.

Hansford, James. *British Book News*, November 1985: 683.

Hatfield, Len. "Changelings and Alien Contact." *Fantasy Review*, May 1986, p. 18.

Jones, D.A.N. "Sergeant Farthing." *London Review of Books*, 17 October 1985, pp. 26–27. Also reviewed is *The Romances of John Fowles*, by Simon Loveday.

Kemp, Peter. "Shakers in Suspense." *Times*, 22 September 1985, p. 44.

Miller, Walter, Jr. "Chariots of the Goddesses, or What?" *New York Times Book Review*, 8 September 1985, p. 11.

Mitgang, Herbert. "Stonehenge Again." *New York Times*, 2 September 1985, p. 34.

Moynahan, Julian. "Fly Casting." *New Republic*, 7 October 1985, pp. 47–49.

Porterfield, Christopher. "Mysterious Movers and Shakers." *Time*, 9 September 1985, pp. 67–68.

Prescott, Peter S. "Five Characters in Search of a Book." *Newsweek*, 7 October 1985, pp. 92–92A.

Rogers, Pat. "Left Lobe and Right." *Times Literary Supplement*, 20 September 1985, p. 1027.

Schieder, Rupert. "Themes and Variations." *Books in Canada*, December 1985, pp. 36–37.

Seidel, Michael. "Rake's Progress: A Magical History Tour." *Wall Street Journal,*
    13 September 1985, p. 24.
Steinfeld, Janis Paul. *World Literature Today* 60 (1986): 470.
Taylor, D. J. *Encounter,* June 1986, pp. 54–55.

Bibliographic Studies

Dixon, Ronald C. "Criticism of John Fowles: A Selected Checklist." *Modern Fic-
    tion Studies* 31 (1985): 205–10.
Evarts, Prescott, Jr. "John Fowles: A Checklist." *Critique* 13.3 (1972): 105–7.
Myers, Karen Magee. "John Fowles: An Annotated Bibliography, 1963–1976."
    Bulletin of Bibliography 32.3 (1976): 162–69.
Olshen, Barry N., and Toni A. Olshen. *John Fowles: A Reference Guide.* Boston:
    G. K. Hall, 1980.
Roberts, Ray A. "John Fowles: A Bibliographical Checklist." *American Book Col-
    lector* 1.5 (1980): 26–37.

INDEX

About the Author

JAMES R. AUBREY is Associate Professor of English at Metropolitan State College of Denver. Specializing in British literature, Dr. Aubrey has written articles for *Victorian Prose, Bucknell Review,* and *Studies in Philology.*